James Cook

A Voyage to the Pacific Ocean

James Cook

A Voyage to the Pacific Ocean

ISBN/EAN: 9783741171123

Manufactured in Europe, USA, Canada, Australia, Japa

Cover: Foto ©Andreas Hilbeck / pixelio.de

Manufactured and distributed by brebook publishing software (www.brebook.com)

James Cook

A Voyage to the Pacific Ocean

A VOYAGE TO THE PACIFIC OCEAN.

UNDERTAKEN,
BY THE COMMAND OF HIS MAJESTY,

FOR MAKING

Discoveries in the Northern Hemisphere.

TO DETERMINE

The POSITION and EXTENT of the WEST SIDE of NORTH AMERICA; its DISTANCE from ASIA; and the PRACTICABILITY of a NORTHERN PASSAGE to EUROPE.

PERFORMED UNDER THE DIRECTION OF

Captains COOK, CLERKE, and GORE,

In his MAJESTY's Ships the RESOLUTION and DISCOVERY.
In the Years 1776, 1777, 1778, 1779, and 1780.

IN THREE VOLUMES.

VOL. I. and II. written by Captain JAMES COOK, F.R.S.
VOL. III. by Captain JAMES KING, LL.D. and F.R.S.

Illustrated with Maps and Charts, from the Original Drawings made by Lieut. HENRY ROBERTS, under the Direction of Captain COOK; and with a great Variety of Portraits of Persons, Views of Places, and Historical Representations of Memorable Incidents, drawn by Mr. WEBBER during the Voyage, and engraved by the most eminent Artists.

Published by Order of the Lords Commissioners of the Admiralty.

VOL. I.

LONDON:

PRINTED BY W. AND A. STRAHAN;
FOR G. NICOL, BOOKSELLER TO HIS MAJESTY, IN THE STRAND;
AND T. CADELL, IN THE STRAND.
MDCCLXXXIV.

CONTENTS

OF THE FIRST VOLUME

INTRODUCTION.	Page i
Inscription to the Memory of Captain JAMES COOK.	lxxxvii
List of the PLATES.	xci

BOOK I.

Transactions from the Beginning of the Voyage till our Departure from New Zealand.

CHAP. I.

VARIOUS *Preparations for the Voyage.—Omai's Behaviour on embarking.—Observations for determining the Longitude of Sheerness, and the North Foreland.—Passage of the Resolution from Deptford to Plymouth.—Employments there.—Complements of the Crews of both Ships, and Names of the Officers.—Observations to fix the Longitude of Plymouth.—Departure of the Resolution.*

Page 1

CHAP. II.

Passage of the Resolution to Teneriffe.—Reception there.—Description of Santa Cruz Road.—Refreshments to be met with.—Observations

for

CONTENTS.

for fixing the Longitude of Teneriffe.—Some Account of the Island.—Botanical Observations.—Cities of Santa Cruz and Laguna.—Agriculture.—Air and Climate.—Commerce.—Inhabitants. 14

CHAP. III.

Departure from Teneriffe.—Danger of the Ship near Bonavista.—Isle of Mayo.—Port Praya.—Precautions against the Rain and sultry weather in the Neighbourhood of the Equator.—Position of the Coast of Brazil.—Arrival at the Cape of Good Hope.—Transactions there.—Junction of the Discovery.—Mr. Anderson's Journey up the Country.—Astronomical Observations.—Nautical Remarks on the Passage from England to the Cape, with regard to the Currents and the Variation. 29

CHAP. IV.

The two Ships leave the Cape of Good Hope.—Two Islands, named Prince Edward's, seen, and their Appearance described.—Kerguelen's Land visited.—Arrival in Christmas Harbour.—Occurrences there.—Description of it. 51

CHAP. V.

Departure from Christmas Harbour.—Range along the Coast, to discover its Position and Extent.—Several Promontories and Bays, and a Peninsula, described and named.—Danger from Shoals.—Another Harbour and a Sound. Mr. Anderson's Observations on the natural Productions, Animals, Soil, &c. of Kerguelen's Land. 70

CHAP. VI.

Passage from Kerguelen's to Van Diemen's Land.—Arrival in Adventure Bay.—Incidents there.—Interviews with the Natives.—Their Persons and Dress described.—Account of their Behaviour.—Table of the Longitude, Latitude, and Variation.—Mr. Anderson's Observations on the natural Productions of the Country, on the Inhabitants, and their Language. 91

CONTENTS.

CHAP. VII.

The Passage from Van Diemen's Land to New Zealand.—Employments in Queen Charlotte's Sound.—Transactions with the Natives there.—Intelligence about the Massacre of the Adventure's Boat's Crew.—Account of the Chief who headed the Party on that Occasion.—Of the two young Men who embark to attend Omai.—Various Remarks on the Inhabitants.—Astronomical and Nautical Observations. 118

CHAP. VIII.

Mr. Anderson's Remarks on the Country near Queen Charlotte's Sound. —The Soil.—Climate.—Weather.—Winds.—Trees.—Plants.— Birds.—Fish.—Other Animals.—Of the Inhabitants—Description of their Persons.—Their Dress.—Ornaments.—Habitations.—Boats. —Food and Cookery.—Arts.—Weapons.—Cruelty to Prisoners.— Various Customs.—Specimen of their Language. 145

BOOK II.

From leaving New Zealand, to our Arrival at Otaheite, or the Society Islands.

CHAP. I.

Prosecution of the Voyage.—Behaviour of the two New Zealanders on board.—Unfavourable winds.—An Island called Mangea discovered. —The Coast of it examined.—Transactions with the Natives.—An Account of their Persons, Dress, and Canoe.—Description of the Island.—A Specimen of the Language.—Disposition of the Inhabitants. 167

CONTENTS.

CHAP. II.

The Discovery of an Island called Wateeoo.—Its Coasts examined.—Visits from the Natives on board the Ships.—Mess. Gore, Burney, and Anderson, with Omai, sent on Shore.— Mr. Anderson's Narrative of their Reception.—Omai's Expedient to prevent their being detained.—His meeting with some of his Countrymen, and their distressful Voyage.—Farther Account of Wateeoo, and of its Inhabitants. 180

CHAP. III.

Wenooa-ette, or Otakootaia, visited.—Account of that Island, and of its Produce. Hervey's Island, or Terougge mou Atooa, found to be inhabited.—Transactions with the Natives.—Their Persons, Dress, Language, Canoes.—Fruitless Attempt to land there.—Reasons for bearing away for the Friendly Islands.—Palmerston's Island touched at.—Description of the two Places where the Boats landed. —Refreshments obtained there.—Conjectures on the Formation of such low Islands.—Arrival at the Friendly Islands. 205

CHAP. IV.

Intercourse with the Natives of Komango, and other Islands.—Arrival at Annamooka.—Transactions there.—Feenou, a principal Chief, from Tongataboo, comes on a Visit.—The Manner of his Reception in the Island, and on board.—Instances of the pilfering Disposition of the Natives.—Some Account of Annamooka.—The Passage from it to Hapaee. 225

CHAP. V.

Arrival of the Ships at Hapaee, and friendly Reception there.—Presents and Solemnities on the Occasion.—Single Combats with Clubs. —Wrestling and Boxing-matches.—Female Combatants.—Marines exercised.—A Dance performed by Men.—Fireworks exhibited.— The Night-entertainments of singing and dancing particularly described. 242

CONTENTS.

CHAP. VI.

Description of Lefooga.—Its cultivated State.—Its Extent.—Transactions there.—A Female Oculist.—Singular Expedients for shaving off the Hair.—The Ships change their Station.—A remarkable Mount and Stone.—Description of Hoolaiva.—Account of Poulaho, King of the Friendly Islands.—Respectful Manner in which he is treated by his People.—Departure from the Hapaee Islands.—Some Account of Kotoo.—Return of the Ships to Annamooka.—Poulaho and Feenou meet.—Arrival at Tongataboo. 256

CHAP. VII.

Friendly Reception at Tongataboo.—Manner of distributing a baked Hog and Kava to Poulaho's Attendants.—The Observatory, &c. erected.—The Village where the Chiefs reside, and the adjoining Country, described.—Interviews with Mareewagee, and Toobou, and the King's Son.—A grand Haiva, or Entertainment of Songs and Dances, given by Mareewagee.—Exhibition of Fire-works.—Manner of Wrestling and Boxing.—Distribution of the Cattle.—Thefts committed by the Natives.—Poulaho, and the other Chiefs, confined on that Account.—Poulaho's Present, and Haiva. 278

CHAP. VIII.

Some of the Officers plundered by the Natives.—A fishing Party.—A Visit to Poulaho.—A Fiatooka described.—Observations on the Country Entertainment at Poulaho's House.—His Mourning Ceremony.—Of the Kava Plant, and the Manner of preparing the Liquor.—Account of Onevy, a little Island.—One of the Natives wounded by a Sentinel.—Messrs. King and Anderson visit the King's Brother.—Their Entertainment.—Another Mourning Ceremony.—Manner of passing the Night.—Remarks on the Country they passed through.—Preparations made for sailing.—An Eclipse of the Sun, imperfectly observed.—Mr. Anderson's Account of the Island, and its Productions. 309

CONTENTS.

CHAP. IX.

A grand Solemnity, called NATCHE, *in Honour of the King's Son, performed.—The Processions and other Ceremonies, during the first Day, described.—The Manner of passing the Night at the King's House.—Continuation of the Solemnity, the next Day.—Conjectures about the Nature of it.—Departure from Tongataboo, and Arrival at Eooa.—Account of that Island, and Transactions there.* 336

CHAP. X.

Advantages derived from visiting the Friendly Islands.—Best Articles for Traffic.—Refreshments that may be procured.—The Number of the Islands, and their Names.—Keppel's and Boscawen's Islands belong to them.—Account of Vavaoo—of Hamoa—of Feejee.—Voyages of the Natives in their Canoes.—Difficulty of procuring exact Information.—Persons of the Inhabitants of both Sexes.—Their Colour. —Diseases.—Their general Character.—Manner of wearing their Hair—of puncturing their Bodies.—Their Clothing and Ornaments. —Personal Cleanliness. 364

CHAP. XI.

Employments of the Women, at the Friendly Islands.—Of the Men.— Agriculture.—Construction of their Houses.—Their working Tools, —Cordage, and fishing Implements.—Musical Instruments.—Weapons.—Food, and Cookery.—Amusements.—Marriage.—Mourning Ceremonies for the Dead.—Their Divinities.—Notions about the Soul, and a future State.—Their Places of Worship.—Government. —Manner of paying Obeisance to the King.—Account of the Royal Family.—Remarks on their Language, and a Specimen of it.—Nautical and other Observations. 390

ERRATUM.

Page 206, line 24, *for* latitude 19° 15′ South, *read* latitude 19° 51′ South.

INTRODUCTION.

THE spirit of discovery, which had long animated the European nations, having, after its arduous and successful exertions, during the fifteenth and sixteenth centuries, gradually subsided, and for a considerable time lain dormant, began to revive in Great Britain in the late reign*; and recovered all its former activity, under the cherishing influence, and munificent encouragement, of his present Majesty.

Soon after his accession to the throne, having happily closed the destructive operations of war, he turned his thoughts to enterprizes more humane, but not less brilliant, adapted to the season of returning peace. While every liberal art, and useful study, flourished under his patronage at home, his superintending care was extended to such branches of knowledge, as required distant examination and inquiry; and his ships, after bringing back victory and conquest from every quarter of the known world, were

* Two voyages for discovering a North West passage, through Hudson's Bay, were then performed; one under the command of Captain Middleton, in his Majesty's ships the Furnace, and the Discovery Pink, in 1741, and 1742. The other under the direction of Captains Smith and Moore, in the ships Dobbs and California, fitted out by subscription, in 1746, and 1747.

INTRODUCTION.

now employed in opening friendly communications with its hitherto unexplored receſſes.

In the proſecution of an object ſo worthy of the Monarch of a great commercial people, one voyage followed another in cloſe ſucceſſion; and, we may add, in regular gradation. What Byron [*] had begun, Wallis [†] and Carteret [‡] ſoon improved. Their ſucceſs gave birth to a far more extenſive plan of diſcovery, carried into execution, in two ſubſequent voyages, conducted by Cook [§]. And that nothing might be left unattempted, though much had been already done, the ſame Commander, whoſe profeſſional ſkill could only be equalled by the perſevering diligence with which he had exerted it, in the courſe of his former reſearches, was called upon, once more, to reſume, or rather to complete, the ſurvey of the globe. Accordingly, another voyage was undertaken in 1776; which, though laſt in the order of time, was far from being the leaſt conſiderable, with reſpect to the extent and importance of its objects; yet, ſtill, far leſs fortunate than any of the former, as thoſe objects

---

[*] Captain, now Admiral, Byron, had, under his command, the Dolphin and Tamer. He ſailed in June 1764, and returned in May 1766.

[†] Captain Wallis had, under his command, the Dolphin and Swallow. He ſailed in Auguſt 1766, and returned, with the Dolphin, in May 1768.

[‡] The Swallow, commanded by Captain Carteret, having been ſeparated from Wallis, and, by keeping a different route, having made different diſcoveries, this may be conſidered as a diſtinct voyage. The Swallow returned to England in March 1769.

[§] Captain Cook, in the Endeavour, ſailed in Auguſt 1768, and returned in July 1771.

In his ſecond voyage, he had the Reſolution and Adventure under his command. They ſailed from England in July 1772, and returned on the 30th of July 1775.

were

INTRODUCTION.

were not accomplished, but at the expence of the valuable life of its Conductor.

When plans, calculated to be of general utility, are carried into execution with partial views, and upon interested motives, it is natural to attempt to confine, within some narrow circle, the advantages which might have been derived to the world at large, by an unreserved disclosure of all that had been effected. And, upon this principle, it has too frequently been considered as found policy, perhaps, in this country, as well as amongst some of our neighbours, to affect to draw a veil of secrecy over the result of enterprizes to discover and explore unknown quarters of the globe. It is to the honour of the present reign, that more liberal views have been now adopted. Our late voyages, from the very extensive objects proposed by them, could not but convey useful information to every European nation; and, indeed, to every nation, however remote, which cultivates commerce, and is acquainted with navigation; and that information has most laudably been afforded. The same enlarged and benevolent spirit, which ordered these several expeditions to be undertaken, has also taken care that the result of their various discoveries should be authentically recorded. And the transactions of the five first voyages round the world having, in due time, been communicated [*], under the authority of his Majesty's naval Minister; those of the sixth, which, besides revisiting many of the former discoveries in the Southern, carried its opera-

---

[*] The account of the four first of these voyages, compiled by Dr. Hawkesworth, from the Journals of the several Commanders, was published in 1773, in Three Volumes quarto; and Captain Cook's own account of the fifth, in 1777, in Two Volumes quarto.

INTRODUCTION.

tions into untrodden paths in the Northern hemisphere, are, under the same sanction, now submitted to the Public in these Volumes.

One great plan of nautical investigation having been pursued throughout, it is obvious, that the several voyages have a close connection, and that an exact recollection of what had been aimed at, and effected, in those that preceded, will throw considerable light on our period. With a view, therefore, to assist the Reader in forming a just estimate of the additional information conveyed by this Publication, it may not be improper to lay before him a short, though comprehensive, abstract of the principal objects that had been previously accomplished, arranged in such a manner, as may serve to unite, into one point of view, the various articles which lie scattered through the voluminous Journals already in the hands of the Public; those compiled by Dr. Hawkesworth; and that which was written by Captain Cook himself. By thus shewing what had been formerly done, how much still remained for subsequent examination, will be more apparent; and it will be better understood on what grounds, though the ships of his Majesty had already circumnavigated the world five different times, in the course of about ten years, another voyage should still be thought expedient.

There will be a farther use in giving such an abstract a place in this Introduction. The plan of discovery, carried on in so many successive expeditions, being now, we may take upon us to say, in a great measure completed; by summing up the final result, we shall be better able to do justice to the benevolent purposes it was designed to answer; and a solid foundation will be laid, on which we may build

a sa-

INTRODUCTION.

a satisfactory answer to a question, sometimes asked by peevish refinement, and ignorant malevolence, What beneficial consequences, if any, have followed, or are likely to follow, to the discoverers, or to the discovered, to the common interests of humanity, or to the increase of useful knowledge, from all our boasted attempts to explore the distant recesses of the globe?

The general object of the several voyages round the world, undertaken by the command of his Majesty, prior to that related in this work, was to search for unknown tracts of land that might exist within the bosom of the immense expanse of ocean that occupies the whole Southern hemisphere.

Within that space, so few researches had been made, before our time, and those few researches had been made so imperfectly, that the result of them, as communicated to the world in any narration, had rather served to create uncertainty, than to convey information; to deceive the credulous, rather than to satisfy the judicious inquirer; by blending the true geography of above half the superficies of the earth, with an endless variety of plausible conjectures, suggested by ingenious speculation; of idle tales, handed down by obscure tradition; or of bold fictions, invented by deliberate falsehood.

It would have been very unfortunate, indeed, if five different circumnavigators of the globe, some of them, at least, if not all, in tracks little known, and less frequented, had produced no discoveries, to reward the difficulties and perils unavoidably encountered. But the following review will furnish the most satisfactory proofs, that his Majesty's instructions have been executed with ability; and that the

repeated

INTRODUCTION.

repeated visits of his ships to the Southern hemisphere, have very considerably added to our stock of geographical knowledge.

1.

The South Atlantic Ocean was the first scene of our operations. Falkland's Islands had been hitherto barely known to exist; but their true position and extent, and every circumstance which could render their existence of any consequence, remained absolutely undecided, till Byron visited them in 1764. And Captain Macbride, who followed him thither two years after, having circumnavigated their coasts, and taken a complete survey, a chart of Falkland's Islands has been constructed, with so much accuracy, that the coasts of Great Britain, itself, are not more authentically laid down upon our maps.

How little was really known of the islands in the South Atlantic, even so late as the time of Lord Anson, we have the most remarkable proofs, in the History of his voyage. Unavoidably led into mistake, by the imperfect materials then in the possession of the world, he had considered Pepys's Island, and Falkland Isles, as distinct places, distant from each other about five degrees of latitude *. Byron's researches have rectified this capital error; and it is now decided, beyond all contradiction, that *future navigators will mispend their time, if they look for Pepys's Island in latitude 47°*; it being now certain, that Pepys's Island is no other than those islands of Falkland †.

* See Lord Anson's Voyage, quarto edition, p. 91.

† These are Captain Cook's words, *Preface to his Voyage*, p. 14.; and the evidence, on which he forms this judgment, may be met with in Hawkesworth's Journal of Byron's Voyage, Vol. I. p. 23, 24,—51, 52, 53, 54.

Besides

INTRODUCTION.

Besides the determination of this considerable point, other lands, situated in the South Atlantic, have been brought forward into view. If the isle of Georgia had been formerly seen by La Roche, in 1675, and by Mr. Guyot, in the ship Lion, in 1756, which seems to be probable, Captain Cook, in 1775, has made us fully acquainted with its extent and true position; and, in the same year, he added to the map of the world Sandwich Land, hitherto not known to exist, and the most Southern discovery that has been ever accomplished[*].

II.

Though the Strait of Magalhaens had been frequently visited, and sailed through, by ships of different nations, before our time, a careful examination of its bays, and harbours, and head-lands; of the numerous islands it contains, and of the coasts, on both sides, that inclose it; and an exact account of the tides, and currents, and soundings, throughout its whole extent, was a task, which, if Sir John Narborough, and others, had not totally omitted, they cannot be said to have recorded so fully, as to preclude the utility of future investigation. This task has been ably and effectually performed by Byron, Wallis, and Carteret; whose transactions in this Strait, and the chart of it, founded on their observations and discoveries, are a most valuable accession to geography.

III.

If the correct information, thus obtained, about every part of this celebrated Strait, should deter future adventurers from involving themselves in the difficulties and

[*] See the Chart of Discoveries in the South Atlantic. Cook's Voyage, Vol. ii. p. 210.

embarrassments

embarrassments of a labyrinth, now known to be so intricate, and the unavoidable source of danger and delay, we have the satisfaction to have discovered, that a safer and more expeditious entrance into the Pacific Ocean, may be reasonably depended upon. The passage round Cape Horn, has been repeatedly tried, both from the East and from the West, and stript of its terrors. We shall, for the future, be less discouraged by the labours and distresses experienced by the squadrons of Lord Anson and Pizarro, when we recollect, that they were obliged to attempt the navigation of those seas at an unfavourable season of the year; and that there was nothing very formidable met with there, when they were traversed by Captain Cook.

To this distinguished navigator was reserved the honour of being the first, who, from a series of the most satisfactory observations, beginning at the West entrance of the Strait of Magalhaens, and carried on, with unwearied diligence, round Tierra del Fuego, through the Strait of Le Maire, has constructed a chart of the Southern extremity of America, from which it will appear, how much former navigators must have been at a loss to guide themselves, and what advantages will now be enjoyed by those who shall hereafter sail round Cape Horn.

IV.

As the voyages of discovery, undertaken by his Majesty's command, have facilitated the access of ships into the Pacific Ocean, they have also greatly enlarged our knowledge of its contents.

Though the immense expanse usually distinguished by this appellation, had been navigated by Europeans for near

INTRODUCTION.

near two centuries and a half*, by far the greater part of it, particularly to the South of the equator, had remained, during all this time, unexplored.

The great aim of Magalhaens, and of the Spaniards in general, its first navigators, being merely to arrive, by this passage, at the Moluccas, and the other Asiatic Spice Islands, every intermediate part of the ocean that did not lie contiguous to their Western track, which was on the North side of the equator, of course escaped due examination; and if Mendana and Quiros, and some nameless conductors of voyages before them †, by deviating from this track, and holding a Westerly one from Callao, within the Southern tropic, were so fortunate as to meet with various islands there, and so sanguine as to consider those islands as marks of the existence of a neighbouring Southern continent; in the exploring of which they flattered themselves they should rival the fame of De Gama and Columbus; these feeble efforts never led to any effectual disclosure of the supposed hidden mine of the New World. On the contrary, their voyages being conducted without a judicious plan, and their discoveries being left imperfect without immediate settlement, or subsequent examination, and scarcely recorded in any well-authenticated or accurate narrations, had been almost forgot, or were so obscurely remembered, as only to serve the purpose of producing perplexing debates about their situation and extent; if not to suggest doubts about their very existence.

* Magalhaens's Voyage was undertaken in 1519.

† See the particulars of their discoveries in Mr. Dalrymple's valuable Collection of Voyages in the South Pacific Ocean.

INTRODUCTION.

It seems, indeed, to have become a very early object of policy in the Spanish councils, to discontinue and to discourage any farther researches in that quarter. Already masters of a larger empire on the continent of America than they could conveniently govern, and of richer mines of the precious metals on that continent than they could convert into use, neither avarice nor ambition furnished reasons for aiming at a fresh accession of dominions. And thus, though settled all along the shores of this Ocean, in a situation so commodious for prosecuting discoveries throughout its wide extent, the Spaniards remained satisfied with a coasting intercourse between their own ports; never stretching across the vast gulph that separates that part of America from Asia, but in an unvarying line of navigation; perhaps in a single annual ship, between Acapulco and Manilla.

The tracks of other European navigators of the South Pacific Ocean, were, in a great measure, regulated by those of the Spaniards; and consequently limited within the same narrow bounds. With the exception, perhaps, of two instances only, those of Le Maire and Roggewein, no ships of another nation had entered this sea, through the Strait of Magalhaens, or round Cape Horn, but for the purposes of clandestine trade with the Spaniards, or of open hostility against them; purposes which could not be answered, without precluding any probable chance of adding much to our stock of discovery. For it was obviously incumbent on all such adventurers, to confine their cruises within a moderate distance of the Spanish settlements; in the vicinity of which alone they could hope to exercise their commerce, or to execute their predatory and military operations. Accordingly, soon after emerging from the Strait, or completing

pleting the circuit of Tierra del Fuego, they began to hold a Northerly course, to the uninhabited island of Juan Fernandez, their usual spot of rendezvous and refreshment. And, after ranging along the continent of America, from Chili to California, they either reversed their course back to the Atlantic; or, if they ventured to extend their voyage, by stretching over to Asia, they never thought of trying experiments in the unfrequented and unexplored parts of the Ocean; but chose the beaten path (if the expression may be used), within the limits of which it was likely that they might meet with a Philippine galleon, to make their voyage profitable to themselves; but could have little prospect, if they had been desirous, of making it useful to the world, by gaining any accession of new land to the Map of the World.

By the natural operation of these causes, it could not but happen, that little progress should be made toward obtaining a full and accurate knowledge of the South Pacific Ocean. Something, however, had been attempted by the industrious, and once enterprising Dutch; to whom we are indebted for three voyages, undertaken for the purposes of discovery; and whose researches, in the Southern latitudes of this Ocean, are much better ascertained than are those of the earlier Spanish navigators above mentioned.

Le Maire and Schouten, in 1616, and Roggewein, in 1722, wisely judging, that nothing new could be gained by adhering to the usual passage on the North side of the line, traversed this Ocean from Cape Horn to the East Indies, crossing the South tropic; a space which had been so seldom, and so ineffectually visited; though popular belief, fortified by philosophical speculation, expected there to reap the richest harvest of discovery.

b 2 Tasman,

INTRODUCTION.

Tasman, in 1642, in his extensive circuit from Batavia, through the South Indian Ocean, entered the South Pacific, at its greatest distance from the American side, where it never had been examined before. And his range continued from a high Southern latitude, Northward to New Guinea, and the islands to the East of it near the equator, produced intermediate discoveries, that have rendered his voyage memorable in the annals of navigation.

But still, upon the whole, what was effected in these three expeditions, served only to shew how large a field was reserved for future and more persevering examination. Their results had, indeed, enabled geographers to diversify the vacant uniformity of former charts of this Ocean, by the insertion of some new Islands. But the number, and the extent of these insertions were so inconsiderable, that they may be said to appear

Rari, nantes in gurgite vasto.

And, if the discoveries were few, those few were made very imperfectly. Some coasts were approached, but not landed upon; and passed without waiting to examine their extent, and connection with those that might exist at no great distance. If others were landed upon, the visits were, in general, so transient, that it was scarcely possible to build upon a foundation, so weakly laid, any information that could even gratify idle curiosity; much less satisfy philosophical inquiry, or contribute greatly to the safety, or to the success of future navigation.

Let us, however, do justice to these beginnings of discovery. To the Dutch we must, at least, ascribe the merit of being our harbingers, though we afterward went beyond them

INTRODUCTION.

them in the road they had first ventured to tread. And with what success his Majesty's ships have, in their repeated voyages, penetrated into the obscurest recesses of the South Pacific Ocean, will appear from the following enumeration of their various and very extensive operations, which have drawn up the veil that had hitherto been thrown over the geography of so great a proportion of the globe.

1. The several lands, of which any account had been given, as seen by any of the preceding navigators, Spanish or Dutch, have been carefully looked for; and most of them (at least such as seemed to be of any consequence) found out and visited; and not visited in a cursory manner, but every means used to correct former mistakes, and to supply former deficiencies, by making accurate inquiries ashore, and taking skilful surveys of their coasts, by sailing round them. Who has not heard, or read, of the boasted *Tierra Australia del Espiritu Santo* of Quiros? But its bold pretensions to be a part of a Southern continent, could not stand Captain Cook's examination, who sailed round it, and assigned it its true position and moderate bounds, in the Archipelago of the New Hebrides [*].

2. Besides perfecting many of the discoveries of their predecessors, our late navigators have enriched geographical knowledge with a long catalogue of their own. The Pacific Ocean, within the South tropic, repeatedly traversed, in every direction, was found to swarm with a seemingly endless profusion of habitable spots of land. Islands scattered through the amazing space

---

[*] Bougainville, in 1768, did no more than discover that the land here was not connected, but composed of islands. Captain Cook, in 1774, explored the whole group. See Cook's Voyage, Vol. ii. p. 96.

INTRODUCTION.

of near fourscore degrees of longitude, separated at various distances, or grouped in numerous clusters, have, at their approach, as it were, started into existence; and such ample accounts have been brought home concerning them and their inhabitants, as may serve every useful purpose of inquiry; and, to use Captain Cook's words, who bore so considerable a share in those discoveries, *have left little more to be done in that part* *.

3. Byron, Wallis, and Carteret, had each of them contributed toward increasing our knowledge of the islands that exist in the Pacific Ocean, within the limits of the Southern tropic; but how far that ocean reached to the West, what lands bounded it on that side, and the connection of those lands with the discoveries of former navigators, was still the reproach of geographers, and remained absolutely unknown, till Captain Cook, during his first voyage in 1770†, brought back the most satisfactory decision of this important question. With a wonderful perseverance, and consummate skill, amidst an uncommon combination of perplexities and dangers, he traced this coast near two thousand miles from the 38° of South latitude, cross the tropic, to its Northern extremity, within 10°½ of the equinoctial, where it was found to join the lands already explored by the Dutch, in several voyages from their Asiatic settlements, and to which they have given the name of New Holland. Those discoveries made in the last century, before Tasman's voyage, had traced the North and the West coasts of this land; and Captain Cook, by his extensive operations on its East side, left little to be done toward completing the full circuit of it. Between Cape Hicks, in latitude 38°, where his examination of this coast began; and that part of Van

* Cook's Voyage, Vol. ii. p. 239.   † See Hawkesworth's Collection, Vol. iii.

Diemen's

INTRODUCTION.

Diemen's Land, from whence Tafman took his departure, was not above fifty-five leagues. It was highly probable, therefore, that they were connected; though Captain Cook cautiously says, that *he could not determine whether* his New South Wales, that is, the East Coast of New Holland, *joins to Van Diemen's Land, or no*[*]. But what was thus left undetermined by the operations of his first voyage, was, in the course of his second, soon cleared up; Captain Furneaux, in the Adventure, during his separation from the Resolution (a fortunate separation as it thus turned out) in 1773, having explored Van Diemen's Land, from its Southern point, along the East coast, far beyond Tafman's station, and on to the latitude 38°, where Captain Cook's examination of it in 1770 had commenced [†].

It is no longer, therefore, a doubt, that we have now a full knowledge of the whole circumference of this vast body of land, this fifth part of the world (if I may so speak), which our late voyages have discovered to be of so amazing a magnitude, that, to use Captain Cook's words, *it is of a larger extent than any other country in the known world, that does not bear the name of a continent* [‡].

4. Tafman having entered the Pacific Ocean, after leaving Van Diemen's Land, had fallen in with a coast to which he gave the name of New Zealand. The extent of this coast, and its position in any direction but a part of its West side, which he sailed along in his course Northward, being left absolutely unknown, it had been a favourite opinion amongst geographers, since his time, that New Zealand was

---
[*] Hawkesworth, Vol. iii. p. 483.
[†] Cook's Voyage, Vol. i. p. 114.
[‡] Hawkesworth, Vol. iii. p. 622.

a part

INTRODUCTION.

a part of a Southern continent, running North and South, from the 33° to the 64° of South latitude, and its Northern coast, stretching across the South Pacific to an immense distance, where its Eastern boundary had been seen by Juan Fernandez, half a century before. Captain Cook's voyage in the Endeavour, has totally destroyed this supposition. Though Tasman must still have the credit of having first seen New Zealand; to Captain Cook solely belongs that of having really explored it. He spent near six months upon its coasts in 1769 and 1770*, circumnavigated it completely, and ascertained its extent and division into two islands†. Repeated visits since that, have perfected this important discovery, which, though now known to be no part of a Southern continent, will, probably, in all future charts of the world, be distinguished as the largest islands that exist in that part of the Southern hemisphere.

5. Whether New Holland did or did not join to New Guinea, was a question involved in much doubt and uncertainty, before Captain Cook's sailing between them, through Endeavour Strait, decided it. We will not hesitate to call this an important acquisition to geography. For though the great sagacity and extensive reading of Mr. Dalrymple, had discovered some traces of such a passage having been found before‡, yet these traces were so obscure, and so little known in the present age, that they had not generally regulated the construction of our charts; the President De

* From October 6, 1769, to March 31, 1770.
† Its Southern extremity nearly in latitude 47°, and its Northern in 35°]. See Captain Cook's chart, in Hawkesworth, Vol. ii. p. 281.
‡ See the track of Torre, in one of Quiros's ships, in 1606, between New Holland and New Guinea, upon Mr. Dalrymple's Chart of Discoveries in the South Pacific Ocean, before 1764.

Brosses,

INTRODUCTION.

Broffes*, who wrote in 1756, and was well verfed in geographical refearches, had not been able to fatisfy himfelf about them; and Monf. de Bougainville, in 1768, who had ventured to fall in with the South coaſt of New Guinea, near ninety leagues to the Weſtward of its South Eaſt point, chofe rather to work thofe ninety leagues directly to windward, at a time when his people were in fuch diſtreſs for proviſions as to eat the feal-fkins from off the yards and rigging, than to run the rifk of finding a paffage, of the exiſtence of which he entertained the ſtrongeſt doubts, by perfevering in his Weſterly courfe †. Captain Cook therefore in this part of his voyage (though he modeſtly difclaims all merit ‡), has eſtabliſhed, beyond future controverfy, a fact of effential fervice to navigation, by opening if not a new, at leaſt an unfrequented and forgotten communication between the South Pacific and Indian Oceans.

6. One more difcovery, for which we are indebted to Captain Carteret, as fimilar in fome degree to that laſt mentioned, may properly fucceed it, in this enumeration. Dampier, in failing round what was fuppofed to be part of the coaſt of New Guinea, difcovered it to belong to a feparate ifland, to which he gave the name of New Britain. But that the land which he named New Britain, fhould be fub-divided again into two feparate large iflands, with many

---

* M. de Broſſes fays of New Guinea: "C'eſt une longue iſle, ou preſqu' iſle, & elle touche à la Nouvelle Hollande." *Navigations aux Terres Auſtrales*, Tom. I. p. 434.

† "Le trifte état où nous étions réduits, ne nous permettoit de chercher en faifant "route à l'oueſt, un paſſage au fud de la Nouvelle Guinée, qui nous frayât par le "Golfe de la Carpentarie une route nouvelle & courte aux îles Moluques. Rien "s'étoit à la verité plus problematique que l'exiſtence de ce paſſage." *Voyage autour du Monde*, p. 259.

‡ Hawkeſworth, Vol. iii. p. 610.

Vol. I. c fmaller

smaller intervening, is a point of geographical information, which, if ever traced by any of the earliest navigators of the South Pacific, had not been handed down to the present age: and its having been ascertained by Captain Carteret, deserves to be mentioned as a discovery, in the strictest sense of the word; a discovery of the utmost importance to navigation. St. George's Channel, through which his ship found a way, between New Britain and New Ireland, from the Pacific into the Indian Ocean, to use the Captain's own words*, "is a much better and shorter passage, whether from the Eastward or Westward, than round all the islands and lands to the Northward †."

V.

The voyages of Byron, Wallis, and Carteret were principally confined to a favourite object of discovery in the South Atlantic, and though accessions to geography were procured by them in the South Pacific, they could do but little toward giving the world a complete view of the contents of that immense expanse of ocean, through which they only held a direct track, on their way homeward by the East-Indies. Cook, indeed, who was appointed to the conduct of the succeeding voyage, had a more accurate examination of the South Pacific intrusted to him. But as the improvement of astronomy went hand in hand, in his instructions, with that of geography, the Captain's solicitude

---

* Hawkesworth, Vol. I. p. 563.

† The position of the Solomon Islands, Mendana's celebrated discovery, will no longer remain a matter in debate amongst geographers, Mr. Dalrymple having, on the most satisfactory evidence, proved, that they are the cluster of islands which comprises what has since been called New Britain, New Ireland, &c. The great light thrown on that cluster by Captain Carteret's discovery, is a strong confirmation of this. See Mr. Dalrymple's Collection of Voyages, Vol. i. p. 16—21.

INTRODUCTION.

to arrive at Otaheite time enough to obferve the *tranfit* of Venus, put it out of his power to deviate from his direct track, in fearch of unknown lands that might lie to the South Eaft of that ifland. By this unavoidable attention to his duty, a very confiderable part of the South Pacific, and that part where the richeft mine of difcovery was fuppofed to exift, remained unvifited and unexplored, during that voyage in the Endeavour. To remedy this, and to clear up a point, which, though many of the learned were confident of, upon principles of fpeculative reafoning, and many of the unlearned admitted, upon what they thought to be credible teftimony, was ftill held to be very problematical, if not abfolutely groundlefs, by others who were lefs fanguine or more incredulous; his Majefty, always ready to forward every inquiry that can add to the ftock of interefting knowledge in every branch, ordered another expedition to be undertaken. The fignal fervices performed by Captain Cook, during his firft voyage, of which we have given the outlines, marked him as the fitteft perfon to finifh an examination which he had already fo fkilfully executed in part. Accordingly, he was fent out in 1772, with two fhips, the Refolution and Adventure, upon the moft enlarged plan of difcovery known in the annals of navigation. For he was inftructed not only to circumnavigate the whole globe, but to circumnavigate it in high Southern latitudes, making fuch traverfes, from time to time, into every corner of the Pacific Ocean not before examined, as might finally and effectually refolve the much agitated queftion about the exiftence of a Southern continent, in any part of the Southern hemifphere acceffible by navigation.

The ample acceffions to geography, by the difcovery of many iflands within the Tropic in the Pacific Ocean, in the

INTRODUCTION.

course of this voyage, which was carried on, with singular perseverance, between three and four years, have been already stated to the reader. But the general search now made, throughout the whole Southern hemisphere, as being the principal object in view, hath been reserved for this separate article. Here, indeed, we are not to take notice of lands that have been discovered, but of seas sailed through, where lands had been supposed to exist. In tracing the route of the Resolution and Adventure, throughout the South Atlantic, the South Indian, and the South Pacific Oceans that environ the globe, and combining it with the route of the Endeavour, we receive what may be called ocular demonstration, that Captain Cook, in his persevering researches, sailed over many an extensive continent, which, though supposed to have been seen by former navigators, at the approach of his ships, sunk into the bosom of the ocean, and, *like the baseless fabric of a vision, left not a rack behind*[*].

It

---

[*] It must be observed, however, that Monsieur le Monier, in the Memoirs of the French Academy of Sciences for 1776, pleads for the existence of Cape Circumcision, seen by Bouvet in 1738, which our English navigator sought for in vain, and supposed to have been only an island of ice. Mr. Wales, in a paper read before the Royal Society, very forcibly replied to M. le Monier's objections; and the attack having been repeated, he has drawn up a more extended defence of this part of Captain Cook's Journal, which he hath very obligingly communicated, and is here inserted.

Arguments, tending to prove that Captain Cook sought for Cape Circumcision under the proper Meridian; and that the Objections which have been made to his Conduct, in this respect, are not well founded.

In the Memoirs of the Royal Academy of Sciences at Paris for 1776, printed in 1779, M. *Le Monier* has made some remarks, with a design to shew that Captain Cook sought the land, usually called Cape Circumcision, in a wrong place; and that, instead of looking for it under the meridian of 9°, or 10° of East longitude, he ought to have looked for it under a meridian which is only 3°, or 3°½ to the Eastward of the

meridian

INTRODUCTION.

It has been urged, that the existence of a Southern continent is necessary to preserve an *equilibrium* between the two meridian of Greenwich: and consequently that this land may exist, notwithstanding all that has yet been done to find it. M. Le Monier has also two additional Memoirs on the same subject, in the volume for 1779, occasioned, as it appears, by some objections which have been made to his former Memoir before the Academy. For some reason or other, the Academy has not thought proper to print the objections which have been made to M. Le Monier's hypothesis; nor has he been particular enough in his two Memoirs, which reply to them, to enable me to say of what importance the objections are. I can only gather, that they contain some exceptions to the quantity by which M. Le Monier affers the variation alters in 10° of longitude, under the parallel of 54° South; and which, I conceive, has little to do in the dispute.

Whether the land, usually called Cape Circumcision, exists or not, is a point of small importance to geography; as the most strenuous afferters of its existence must allow it to be a very inconsiderable island, and of no use. This, therefore, is not, in itself, a matter worthy of dispute: but, in afferting this, M. Le Monier has, and I am sorry to observe it, with some asperity too, particularly in his second Memoir, endeavoured to censure the judgment and conduct of Captain Cook, whose memory I have every reason to revere, as well as the judgment of those who were with him; and, on this account, I cannot help feeling myself called on to explain the motives which induced Captain Cook to place no dependance on the arguments, now adduced by M. Le Monier, in support of his supposition; and which, M. Le Monier must know, were not unattended to, at that time, from what the Captain has said, p. 236. Vol. II. of his Account of the Voyage. And it may be proper to observe here, that what fell from Captain Cook, on this subject, was to shew that this circumstance was then attended to, and not to throw blame on M. Bouvet, for whose memory and abilities Captain Cook entertained great respect: nor is it incompatible with the utmost respect, for a man to have a favourable opinion of his own labours; or to endeavour to shew why he thinks the disagreement between them and those of another person, when there is one, does not arise from an error committed by himself. There could, therefore, be no occasion for M. Le Monier to express himself as he has done in several parts of his second Memoir.

The substance of M. Le Monier's argument is this. In 1739, when M. Bouvet's discovery is supposed to have been made, the methods for determining the longitude of a ship at sea were very defective; and, of course, the longitude of any land which happened accidentally to be seen by one, was equally uncertain. On a presumption that this was the case with respect to Cape Circumcision, M. Le Monier enquires into the quantity of the variation of the magnetic needle, observed by M. Bouvet at that place, and also into observations of the same kind, made at other places in the neighbourhood of it, about the same time, as well as both before and since. And by comparing these observations together, he concludes, that at the time when Captain Cook was

in

INTRODUCTION.

two hemispheres. But however plausible this theory may seem, at first sight, experience has abundantly detected its fallacy.

In these seas, the variation of the needle at Cape Circumcision must have been 10° Westerly; whereas, in the most Westerly point of Captain Cook's track, where he was sufficiently near the parallel of 54° South, to have seen land situated in it, the variation was 13° ¼ Westerly. This difference of 3° ¾, in the variation, answers to about 7° of longitude, in this part of the parallel of 54° South: and by so much did Captain Cook fall in with this parallel to the Eastward of what he ought to have done to see the land in question. "Hence (M. Le Monier infers), that it is not surprizing the British navigator should not find Cape Circumcision under a meridian which is 18° ¼ to the Eastward of Ferro, when it is really situated under a meridian which is but 11° ¼ to the Eastward of it."

In replying to these allegations, I shall, first, shew, that, granting the dependence which *M. Le Monier* supposes may be placed on observations of the variation made at sea, he has stated the quantity of the variation, observed on board the Resolution, very erroneously.

Secondly, I shall prove, beyond contradiction, that observations of the variation, made at sea, cannot be depended on, for the purposes to which *M. Le Monier* has applied them.

And, lastly, that no material error had crept into *M. Bayly*'s reckoning; but that if any error did exist, it must have been of a contrary nature to that which *M. Le Monier* supposes.

That *M. Le Monier* has not given altogether a true representation of the matter, will appear from hence. On the 16th of February, at noon *, the Resolution was in latitude 54° 31′ South, which is sufficiently near the parallel of 54° South, to see high land, the Northern extremity of which lies to the Southward of that parallel; and at that time we were in 6° East of Greenwich, or 25° ¼ East of the island of Ferro: that is, 4° ¾ less than is assigned for our situation by *M. Le Monier*. On the evening of the same day, the ship being in latitude 54° 24′, and longitude 6° 30′, or 24° ¼ East of Ferro, the variation was no more than 12° 7 West, which also is near a degree and half less than *M. Le Monier* says it was, when we first arrived in a proper parallel for seeing Cape Circumcision. It is true, the next morning, in latitude 54° 21′ South, longitude 8° 6′ East, we had 13° 42′ West variation; but this was after we had run more than two degrees within sight of the parallel of 54° South. It is, moreover, highly probable, that both these variations were too great; for, on the 27th, in the evening, latitude 54° 25′ South, and longitude 9° 10′ East; that is, 1° ¼

more

---

* I here go by the dates in "The Original Astronomical Observations," printed by order of the Board of Longitude; which, after the 14th of February 1775, differ one day from Captain Cook's date.

INTRODUCTION.

fallacy. In consequence of Captain Cook's voyage, now under consideration, we have a thorough knowledge of the state

move to the Eastward, and after we had run 3° ½ on the parallel we were then on, the variation was no more than 13° 16′ West. It is also worthy of remark, that on the 14th, in the evening, latitude 56° 14½′ South, and longitude 4° 50′ East, which is but 1° 10′ to the Westward of the point, where the Resolution came first into a proper situation to see land, situated in the parallel of 54° South, the variation observed was no more than 6° 30′ West. And we may further add, that on the 1st of March, 1774, the Adventure had no more than 12° ½ West variation, though she was then considerably both to the Northward and Eastward of our situation on the 17th of February, in the morning, on both which accounts the variation ought to have been greater, instead of a whole degree less. From all these circumstances, there can be little doubt but that the two variations, observed by us on the 16th and 17th of February, were too great; or that the variation, at the point where the Resolution first came sufficiently near the parallel of 54° South, to see land, the Northern extremity of which is situated in that parallel, could not be more than 11° ½ West, instead of 13° ½, as *M. Le Monier* has represented it.

Under this head of enquiry I may also observe, that although the Resolution was too much to the Southward of the parallel of 54° South, when she crossed the meridian which is 21° ½ to the Eastward of Ferro; that is, 3° ½ East of Greenwich, the longitude which *M. Le Monier* assigns for Cape Circumcision, to see if it had been in that situation; yet her comfort, the Adventure, was for several degrees on each side of that meridian, and especially when she had 10° ½ of West variation, full as near to the parallel of 54° South, as *M. Bouvet* was to the land when he saw it *: and on the day that she actually passed that meridian, had fine clear weather †. Hence, therefore, granting *M. Le Monier* his own arguments, which, however, I have proved to be erroneous; and that observations made at sea, for the variation of the compass, may be depended on for the purpose of finding the longitude, it is utterly impossible that both the Resolution and Adventure could have passed Cape Circumcision without seeing it. But I shall now shew, that those observations are liable to a much greater error than the whole quantity, so vigorously insisted on by this gentleman.

I will not here run the risk of incurring *M. Le Monier*'s displeasure, by calling the accuracy of *M. Bouvet*'s observations in question; but will admit every thing that he himself can think due to the instruments and observations of that deserving navigator. It is enough for my argument, and it is but too evident, from the observations themselves, that ours were by no means capable of determining the variation to so small a quantity

---

* See The Original Astronomical Observations, p. 185, and Bouvet's Voyage, published by Mr. Dalrymple, p. 4, and 11.

† See the Observations, p. 212.

INTRODUCTION.

ftate of the Southern hemifphere, and can pronounce with certainty, that the *equilibrium* of the globe is effectually preferved,

quantity as that which *M. Le Monier* refts his whole caufe upon; and if fo, his arguments, which depend wholly on a fuppofition, that not only they, but *M. Barow's* alfo, were capable of determining it with the utmoft exactnefs, muft fall to the ground.

1ft, It appears, from various inftances, that the variations obferved by the fame compafs would differ 3° to 5°, 6°, and fometimes even 10°, from no other caufe whatever, but putting the fhip's head a contrary way [a].

2d, That the fame compafs, in the fame fituation in every refpect, within a few miles, but at two different times of the fame day, would give variations differing from one another, 3°, 4°, 5°, 6°, and even 7° [b].

3d, That the fame compafs, on the fame day, and in the hands of the fame obferver, will give variations differing from one another by 5°, on board the fame fhip, when under fail, and when at anchor in a road-ftead [c].

4th, Compaffes, made by the fame artift, at the fame time and place, but on board different fhips, differed 3°, 4°, and even 5° in the variation [d].

5th, The fame Compaffes, on board the fame fhip, and within a few miles of the fame fituation, but at different times of our being there, gave variations differing by 4° and 5°, or upwards [e].

6th, Different

---

[a] See the Original Aftronomical Obfervations, made in the fecond Voyage, March 18, 1773, p. 372. January 14, 1774, p. 373, and July 28, p. 378.

[b] Obfervations in the fecond Voyage, February 1, 1773, p. 371, and January 19, 1775, p. 382. Alfo Obfervations in laft Voyage, July 17, 1776, p. 179. Auguft 30, p. 181. January 24, 1777, p. 192, and September 15, 1778, p. 205.

[c] Aftronomical obfervations of fecond Voyage, July 14, 1775, p. 385.

[d] Compare the Aftronomical Obfervations, made in the fecond Voyage, Auguft 3, and 9, and September 4, 1772, p. 182, with thofe of the fame dates, p. 369. Thofe of January 11, and 14, and February 7, 1775, p. 181, with thofe of the fame dates, p. 371. Alfo Aftronomical Obfervations, made in the laft Voyage, of December 17, 1776, p. 191. February 22, 1778, p. 201. May 5, and 8, p. 155. July 9, and 24, 1779, p. 209, and January 16, 1780, p. 212, with thofe of the fame dates, p. 191, 193, 194, 197, and 198.

[e] Compare Aftronomical Obfervations, made in the fecond Voyage, February 10, p. 375, with Obfervations of December 11, 1774, p. 381. Alfo Obfervations, made in the laft Voyage, May 3, and June 18, 1779, p. 208.

INTRODUCTION.

preserved, though the proportion of sea actually sailed through, leaves no sufficient space for the corresponding mass

6th, Different compasses, at the same time, on board the same ship, and in every respect under the same circumstances, will give variations differing from one another, $3°$, $4°$, $5°$, and $6°$ *.

These differences, several of which happened very near the place in question, are all of them at least equal to, most of them much greater, and some of them double that which *M. Le Monier* founds his argument on, even according to his own account of it, which I have already shewn is by no means admissible, and, therefore, totally invalidate it. To allege that the instruments made use of in Captain Cook's two voyages were bad, or that the observers were not expert in the use of them, will answer no purpose: they are the instruments and observers which *M. Le Monier*'s argument must rest on; and, therefore, let those of the French, or any other navigators, have been ever so much better than they were (which few will be hardy enough to assert, and fewer still found weak enough to believe), it will avail nothing to the point in dispute, which must evidently fall to the ground, if the observations made for finding the variation in Captain Cook's voyage are not sufficient to support it. What then must become of it, if *M. Borner*'s observations, of this kind, were liable to an equal, or a greater error? which, without any reasonable cause for offence, we might suppose they were.

It is not necessary to account for these differences in the observed variations in this place, nor yet to point out the reasons why such anomalies have not been noticed in observations of this kind before. I shall, however, remark, that I have hinted at some of the causes in my introduction to the observations which were made in Captain Cook's second voyage; and many others will readily offer themselves to persons who have had much practice in making these observations, and who have attentively considered the principles on which the instruments are constructed, and the manner in which they are fabricated. Nor is it at all surprising, that the errors to which the instruments and observations of this kind are liable, should not have been discovered before, since no navigators before us ever gave the same opportunity, by multiplying their observations, and making them under such a variety of circumstances as we did.

Having now fully shewn, that the circumstances, brought forward by *M. Le Monier*, in support of his argument, are neither such as can be depended on, nor yet

fairly

---

* Observations made in the second Voyage, February 2, 1773, p. 371. March 18, p. 372. and January 14, 1774, p. 375. See also Observations made last Voyage, August 18, 1776, p. 180. October 7, and 14, p. 189. and 190. December 11, p. ibid. January 14, 1777, p. 192. March 10, p. 193. July 9, and 17, 1779, p. 209. January 10, 1780, p. 212. March 14, p. 213. and May 19, p. 233.

VOL. I.   d

INTRODUCTION.

mass of land, which, on speculative arguments had been maintained to be necessary [*].

If fairly represented, I shall next attempt to demonstrate, that it is utterly improbable M. Bouvet could be out, in his account of longitude, so much as is here supposed, in the short run which had been made from the island of St. Catharine, the place they took their departure from: on the contrary, that there is sufficient reason to believe the error, of whatever magnitude it might be, was of a different nature from that contended for, and that the two ships, instead of being to the Westward of their account of longitude, were actually to the Eastward of it. For, according to their Journals, extracted from the archives of the French East-India Company, by M. D'Après, printed under his inspection, and published by Mr. Dalrymple, F. R. S. amongst other voyages made for the purpose of examining the Southern parts of the Atlantic Ocean, the longitude, according to the Eagle's run from St. Catherine's, was 26° 27′, and according to the Mary's, 26° 20′ East of Teneriff; that is, 9° 57′, and 9° 50′ East of Greenwich, or 27° 45′, and 27° 36′ East of Ferro. But the Mary, which went to the Cape of Good Hope, made 7° 15′ East longitude from the land in question, to that place. Consequently the Cape of Good Hope being in longitude 18° 23′ East of Greenwich, Cape Circumcision will be in 11° 10′ East of Greenwich, or 1° 20′ more to the Eastward than the run by the same ship from the island of St. Catherine's makes it. Again, the Eagle made the difference of longitude between Cape Circumcision, and the island of Rodrigues, 49° 44′ : and by the observations of M. Pingré, this island is in 62° 50′ of East longitude from Greenwich :: Cape Circumcision is therefore in 13° 6′ East of Greenwich, or 2° 9′ more to the Eastward than by the Eagle's run from St. Catherine's. Hence, therefore, as the longitude of this land, resulting from a comparison of that shewn by each of the ships, on their making land at places where the longitude is exceedingly well determined, is greater than that which results from their run from St. Catherine's, the longitude of which is not known with certainty within several degrees, we may infer, with great safety, that whatever the quantity of M. Bouvet's error might be, when he is supposed to have seen Cape Circumcision, it must have been in defect, and not in excess, as M. Le Monnier supposes it.

Christ's Hospital,   W. WALES.
April 20, 1784.

[*] The judgment of the ingenious Author of *Recherches for les Américains*, on this question, seems to be very deserving of a place here: " Qu'on calcule, comme on " voudra, on sera toujours contraints d'avouer, qu'il y a une plus grande portion de " continent située dans la latitude septentrionale, que dans la latitude australe.

" C'est fort mal à-propos, qu'on a soutenu que cette répartition inégale ne sauroit " exister, sous prétexte que le globe perdroit son équilibre, faute d'un contrepoids suf-
" fisant

INTRODUCTION.

If former navigators have added more land to the known globe than Captain Cook, to him, at least, was reserved the honour of being foremost in disclosing to us the extent of sea that covers its surface. His own summary view of the transactions of this voyage, will be a proper conclusion to these remarks: " I had now made the circuit of the " Southern Ocean in a high latitude, and traversed it in " such a manner as to leave not the least room for there " being a continent, unless near the pole, and out of the " reach of navigation. By twice visiting the Tropical Sea, " I had not only settled the situation of some old discove- " ries, but made there many new ones, and left, I conceive, " very little to be done, even in that part. Thus I flatter " myself, that the intention of the voyage has, in every re- " spect, been fully answered; the Southern hemisphere " sufficiently explored; and a final end put to the searching " after a Southern continent, which has, at times, engrossed " the attention of some of the Maritime Powers for near " two centuries past, and been a favourite theory amongst " the geographers of all ages [*]."

Thus far, therefore, the voyages to disclose new tracks of navigation, and to reform old defects in geography, appear to have been prosecuted with a satisfactory share of success. A perusal of the foregoing summary of what had been done, will enable every one to judge what was still

---

" Étant au pole méridionale. Il est vrai qu'un pied cube d'eau salée ne pèse pas au- " tant qu'un pied cube de terre; mais on auroit dû réfléchir, qu'il peut y avoir sous " l'océan des lits & des couches de matières, dont la pésanteur spécifique varie à " l'infini, & que le peu de profondeur d'une mer, versée sur une grande surface, con- " trebalance les endroits où il y a moins de mer, mais où elle est plus profonde." *Recherches Philosophiques*, Tom. ii. p. 375.

[*] Cook's Voyage, Vol. ii. p. 239.

INTRODUCTION.

wanting to complete the great plan of discovery. The Southern hemisphere had, indeed, been repeatedly visited, and its utmost accessible extremities been surveyed. But much uncertainty, and, of course, great variety of opinion, subsisted, as to the navigable extremities of our own hemisphere; particularly, as to the existence, or, at least, as to the practicability of a Northern passage between the Atlantic and Pacific Oceans, either by sailing Eastward, round Asia, or Westward, round North America.

It was obvious, that if such a passage could be effected, voyages to Japan and China, and, indeed, to the East Indies in general, would be much shortened; and consequently become more profitable, than by making the tedious circuit of the Cape of Good Hope. Accordingly, it became a favourite object of the English to effectuate this, above two centuries ago; and (to say nothing of Cabot's original attempt, in 1497, which ended in the discovery of Newfoundland, and the Labradore coast) from Frobisher's first voyage to find a Western passage, in 1576, to those of James and of Fox, in 1631, repeated trials had been made by our enterprizing adventurers. But though farther knowledge of the Northern extent of America was obtained in the course of these voyages, by the discovery of Hudson's and Baffin's Bays, the wished-for passage, on that side, into the Pacific Ocean, was still unattained. Our countrymen, and the Dutch, were equally unsuccessful, in various attempts, to find this passage in an Eastern direction. Wood's failure, in 1676, seems to have closed the long list of unfortunate Northern expeditions in that century; and the discovery, if not absolutely despaired of, by having been so often missed, ceased, for many years, to be sought for.

Mr.

INTRODUCTION.

Mr. Dobbs, a warm advocate for the probability of a North West passage through Hudson's Bay, in our own time, once more recalled the attention of this country to that undertaking; and, by his active zeal, and persevering solicitation, renewed the spirit of discovery. But it was renewed in vain. For Captain Middleton, sent out by Government in 1741, and Captains Smith and Moore, by a private society, in 1746, though encouraged by an act of Parliament passed in the preceding year, that annexed a reward of twenty thousand pounds to the discovery of a passage, returned from Hudson's Bay with reports of their proceedings, that left the accomplishment of this favourite object at as great a distance as ever.

When researches of this kind, no longer left to the solicitation of an individual, or to the subscriptions of private adventurers, became cherished by the Royal attention, in the present reign, and warmly promoted by the Minister at the head of the naval department, it was impossible, while so much was done toward exploring the remotest corners of the Southern hemisphere, that the Northern passage should not be attempted. Accordingly, while Captain Cook was prosecuting his voyage toward the South Pole, in 1773, Lord Mulgrave sailed with two ships, *to determine how far navigation was practicable toward the North Pole*. And though his Lordship met with the same insuperable bar to his progress, which former navigators had experienced [*], the hopes of opening a communication between the Pacific and Atlantic Oceans, by a Northerly course, were not abandoned;

---
[*] See the history of former attempts to sail toward the North Pole, in the Introduction to Lord Mulgrave's Journal. Mr. Barrington has collected several instances of ships advancing to very high latitudes. See his Miscellanies, p. 1—124.

INTRODUCTION.

and a voyage for that purpose, was ordered to be undertaken.

The operations proposed to be pursued, were so new, so extensive, and so various, that the skill and experience of Captain Cook, it was thought, would be requisite to conduct them. Without being liable to any charge of want of zeal for the public service, he might have passed the rest of his days in the command to which he had been appointed in Greenwich Hospital, there to enjoy the fame he had dearly earned in two circumnavigations of the world. But he cheerfully relinquished this honourable station at home; and, happy that the Earl of Sandwich had not cast his eye upon any other Commander, engaged in the conduct of the expedition, the history of which is presented to the Public in these Volumes; an expedition that would expose him to the toils and perils of a third circumnavigation, by a track hitherto unattempted. Every former navigator round the globe had made his passage home to Europe by the Cape of Good Hope; the arduous task was now assigned to Captain Cook, of attempting it, by reaching the high Northern latitudes between Asia and America. So that the usual plan of discovery was reversed; and, instead of a passage from the Atlantic to the Pacific, one from the latter into the former was to be tried. For it was wisely foreseen, that whatever openings or inlets there might be on the East side of America, which lie in a direction which could give any hopes of a passage, the ultimate success of it would still depend upon there being an open sea between the West side of that continent, and the extremities of Asia. Captain Cook, therefore, was ordered to proceed into the Pacific Ocean, through the chain of his new islands in the Southern tropic,

INTRODUCTION.

and having croſſed the equator into its Northern Parts, then to hold ſuch a courſe as might probably fix many intereſting points in geography, and produce intermediate diſcoveries, in his progreſs Northward to the principal ſcene of his operations.

But the plan of the voyage, and the various objects it embraced, will beſt appear from the Inſtructions under which Captain Cook ſailed; and the inſertion of them here, will convey ſuch authentic information, as may enable the Reader to judge with preciſion how far they have been carried into execution.

By the COMMISSIONERS for executing the Office of Lord High Admiral of GREAT BRITAIN and IRELAND, &c.

SECRET INSTRUCTIONS for Captain JAMES COOK, Commander of his Majeſty's Sloop the RESOLUTION.

*W*HEREAS the Earl of Sandwich has ſignified to us his Majeſty's pleaſure, that an attempt ſhould be made to find out a Northern paſſage by ſea from the Pacific to the Atlantic Ocean; and whereas we have, in purſuance thereof, cauſed his Majeſty's ſloops Reſolution and Diſcovery to be fitted, in all reſpects, proper to proceed upon a voyage for the purpoſe above-mentioned, and, from the experience we have had of your abilities and good conduct in your late voyages, have thought fit to intruſt you with the conduct of the preſent intended voyage, and with that view appointed you to command the firſt mentioned ſloop, and directed Captain Clerke, who commands the other, to follow your orders for his farther proceedings; You are hereby required and directed to proceed with the ſaid two ſloops directly to the Cape of Good-Hope, unleſs you ſhall judge it neceſſary to ſtop at Madeira, the Cape de Verd, or Canary Iſlands, to take in wine for the uſe of their companies, in which caſe you are at liberty to do ſo, taking care to remain there no longer than may be neceſſary for that purpoſe.

On

INTRODUCTION.

On your arrival at the Cape of Good Hope, you are to refresh the sloops companies, and to cause the sloops to be supplied with as much provisions and water as they can conveniently stow.

You are, if possible, to leave the Cape of Good Hope by the end of October, or the beginning of November next, and proceed to the Southward in search of some islands said to have been lately seen by the French, in the latitude of 48° of South, and about the meridian of Mauritius. In case you find those islands, you are to examine them thoroughly for a good harbour; and upon discovering one, make the necessary observations to facilitate the finding it again; as a good port, in that situation, may hereafter prove very useful, although it should afford little or nothing more than shelter, wood, and water. You are not, however, to spend too much time in looking out for those islands, or in the examination of them, if found, but proceed to Otaheite, or the Society Isles (touching at New Zealand in your way thither, if you should judge it necessary and convenient), and taking care to arrive there time enough to admit of your giving the sloops companies the refreshments they may stand in need of, before you prosecute the farther object of these instructions.

Upon your arrival at Otaheite, or the Society Isles, you are to land Omiah at such of them as he may chuse, and to leave him there.

You are to distribute among the Chiefs of those islands such part of the presents with which you have been supplied, as you shall judge proper, reserving the remainder to distribute among the natives of the countries you may discover in the Northern Hemisphere: And having refreshed the people belonging to the sloops under your command, and taken on board such wood and water as they may respectively stand in need of, you are to leave those islands in the beginning of February, or sooner if you shall judge it necessary, and then proceed in as direct a course as you can to the coast of New Albion, endeavouring to fall in with it in the latitude of 45° of North; and taking care, in your way thither, not to lose any time in search of new lands, or to stop at any you may fall in with, unless you find it necessary to recruit your wood and water.

You are also, in your way thither, strictly enjoined not to touch upon any part of the Spanish dominions on the Western continent of America, unless driven thither by some unavoidable accident; in which case you are to stay no longer there than shall be absolutely necessary, and to be very careful not to give any umbrage or offence to any of the inhabitants or subjects of his Catholic Majesty. And if, in your farther progress to the Northward, as hereafter directed, you find any subjects of any European Prince or State upon any part of the coast you may think proper to visit, you are not to disturb them, or give them

INTRODUCTION.

them any just cause of offence, but, on the contrary, to treat them with civility and friendship.

Upon your arrival on the coast of New Albion, you are to put into the first convenient port to recruit your wood and water, and procure refreshments, and then to proceed Northward along the coast, as far as the latitude of 65°, or farther, if you are not obstructed by lands or ice; taking care not to lose any time in exploring rivers or inlets, or upon any other account, until you get into the before-mentioned latitude of 65°, where we could wish you to arrive in the month of June next. When you get that length, you are very carefully to search for, and to explore, such rivers or inlets as may appear to be of a considerable extent, and pointing towards Hudson's or Baffin's Bays; and if, from your own observations, or from any information you may receive from the natives (who, there is reason to believe, are the same race of people, and speak the same language, of which you are furnished with a Vocabulary, as the Esquimaux), there shall appear to be a certainty, or even a probability, of a water passage into the afore-mentioned bays, or either of them, you are, in such case, to use your utmost endeavours to pass through with one or both of the sloops, unless you shall be of opinion that the passage may be effected with more certainty, or with greater probability, by smaller vessels; in which case you are to set up the frames of one or both the small vessels with which you are provided, and, when they are put together, and are properly fitted, stored, and victualled, you are to dispatch one or both of them, under the care of proper officers, with a sufficient number of petty officers, men, and boats, in order to attempt the said passage; with such instructions for their rejoining you, if they should fail, or for their farther proceedings, if they should succeed in the attempt, as you shall judge most proper. But, nevertheless, if you shall find it more eligible to pursue any other measures than those above pointed out, in order to make a discovery of the before-mentioned passage (if any such there be), you are at liberty, and we leave it to your discretion, to pursue such measures accordingly.

In case you shall be satisfied that there is no passage through to the above-mentioned bays, sufficient for the purposes of navigation, you are, at the proper season of the year, to repair to the port of St. Peter and St. Paul in Kamtschatka, or wherever else you shall judge more proper, in order to refresh your people and pass the Winter; and, in the Spring of the ensuing year 1778, to proceed from thence to the Northward, as far as, in your prudence, you may think proper, in farther search of a North East, or North West passage, from the Pacific Ocean into the Atlantic Ocean, or the North Sea: and if, from

INTRODUCTION.

your own observation, or any information you may receive, there shall appear to be a probability of such passage, you are to proceed as above directed: and, having discovered such passage, or failed in the attempt, make the best of your way back to England, by such route as you may think best for the improvement of geography and navigation, repairing to Spithead with both sloops, where they are to remain till further order.

At whatever places you may touch in the course of your voyage, where accurate observations of the nature hereafter mentioned have not already been made, you are, as far as your time will allow, very carefully to observe the true situation of such places, both in latitude and longitude; the variation of the needle; bearings of head-lands; height, direction, and course of the tides and currents; depths and soundings of the sea; shoals, rocks, &c., and also to survey, make charts, and take views of such bays, harbours, and different parts of the coast, and to make such notations thereon, as may be useful either to navigation or commerce. You are also carefully to observe the nature of the soil, and the produce thereof; the animals and fowls that inhabit or frequent it; the fishes that are to be found in the rivers or upon the coast, and in what plenty; and, in case there are any peculiar to such places, to describe them as minutely, and to make as accurate drawings of them, as you can: and, if you find any metals, minerals, or valuable stones, or any extraneous fossils, you are to bring home specimens of each; as also of the seeds of such trees, shrubs, plants, fruits, and grains, peculiar to those places, as you may be able to collect, and to transmit them to our Secretary, that proper examination and experiments may be made of them. You are likewise to observe the genius, temper, disposition, and number of the natives and inhabitants, where you find any; and to endeavour, by all proper means, to cultivate a friendship with them; making them presents of such trinkets as you may have on board, and they may like best; inviting them to traffic; and shewing them every kind of civility and regard; but taking care, nevertheless, not to suffer yourself to be surprized by them, but to be always on your guard against any accidents.

You are also, with the consent of the natives, to take possession, in the name of the King of Great Britain, of convenient situations in such countries as you may discover, that have not already been discovered or visited by any other European power; and to distribute among the inhabitants such things as will remain as traces and testimonies of your having been there: but if you find the countries so discovered are uninhabited, you are to take possession of them for his Majesty, by setting up proper marks and inscriptions, as first discoverers and possessors.

But

INTRODUCTION.

But forasmuch as, in undertakings of this nature, several emergencies may arise not to be foreseen, and therefore not particularly to be provided for by instructions before-hand; you are, in all such cases, to proceed as you shall judge most advantageous to the service on which you are employed.

You are, by all opportunities, to send to our Secretary, for our information, accounts of your proceedings, and copies of the surveys and drawings you shall have made; and upon your arrival in England, you are immediately to repair to this office, in order to lay before us a full account of your proceedings in the whole course of your voyage; taking care, before you leave the sloop, to demand from the officers and petty officers, the log-books and journals they may have kept, and to seal them up for our inspection; and enjoining them, and the whole crew, not to divulge where they have been, until they shall have permission so to do: and you are to direct Captain Clerk to do the same, with respect to the officers, petty officers, and crew of the Discovery.

If any accident should happen to the Resolution in the course of the voyage, so as to disable her from proceeding any farther, you are, in such case, to remove yourself and her crew into the Discovery, and to prosecute your voyage in her; her Commander being hereby strictly required to receive you on board, and to obey your orders, the same, in every respect, as when you were actually on board the Resolution: And, in case of your inability, by sickness or otherwise, to carry these instructions into execution, you are to be careful to leave them with the next officer in command, who is hereby required to execute them in the best manner he can.

Given under our hands the 6th day of July, 1776,

SANDWICH.
C. SPENCER.
H. PALLISER.

By command of their Lordships,
PH. STEPHENS.

Besides ordering Captain Cook to sail on this important voyage, Government, in earnest about the object of it, adopted a measure, which, while it could not but have a powerful

powerful operation on the crews of the Resolution and Discovery, by adding the motives of interest, to the obligations of duty; at the same time encouraged all his Majesty's subjects to engage in attempts toward the proposed discovery. By the act of parliament, passed in 1745*, a reward of twenty thousand pounds had been held out. But it had been held out only to the ships *belonging to any of his Majesty's subjects*, exclusive of his Majesty's own ships. The act had a still more capital defect. It held out this reward only to such ships as should discover a passage *through Hudson's Bay*; and, as we shall soon take occasion to explain, it was, by this time, pretty certain, that no such passage existed within those limits. Effectual care was taken to remedy both these defects, by passing a new law; which, after reciting the provisions of the former, proceeds as follows: " And " whereas many advantages, both to commerce and science, " may be also expected from the discovery of *any Northern* " *passage* for vessels by sea, between the Atlantic and Pacific " Oceans—be it enacted, That if any ship belonging to any " of his Majesty's subjects, or *to his Majesty*, shall find out, " and sail through, any passage by sea, between the Atlan- " tic and Pacific Oceans, in *any direction*, or parallel of the " Northern hemisphere, to the Northward of the 52° of " Northern latitude, the owners of such ships, if belong- " ing to any of his Majesty's subjects, or *the commander, offi-* " *cers, and seamen, of such ship belonging to his Majesty*, shall re- " ceive, as a reward for such discovery, the sum of twenty " thousand pounds.

" And whereas ships employed, both in the Spitzbergen " Seas, and in Davis's Straits, have frequent opportunities

* See the Statutes at Large, 18 George II. chap. 17.

" of

INTRODUCTION.

" of approaching the North Pole, though they have not
" time, during the courfe of one fummer, to penetrate into
" the Pacific Ocean: and whereas fuch approaches may
" greatly tend to the difcovery of a communication between
" the Atlantic and Pacific Oceans, as well as be attended
" with many advantages to commerce and fcience, &c. be
" it enacted, That if any fhip fhall approach to within 1°
" of the North Pole, the owner, &c. or commander, &c.
" fo approaching, fhall receive, as a reward for fuch firft
" approach, the fum of five thoufand pounds *."

That nothing might be omitted that could facilitate the fuccefs of Captain Cook's expedition, fome time before he failed, In the beginning of the fummer of 1776, Lieutenant Pickerfgill, appointed Commander of his Majefty's armed brig the Lion, was ordered " to proceed to Davis's Straits, " for the protection of the Britifh whale fifhers;" and that firft object being fecured, " he was then required and di-
" rected to proceed up Baffin's Bay, and explore the coafts
" thereof, as far as in his judgment the fame could be done
" without apparent rifk, taking care to leave the above
" mentioned Bay fo timely, as to fecure his return to Eng-
" land in the fall of the year;" and it was farther enjoined to him, " to make nautical remarks of every kind, and to
" employ Mr. Lane (Mafter of the veffel under his com-
" mand) in furveying, making charts, and taking views of
" the feveral bays, harbours, and different parts of the coafts
" which he might vifit, and in making fuch notations thereon
" as might be ufeful to geography and navigation †."

* See the Statutes at Large, 1776, 16 George III. chap. 6.
† From his MS. Inftructions, dated May 14, 1776.

Pickerfgill,

INTRODUCTION

Pickersgill, we see, was not to attempt the discovery of the passage. He was directed to explore the coasts of Baffin's Bay, with a view only to bring back, the same year, some information, which might be an useful direction toward planning an intended voyage into that bay the ensuing summer, to try for the discovery of a passage on that side, with a view to co-operate with Captain Cook, who, it was supposed (from the tenor of his Instructions) would be trying for this passage, about the same time, from the opposite side of America.

Pickersgill, obeying his instructions, at least in this instance, did return that year; but there were sufficient reasons for not sending him out again; and the command of the next expedition into Baffin's Bay was conferred on Lieutenant Young; whose Instructions, having an immediate connection with our voyage, are here inserted.

EXTRACT of INSTRUCTIONS to Lieutenant YOUNG, commanding the LION armed Vessel, dated 13th March 1777.

Resolution, Discovery.

WHEREAS, in pursuance of the King's pleasure, signified to us by the Earl of Sandwich, his Majesty's sloops named in the margin have been sent out under the command of Captain Cook, in order, during this and the ensuing year, to attempt a discovery of a Northern passage, by sea, from the Pacific to the Atlantic Ocean; and, for that purpose, to run up as high as the latitude of 65° North, where it is hoped he will be able to arrive in the month of June next; and there, and as much farther to the Northward as in his prudence he shall think proper, very carefully to search for and explore such rivers or inlets as may appear to be of a considerable extent, and pointing to Hudson's or Baffin's Bays, or the North Sea; and, upon finding any passage through,

INTRODUCTION.

through, sufficient for the purposes of navigation, to attempt such passage with one or both of the sloops, or, if they are judged to be too large, with smaller vessels, the frames of which have been sent out with him for that purpose: And whereas, in pursuance of his Majesty's further pleasure, signified as aforesaid, the armed vessel under your command hath been fitted in order to proceed to Baffin's Bay, with a view to explore the Western parts thereof, and to endeavour to find a passage, on that side, from the Atlantic to the Pacific Ocean, and we have thought fit to intrust you with the conduct of that voyage; You are therefore hereby required and directed to put to sea in the said armed vessel, without a moment's loss of time, and make the best of your way into Baffin's Bay, and so use your best endeavours to explore the Western shores thereof, as far as in your judgment the same can be done, without apparent risque, and to examine such considerable rivers or inlets as you may discover; and, in case you find any, through which there may be a probability of passing into the Pacific Ocean, you are to attempt such passage; and if you succeed in the attempt, and shall be able to repass it again, so as to return to England this year, you are to make the best of your way to Spithead, or the Nore, and remain there until you receive further order; sending us an account of your arrival and proceedings. But if you shall succeed in the attempt, and shall find the season too far advanced for you to return the same way, you are then to look out for the most convenient place to winter in, and to endeavour to return by the said passage as early in the next year as the season will admit, and then to make the best of your way to England, as above directed.

In case, however, you should not find, or should be satisfied there is not any probability of finding, any such passage, or, finding it, you should not be able to get through in the vessel you command, you are then to return to England, as before mentioned, unless you shall find any branch of the sea leading to the Westward which you shall judge likely to afford a communication between the Atlantic and Pacific Oceans, and which you shall not be able to explore in the course of this year, it being, in that case, left to your discretion to stay the Winter in the most commodious situation you can find, in order to pursue the discovery next year, if you shall find it advisable so to do; and, having discovered such passage, or not succeeded in the attempt, you are to make the best of your way to England, as above directed.

INTRODUCTION.

It was natural to hope, that something would have been done in one or other, or in both these voyages of the Lion, that might have opened our views with regard to the practicability of a passage from this side of America. But, unfortunately, the execution did not answer the expectations conceived. Pickersgill, who had acquired professional experience when acting under Captain Cook, justly merited the censure he received, for improper behaviour when intrusted with command in Davis's Straits; and the talents of Young, as it afterward appeared, were more adapted to contribute to the glory of a victory, as Commander of a line of battle ship, than to add to geographical discoveries, by encountering mountains of ice, and exploring unknown coasts [*].

Both Pickersgill and Young having been ordered to proceed into Baffin's Bay; and Captain Cook being directed not to begin his search till he should arrive in the latitude of 65°, it may not be improper to say something here of the reasons which weighed with those who planned the voyages, and framed the instructions, to carry their views so far Northward, as the proper situation, where the passage, if it existed at all, was likely to be attempted with success. It may be asked, Why was Hudson's Bay neglected on our side of America; and why was not Captain Cook ordered to begin his search on its opposite side, in much lower lati-

[*] In the Philosophical Transactions, Vol. lxviii. p. 1057, we have the track of Pickersgill's voyage, which, probably, may be of use to our Greenland ships, as it contains many observations for fixing the longitude and latitude of the coasts in Davis's Straits. But it appears that he never entered Baffin's Bay, the highest Northern latitude to which he advanced being 68° 14'. As to Young's proceedings, having failed absolutely in making any discovery, it is of less consequence, that no communication of his journal could be procured.

tudes?

INTRODUCTION.

tudes? Particularly, why not explore the strait leading into the Western sea of John de Fuca, between the latitudes of 47° and 48°; the Archipelago of St. Lazarus of Admiral de Fonte, between 50° and 55°; and the rivers and lakes through which he found a passage North Eastward, till he met with a ship from Boston?

As to the pretended discoveries of de Fuca, the Greek Pilot, or of de Fonte, the Spanish Admiral, though they have sometimes found their way into fictitious maps, or have been warmly contended for by the espousers of fanciful systems; to have directed Captain Cook to spend any time in tracing them, would have been as wise a measure as if he had been directed to trace the situation of Lilliput or Brobdignac. The latter are, indeed, confessedly, mere objects of imagination; and the former, destitute of any sufficient external evidence, bear so many striking marks of internal absurdity, as warrant our pronouncing them to be the fabric of imposture. Captain Cook's instructions were founded on an accurate knowledge of what had been already done, and of what still remained to do; and this knowledge pointed out the inutility of beginning his search for a passage till his arrival in the latitude of 65°; of which every fair and capable inquirer will be abundantly convinced, by an attention to the following particulars.

Middleton, who commanded the expedition in 1741 and 1742, into Hudson's Bay, had proceeded farther North than any of his predecessors in that navigation. But though, from his former acquaintance with that Bay, to which he had frequently sailed in the service of the company, he had entertained hopes of finding out a passage through it into the Pacific Ocean, the observations which he was now enabled

INTRODUCTION.

enabled to make, induced him to change his opinion; and, on his return to England, he made an unfavourable report. Mr. Dobbs, the patron of the enterprize, did not acquiesce in this; and, fortified in his original idea of the practicability of the passage, by the testimony of some of Middleton's officers, he appealed to the Public, accusing him of having misrepresented facts, and of having, from interested motives, in concert with the Hudson's Bay Company, decided against the practicability of the passage, though the discoveries of his own voyage had put it within his reach.

He had, between the latitude of 65° and 66°, found a very considerable inlet running Westward, into which he entered with his ships; and, "after repeated trials of the tides, and "endeavours to discover the nature and course of the open- "ing, for three weeks successively, he found the flood con- "stantly to come from the Eastward, and that it was a large "river he had got into," to which he gave the name of Wager River *.

The accuracy, or rather the fidelity of this report was denied by Mr. Dobbs, who contended that this opening *is a Strait, and not a fresh water river*, and that Middleton, if he had examined it properly, would have found a passage through it to the Western American Ocean. The failure of this voyage, therefore, only served to furnish our zealous advocate for the discovery, with new arguments for attempting it once more; and he had the good fortune, after getting the reward of twenty thousand pounds established by act of parliament, to prevail upon a society of gentlemen and merchants to fit out the Dobbs and California;

* See the Abstract of his Journal, published by Mr. Dobbs.

which

which ships, it was hoped, would be able to find their way into the Pacific Ocean, by the very opening which Middleton's voyage had pointed out, and which he was believed to have misrepresented.

This renovation of hope only produced fresh disappointment. For it is well known, that the voyage of the Dobbs and California, instead of confuting, strongly confirmed all that Middleton had asserted. The supposed Strait was found to be nothing more than a fresh water river, and its utmost Western navigable boundaries were now ascertained, by accurate examination. But though Wager's Strait had thus disappointed our hopes, as had also done Rankin's Inlet, which was now found to be a close Bay; and though other arguments, founded on the supposed course of the tides in Hudson's Bay, appeared to be groundless; such is our attachment to an opinion once adopted, that, even after the unsuccessful issue of the voyage of the Dobbs and California, a passage through some other place in that Bay was, by many, considered as attainable; and, particularly, Chesterfield's (formerly called Bowden's) Inlet, lying between latitude 63° and 64°, succeeded Wager's Strait, in the sanguine expectations of those who remained unconvinced by former disappointments. Mr. Ellis, who was on board the ships, and who wrote the history of the voyage, holds up this as one of the places where the passage may be sought for, *upon very rational grounds, and with very good effects* *. He also mentions Repulse Bay, nearly in latitude 67°; but as to this he speaks less confidently; only saying, that by an attempt there, we might probably *approach nearer to the discovery* †. He had good reason for thus guarding his expression; for

* Ellis's Voyage, p. 318.   † Ibid. p. 330.

INTRODUCTION.

the committee, who directed this voyage, admitting the impracticability of effecting a passage at Repulse Bay, had refused allowing the ships to go into it, *being satisfied as to that place* *.

Setting Repulse Bay, therefore, aside, within which we have no reason for believing that any Inlet exists, there remained no part of Hudson's Bay to be searched, but Chesterfield's Inlet, and a small track of coast between the latitude 62°, and what is called the South Point of Main, which had been left unexplored by the Dobbs and California.

But this last gleam of hope has now disappeared. The aversion of the Hudson's Bay Company, to contribute any thing to the discovery of a North West passage, had been loudly reported by Mr. Dobbs; and the Public seemed to believe that the charge was well founded. But still, in justice to them, it must be allowed, that, in 1720, they had sent Messrs. Knight and Barlow, in a sloop on this very discovery; but these unfortunate people were never more heard of. Mr. Scroggs, who sailed in search of them, in 1722, only brought back proofs of their shipwreck, but no fresh intelligence about a passage, which he was also to look for. They also sent a sloop, and a shallop, to try for this discovery, in 1737; but to no purpose. If obstructions were thrown in the way of Captain Middleton, and of the Commanders of the Dobbs and California, the Governor and Committee of the Hudson's Bay Company, since that time, we must acknowledge, have made amends for the narrow

* Account of the Voyage, by the Clerk of the California, Vol. II. p. 273. Mr. Dobbs himself says, That he thought the passage would be impracticable, or, at least, very difficult, in case there was the farther North than 67°.
Account of Hudson's Bay, p. 99.

prejudices

INTRODUCTION.

prejudices of their predecessors; and we have it in our power to appeal to facts, which abundantly testify, that every thing has been done by them, that could be required by the Public, toward perfecting the search for a North West passage.

In the year 1761, Captain Christopher sailed from Fort Churchill, in the sloop Churchill; and his voyage was not quite fruitless; for he sailed up Chesterfield's Inlet, through which a passage had, by Mr. Ellis's account of it, been so generally expected. But when the water turned brackish, which marked that he was not in a strait, but in a river, he returned.

To leave no room for a variety of opinion, however, he was ordered to repeat the voyage the ensuing summer, in the same sloop, and Mr. Norton, in a cutter, was appointed to attend him. By the favour of the Governor and Committee of the Company, the Journals of Captain Christopher, and of Mr. Norton, and Captain Christopher's chart of the Inlet, have been readily communicated. From these authentic documents, it appears that the search and examination of Chesterfield's Inlet was now completed. It was found to end in a fresh water lake, at the distance of about one hundred and seventy miles from the sea. This lake was found also to be about twenty-one leagues long, and from five to ten broad, and to be completely closed up on every side, except to the West, where there was a little rivulet; to survey the state of which, Mr. Norton and the crew of the cutter having landed, and marched up the country, saw that it soon terminated in three falls, one above another, and not water for a small boat over them; and ridges, mostly dry from side to side, for five or six miles higher.

Thus

INTRODUCTION.

Thus ends Chesterfield's Inlet, and all Mr. Ellis's expectations of a passage through it to the Western Ocean. The other part of the coast, from latitude 62°, to the South Point of Main, within which limits hopes were also entertained of finding a passage, have, of late years, been thoroughly explored. It is here that Pistol Bay is situated; which the author who has writ last in this country, on the *probability of a North West passage*[*], speaks of as the only remaining part of Hudson's Bay where this Western communication may exist. But this has been also examined; and, on the authority of Captain Christopher, we can assure the Reader, that there is no inlet of any consequence in all that part of the coast. Nay, he has, in an open boat, sailed round the bottom of what is called Pistol Bay, and, instead of a passage to a Western Sea, found it does not run above three or four miles inland.

Besides these voyages by sea, which satisfy us that we must not look for a passage to the South of 67° of latitude; we are indebted to the Hudson's Bay Company, for a journey by land, which has thrown much additional light on this matter, by affording what may be called demonstration, how much farther North, at least in some part of their voyage, ships must hold their course, before they can pass from one side of America to the other. The Northern Indians, who come down to the Company's forts for trade, had brought to the knowledge of our people, the existence of a river; which, from copper abounding near it, had got the name of the *Copper-mine River*. We read much about

---
[*] Printed for Jefferys, in 1768. His words are, "There remains then to be searched for the discovery of a passage, the opening called Pistol Bay, in Hudson's Bay." P. 122.

this

this river in Mr. Dobbs's publications, and he considers the Indian accounts of it as favourable to his system. The Company being desirous of examining the matter with precision, ordered their Governor of Prince of Wales's Fort, to send a proper person to travel by land, under the escort of some trusty Northern Indians, with orders to proceed to this famous river, to take an accurate survey of its course, and to trace it to the sea, into which it empties itself. Mr. Hearne, a young gentleman in their service, who, having been an officer in the Navy, was well qualified to make observations for fixing the longitude and latitude, and make drawings of the country he should pass through, and of the river which he was to examine, was appointed for this service.

Accordingly, he set out from Fort Prince of Wales, on Churchill River, in latitude 58° 50′, on the 7th of December 1770; and the whole of his proceedings, from time to time, are faithfully preserved in his written Journal. The publication of this would not be an unacceptable present to the world, as it draws a plain artless picture of the savage modes of life, the scanty means of subsistence, and indeed of the singular wretchedness, in every respect, of the various tribes, who, without fixed habitations, pass their miserable lives, roving throughout the dreary deserts, and over the frozen lakes of the immense tract of continent through which Mr. Hearne passed, and which he may be said to have added to the geography of the globe. His general course was to the North West. In the month of June 1771, being then at a place called *Conge catha wha Chaga*, he had, to use his own words, *two good observations, both by meridian and double altitudes, the mean of which determines this place to be in latitude 68° 46′ North, and, by account, in longitude 24° 2′ West*

West of Churchill River. On the 13th of July (having left *Conge catha wha Choza* on the 2d, and travelling still to the West of North) he reached the Copper-mine River; and was not a little surprized to find it differ so much from the descriptions given of it by the natives at the fort; for, instead of being likely to be navigable for a ship, it is, at this part, scarcely navigable for an indian canoe; three falls being in sight, at one view, and being choaked up with shoals and stony ridges.

Here Mr. Hearne began his survey of the river. This he continued till he arrived at its mouth, near which his Northern Indians massacred twenty-one Esquimaux, whom they surprized in their tents. We shall give Mr. Hearne's account of his arrival at the sea, in his own words. "After
" the Indians had plundered the tents of the Esquimaux of
" all the copper, &c. they were then again ready to assist
" me in making an end to the survey; the sea then in sight
" from the North West by West to the North East, distant
" about eight miles. It was then about five in the morning of
" the 17th, when I again proceeded to survey the river to
" the mouth, still found, in every respect, no ways likely,
" or a possibility of being made navigable, being full of
" shoals and falls; and, at the entrance, the river emptying
" itself over a dry flat of the shore. For the tide was then
" out, and seemed, by the edges of the ice, to flow about
" twelve or fourteen feet, which will only reach a little
" within the river's mouth. That being the case, the wa-
" ter in the river had not the least brackish taste. But I am
" sure of its being the sea, or some part thereof, by the
" quantity of whale-bone and seal skins the Esquimaux had
" at their tents; as also the number of seals which I saw
" upon the ice. The sea, at the river's mouth, was full
" of

INTRODUCTION.

" of iſlands and ſhoals, as far as I could ſee, by the aſſiſt-
" ance of a pocket teleſcope; and the ice was not yet broken
" up, only thawed away about three quarters of a mile
" from the ſhore, and a little way round the iſlands and
" ſhoals.

" By the time I had completed this ſurvey, it was about
" one in the morning of the 18th; but in theſe high la-
" titudes, and this time of the year, the ſun is always a
" good height above the horizon. It then came on a thick
" drizzling rain, with a thick fog; and, as finding the river
" and ſea, in every reſpect, not likely to be of any utility,
" I did not think it worth while to wait for fair weather, to
" determine the latitude exactly by an obſervation. But, by
" the extraordinary care I took in obſerving the courſes and
" diſtances, walked from *Congecathawhachaaga*, where I had
" two good obſervations, the latitude may be depended on,
" within twenty miles at fartheſt."

From the map which Mr. Hearne conſtructed of the country through which he paſſed, in this ſingular journey, and which we have been permitted to copy upon our general chart, it appears that the mouth of the copper-mine river lies in the latitude 72°, and above 25° Weſt longitude from the fort, from whence he took his departure [*].

The conſequences reſulting from this extenſive diſcovery, are obvious. We now ſee that the continent of North America ſtretches from Hudſon's Bay ſo far to the North Weſt,

---

[*] Mr. Hearne's journey, back from the copper-mine river, to Fort Prince of Wales, laſted till June 30, 1772. From his firſt ſetting out till his return, he had employed near a year and ſeven months. The unparalleled hardſhips he ſuffered, and the eſſential ſervice he performed, met with a ſuitable reward from his maſters, and he is now the Governor of Fort Prince of Wales, where he was taken priſoner by the French in 1782; and laſt ſummer returned to his ſtation.

VOL. I.   g   that

INTRODUCTION.

that Mr. Hearne had travelled near thirteen hundred miles before he arrived at the sea. His most Western distance from the coast of Hudson's Bay was near six hundred miles [*]; and that his Indian guides were well apprized of a vast tract of continent stretching farther on in that direction, is certain from many circumstances mentioned in his journal; one of which, as besides establishing this fact, it presents us with a very striking picture of savage life, has been transcribed in the following note [†].

What

[*] The Hudson's Bay company have a trading post called *Hudson's House*, above five hundred miles up the country, in lat. 53° 0' 32", and in long. 106° 17' 30".

[†] This day, Jan. 11, 1772, as the Indians were hunting, some of them saw a strange snow-shoe track, which they followed, and at a considerable distance came to a little hut, where they found a young woman sitting alone. They brought her to the tents; and, on examining her, found that she was one of the Western Dog-ribbed Indians, and had been taken prisoner by the Arathapescow Indians in the summer 1770; and when the Indians, who took her prisoner, were near this part in the summer 1771, she eloped from them, with an intent to return to her own country; but it being so far off, and, after being taken prisoner, having come the whole way in canoes, with the winding of rivers and lakes, she had forgot the way; and had been in this little hut ever since the first setting in of the fall. By her account of the moons past, since her elopement, it appears to be the middle of last July when she left the Arathapescow Indians, and had not seen a human face ever since. She supported herself very well by snaring of rabbits, partridges, and squirrels, and was now in good health and flesh; and, I think, as fine a woman of a real Indian, as I have seen in any part of North America. She had nothing to make snares of but the sinews of rabbits legs and feet, which she twisted together for that purpose; and of the rabbits skins had made herself a neat and warm winter's clothing. The stock of materials she took with her when she eloped, consisted of about five inches of an iron hoop for a knife; a stone steel, and other hard stones as flints, together with other fire tackle, as tinder, &c.; about an inch and half of the shank of the shoring of an arrow, of iron, of which she made an awl. She had not been long at the tents, when half a score of men wrestled to see who should have her for their wife. She says, when the Arathapescow Indians took her prisoner, that they stole on the tents in the night, when the inhabitants were all asleep, and killed every soul except herself and three other young women. Her father, mother, and husband were in the same tent with her, and they were all killed. Her child, of about five months old, she took with her, wrapped in a bundle of her clothing, undiscovered, in the night. But when arrived at the place where the Arathapescows had left their wives, which was not far off, it being then day-break, these

Indians

INTRODUCTION.

What is now, for the first time, authentically laid before the Public, with regard to the discoveries made by the Hudson's Bay Company, was well known to the noble Lord who presided at the board of Admiralty, when this voyage was undertaken; and the intimate connection of those discoveries with the Plan of the Voyage, of course, regulated the instructions given to Captain Cook.

And now, may we not take it upon us to appeal to every candid and capable Inquirer, whether that part of the Instructions which directed the Captain *not to lose time, in exploring rivers or inlets, or upon any other account, till he got into the latitude* of 65°, was not framed judiciously; as there were such indubitable proofs that no passage existed so far to the South as any part of Hudson's Bay, and that, if a passage could be effected at all, part of it, at least, must be traversed by the ships as far to the Northward as the latitude 72°, where Mr. Hearne arrived at the sea?

We may add as a farther consideration, in support of this article of the Instructions, that Beering's Asiatic discoveries, in 1728, having traced that continent to the latitude of 67°, Captain Cook's approach toward that latitude was to be wished for, that he might be enabled to bring back more

---

Indian women immediately began to examine her bundle; and having there found the child, took it from her and killed it immediately. The relation of this shocking scene only served the savages of my gang for laughter. Her country is so far to the *Westward*, that she says she never saw any iron, or other kind of metal, till taken prisoner; those of her tribe making their hatchets and chisels of deers horns, and knives of stone and bone; their arrows are shod with a kind of slate, bones, and deers horns; and their instruments, to make their wood work, are nothing but beavers teeth. They have frequently heard of the useful materials the nations to the East of them are supplied with from the English; but, instead of drawing nearer to be in the way of trading for iron work, &c. are obliged to retreat farther back, to avoid the Arathapescow Indians, as they make surprising slaughter amongst them every year, both winter and summer. HEARNE's MS. Journal.

INTRODUCTION.

authentic information than the world had hitherto obtained, about the relative situation and vicinity of the two continents, which was absolutely necessary to be known, before the practicability of sailing between the Pacific and Atlantic Oceans, in any Northern direction, could be ascertained.

After all, that search, in a lower latitude, which they who give credit (if any such there now be) to the pretended discoveries of de Fonte, affect to wish had been recommended to Captain Cook, has (if that will cure them of their credulity) been satisfactorily made. The Spaniards, roused from their lethargy by our voyages, and having caught a spark of enterprize from our repeated visits to the Pacific Ocean, have followed us more than once into the line of our discoveries within the Southern tropic; and have also fitted out expeditions to explore the American continent to the North of California. It is to be lamented, that there should be any reasons why the transactions of those Spanish voyages have not been fully disclosed, with the same liberal spirit of information which other nations have adopted. But, fortunately, this excessive caution of the court of Spain has been defeated, at least in one instance, by the publication of an authentic Journal of their last voyage of discovery upon the coast of America, in 1775, for which the world is indebted to the Honourable Mr. Daines Barrington. This publication, which conveys some information of real consequence to geography, and has therefore been referred to more than once in the following work, is particularly valuable in this respect, that some parts of the coast which Captain Cook, in his progress Northward, was prevented, by unfavourable winds, from approaching, were seen and examined by the Spanish ships who preceded him; and the perusal of the following extract from their Journal, may

INTRODUCTION,

may be recommended to those (if any such there be) who would represent it as an imperfection in Captain Cook's voyage, that he had not an opportunity of examining the coast of America, in the latitude assigned to the discoveries of Admiral Fonte. "We now attempted to find out the "straits of Admiral Fonte, though, as yet, we had not dis- "covered the Archipelago of St. Lazarus, through which he "is said to have sailed. With this intent, we searched every "bay and recess of the coast, and sailed round every head- "land, lying to in the night, that we might not lose sight "of this entrance. *After these pains taken, and being favoured* "*by a North West wind, it may be pronounced that no such straits* "*are to be found* *."

In this Journal, the Spaniards boast of "having reached "so high a latitude as 58°, beyond what any other naviga- "tors had been able to effect in those seas †." Without diminishing the merit of their performance, we may be permitted to say that it will appear very inconsiderable, indeed, in comparison of what Captain Cook effected, in the voyage of which an account is given in these volumes. Besides exploring the land in the South Indian Ocean, of which Kerguelen, in two voyages, had been able to obtain but a very imperfect knowledge; adding also many considerable accessions to the geography of the Friendly Islands; and discovering the noble group, now called Sandwich Islands, in the Northern part of the Pacific Ocean, of which not the faintest trace can be met with in the account of any former voyage; besides these preliminary discoveries, the Reader of the following work will find, that in

* Journal of a voyage in 1775 by Don Francisco Antonio Maurele, in Mr. Barrington's Miscellanies, p. 508.

† *Ibid*. p. 507. We learn from Maurelle's Journal that another voyage had been some time before performed upon the coast of America; but the utmost Northern progress of it was to latitude 55°.

one

liv   INTRODUCTION.

one summer, our English Navigator discovered a much larger proportion of the North West coast of America than the Spaniards, though settled in the neighbourhood, had, in all their attempts, for above two hundred years, been able to do; That he has put it beyond all doubt that Beering and Tscherikoff had really discovered the continent of America in 1741, and has also established the prolongation of that continent Westward opposite Kamtschatka, which speculative writers, wedded to favourite systems, had affected so much to disbelieve*, and which, though admitted by Muller, had, since he wrote, been considered as disproved by later Russian discoveries †; That, besides ascertaining the true position of the Western coasts of America, with some inconsiderable interruptions, from latitude 44° up to beyond the latitude 70°, he has also ascertained the position of the North Eastern extremity of Asia, by confirming Beering's discoveries in 1728, and adding extensive accessions of his own; That he has given us more authentic information concerning the islands lying between the two continents, than the Kamtschatka traders, ever since Beering first taught them to venture on this sea, had been able to procure ‡; That, by fixing the relative

* Dr. Campbell, speaking of Beering's voyage in 1741, says, "Nothing can be plainer than this truth, that his discovery does not warrant any such supposition, as that the country he touched at was a great continent making part of North America."

† See Coxe's Russian Discoveries, p. 26, 27, &c. The fictions of speculative geographers in the Southern hemisphere, have been continents; in the Northern hemisphere, they have been seas. It may be observed, therefore, that if Captain Cook in his first voyages annihilated imaginary Southern lands, he has made amends for the havock, in his third voyage, by annihilating imaginary Northern seas, and filling up the vast space, which had been allotted to them, with the solid contents of his new discoveries of American land farther West and North than had hitherto been traced.

‡ The Russians seem to owe much to England, in matters of this sort. It is singular enough that one of our countrymen, Dr. Campbell [See his edition of Harris's voyages,

INTRODUCTION.

lative situation of Asia and America, and discovering the narrow bounds of the strait that divides them, he has thrown a blaze of light upon this important part of the geography of the globe, and solved the puzzling problem about the peopling of America, by tribes destitute of the necessary means to attempt long navigations; and, lastly, That, though the principal object of the voyage failed, the world will be greatly benefited even by the failure, as it has brought us to the knowledge of the existence of the impediments, which future navigators may expect to meet with in attempting to go to the East Indies through Beering's strait.

The extended review we have taken of the preceding voyages, and the general outline we have sketched out, of the transactions of the last, which are recorded at full length in these volumes, will not, it is hoped, be considered as a prolix, or unnecessary detail. It will serve to give a just notion of the whole plan of discovery executed by his Majesty's commands. And it appearing that much was aimed at, and much accomplished, in the unknown parts of the globe, in both hemispheres, there needs no other consideration, to give full satisfaction to those who possess an enlarged way of thinking, that a variety of useful purposes must have been effected by these researches. But

voyages, Vol. ii. p. 1021.) has preserved many valuable particulars of Beering's first voyage, of which Muller himself, the Historian of their earlier discoveries, makes no mention; that it should be another of our countrymen, Mr. Coxe, who first published a satisfactory account of their later discoveries; and that the King of Great Britain's ships should traverse the globe in 1778, to confirm to the Russian empire, the possession of near thirty degrees, or above six hundred miles of continent, which Mr. Engel, in his zeal for the predicability of a North East passage, would prune away from the length of Asia to the Eastward. See his *Mémoires Geographiques*, &c. Lausanne 1765; which, however, contains much real information; and many parts of which are confirmed by Captain Cook's American discoveries.

there

INTRODUCTION.

there are others, no doubt, who, too diffident of their own abilities, or too indolent to exert them, would wish to have their reflections assisted, by pointing out what those useful purposes are. For the use of such, the following enumeration of particulars is entered upon. And if there should be any, who affect to undervalue the plan, or the execution of our voyages, what shall now be offered, if it do not convince them, may, at least, check the influence of their unfavourable decision.

1. It may be fairly considered, as one great advantage accruing to the world from our late surveys of the globe, that they have confuted fanciful theories, too likely to give birth to impracticable undertakings.

After Captain Cook's persevering and fruitless traverses through every corner of the Southern hemisphere, who, for the future, will pay any attention to the ingenious reveries of Campbell, de Brosses, and de Buffon? or hope to establish an intercourse with such a continent as Maupertuis's fruitful imagination had pictured? A continent equal, at least, in extent, to all the civilized countries in the known Northern hemisphere, where new men, new animals, new productions of every kind, might be brought forward to our view, and discoveries be made, which would open inexhaustible treasures of commerce [a]. We can now boldly take it upon us to discourage all expeditions, formed on such reasonings of speculative philosophers, into a quarter of the globe,

[a] See Maupertuis's Letter to the King of Prussia. The author of the Preliminary Discourse to Bougainville's *Voyage aux Isles Moluines*, computes that the Southern continent (for the existence of which, he owns, we must depend more on the conjectures of philosophers, than on the testimony of voyagers) contains eight or ten millions of square leagues.

† where

where our perfevering Englifh navigator, inftead of this promifed fairy land, found nothing but barren rocks, fcarcely affording fhelter to penguins and feals; and dreary feas, and mountains of ice, occupying the immenfe fpace allotted to imaginary paradifes, and the only treafures there to be difcovered, to reward the toil, and to compenfate the dangers of the unavailing fearch.

Or, if we carry our reflections into the Northern hemifphere, could Mr. Dobbs have made a fingle convert, much lefs could he have been the fuccefsful folicitor of two different expeditions, and have met with encouragement from the legiflature, with regard to his favourite paffage through Hudfon's Bay, if Captain Chriftopher had previoufly explored its coafts, and if Mr. Hearne had walked over the immenfe continent behind it? Whether, after Captain Cook's and Captain Clerke's difcoveries on the Weft fide of America, and their report of the ftate of Beering's Strait, there can be fufficient encouragement to make future attempts to penetrate into the Pacific Ocean in any Northern direction, is a queftion, for the decifion of which the Public will be indebted to this work.

2. But our voyages will benefit the world, not only by difcouraging future unprofitable fearches, but alfo by leffening the dangers and diftreffes formerly experienced in thofe feas, which are within the line of commerce and navigation, now actually fubfifting. In how many inftances have the miftakes of former navigators, in fixing the true fituations of important places, been rectified? What acceffion to the variation chart? How many nautical obfervations have been collected, and are now ready to be confulted, in directing a fhip's courfe, along rocky fhores, through nar-

INTRODUCTION.

row straits, amidst perplexing currents, and dangerous shoals? But, above all, what numbers of new bays, and harbours, and anchoring-places, are now, for the first time, brought forward, where ships may be sheltered, and their crews find tolerable refreshments? To enumerate all these would be to transcribe great part of the journals of our several Commanders, whose labours will endear them to every navigator, whom trade or war may carry into their tracks. Every nation that sends a ship to sea, will partake of the benefit; but Great Britain herself, whose commerce is boundless, must take the lead in reaping the full advantage of her own discoveries.

In consequence of all these various improvements, lessening the apprehensions of engaging in long voyages, may we not reasonably indulge the pleasing hope, that fresh branches of commerce may, even in our own time, be attempted, and successfully carried on? Our hardy adventurers in the whale-fishery, have already found their way, within these few years, into the South Atlantic; and who knows what fresh sources of commerce may still be opened, if the prospect of gain can be added, to keep alive the spirit of enterprize? If the situation of Great Britain be too remote, other trading nations will assuredly avail themselves of our discoveries. We may soon expect to hear that the Russians, now instructed by us where to find the American continent, have extended their voyages from the Fox Islands to Cook's River, and Prince William's Sound. And if Spain itself should not be tempted to trade from its most Northern Mexican ports, by the fresh mine of wealth discovered in the furs of King George's Sound, which they may transport in their Manilla ships, as a favourite commodity for the

Chinese

INTRODUCTION.

Chinese market; that market may probably be supplied by a direct trade to America, from Canton itself, with those valuable articles which the inhabitants of China have hitherto received, only by the tedious and expensive circuit of Kamtschatka and Kiachta.

These and many other commercial improvements may reasonably be expected to result from the British discoveries, even in our own times. But if we look forward to future ages, and to future changes in the history of commerce, by recollecting its various past revolutions and migrations, we may be allowed to please ourselves with the idea of its finding its way, at last, throughout the extent of the regions with which our voyages have opened an intercourse; and there will be abundant reason to subscribe to Captain Cook's observation with regard to New Zealand, which may be applied to other tracks of land explored by him, that "although they be far remote from the present trading "world, we can, by no means, tell what use future ages "may make of the discoveries made by the present*." In this point of view, surely, the utility of the late voyages must stand confessed; and we may be permitted to say, that the history of their operations, which will be completed in these volumes, has the justest pretensions to be called *ærium is æsi*, as it will convey to latest posterity a treasure of interesting information.

3. Admitting, however, that we may have expressed too sanguine expectations of commercial advantages, either within our own reach, or gradually to be unfolded at some future period, as the result of our voyages of discovery; we

* Cook's Voyage, Vol. I. p. 92.

INTRODUCTION.

may still be allowed to consider them as a laudable effort to add to the stock of human knowledge, with regard to an object which cannot but deserve the attention of enlightened man. To exert our faculties in devising ingenious modes of satisfying ourselves about the magnitude and distance of the sun; to extend our acquaintance with the system to which that luminary is the common centre, by tracing the revolutions of a new planet, or the appearance of a new comet; to carry our bold researches through all the immensity of space, where world beyond world rises to the view of the astonished observer; these are employments which none but those incapable of pursuing them can depreciate, and which every one capable of pursuing them must delight in, as a dignified exercise of the powers of the human mind. But while we direct our studies to distant worlds, which, after all our exertions, we must content ourselves with having barely discovered to exist, it would be a strange neglect, indeed, and would argue a most culpable want of rational curiosity, if we did not use our best endeavours to arrive at a full acquaintance with the contents of our own planet; of that little spot in the immense universe, on which we have been placed, and the utmost limits of which, at least its habitable parts, we possess the means of ascertaining, and describing, by actual examination.

So naturally doth this reflection present itself, that to know something of the terraqueous globe, is a favourite object with every one who can taste the lowest rudiments of learning. Let us not therefore think so meanly of the times in which we live, as to suppose it possible that full justice will not be done to the noble plan of discovery, so steadily and so successfully carried on, since the accession of his Majesty;

which

INTRODUCTION.

which cannot fail to be confidered, in every fucceeding age, as a fplendid period in the hiftory of our country, and to add to our national glory, by diftinguifhing Great Britain as taking the lead in the moft arduous undertakings for the common benefit of the human race. Before thefe voyages took place, nearly half the furface of the globe we inhabit was hid in obfcurity and confufion. What is ftill wanting to complete our geography, may juftly be termed the *minutiæ* of that fcience.

4. Let us now carry our thoughts fomewhat farther. It is fortunate for the interefts of knowledge, that acquifitions in any one branch, generally, and indeed unavoidably, lead to acquifitions in other branches, perhaps of ftill greater confequence; and that we cannot even gratify mere curiofity, without being rewarded with valuable inftruction. This obfervation applies to the fubject before us. Voyages, in which new oceans have been traverfed, and in which new countries have been vifited, can fcarcely ever be performed, without bringing forward to our view frefh objects of fcience. Even when we are to take our report of what was difcovered, from the mere failor, whofe knowledge fcarcely goes beyond the narrow limits of his own profeffion, and whofe inquiries are not directed by philofophical difcernment, it will be unfortunate indeed, if fomething hath not been remarked, by which the fcholar may profit, and ufeful acceffions be made to our old ftock of information. And if this be the cafe in general, how much more muft be gained by the particular voyages now under confideration? Befides naval officers equally fkilled to examine the coafts they might approach, as to delineate them accurately upon

their charts, artists* were engaged, who, by their drawings might illustrate what could only be imperfectly described; mathematicians†, who might treasure up an extensive series of scientific observations; and persons versed in the various departments of the history of nature, who might collect, or record, all that they should find new and valuable, throughout the wide extent of their researches. But while most of these associates of our naval discoverers, were liberally rewarded by the Public, there was one gentleman, who thinking it the noblest reward he could receive, to have an opportunity of making the ample fortune he inherited from his ancestors, subservient to the improvement of science, stepped forward of his own accord, and submitting to the hardships and dangers of a circumnavigation of the globe, accompanied Captain Cook in the Endeavour. The learned world, I may also say the unlearned, will never forget the obligations which it owes to Sir Joseph Banks.

What real acquisitions have been gained, by this munificent attention to science, cannot be better expressed than in the words of Mr. Wales, who engaged in one of these voyages himself, and contributed largely to the benefits derived from them.

"That branch of natural knowledge which may be "called *nautical astronomy*, was undoubtedly in its infancy,

---

* Mess. Hodges and Webber, whose drawings have ornamented and illustrated this and Captain Cook's second voyage.

† Mr. Green, in the Endeavour; Messrs. Wales and Bayly, in the Resolution and Adventure; Mr. Bayly, a second time, jointly with Captains Cook and King in this voyage; and Mr. Lyons, who accompanied Lord Mulgrave. The observations of Messrs. Wales and Bayly, during Captain Cook's second voyage, are already in the hands of the Public, by the favour of the Board of Longitude; and those of Captains Cook and King, and Mr. Bayly, during this last, will appear immediately after our Publication.

"when

INTRODUCTION.

lxiii

"when these voyages were first undertaken. Both instru-
"ments and observers, which deserved the name, were very
"rare; and so late as the year 1770, it was found necessary,
"in the appendix to *Mayer's Tables*, published by the Board
"of Longitude, to state facts, in contradiction to the asser-
"tions of so celebrated an astronomer as the Abbé de la
"Caille, that the altitude of the sun at noon, the easiest and
"most simple of all observations, could not be taken with
"certainty to a less quantity than five, six, seven, or even
"eight minutes*. But those who will give themselves the
"trouble to look into the *astronomical observations*, made in
"Captain Cook's last voyage, will find, that there were few,
"even of the petty officers, who could not observe the
"distance of the moon from the sun, or a star, the most de-
"licate of all observations, with sufficient accuracy. It
"may be added, that the method of making and computing
"observations for finding the variation of the compass, is
"better known, and more frequently practised by those
"who have been on these voyages, than by most others.
"Nor is there, perhaps, a person who ranks as an officer,

* The Abbé's words are, "Si ceux qui promettent une si grande precision dans
"ces sortes de méthodes, avoient navigué quelque temps, ils auroient vû souvent, que
"dans l'observation la plus simple de toutes, qui est celle de la hauteur du soleil à
"midi, deux observations, munis de bons quartiers de reflexion, bien rectifiés, dif-
"ferent entr'eux, lorsqu'ils obsèrvent chacun à part, de 5', 6', 7', & 8'."
Ephemer. 1755—1765. *Introduction*, p. 31.

It must be, however, mentioned, in justice to M. de la Caille, that he attempted
to introduce the lunar method of discovering the longitude, and proposed a plan of
calculations of the moon's distance from the sun and fixed stars; but through the
imperfection of his instruments, his success was much less than that method was capable of affording. The bringing it into general use was reserved for Dr. Maskelyne,
our Astronomer Royal. See the preface to the *Tables for correcting the Effects of Re-
fraction and Parallax*, published by the Board of Longitude, under the Direction of
Dr. Shepherd, Plumian Professor of Astronomy and Experimental Philosophy at Cam-
bridge, in 1772.

"and

INTRODUCTION.

" and has been concerned in them, who would not, what-
" ever his real skill may be, feel ashamed to have it thought
" that he did not know how to observe for, and compute
" the time at sea; though, but a short while before these
" voyages were set on foot, such a thing was scarcely ever
" heard of amongst seamen; and even first-rate astro-
" nomers doubted the possibility of doing it with sufficient
" exactness*.

" The number of places, at which the rise and times of
" flowing of tides have been observed, in these voyages, is
" very great; and hence an important article of useful
" knowledge is afforded. In these observations, some very
" curious and even unexpected circumstances have offered

* In addition to Mr. Wales's Remark, it may be observed, that the proficiency of our naval officers in taking observations at sea, must ultimately be attributed to the great attention paid to this important object by the Board of Longitude at home; liberal rewards having been given to mathematicians for perfecting the lunar tables, and facilitating calculations; to artists for constructing more accurate instruments for observing, and watches better adapted to keeping time at sea. It appears, therefore, that the voyages of discovery, and the operations of the board of longitude went hand in hand; and they must be combined, in order to form a just estimate of the extent of the plan carried into execution since his Majesty's accession, for improving astronomy and navigation. But, besides the establishment of the Board of Longitude on its present footing, which has had such important consequences, it must also be ever acknowledged, that his present Majesty has extended his royal patronage to every branch of the liberal arts and useful sciences. The munificent present to the Royal Society for defraying the expense of observing the transit of Venus;—the institution of the Academy of Painting and Sculpture;—the magnificent apartments allotted to the Royal and Antiquary Societies, and to the Royal Academy, at Somerset Place;—the support of the Garden of Exotics at Kew, to improve which, Mr. Mason was sent to the extremities of Africa;—the substantial encouragement afforded to learned men and learned works, in various departments; and particularly, that afforded to Mr. Herschell, which has enabled him to devote himself intirely to the improvement of astronomy; these, and many other instances which might be enumerated, would have greatly distinguished his Majesty's reign, even if he had not been the patron of those successful attempts to perfect geography and navigation by so many voyages of discovery.

" them-

INTRODUCTION.

"themfelves to our confideration. It will be fufficient to
" inftance the exceedingly fmall height to which the tide
" rifes, in the middle of the great Pacific Ocean; where it
" falls fhort, two-thirds at leaft, of what might have been
" expected from theory and calculation.

" The direction and force of currents at fea, make alfo
" an important object. Thefe voyages will be found to
" contain much ufeful information on this head; as well
" relating to feas nearer home, and which, in confequence,
" are navigated every day, as to thofe which are more re-
" mote, but where, notwithftanding, the knowledge of thefe
" things may be of great fervice to thofe who are deftined
" to navigate them hereafter. To this head alfo we may refer
" the great number of experiments which have been made
" for inquiring into the depth of the fea, its temperature,
" and faltnefs at different depths, and in a variety of places
" and climates.

" An extenfive foundation has alfo been laid for improve-
" ments in magnetifm, for difcovering the caufe and nature
" of the polarity of the needle, and a theory of its varia-
" tions, by the number and variety of the obfervations and
" experiments which have been made, both on the variation
" and dip, in almoft all parts of the world. Experiments alfo
" have been made, in confequence of the late voyages, on
" the effects of gravity, in different and very diftant places,
" which may ferve to increafe our ftock of natural know-
" ledge. From the fame fource of information we have
" learned, that the phænomenon, ufually called the *aurora*
" *borealis*, is not peculiar to high Northern latitudes, but be-
" longs, equally, to all cold climates, whether they be North
" or South.

Vol. I.   i   " But,

INTRODUCTION.

"But, perhaps, no part of knowledge has been so great
"a gainer by the late voyages, as that of botany. We
"are told * that, at least, twelve hundred new plants have
"been added to the known system; and that very con-
"siderable additions have been made to every other branch
"of natural history, by the great skill and industry of Sir
"Joseph Banks, and the other gentlemen † who have accom-
"panied Captain Cook for that purpose."

To our naval 'officers in general, or to their learned associates in the expeditions, all the foregoing improvements of
knowledge may be traced; but there is one very singular
improvement indeed, still behind, for which, as we are solely
indebted to Captain Cook, let us state it in his own words:
"Whatever may be the public judgment about other mat-
"ters, it is with real satisfaction, and without claiming any
"merit but that of attention to my duty, that I can con-
"clude this account with an observation, which facts en-
"able me to make, that our having discovered the possibi-
"lity of preserving health amongst a numerous ship's com-
"pany, for such a length of time, in such varieties of cli-
"mate, and amidst such continued hardships and fatigues,
"will make this voyage remarkable, in the opinion of
"every benevolent person, when the disputes about a South-
"ern continent shall have ceased to engage the attention,
"and to divide the judgment of philosophers ‡."

* See Dr. Shepherd's Preface, as above.

† Dr. Solander, Dr. Forster and his son, and Dr. Sparrman. Dr. Forster has given us a specimen of the botanical discoveries of his voyage in the *Characteres Generum Plantarum*, &c. and much curious philosophical matter is contained in his *Observations made in a Voyage round the World.* Dr. Sparrman also, on his return to Sweden, favoured us with a publication, in which he expatiates on the advantages accruing to natural history, to astronomy, geography, general physics, and navigation, from our South Sea voyages.

‡ Cook's Voyage, Vol. ii. p. 293.

5. But

INTRODUCTION.

5. But while our late voyages have opened so many channels to an increase of knowledge in the several articles already enumerated; while they have extended our acquaintance with the contents of the globe; while they have facilitated old tracks, and have opened new ones for commerce; while they have been the means of improving the skill of the navigator, and the science of the astronomer; while they have procured to us so valuable accessions in the several departments of natural history, and furnished such opportunities of teaching us how to preserve the healths and lives of seamen, let us not forget another very important object of study, for which they have afforded to the speculative philosopher ample materials: I mean the study of human nature in various situations, equally interesting as they are uncommon.

However remote or secluded from frequent intercourse with more polished nations, the inhabitants of any parts of the world be, if history or our own observation should make it evident that they have been formerly visited, and that foreign manners and opinions, and languages, have been blended with their own, little use can be made of what is observed amongst such people, toward drawing a real picture of man in his natural uncultivated state. This seems to be the situation of the inhabitants of most of the islands that lie contiguous to the continent of Asia, and of whose manners and institutions the Europeans, who occasionally visit them, have frequently given us accounts. But the islands which our enterprising discoverers visited in the centre of the South Pacific Ocean, and are, indeed, the principal scenes of their operations, were untrodden ground. The inhabitants, as far as could be observed, were unmixed with any different tribe, by occasional intercourse, subsequent to their

original

INTRODUCTION.

original settlement there; left intirely to their own powers for every art of life; and to their own remote traditions for every political or religious custom or institution; uninformed by science; unimproved by education; in short, a fit soil from whence a careful observer could collect facts for forming a judgment, how far unassisted human nature will be apt to degenerate; and in what respects it can ever be able to excel. Who could have thought, that the brutal ferocity of feeding upon human flesh, and the horrid superstition of offering human sacrifices, should be found to exist amongst the natives lately discovered in the Pacific Ocean, who, in other respects, appear to be no strangers to the fine feelings of humanity, to have arrived at a certain stage of social life, and to be habituated to subordination and government which tend so naturally to repress the ebullitions of wild passion, and expand the latent powers of the understanding?

Or, if we turn from this melancholy picture, which will suggest copious matter for philosophical speculation, can we, without astonishment, observe to what a degree of perfection the same tribe (and indeed we may here join, in some of those instances, the American tribes visited in the course of the present voyage) have carried their favourite amusements, the plaintive songs of their women; their dramatic entertainments, their dances, their Olympian games, as we may call them; the orations of their Chiefs; the chants of their priests; the solemnity of their religious processions; their arts and manufactures; their ingenious contrivances to supply the want of proper materials, and of effective tools and machines; and the wonderful productions of their persevering labour under a complication of disadvantages; their cloth and their mats; their weapons; their fishing-ing-inftruments; their ornaments; their utenfils; which in defign and in execution, may vie with whatever modern Europe, or claffical antiquity can exhibit!

It is a favourite ftudy with the fcholar to trace the remains of Grecian or Roman workmanfhip; he turns over his Montfaucon with learned fatisfaction; and he gazes with rapture on the noble collection of Sir William Hamilton. The amufement is rational and inftructive. But will not his curiofity be more awakened, will he not find even more real matter for important reflection, by paffing an hour in furveying the numerous fpecimens of the ingenuity our newly difcovered friends brought from the utmoft receffes of the globe, to enrich the Britifh Mufeum, and the valuable repofitory of Sir Afhton Lever! If the curiofities of Sir Afhton's Sandwich-room alone, were the only acquifition gained by our vifits to the Pacific Ocean, who that has tafte to admire, or even eyes to behold, could hefitate to pronounce, that Captain Cook had not failed in vain! The expence of his three voyages did not, perhaps, far exceed that of digging out the buried contents of Herculaneum. And we may add, that the *novelties* of the Society or Sandwich iflands, feem better calculated to engage the attention of the ftudious in our times, than the *antiquities*, which exhibit proofs of Roman magnificence.

The grounds for making this remark cannot be better explained, than in the words of a very ingenious writer; " In an age (fays Mr. Warton *), advanced to the higheft " degree of refinement, that fpecies of curiofity com- " mences, which is bufied in contemplating the progrefs of " focial life, in difplaying the gradation of fociety, and in

* Preface to his Hiftory of Englifh Poetry.

† " tracing

INTRODUCTION.

"tracing the gradations from barbarism to civility. That these
"speculations should become the favourite topics of such a
"period is extremely natural. We look back on the savage
"condition of our ancestors with the triumph of superiority;
"and are pleased to mark the steps by which we have been
"raised from rudeness to elegance; and our reflections on
"this subject are accompanied with a conscious pride,
"arising, in a great measure, from a tacit comparison of
"the infinite disproportion between the feeble efforts of
"remote ages, and our present improvements in know-
"ledge. In the mean time, the manners, monuments,
"customs, practices, and opinions of antiquity, by forming
"so strong a contrast with those of our own times, and
"by exhibiting human nature and human inventions in
"new lights, in unexpected appearances, and in various
"forms, are objects which forcibly strike a feeling imagi-
"nation. Nor does this spectacle afford nothing more than
"a fruitless gratification to the fancy. It teaches us to set
"a just estimation on our own acquisitions, and encourages
"us to cherish that cultivation, which is so closely connected
"with the existence and the exercise of every social virtue."
We need not here observe, that the *manners, monuments, customs,
practices, and opinions* of the present inhabitants of the Pacific
Ocean, or of the West side of North America, form *the
strongest contrast* with those of our own time in enlightened
Europe; and that *a feeling imagination* will probably be more
struck with the narration of the ceremonies of a *Natche* at
Tongataboo, than of a Gothic tournament at London; with
the contemplation of the colossuses of Easter Island, than of
the mysterious remains of Stonehenge.

Many singularities, respecting what may be called the
natural history of the human species, in different climates,
will,

will, on the authority of our late navigators, open abundant sources for philosophical discussion. One question of this sort, in particular, which had formerly divided the opinions of the inquisitive, as to the existence, if not of " giants on the earth," at least of a race (inhabiting a district bordering on the North side of the strait of Magalhaens), whose stature considerably exceeds that of the bulk of mankind, will no longer be doubted or disbelieved. And the ingenious objections of the sceptical author of *Recherches sur les Américains* *, will weigh nothing in the balance against the concurrent and accurate testimony of Byron, Wallis, and Carteret.

Perhaps there cannot be a more interesting inquiry than to trace the migrations of the various families or tribes that have peopled the globe; and in no respect have our late voyages been more fertile in curious discoveries. It was known in general (and I shall use the words of Kæmpfer †), that the Asiatic nation called Malayans, " in former times, " had by much the greatest trade in the Indies, and fre- " quented with their merchant ships, not only all the coasts " of Asia, but ventured even over to the coasts of Africa, " particularly to the great island of Madagascar ‡. The title

---

* Tom. i. p. 331.

† History of Japan, Vol. i. p. 93.

‡ That the Malayans have not only frequented Madagascar, but have also been the progenitors of some of the present race of inhabitants there, is confirmed to us by the testimony of Monsieur de Pages, who visited that island so late as 1774. " Ils " n'ont paru provenir des diverses Races ; leur couleur, leurs cheveux, et leur corps " l'indiquent. Ceux que je n'ai pas cru originaires des anciens naturels du pays, sont " petits et trapus ; ils ont les cheveux presque unis ; et font ailleurs comme les Ma- " layes, avec qui ils ont, en général, une espece de resemblance."

Voyages de M. des Pages, T. ii. p. 90.

" which

INTRODUCTION.

" which the king of the Malayans assumed to himself, of
" *Lord of the Winds and Seas to the East and to the West*, is an evi-
" dent proof of this; but much more the Malayan language,
" which spread most all over the East, much after the same
" manner as formerly the Latin, and of late the French, did
" all over Europe." Thus far, I say, was known. But that
from Madagascar to the Marqueses and Easter Island, that
is, nearly from the East side of Africa, till we approach toward the West side of America, a space including above
half the circumference of the globe, the same tribe or nation, the Phoenicians, as we may call them, of the Oriental
world, should have made their settlements, and founded
colonies throughout almost every intermediate stage of this
immense tract, in islands at amazing distances from the
mother continent, and ignorant of each others existence;
this is an historical fact, which could be but very imperfectly known before Captain Cook's two first voyages discovered so many new inhabited spots of land lurking in the
bosom of the South Pacific Ocean; and it is a fact which
does not rest solely on similarity of customs and institutions,
but has been established by the most satisfactory of all
proofs, that drawn from affinity of language. Mr. Marsden,
who seems to have considered this curious subject with
much attention, says, that *the links of the latitudinal chain remain yet to be traced* [*]. The discovery of the Sandwich Islands
in

[*] Archæolog. Vol. vi. p. 155. See also his History of Sumatra, p. 166. from
which the following passage is transcribed. " Besides the Malaye, there are a va-
" riety of languages spoken on Sumatra, which, however, have not only a manifest
" affinity among themselves, but also to that general language which is found to
" prevail in, and to be indigenous to, all the islands of the Eastern seas; from Ma-
" dagascar to the remotest of Captain Cook's discoveries, comprehending a wider
" extent than the Roman or any other tongue has yet boasted. In different places,
" it has been more or less mixed and corrupted; but between the most dissimilar
" branches,

INTRODUCTION.

in this laſt voyage, has added ſome links to the chain. But Captain Cook had not an opportunity of carrying his reſearches into the more Weſterly parts of the North Pacific. The Reader, therefore, of the following work will not, perhaps, think that the Editor was idly employed when he ſubjoined ſome notes, which contain abundant proof that the inhabitants of the Ladrones, or Marianne iſlands, and thoſe of the Carolines, are to be traced to the ſame common ſource, with thoſe of the iſlands viſited by our ſhips. With the like view, of exhibiting a ſtriking picture of the amazing extent of this Oriental language, which marks, if not a common original, at leaſt an intimate intercourſe between the inhabitants of places ſo very remote from each other, he has inſerted a comparative table of their numerals, upon a more enlarged plan than any that has hitherto been executed [*].

Our Britiſh diſcoverers have not only thrown a blaze of light on the migrations of the tribe which has ſo wonderfully ſpread itſelf throughout the iſlands in the Eaſtern Ocean; but they have alſo favoured us with much curious information concerning another of the families of the earth, whoſe lot has fallen in leſs hoſpitable climates. We ſpeak of the Eſquimaux, hitherto only found ſeated on the coaſts of Labradore and Hudſon's Bay, and who differ in ſeveral

---

"branches, an eminent ſameneſs of many radical words is apparent; and in ſome "very diſtant from each other, in point of ſituation: As, for inſtance, the Philip-"pines and Madagaſcar, the deviation of the words is ſcarcely more than is obſerved "in the dialects of neighbouring provinces of the ſame kingdom."

[*] We are indebted to Sir Joſeph Banks, for a general outline of this, in Hawkeſworth's Collection, Vol. iii. p. 777. The Reader will find our enlarged Table at the end of the third volume, Appendix, No. 2.

INTRODUCTION.

characteristic marks from the inland inhabitants of North America. That the Greenlanders and they agree in every circumstance of customs, and manners, and language, which are demonstrations of an original identity of nation, had been discovered about twenty years ago*. Mr. Hearne, in 1772, traced this unhappy race farther back, toward that part of the globe from whence they had originally coasted along in their skin boats, having met with some of them at the mouth of the Coppermine River, in the latitude of 72°, and near five hundred leagues farther West than Pickersgill's most Westerly station in Davis's Strait. Their being the same tribe who now actually inhabit the islands and coasts on the West side of North America, opposite Kamtschatka, was a discovery, the completion of which was reserved for Captain Cook. The Reader of the following work will find them at Norton Sound; and at Oonalashka, and Prince William's Sound; that is, near 1500 leagues distant from their stations in Greenland, and on the Labradore coast. And lest similitude of manners should be thought to deceive us, a table exhibiting proofs of affinity of language, which was drawn up by Captain Cook, and is inserted in this work †, will remove every doubt from the mind of the most scrupulous inquirer after truth.

There are other doubts of a more important kind, which, it may be hoped, will now no longer perplex the ignorant,

* See Cranix's History of Greenland, Vol. i. p. 262; where we are told that the Moravian Brethren, who, with the consent and furtherance of Sir Hugh Palliser, then Governor of Newfoundland, visited the Esquimaux on the Labradore coast, found that their language, and that of the Greenlanders, do not differ so much as that of the High and Low Dutch.

† See Appendix, No. 6. The Greenlanders, as Cranix tells us, call themselves *Kareliti*; a word not very unlike *Konegyst*, the name, assumed by the inhabitants of Kodiack, one of the Schumagin islands, as Staehlin informs us.

or

or furnish matter of cavil to the ill-intentioned. After the great discovery, or at least the full confirmation of the great discovery, of the vicinity of the two continents of Asia and America, we trust that we shall not be any more ridiculed, for believing that the former could easily furnish its inhabitants to the latter. And thus, to all the various good purposes already enumerated, as answered by our late voyages, we may add this last, though not the least important, that they have done service to religion, by robbing infidelity of a favourite objection to the credibility of the Mosaic account of *the peopling of the earth* *.

6. Hitherto we have considered our voyages as having benefited the *discoverers*. But it will be asked, Have they conveyed, or are they likely ever to convey, any benefit to the *discovered*? It would afford exquisite satisfaction to every benevolent mind, to be instructed in facts, which might enable us, without hesitation, to answer this question in the affirmative. And yet, perhaps, we may indulge the pleasing hope, that, even in this respect, our ships have not failed in vain. Other discoveries of new countries have, in effect, been wars, or rather massacres; nations have been no sooner found out, than they have been extirpated; and the horrid cruelties of the conquerors of Mexico and Peru

---

* A contempt of Revelation is generally the result of ignorance, conceited of its possessing superior knowledge. Observe how the Author of *Recherches Philosophiques sur les Américains*, expresses himself on this very point. "Cette distance que "Mr. Antermony veut trouver si peu importante, est à-peu-près de huit cent lieues "Gondoles ou travers d'un ocean perilleux, et impossible à franchir avec des canots "aussi chetifs et aussi fragiles que le sont, au rapport d'Yfbrand Ides, les chaloupes "des Tongufes," &c. &c. T. i. p. 156. Had this writer known that the two continents are not above *thirteen* leagues (instead of *eight hundred*) distant from each other, and that, even in that narrow space of sea, there are intervening islands, he would not have ventured to urge this argument in opposition to Mr. Bell's notion of the quarter from which North America received its original inhabitants.

can

can never be remembered, without blushing for religion and human nature. But when the recesses of the globe are investigated, not to enlarge private dominion, but to promote general knowledge; when we visit new tribes of our fellow-creatures as friends; and wish only to learn that they exist, in order to bring them within the pale of the offices of humanity, and to relieve the wants of their imperfect state of society, by communicating to them our superior attainments; voyages of discovery planned with such benevolent views by George the Third, and executed by Cook, have not, we trust, totally failed in this respect. Our repeated visits, and long continued intercourse with the natives of the Friendly, Society, and Sandwich Islands, cannot but have darted some rays of light on the infant minds of those poor people. The uncommon objects they have thus had opportunities of observing and admiring, will naturally tend to enlarge their stock of ideas, and to furnish new materials for the exercise of their reason. Comparing themselves with their visiters, they cannot but be struck with the deepest conviction of their own inferiority, and be impelled, by the strongest motives, to strive to emerge from it, and to rise nearer to a level with those children of the Sun who deigned to look upon them, and left behind so many specimens of their generous and humane attention. The very introduction of our useful animals and vegetables, by adding fresh means of subsistence, will have added to their comforts of life, and immediate enjoyments; and if this be the only benefit they are ever to receive, who will pronounce that much has not been gained? But may we not carry our wishes and our hopes still farther! Great Britain itself, when first visited by the Phœnicians, was inhabited by painted Savages, not, perhaps, blessed with higher attainments

ments than are possessed by the present natives of New Zealand; certainly less civilized than those of Tongataboo or Otaheite. Our having opened an intercourse with them, is the first step toward their improvement. Who knows, but that our late voyages may be the means appointed by Providence, of spreading, in due time, the blessings of civilization, amongst the numerous tribes of the South Pacific Ocean; of abolishing their horrid repasts and their horrid rites; and of laying the foundation for future and more effectual plans, to prepare them for holding an honourable station amongst the nations of the earth? This, at least, is certain, that our having, as it were, brought them into existence by our extensive researches, will suggest to us fresh motives of devout gratitude to the Supreme Being, for having blessed us with advantages hitherto withheld from so great a proportion of the human race; and will operate powerfully to incite us to persevere in every feasible attempt, to be his instruments in rescuing millions of fellow-creatures from their present state of humiliation.

The several topics, which occurred, as suitable to this general Introduction, being now discussed, nothing remains but to state a few particulars, about which the reader of these volumes has a right to expect some information.

Captain Cook, knowing, before he sailed upon this last expedition, that it was expected from him to *relate*, as well as to *execute*, its operations, had taken care to prepare such a journal as might be made use of for publication. This journal, which exists in his own hand-writing, has been faithfully adhered to. It is not a bare extract from his log-books, but contains many remarks which, it appears, had not been inserted by him in the nautical register; and it is

INTRODUCTION.

also enriched with confiderable communications from Mr. Anderfon, Surgeon of the Refolution. The confeffed abilities, and great affiduity, of Mr. Anderfon, in obferving every thing that related either to natural hiftory, or to manners and language; and the defire which, it is well known, Captain Cook, on all occafions, fhewed to have the affiftance of that gentleman, ftamped a great value on his collections. That nothing, therefore, might be wanting to convey to the Public the beft poffible account of the tranfactions of the Voyage, his journal, by the order of Lord Sandwich, was alfo put into the hands of the Editor, who was authorized and directed to avail himfelf of the information it might be found to contain, about matters imperfectly touched, or altogether omitted, in Captain Cook's manufcript. This tafk has been executed in fuch a manner, that the reader will fcarcely ever be at a lofs to diftinguifh in what inftances recourfe has been had to Mr. Anderfon. To preclude, if poffible, any miftake, the copy of the firft and fecond volumes, before it went to the printer, was fubmitted to Captain King; and after it had been read over and corrected by one fo well qualified to point out any inaccuracies, the Earl of Sandwich had the goodnefs to give it a perufal. As to the third volume, nothing more need be faid, than that it was completely prepared for the prefs by Captain King himfelf. All that the Editor of the work has to anfwer for, are the notes occafionally introduced in the courfe of the two volumes, contributed by Captain Cook; and this introduction, which was intended as a kind of epilogue to our Voyages of difcovery. He muft be permitted, however, to fay, that he confiders himfelf as intitled to no inconfiderable fhare of candid indulgence from the Public; having engaged in a very tedious and trouble-

INTRODUCTION.

some undertaking upon the most *disinterested* motives; his only reward being the satisfaction he feels, in having been able to do an essential service to the family of our great navigator, who had honoured him, in the journal of this voyage, with the appellation of Friend.

They who have repeatedly asked why this publication has been so long delayed, need only look at the volumes, and their attendant illustrations and ornaments, to be satisfied that it might, with at least equal reason, be wondered at, that it has not been delayed longer. The Journal of Captain Cook, from the first moment that it came into the hands of the Editor, had been ready for the Press; and Captain King had left with him his part of the narrative, so long ago as his departure for the West Indies, when he commanded the Resistance man of war. But much, besides, remained to be done. The charts, particularly the general one, were to be prepared by Mr. Roberts, who gives an account of his work in the note *; the very numerous and elegant drawings of Mr.

---

* Soon after our departure from England, I was instructed by Captain Cook to complete a map of the world as a general chart, from the best materials he was in possession of for that purpose; and before his death this business was in a great measure accomplished: That is, the grand outline of the whole was arranged, leaving only those parts vacant or unfinished, which he expected to fill in with and explore. But on our return home, when the fruits of our voyage were ordered by the Lords Commissioners of the Admiralty to be published, the care of the general chart being consigned to me, I was directed to prepare it from the latest and best authorities; and also to introduce Captain Cook's three successive tracks, that all his discoveries, and the different routes he had taken might appear together; by this means to give a general idea of the whole. This task having been performed by me, it is necessary, for the information of the Reader, to state the heads of the several authorities which I have followed in such parts of the chart as differ from what was drawn up immediately under the inspection of Captain Cook: And when the Public are made acquainted, that many materials, necessary to complete and elucidate the work, were not, at the time, on board the Resolution, or in his possession, the reason will appear

INTRODUCTION.

Mr. Webber were to be reduced by him to the proper size; artists were next to be found out who would undertake to engrave

pear very obvious, why these alterations and additions were introduced contrary to the original drawing.

First then, I have followed closely the very excellent and correct charts of the Northern Atlantic Ocean, published by Messrs. de Verdun de la Crenne, de Borda, et Pringré in 1775 and 1776; which comprise the coast of Norway from the Sud Hock, in the latitude of 62 degrees North, to Trelleburg, Denmark, the coast of Holland, North coast of Great Britain, Orkneys, Shetland, Ferro Isles, Iceland, coasts of France, Spain, and Portugal, to Cape St. Maria on the coast of Africa; including the Azores, Canaries, Cape de Verd, Antilles, and West India islands from Barbadoes to the East end of Cuba; the North part of Newfoundland and the Labradore coast, as far as the latitude of 57° degrees North.

Ireland, and part of the coast of Scotland, is laid down from Mr. Mackensie's late surveys; and the South coast of England from a chart published by Mr. Faden in 1780, taken from Mr. l'Abbé Dicquemare.

The North part of the coast of Labradore, from the latitude of 57.° North, to Button's Islands in the entrance of Hudson's Strait, is taken from Monsieur Bellin's chart, as is also the North coast of Norway and Lapland, including the White Sea, Gulf of Bothnia, Baltic Sea, and the East coast of Greenland.

The Gulf of Finland, from a large (MS) chart, now engraving for the use of some private merchants.

The West India islands, from the East end of Cuba to the West end, including Jamaica and the Bahama islands, are from a chart published in London by Sayer and Bennett, in 1779.

The South side of Cuba from Point Gorda to Cape de Cruz, is laid down from Monsieur Bellin, in 1762.

The coasts of Newfoundland, and the Gulf of St. Laurence, from the surveys made by Captain Cook, and Messrs. Gilbert and Lane.

Nova Scotia, Cape Breton, Island of St. John, River St. Laurence, Canada, and New England to the River Delaware, from J. F. W. des Barres, Esq; in 1777 and 1778; and charts published in France by order of the King, in 1780, intituled, Neptune Americo-Septentrional, &c. And from these charts also are taken the coasts of Pensylvania, New Jersey, Maryland, Virginia, North and South Carolina, Georgia, East and West Florida, as well as the interior parts of the country to the East side of Lake Ontario.

The other parts of this lake, as likewise Lakes Erie, Huron, Michigan, and Superior, were copied from Mr. Green's maps of America: The Northern part of this last mentioned lake is found from the astronomical observations made by order of the Hudson's Bay Company, at Missippicotton House.

The

INTRODUCTION.

engrave them; the prior engagements of those artists were to be fulfilled before they could begin; the labour and skill

The whole of Hudson's Bay I took from a chart, compiled by Mr. Marley, from all the most authentic maps he could procure of those parts with which I was favoured by Samuel Wegg, Esq; F. R. S. and Governor of that Company, who also politely furnished me with Mr. Hearne's Journals, and the map of his route to the Coppermine River, which is faithfully inserted on the chart, together with the survey of Chesterfield Inlet made by Captain Christopher and Mr. Moses Norton, in 1762; and the discoveries from York Fort to Cumberland, and Hudson Houses (this last is the most Western settlement belonging to the Company), extending to Lake Winipeg, from the drafts of Mr. Philip Turnor, made in 1778 and 1779, corrected by astronomical observations. And from this lake, the disposition of the other lakes to the Southward of it, and which communicate with it, is formed, and laid down from a map constructed by Mr. Spurrel, in the Company's service. The Albany and Moose rivers to Gloucester House, and to Lake Abbitibbe and Superior, are also drawn from a map of Mr. Turnor's, adjusted by observations for the longitudes.

The West coast of Greenland, as chiefly laid down from the observations made by Lieut. R. Pickersgill in the Lion brig in 1776, which determine the line of the coast only, as the immense quantities of ice choak up every bay and inlet on this coast, which formerly were, in the summer season, quite free and open.

From the mouth of the Mississippi River, including its source, and the other rivers branching from it; all the coast of New Leon to Cape Rozo, and the Western coast of America, from Cape Corrientes to the Great Bay of Tecuantepec, is taken from Monsieur D'Anville.

The Gulf of California I have laid down from a German publication in 1773, put into my hands by Sir Joseph Banks, Bart. P. R. S.; and the Western side of it is brought together from a Spanish MS. chart with which A. Dalrymple, Esq; F. R. S. obliged me.

The coast of Brazil from Sierra to Cape Frio, is copied from a small chart of that part by Mr. Dalrymple.

For the Southern part of Africa, from the Cape of Good Hope to Point Natal, I have taken the authority of the chart of Major J. Rennels, F. R. S. shewing the extent of the bank of Lagulhas.

For the existence of the small islands, shoals, and banks to the Eastward of Madagascar, together with the Archipelago of the Maldive and Laccidive Islands; for the coasts of Mallacca, part of Cambodia, and the Island Sumatra, I have used the latest authority of Monsieur D'Après de Manneville's publications in the Neptune Oriental.

The coasts of Guzerat, Malabar, Coromandel, and the opposite shore, containing the Great Bay of Bengal, and the Island of Ceylon, and exhibiting the Heads of

Vol. I.   I   the

INTRODUCTION.

to be exerted in finishing many of them, rendered this a tedious operation; paper fit for printing them upon was to be procured from abroad; and after all these various and unavoidable difficulties were surmounted, much time was necessarily required for executing a numerous impression of the long list of plates, with so much care as might do justice both to Mr. Webber, and to his several engravers. When all these circumstances are taken into consideration, we trust that we shall hear no more of the delay; and only be grate-

the Ganges, and Barrampooter or Sanpoo Rivers, are inferred from the work of the ingenious Author of the map of Hindoostan, published in 1782.

The China sea is laid down from the chart published by Mr. Dalrymple; but the longitudes of Pulo Sapata, Pulo Condore, Pulo Timoan, Straits of Banca and Sunda, and the parts we saw are as settled by us, together with the East coast of Niphon, the principal of the Japanese Islands.

The Jeso and Kurile islands, the East coast of Asia and Kamtschatka, as well as the sea of Okotsk, and the islands lying between Kamtschatka and America that were not seen in the voyage, are taken from a Russian MS. chart, got by us at the Island of Oonalashka.

The Northern countries from Cape Kanin, near the White Sea, as far East as the River Lena, I have given from the Great Russian Map, published at Petersburg in 1776, including the Euxine, Caspian, and Aral Seas, as also the principal lakes to the Eastward; the intent of which is to shew the source of the large rivers that empty themselves into the different oceans and seas.

Every other part of the chart not mentioned in this account, is as originally placed by Captain Cook.

The whole has been corrected from the latest astronomical observations, selected from the Tables compiled by Mr. William Wales, F. R. S. and mathematical master of Christ's Hospital, for the Nautical Almanack: From those in the Mariner's Guide by the Rev. Dr. Maskelyne, F. R. S. and Astronomer Royal, published in 1775; From the Connoissance des Temps for 1780 and 1781; From Professor Mayer's Geographical Table; From the Voyages of Messrs. d'Eveux de Fleurieu, Verdun, de Borda, and Chabert, &c.; From the Table lately published by Mr. Dalrymple for the use of the East India ships; From the Philosophical Transactions of the Royal Society; and from the Observations of our late Navigators,

HEN^Y. ROBERTS.

SHOREHAM, SUSSEX, May 1st, 1784.

ful to that munificent Patron of Science, who not only directed the history of the voyage to be published; but to be published with such a splendid train of ornaments, at the public expence, as will still add to the merit of having ordered the voyage itself to be undertaken.

And here it seems to be incumbent upon us to add, as another instance of munificent attention, that care has been taken to mark, in the most significant manner, the just sense entertained of the humane and liberal relief afforded to our ships in Kamtschatka. Colonel Behm, the commandant of that province, has not been rewarded merely by the pleasure which a benevolent mind feels in reflecting upon the blessings it confers; but has been thanked in a manner equally consistent with the dignity of his own sovereign and of ours, to whose subjects he extended protection. A magnificent piece of plate was presented to him, with an inscription worthy of a place in the same book where the history of his humanity to our countrymen is recorded, and which, while it does honour to our national gratitude, deserves also to be preserved as a monument of our national taste for elegant composition. It is as follows:

VIRO EGREGIO MAGNO DE BEHM; *qui, Imperatricis Augustissimae Catherinae auspiciis, summáque animi benignitate, seva, quibus praerat, Kamtschatkae littora, navibus nauticísque Britannicis, hospita praebuit; eósque, in terminis, si qui essent Imperio Russico, frustra explorandis, mala multa perpessos, iteratá vice excepit, refecit, recreavit, et commeatú omni cumulatí auctos dimisit;* REI NAVALIS BRITANNICAE SEPTEMVIRI *in aliquam benevolentiae tam insignis memoriam, amicissimo, gratissimóque animo, suo, patriaeque nomine,* D. D. D.
MDCCLXXXI.

INTRODUCTION.

This public testimony of gratitude, reminds the Editor, that there are similar calls upon himself. He owes much to Captain King for his advice and direction, in a variety of instances, where Captain Cook's Journal required explanations; for filling up several blanks with the proper longitude and latitude; and for supplying deficiencies in the tables of astronomical observations.

Lieutenant Roberts was also frequently consulted, and was always found to be a ready and effectual assistant, when any nautical difficulties were to be cleared up.

But particular obligations are due to Mr. Wales, who, besides the valuable communications which have been adopted in this Introduction, seconded most liberally the Editor's views of serving Mrs. Cook, by cheerfully taking upon himself the whole trouble of digesting, from the log books, the tables of the route of the ships, which add so greatly to the intrinsic merit of this publication.

Mr. Wegg, besides sharing in the thanks so justly due to the committee of the Hudson's Bay Company, for their unreserved communications, was particularly obliging to the Editor, by giving him repeated opportunities of conversing with Governor Hearne, and Captain Christopher.

The Honourable Mr. Daines Barrington had the goodness to interest himself, with his usual zeal for every work of public utility, in procuring some necessary information, and suggesting some valuable hints which were adopted.

It would be great injustice not to express our acknowledgments to Mr. Pennant, who, besides enriching the third volume with references to his *Arctic Zoology*, the publication of which will be an important accession to Natural History,

also

INTRODUCTION.

alſo communicated ſome very authentic and ſatisfactory manuſcript accounts of the Ruſſian diſcoveries.

The vocabularies of the Friendly and Sandwich Iſlands, and of the natives of Nootka, had been furniſhed to Captain Cook, by his moſt uſeful aſſociate in the voyage, Mr. Anderſon; and a fourth, in which the language of the Eſquimaux is compared with that of the Americans on the oppoſite ſide of the continent, had been prepared by the Captain himſelf. But the comparative Table of Numerals, which is marked No. 2. in the Appendix, was very obligingly drawn up, at the requeſt of the Editor, by Mr. Bryant, who, in his ſtudy, has followed Captain Cook, and, indeed, every traveller and hiſtorian, of every age, into every part of the globe. The Public will conſider this Table as a very ſtriking illuſtration of the wonderful migrations of a nation, about whom ſo much additional information has been gained by our voyages, and be ready to acknowledge it as a very uſeful communication.

One more communication remains to be not only acknowledged, but to be inſerted at the cloſe of this Introduction. The *teſtimonies* of learned contemporaries, in commendation of a deceaſed Author, are frequently diſplayed in the front of his book. It is with the greateſt propriety, therefore, that we prefix to this poſthumous work of Captain Cook the *teſtimony* of one of his own profeſſion, not more diſtinguiſhed by the elevation of rank, than by the dignity of private virtues. As he wiſhes to remain concealed, perhaps this alluſion, for which we intreat his indulgence, may have given too exact direction to the eyes of the Public where to look for ſuch a character. Let us, however, reſt ſatiſfied with the intrinſic merit of a compoſition,

conveyed

INTRODUCTION.

conveyed under the injunction of secrecy; and conclude our long preliminary dissertation with expressing a wish, or rather a well-grounded hope, that this volume may not be the only place where posterity can meet with a monumental inscription, commemorative of a man, in recounting and applauding whose services, the whole of enlightened Europe will equally concur with Great Britain.

TO

[lxxxvii]

TO THE MEMORY OF
Captain JAMES COOK,

The ablest and most renowned Navigator this
or any country hath produced.

HE raised himself, solely by his merit, from a very obscure birth, to the rank of Post Captain in the royal navy, and was, unfortunately, killed by the Savages of the island Owhybee, on the 14th of February 1779; which island he had, not long before, discovered, when prosecuting his third voyage round the globe.

He possessed, in an eminent degree, all the qualifications requisite for his profession and great undertakings; together with the amiable and worthy qualities of the best men.

Cool and deliberate in judging; sagacious in determining; active in executing; steady and persevering in enterprising from vigilance and unremitting caution; unsubdued by labour, difficulties, and disappointments; fertile in expedients; never wanting presence of mind; always possessing himself, and the full use of a sound understanding.

Mild, just, but exact in discipline: he was a father to his people, who were attached to him from affection, and obedient from confidence.

His knowledge, his experience, his sagacity, rendered him so intirely master of his subject, that the greatest obstacles were surmounted, and the most dangerous navigations became easy, and almost safe, under his direction.

His

INSCRIPTION TO THE

He explored the Southern hemisphere to a much higher latitude than had ever been reached, and with fewer accidents than frequently befal those who navigate the coasts of this island.

By his benevolent and unabating attention to the welfare of his ship's company, he discovered and introduced a system for the preservation of the health of seamen in long voyages, which has proved wonderfully efficacious: for in his second voyage round the world, which continued upwards of three years, he lost only one man by distemper, of one hundred and eighteen, of which his company consisted.

The death of this eminent and valuable man was a loss to mankind in general; and particularly to be deplored by every nation that respects useful accomplishments, that honours science, and loves the benevolent and amiable affections of the heart. It is still more to be deplored by this country, which may justly boast of having produced a man hitherto unequalled for nautical talents; and that sorrow is further aggravated by the reflection, that his country was deprived of this ornament by the enmity of a people, from whom, indeed, it might have been dreaded, but from whom it was not deserved. For, actuated always by the most attentive care and tender compassion for the savages in general, this excellent man was ever assiduously endeavouring, by kind treatment, to dissipate their fears, and court their friendship; overlooking their thefts and treacheries, and frequently interposing, at the hazard of his life, to protect them from the sudden resentment of his own injured people.

The object of his last mission was to discover and ascertain the boundaries of Asia and America, and to penetrate into the Northern Ocean by the North East Cape of Asia.

Traveller! contemplate, admire, revere, and emulate this great master in his profession; whose skill and labours have enlarged natural philosophy; have extended nautical science; and have disclosed the long concealed and admirable arrangements of the Almighty in the formation of this globe, and, at the same time, the arrogance of mortals, in presuming to account, by their speculations, for the laws by which he was pleased to create it. It is now discovered, beyond all doubt, that the same Great Being who created the universe by his fiat, by the same ordained our earth to keep a just poise, without a corresponding Southern continent—and it does so! " He stretcheth out the North over the empty " place, and hangeth the earth upon nothing." Job, xxvi. 7.

If the arduous but exact researches of this extraordinary man have not discovered a new world, they have discovered seas unnavigated and unknown before. They have made us acquainted with islands, people and productions, of which we had no conception. And if he has not been so fortunate as Americus to give his name to a continent, his pretensions to such a distinction remain unrivalled; and he will be revered, while there remains a page of his own modest account of his voyages, and as long as mariners and geographers shall be instructed, by his new map of the Southern hemisphere, to trace the various courses and discoveries he has made.

If public services merit public acknowledgments; if the man who adorned and raised the fame of his country is deserving of honours, then Captain COOK deserves to have a monument raised to his memory, by a generous and grateful nation.

Virtutis uberrimum alimentum est honos.
VAL. MAXIMUS, Lib. 2. Cap. 6.

[xci]

LIST OF THE PLATES,

With DIRECTIONS for placing them.

[As many of the Purchasers of this Work may choose to preserve the larger-sized Plates in a separate volume in folio, these have been here marked with Asterisks; and Bookfellers are cautioned not to have them bound up, with the rest of the Plates, in the places of these volumes pointed out by the respective References, unless they receive particular directions for that purpose.]

VOL. I.

Page		Plate N°
1	*General Chart exhibiting Captain Cook's discoveries	I.
51	Chart of Kerguelen's Land, with a sketch of Prince Edward's Islands	II.
61	Sketches of Christmas Harbour, and Port Palliser in Kerguelen's Land	III.
71	*View of Christmas Harbour in Kerguelen's Land	IV.
83	Views on the Coast of Kerguelen's Land †	LXXXII.
91	Chart and Views of Van Diemen's Land	V.
96	*A Man of Van Diemen's Land	VI.
101	*A Woman of Van Diemen's Land	VII.
109	*An Opossum of Van Diemen's Land	VIII.

† A few of the Plates are not numbered in the order in which they are to be placed, but no inconvenience can ensue, as the references to the Pages of each Volume will remedy this unavoidable imperfection.

m 2

LIST OF THE PLATES.

Page		Plate Nº
117	* Plan of Adventure Bay, in Van Diemen's Land	IX.
157	* The Inside of a Hippah, in New Zealand	X.
173	* A Man of Mangea	XI.
225	Chart of the Friendly Islands	XII.
230	* View at Anamooka	XIII.
244	* The Reception of Captain Cook in Hapaee	XIV.
246	* A boxing match in Hapaee	XV.
249	* A Night Dance by Men in Hapaee	XVI.
250	* A Night Dance by Women in Hapaee	XVII.
264	* Poulaho, King of the Friendly Islands	XVIII.
277	Sketch of Tongataboo Harbour	XIX.
312	* Poulaho, King of the Friendly Islands, drinking Kava	XX.
314	* A *Fiatooka* or *Morai*, in Tongataboo	XXI.
337	* The *Natche*, a Ceremony in honour of the King's Son, in Tongataboo	XXII.
355	A Woman of Eaoo or Eooa	XXIII.

VOL. II.

5	Sketches of Mangea, Vol. i. p. 170;—of Wateeoo, Vol. i. p. 180;—of Wenooa ette, Vol. i. p. 205;—and of Toobouai	XXIV.
32	* A Human Sacrifice in a *Morai*, in Otaheite	XXV.
51	* A young Woman of Otaheite bringing a present	XXVII.
52	* The Body of Tee, a Chief, as preserved after death, in Otaheite	XXVI.
58	* A Dance, in Otaheite	XXVIII.
69	* A young Woman of Otaheite, dancing	XXIX.
79	Sketch of two Harbours on the North side of Eimeo	XXX.

LIST OF THE PLATES.

Page		Plate N°
91	*A view of Huaheine	XXXI.
179	Christmas Island	XXXII.
200	*A *Morai* in Atooi	XXXIII.
202	*The Inside of the House in the *Morai*, in Atooi	XXXIV.
205	*An Inland View in Atooi	XXXV.
258	Views on the West coast of North America	LXXXVI.
269	*Chart of the North West coast of North America, and North East coast of Asia	XXXVI.
279	Sketch of Nootka Sound	XXXVII.
295	*A Sea Otter	XLIII.
301	*A man of Nootka Sound	XXXVIII.
303	*A woman of Nootka Sound	XXXIX.
306	*Various Articles at Nootka Sound	XL.

  1 A bird, made of wood, hollow, with stones in the inside, which the Natives shake when they dance.
  2 A Seal's head, made of wood, worn upon their heads.
  3 A bird's head, composed of wood and feathers, also worn upon their heads.
  4 Another for the same purpose, and ornamented with green talc.

313	*View of the Habitations in Nootka Sound	XLI.
317	*The Inside of a House in Nootka Sound	XLII.
353	Chart of Cook's River, and Prince William's Sound	XLIV.
361	*A view of Snug Corner Cove in Prince William's Sound	XLV.
367	*A Man of Prince William's Sound	XLVI.
369	*A Woman of Prince William's Sound	XLVII.

LIST OF THE PLATES.

Page		Plate N°
410	Views on the West coast of North America, to the Westward of Cook's River	LXXXVII.
421	*A Man of Oonalashka	XLVIII.
422	*A woman of Oonalashka	XLIX.
423	*Canoes of Oonalashka	L.
424	Sketch of Samganoodha Harbour at the Island Oonalashka	LV.
447	*The Tschuktschi, or Tschutski, and their Habitations	LI.
457	*Sea Horses	LII.
467	Chart of Norton Sound and Beering's Strait	LIII.
471	Views on the coast of Asia	LXXXIV.
484	*Inhabitants of Norton Sound, and their Habitations	LIV.
510	*Caps of the natives of Oonalashka	LVI.
512	*Natives of Oonalashka, and their habitations	LVII.
514	*The Inside of a House in Oonalashka	LVIII.
530	Views of the Sandwich Islands	LXXXIII.

VOL. III.

1	Chart of the Sandwich Islands, and view of Karakakooa Bay	LIX.
13	*An Offering before Captain Cook in the Sandwich Islands	LX.
17	*Tereoboo or Terreeoboo, King of Owhyhee, bringing presents to Captain Cook	LXI.
27	*A Man of the Sandwich Islands, dancing	LXII.
54	*A view of Karakakooa in Owhyhee	LXVIII.
125	*A young woman of the Sandwich Islands	LXIII.

LIST OF THE PLATES.

Page		Plate N°
126	*A Man of the Sandwich Islands, with his helmet	LXIV.
139	*A Canoe of the Sandwich Islands, the Rowers masked	LXV.
140	*A Man of the Sandwich Islands in a mask	LXVI.
151	*Various Articles at the Sandwich Islands	LXVII.

    N° 1 A wooden Instrument or Weapon, set round with the teeth of Sharks, with which they cut up their prisoners.
        2 Another, for the same purpose.
        3 A musical Instrument; the upper part wicker-work, covered with feathers; the bottom part a gourd with stones in it, which the dancer shakes about.—See Plate LXII.
        4 An Idol upon wicker-work, covered with feathers; the eyes mother of pearl, with a black nut; the mouth set with teeth of dogs.
        5 A Bracelet, composed of the tusks of hogs.
        6 A wooden Dagger called *Pahooah*.

Page		Plate N°
184	Sketch of Awatska Bay in Kamtschatka	LXIX.
201	*A Man in Kamtschatka travelling in winter	LXX.
212	*A Sledge in Kamtschatka	LXXI.
215	*A view at Bolcheretskoi in Kamtschatka	LXXII.
252	*A white Bear	LXXIII.
282	*A view of the Town and Harbour of St. Peter and St. Paul, in Kamtschatka	LXXIV.
313	Views on the coast of Kamtschatka	LXXXV.
359	*A Man of Kamtschatka	LXXV.
360	*A Woman of Kamtschatka	LXXVI.
574	*Summer and Winter Habitations in Kamtschatka	LXXVII.

LIST OF THE PLATES.

Page		Plate N°
376	*The Inside of a Winter Habitation in Kamtschatka	LXXVIII.
397	Chart of the Coast of Japan	LXXIX.
409	Sketch of Sulphur Island	LXXX.
420	Sketch of the Typa and Macao	LXXXI.

[N. B. The longitude in these volumes is reckoned from the meridian of Greenwich, and after passing it to the East, in the South Atlantic, is carried on Easterly beyond the 180th degree, to the utmost extent of the voyage; and back, to the same meridian.]

A VOYAGE

A

VOYAGE

TO THE

PACIFIC OCEAN.

BOOK I.

Transactions from the Beginning of the Voyage till our Departure from New Zealand.

CHAP. I.

Various Preparations for the Voyage.—Omai's Behaviour on embarking.—Observations for determining the Longitude of Sheerness, and the North Foreland.—Passage of the Resolution from Deptford to Plymouth.—Employments there.—Complements of the Crews of both Ships, and Names of the Officers.—Observations to fix the Longitude of Plymouth.—Departure of the Resolution.

HAVING, on the ninth Day of February 1776, received a commission to command his Majesty's sloop the Resolution, I went on board the next day, hoisted the pendant, and began to enter men. At the same time, the Discovery, of three hundred tons burthen, was purchased

1776.
February.

purchased into the service, and the command of her given to Captain Clerke, who had been my second Lieutenant on board the Resolution, in my second voyage round the world, from which we had lately returned.

These two ships were, at this time, in the dock at Deptford, under the hands of the shipwrights; being ordered to be equipped to make farther discoveries in the Pacific Ocean, under my direction.

March.
Saturday 9.

On the 9th of March, the Resolution was hauled out of dock into the River; where we completed her rigging, and took on board the stores and provisions requisite for a voyage of such duration. Both ships, indeed, were supplied with as much of every necessary article as we could conveniently stow, and with the best of every kind that could be procured. And, besides this, every thing that had been found, by the experience acquired during our former extensive voyages, to be of any utility in preserving the health of seamen, was supplied in abundance.

May.
Monday 6.

It was our intention to have sailed to Long Reach on the 6th of May, when a pilot came on board to carry us thither; but it was the 29th before the wind would permit us to

Thursday 30.

move; and the 30th before we arrived at that station, where our artillery, powder, shot, and other ordnance stores were received.

June.

While we lay in Long Reach, thus employed, the Earl of Sandwich, Sir Hugh Palliser, and others of the Board of Admiralty, as the last mark of the very great attention they had all along shewn to this equipment, paid us a visit on

Saturday 8.

the 8th of June, to examine whether every thing had been completed conformably to their intentions and orders, and to the satisfaction of all who were to embark in the voyage.

They,

They, and several other Noblemen and Gentlemen their friends, honoured me with their company at dinner on that day; and, on their coming on board, and also on their going ashore, we saluted them with seventeen guns, and three cheers.

With the benevolent view of conveying some permanent benefit to the inhabitants of Otaheite, and of the other islands in the Pacific Ocean, whom we might happen to visit, his Majesty having commanded some useful animals to be carried out, we took on board, on the 10th, a bull, two cows with their calves, and some sheep, with hay and corn for their subsistence; intending to add to these, other useful animals, when I should arrive at the Cape of Good Hope.

I was also, from the same laudable motives, furnished with a sufficient quantity of such of our European garden seeds, as could not fail to be a valuable present to our newly-discovered islands, by adding fresh supplies of food to their own vegetable productions.

Many other articles, calculated to improve the condition of our friends in the other hemisphere in various ways, were, at the same time, delivered to us by order of the Board of Admiralty. And both ships were provided with a proper assortment of iron tools and trinkets, as the means of enabling us to traffic, and to cultivate a friendly intercourse with the inhabitants of such new countries as we might be fortunate enough to meet with.

The same humane attention was extended to our own wants. Some additional cloathing, adapted to a cold climate, was ordered for our crews: and nothing was denied to us that could be supposed in the least conducive to health, or even to conveuience.

1776.
June.

Tuesday 11.

Nor did the extraordinary care of those at the head of the naval department stop here. They were equally solicitous to afford us every assistance towards rendering our voyage of public utility. Accordingly, we received on board, next day, several astronomical and nautical instruments, which the Board of Longitude intrusted to me, and to Mr. King, my second Lieutenant; we having engaged to that Board to make all the necessary observations, during the voyage, for the improvement of astronomy and navigation; and, by our joint labours, to supply the place of a professed observator. Such a person had been originally intended to be sent out in my ship.

The Board, likewise, put into our possession the same watch, or time-keeper, which I had carried out in my last voyage, and had performed its part so well. It was a copy of Mr. Harrison's, constructed by Mr. Kendall. This day, at noon, it was found to be too slow for mean time at Greenwich, by 3′, 31″, 890; and by its rate of going, it lost, on mean time, 1″, 209 per day.

Another time-keeper, and the same number and sort of instruments for making observations, were put on board the Discovery, under the care of Mr. William Bailey; who, having already given satisfactory proofs of his skill and diligence as an observator, while employed in Captain Furneaux's ship, during the late voyage, was engaged a second time, in that capacity, to embark with Captain Clerke.

Mr. Anderson, my surgeon, who, to skill in his immediate profession, added great proficiency in natural history, was as willing as he was well qualified, to describe every thing in that branch of science which should occur worthy of notice. As he had already visited the South Sea islands in the same ship, and been of singular service, by enabling me to

enrich

enrich my relation of that voyage with various useful remarks on men and things*, I reasonably expected to derive considerable assistance from him, in recording our new proceedings.

I had several young men amongst my sea-officers who, under my direction, could be usefully employed in constructing charts, in taking views of the coasts and headlands near which we should pass, and in drawing plans of the bays and harbours in which we should anchor. A constant attention to this I knew to be highly requisite, if we would render our discoveries profitable to future navigators.

And, that we might go out with every help that could serve to make the result of our voyage entertaining to the generality of readers, as well as instructive to the sailor and scholar, Mr. Webber was pitched upon, and engaged to embark with me, for the express purpose of supplying the unavoidable imperfections of written accounts, by enabling us to preserve, and to bring home, such drawings of the most memorable scenes of our transactions, as could only be executed by a professed and skilful artist.

Every preparation being now completed, I received an order to proceed to Plymouth, and to take the Discovery under my command. I accordingly gave Captain Clerke two orders; one to put himself under my command, and the other to carry his ship round to Plymouth.

On the 15th, the Resolution sailed from Long Reach, with the Discovery in company, and the same evening they

* The very copious Vocabulary of the language of Otaheite, and the comparative specimen of the languages of the several other islands visited during the former voyage, and published in Captain Cook's account of it, were furnished by Mr. Anderson.

anchored

anchored at the Nore. Next day the Discovery proceeded, in obedience to my order; but the Resolution was ordered to remain at the Nore till I should join her, being at this time in London.

As we were to touch at Otaheite and the Society Islands, in our way to the intended scene of our fresh operations, it had been determined not to omit this opportunity (the only one ever likely to happen) of carrying Omai back to his native country. Accordingly, every thing being ready for our departure, he and I set out together from London on the 24th, at six o'clock in the morning. We reached Chatham between ten and eleven o'clock; and, after dining with Commissioner Proby, he very obligingly ordered his yacht to carry us to Sheerness, where my boat was waiting to take us on board.

Omai left London with a mixture of regret and satisfaction. When we talked about England, and about those who, during his stay, had honoured him with their protection or friendship, I could observe that his spirits were sensibly affected, and that it was with difficulty he could refrain from tears. But, the instant the conversation turned to his own islands, his eyes began to sparkle with joy. He was deeply impressed with a sense of the good treatment he had met with in England, and entertained the highest ideas of the country and of the people. But the pleasing prospect he now had before him of returning home, loaded with what, he well knew, would be esteemed invaluable treasures there, and the flattering hope which the possession of these gave him, of attaining to a distinguished superiority amongst his countrymen, were considerations which operated, by degrees, to suppress every uneasy sensation; and he seemed to be quite happy when he got on board the ship.

He

He was furnished, by his Majesty, with an ample provision of every article which, during our intercourse with his country, we had observed to be in any estimation there, either as useful or as ornamental. He had, besides, received many presents of the same nature from Lord Sandwich, Mr.[*] Banks, and several other Gentlemen and Ladies of his acquaintance. In short, every method had been employed, both during his abode in England, and at his departure, to make him the instrument of conveying to the inhabitants of the islands of the Pacific Ocean, the most exalted opinion of the greatness and generosity of the British nation.

While the Resolution lay at the Nore, Mr. King made several observations for finding the longitude by the watch. The mean of them all, gave 0° 44′ 0″, for the longitude of the ship. This, reduced to Sheerness, by the bearing and estimated distance, will make that place to be 0° 37′ 0″ East of Greenwich; which is more by seven miles than Mr. Lyons made it, by the watch which Lord Mulgrave had with him, on his voyage towards the North Pole. Whoever knows any thing of the distance between Sheerness and Greenwich, will be a judge which of these two observations is nearest the truth.

The variation of the needle here, by a mean of different sets, taken with different compasses, was 20° 37′ West.

On the 25th, about noon, we weighed anchor, and made sail for the Downs, through the Queen's Channel, with a gentle breeze at North West by West. At nine in the evening we anchored, with the North Foreland bearing South by East, and Margate Point South West by South.

[*] Now Sir Joseph.

1776.
June.
Wednes. 26.

Next morning, at two o'clock, we weighed and stood round the Foreland; and when it bore North, allowing for the variation of the compass, the watch gave 1° 24' East longitude, which, reduced to the Foreland, will be 1° 21' East. Lunar observations made the preceding evening, fixed it at 1° 20' East. At eight o'clock the same morning, we anchored in the Downs. Two boats had been built for us at Deal, and I immediately sent on shore for them. I was told that many people had assembled there to see Omai; but, to their great disappointment, he did not land.

Thursday 27.

Having received the boats on board, and a light breeze at South South East springing up, we got under sail the next day at two o'clock in the afternoon. But the breeze soon died away, and we were obliged to anchor again till ten o'clock at night. We then weighed, with the wind at East, and proceeded down the channel.

Sunday 30.

On the 30th, at three o'clock in the afternoon, we anchored in Plymouth Sound, where the Discovery had arrived only three days before. I saluted Admiral Amherst, whose flag was flying on board the Ocean, with thirteen guns, and he returned the compliment with eleven.

July.
Monday 1.
Tuesday 2.

It was the first object of our care, on arriving at Plymouth, to replace the water and provisions that we had expended, and to receive on board a supply of Port Wine. This was the employment which occupied us on the 1st and 2d of July.

During our stay here, the crews were served with fresh beef every day. And I should not do justice to Mr. Ommanney, the Agent Victualler, if I did not take this opportunity to mention, that he shewed a very obliging readiness to furnish me with the best of every thing that lay within his department.

partment. I had been under the like obligations to him on my setting out upon my last voyage. Commissioner Ourry, with equal zeal for the service, gave us every assistance that we wanted from the naval yard.

It could not but occur to us as a singular and affecting circumstance, that at the very instant of our departure upon a voyage, the object of which was to benefit Europe by making fresh discoveries in North America, there should be the unhappy necessity of employing others of his Majesty's ships, and of conveying numerous bodies of land forces, to secure the obedience of those parts of that continent which had been discovered and settled by our countrymen in the last century. On the 6th, his Majesty's ships Diamond, Ambuscade, and Unicorn, with a fleet of transports, consisting of sixty-two sail, bound to America, with the last division of the Hessian troops, and some horse, were forced into the Sound by a strong North West Wind.

On the 8th, I received, by express, my instructions * for the voyage, and an order to proceed to the Cape of Good Hope with the Resolution. I was also directed to leave an order for Captain Clerke to follow us, as soon as he should join his ship; he being, at this time, detained in London.

Our first discoverers of the New World, and navigators of the Indian and Pacific Oceans, were justly thought to have exerted such uncommon abilities, and to have accomplished such perilous enterprizes, that their names have been handed down to posterity as so many Argonauts. Nay, even the hulks of the ships that carried them, though not converted into constellations in the Heavens, used to be honoured and visited as sacred reliques upon earth. We, in the pre-

* See the instructions, in the Introduction.

Vol. I.   C   sent

1776.
July.

sent age of improved navigation, who have been instructed by their labours, and have followed them as our guides, have no such claim to fame. Some merit, however, being still, in the public opinion, considered as due to those who sail to unexplored quarters of the globe, in conformity to this favourable judgment, I prefixed to the account of my last voyage the names of the officers of both my ships, and a table of the number of their respective crews. The like information will be expected from me at present.

The Resolution was fitted out with the same complement of officers and men she had before; and the Discovery's establishment varied from that of the Adventure, in the single instance of her having no marine officer on board. This arrangement was to be finally completed at Plymouth; and, on the 9th, we received the party of marines allotted for our voyage. Colonel Bell, who commanded the division at this port, gave me such men for the detachment as I had reason to be satisfied with. And the supernumerary seamen, occasioned by this reinforcement, being turned over into the Ocean man of war, our several complements remained fixed, as represented in the following table:

Tuesday 9.

THE PACIFIC OCEAN.

1776. July.

RESOLUTION.			DISCOVERY.	
Officers and Men.	N°	Officers Names.	N°	Officers Names.
Captain,	1	James Cook.	1	Charles Clerke.
Lieutenants,	3	John Gore.	2	James Burney.
		James King.		John Rickman.
		John Williamson.		
Master,	1	William Bligh.	1	Thomas Edgar.
Boatswain,	1	William Ewin.	1	Eneas Atkins.
Carpenter,	1	James Clevely.	1	Peter Reynolds.
Gunner,	1	Robert Anderson.	1	William Peckover.
Surgeon,	1	William Anderson.	1	John Law.
Master's Mates,	3		2	
Midshipmen,	6		4	
Surgeon's Mates,	2		2	
Captain's Clerk,	1		1	
Master at Arms,	1		1	
Corporal,	1			
Armourer,	1		1	
Ditto Mate,	1		1	
Sail Maker,	1		1	
Ditto Mate,	1		1	
Boatswain's Mates,	3		2	
Carpenter's Ditto,	3		2	
Gunner's Ditto,	2		1	
Carpenter's Crew,	4		4	
Cook,	1		1	
Ditto Mate,	1			
Quarter Masters,	6		4	
Able Seamen,	45		33	
		Marines.		
Lieutenant,	1	Molesworth Philips.		
Serjeant,	1		1	
Corporals,	2		1	
Drummer,	1		1	
Private,	15		8	
Total,	112		80	

1776.
July.
Wednef. 10.

On the 10th, the Commissioner and Pay Clerks came on board, and paid the officers and crew up to the 30th of last month. The petty officers and seamen had, besides, two months wages in advance. Such indulgence to the latter, is no more than what is customary in the navy. But the payment of what was due to the superior officers was humanely ordered by the Admiralty, in consideration of our peculiar situation, that we might be better able to defray the very great expence of furnishing ourselves with a stock of necessaries for a voyage which, probably, would be of unusual duration, and to regions where no supply could be expected.

Thursday 11.

Nothing now obstructing my departure but a contrary wind, which blew strong at South West, in the morning of the 11th, I delivered into the hands of Mr. Burney, first Lieutenant of the Discovery, Captain Clerke's sailing orders; a copy of which I also left with the Officer * commanding his Majesty's ships at Plymouth, to be delivered to the Captain immediately on his arrival. In the afternoon, the wind moderating, we weighed with the ebb, and got farther out, beyond all the shipping in the Sound; where, after making an unsuccessful attempt to get to sea, we were detained most of the following day, which was employed in receiving on board a supply of water; and, by the same vessel that brought it, all the empty casks were returned.

Friday 12.

As I did not imagine my stay at Plymouth would have been so long as it proved, we did not get our instruments on shore to make the necessary observations for ascertaining the longitude by the watch. For the same reason, Mr. Baily did not set about this, till he found that the Discovery would,

* Captain Le Crais, Admiral Amherst having struck his flag some days before.

probably,

probably, be detained some days after us. He then placed his quadrant upon Drake's Island; and had time, before the Resolution sailed, to make observations sufficient for the purpose we had in view. Our watch made the island to lie 4° 14', and his, 4° 13½', West of Greenwich. Its latitude, as found by Messrs. Wales and Baily, on the last voyage, is 50° 21' 30" North.

We weighed again at eight in the evening, and stood out of the Sound, with a gentle breeze at North West by West.

CHAP.

CHAP. II.

Paſſage of the Reſolution to Teneriffe.—Reception there.—Deſcription of Santa Cruz Road.—Refreſhments to be met with.—Obſervations for fixing the Longitude of Teneriffe.—Some Account of the Iſland.—Botanical Obſervations.—Cities of Santa Cruz and Laguna.—Agriculture.—Air and Climate.—Commerce.—Inhabitants.

1776.
July.
Friday 12.
Sunday 14.

WE had not been long out of Plymouth Sound, before the wind came more weſterly, and blew freſh, ſo that we were obliged to ply down the Channel; and it was not till the 14th, at eight in the evening, that we were off the Lizard.

Tueſday 16.

On the 16th, at noon, St. Agnes's Light-houſe on the Iſles of Scilly, bore North Weſt by Weſt, diſtant ſeven or eight miles. Our latitude was, now, 49° 53′ 30″ North, and our longitude, by the watch, 6° 11′ Weſt. Hence, I reckon that St. Agnes's Light-houſe is in 49° 57′ 30″ North latitude, and in 6° 20′ of Weſt longitude.

Wedneſ. 17.
Thurſday 18.

On the 17th * and 18th we were off Uſhant, and found the longitude of the iſland to be, by the watch, 5° 18′ 37″ Weſt. The variation was 23° 0′ 50″, in the ſame direction.

* It appears from Captain Cook's log-book, that he began his judicious operations for preſerving the health of his crew, very early in the voyage. On the 17th, the ſhip was ſmoked between decks with gun-powder. The ſpare ſails alſo were then well aired.

With

With a strong gale at South, on the 19th, we stood to the 1776. westward, till eight o'clock in the morning; when, the wind July. shifting to the West and North West, we tacked and stretch- Friday 19. ed to the Southward. At this time, we saw nine sail of large ships, which we judged to be French men of war. They took no particular notice of us, nor we of them.

At ten o'clock in the morning of the 22d, we saw Cape Monday 22. Ortegal; which at noon bore South East, half South, about four leagues distant. At this time we were in the latitude of 44° 6′ North; and our longitude, by the watch, was 8° 23′ West.

After two days of calm weather we passed Cape Finisterre, on the afternoon of the 24th, with a fine gale at Wednesf. 24. North North East. The longitude of this Cape, by the watch, is 9° 29′ West; and, by the mean of forty-one lunar observations, made before and after we passed it, and reduced to it by the watch, the result was 9° 19′ 12″.

On the 30th, at six minutes and thirty-eight seconds past Tuesday 30. ten o'clock at night, apparent time, I observed, with a night telescope, the moon totally eclipsed. By the *ephemeris*, the same happened at Greenwich at nine minutes past eleven o'clock; the difference being one hour, two minutes, and twenty-two seconds, or 15° 35′ 30″ of longitude. The watch, for the same time, gave 15° 26′ 45″ longitude West; and latitude 51° 10′ North. No other observation could be made on this eclipse, as the moon was hid behind the clouds the greater part of the time; and, in particular, when the beginning and end of total darkness, and the end of the eclipse, happened.

Finding that we had not hay and corn sufficient for the subsistence of the flock of animals on board, till our arrival

at

1778.
July.

Wednes. 31.

August.
Thursday 1.

at the Cape of Good Hope, I determined to touch at Teneriffe, to get a supply of these, and of the usual refreshments for ourselves; thinking that island, for such purposes, better adapted than Madeira. At four in the afternoon of the 31st, we saw Teneriffe, and steered for the eastern part. At nine, being near it, we hauled up, and stood off and on during the night.

At day-light, on the morning of the 1st of August, we sailed round the East Point of the island; and, about eight o'clock, anchored on the South East side of it, in the Road of Santa Cruz, in twenty-three fathoms water; the bottom, sand and owze. Punta de Nago, the East point of the Road, bore North 64° East; St. Francis's church, remarkable for its high steeple, West South West; the Pic, South 65° West; and the South West point of the Road, on which stands a fort or castle, South 39° West. In this situation, we moored North East and South West, with a cable each way, being near half a mile from the shore.

We found, riding in this Road, La Boussole, a French frigate, commanded by the *Chevalier de Borda*; two brigantines of the same nation; an English brigantine from London, bound to Senegal; and fourteen sail of Spanish vessels.

No sooner had we anchored, than we were visited by the Master of the Port, who satisfied himself with asking the ship's name. Upon his leaving us, I sent an officer ashore, to present my respects to the Governor; and to ask his leave to take in water, and to purchase such articles as we were in want of. All this he granted with the greatest politeness; and, soon after, sent an officer on board, to compliment me on my arrival. In the afternoon, I waited upon him in person, accompanied by some of my officers; and, before I returned

returned to my ship, bespoke some corn and straw for the live stock; ordered a quantity of wine from Mr. M'Carrick, the contractor, and made an agreement with the master of a Spanish boat to supply us with water, as I found that we could not do it ourselves.

1776.
August.

The road of Santa Cruz is situated before the town of the same name, on the South East side of the island. It is, as I am told, the principal road of Teneriffe, for shelter, capacity, and the goodness of its bottom. It lies entirely open to the South East and South winds. But these winds are never of long continuance; and, they say, there is not an instance * of a ship driving from her anchors on shore. This may, in part, be owing to the great care they take in mooring them; for I observed, that all the ships we met with there, had four anchors out; two to the North East, and two to the South West; and their cables buoyed up with casks. Ours suffered a little by not observing this last precaution.

At the South West part of the road, a stone pier runs out into the sea from the town, for the convenience of loading and landing of goods. To this pier, the water that supplies the shipping is conveyed. This, as also what the inhabitants of Santa Cruz use, is derived from a rivulet that runs from the hills, the greatest part of which comes into the town in wooden spouts or troughs, that are supported by slender posts, and the remainder doth not reach the sea; though it is evident, from the size of the channel, that

---

* Though no such instance was known to those from whom Captain Cook had this information, we learn from Glas, that *some years before* he was at Teneriffe, almost all the shipping in the road were driven on shore. See Glas's *Hist. of the Canary Islands*, p. 235. We may well suppose the precautions now used, have prevented any more such accidents happening. This will sufficiently justify Captain Cook's account.

Vol. I.   D   sometimes

1776.
August

sometimes large torrents rush down. At this time these troughs were repairing, so that fresh water, which is very good here, was scarce.

Were we to judge from the appearance of the country in the neighbourhood of Santa Cruz, it might be concluded that Teneriffe is a barren spot, insufficient to maintain even its own inhabitants. The ample supplies, however, which we received, convinced us that they had enough to spare for visitors. Besides wine, which is the chief produce of the island, beef may be had at a moderate price. The oxen are small and boney, and weigh about ninety pounds a quarter. The meat is but lean, and was, at present, sold for half a bit (three pence sterling) a pound. I, unadvisedly, bought the bullocks alive, and paid considerably more. Hogs, sheep, goats and poultry, are likewise to be bought at the same moderate rate; and fruits are in great plenty. At this time we had grapes, figs, pears, mulberries, plantains, and musk melons. There is a variety of other fruits produced here, though not in season at this time. Their pumpkins, onions, and potatoes, are exceedingly good of their kind, and keep better at sea than any I ever before met with.

The Indian corn, which is also their produce, cost me about three shillings and sixpence a bushel; and the fruits and roots were, in general, very cheap. They have not any plentiful supply of fish from the adjoining sea; but a very considerable fishery is carried on by their vessels upon the coast of Barbary; and the produce of it sells at a reasonable price. Upon the whole, I found Teneriffe to be a more eligible place than Madeira, for ships bound on long voyages to touch at; though the wine of the latter, according to my taste,

taste, is as much superior to that of the former, as strong beer is to small. To compensate for this, the difference of prices is considerable; for the best Teneriffe wine was now sold for twelve pounds a pipe; whereas a pipe of the best Madeira would have cost considerably more than double that sum [*].

The Chevalier de Borda, Commander of the French frigate now lying in Santa Cruz road, was employed, in conjunction with Mr. Varila, a Spanish Gentleman, in making astronomical observations for ascertaining the going of two time-keepers which they had on board their ship. For this purpose, they had a tent pitched on the pier head, where they made their observations, and compared their watches, every day at noon, with the clock on shore, by signals. These signals the Chevalier very obligingly communicated to us; so that we could compare our watch at the same time. But our stay was too short, to profit much by his kindness.

The three days comparisons which we made, assured us that the watch had not materially, if at all, altered her rate of going; and gave us the same longitude, within a very few seconds, that was obtained by finding the time from observations of the sun's altitude from the horizon of the sea. The watch, from a mean of these observations, on the 1st, 2d, and 3d of August, made the longitude 16° 31′

---

[*] Formerly, there was made at Teneriffe a great quantity of Canary sack, which the French call *Vin de Malvoisie*; and we, corruptly after them, name Malmsey (from Malvesia, a town in the Morea, famous for such luscious wine). In the last century, and still later, much of this was imported into England; but little wine is now made there, but of the sort described by Captain Cook. Not more than fifty pipes of the rich Canary was annually made in Glas's time; and he says, they now gather the grapes when green, and make a dry hard wine of them, fit for hot climates, p. 262.

West; and, in like manner, the latitude was found to be 28° 30′ 11″ North.

Mr. Varila informed us, that the true longitude was 18° 35′ 30″, from Paris, which is only 16° 16′ 30″ from Greenwich; less than what our watch gave by 14′ 30″. But, far from looking upon this as an error in the watch, I rather think it a confirmation of its having gone well; and that the longitude by it may be nearer the truth than any other. It is farther confirmed by the lunar observations that we made in the road, which gave 16° 37′ 10″. Those made before we arrived, and reduced to the road by the watch, gave 16° 33′ 30″: and those made after we left it, and reduced back in the same manner, gave 16° 28′. The mean of the three is 16° 30′ 40″.

To reduce these several longitudes, and the latitude, to the Pic of Teneriffe, one of the most noted points of land with Geographers (to obtain the true situation of which, I have entered into this particular discussion), I had recourse to the bearing, and a few hours of the ship's run after leaving Santa Cruz road; and found it to be 12′ 11″ South of the road, and 29′ 30″ of longitude West of it. As the base, which helped to determine this, was partly estimated, it is liable to some error; but I think I cannot be much mistaken. Dr. Maskelyne, in his *British Mariner's Guide*, places the Pic in the latitude of 28° 12′ 54″. This, with the bearing from the road, will give the difference of longitude 43′, which considerably exceeds the distance they reckon the Pic to be from Santa Cruz. I made the latitude of the Pic to be 28° 18′ North. Upon that supposition, its longitude will be as follows:

By

THE PACIFIC OCEAN.

By {The Time-keeper - 17° 0' 30"}
   {Lunar obfervations - 16° 30' 20"} Weſt.
   {Mr. Varila - - 16° 46' 0"}

1776. Auguſt.

But if the latitude of it is 28° 12' 54", as in the *Britiſh Mariner's Guide*, its longitude will be 13' 30" more weſterly.

The variation, when we were at anchor in the road, by the mean of all our compaſſes, was found to be 14° 41' 20" Weſt. The dip of the North end of the needle was 61° 52' 30".

Some of Mr. Anderſon's remarks on the natural appearances of Teneriffe, and its productions; and what he obſerved himſelf, or learnt by information, about the general ſtate of the iſland, will be of uſe, particularly in marking what changes may have happened there ſince Mr. Glas viſited it. They here follow in his own words:

"While we were ſtanding in for the land, the weather being perfectly clear, we had an opportunity of ſeeing the celebrated Pic of Teneriffe. But, I own, I was much diſappointed in my expectation with reſpect to its appearance. It is, certainly, far from equalling the noble figure of Pico, one of the weſtern iſles which I have ſeen; though its perpendicular height may be greater. This circumſtance, perhaps, ariſes from its being ſurrounded by other very high hills; whereas Pico ſtands without a rival.

Behind the city of Santa Cruz, the country riſes gradually, and is of a moderate height. Beyond this, to the South Weſtward, it becomes higher, and continues to riſe towards the Pic, which, from the road, appears but little higher than the ſurrounding hills. From thence it ſeems to decreaſe, though not ſuddenly, as far as the eye can reach. From a ſuppoſition that we ſhould not ſtay above one day,

I was

1776.
August.

I was obliged to contract my excursions into the country; otherwise, I had proposed to visit the top of this famous mountain *.

To the eastward of Santa Cruz, the island appears perfectly barren. Ridges of hills run towards the sea; between which ridges are deep valleys, terminating at mountains or hills that run across, and are higher than the former. Those that run towards the sea, are marked by impressions on their sides, which make them appear as a succession of conic hills, with their tops very rugged. The higher ones that run across, are more uniform in their appearance.

In the forenoon of the 1st of August, after we had anchored in the road, I went on shore to one of these valleys, with an intention to reach the top of the remoter hills, which seemed covered with wood; but time would not allow me to get farther than their foot. After walking about three miles, I found no alteration in the appearance of the lower hills; which produce great quantities of the *euphorbia Canariensis*. It is surprising that this large succulent plant, should thrive on so burnt-up a soil. When broken, which is easily done, the quantity of juice is very great; and it might be supposed that, when dried, it would shrivel to nothing; yet it is a pretty tough, though soft and light

---

* See an account of a journey to the top of the Pic of Teneriffe, in *Sprat's History of the Royal Society*, p. 200, &c. *Glas* also went to the top of it. *History of the Canary Islands*, p. 252 to 259. In the *Philosophical Transactions*, vol. xlvii. p. 353 — 356, we have *Observations made, in going up the Pic of Teneriffe, by Dr. T. Heberden*. The Doctor makes its height, above the level of the sea, to be 2566 fathoms, or 15,396 English feet; and says, that this was confirmed by two subsequent observations by himself, and another made by Mr. Crosse, the Consul. And yet, I find, that the Chevalier de Borda, who measured the height of this mountain in August 1776, makes it to be only 1911 French toises, or 12,340 English feet. See Doctor Forster's *Observations during a Voyage round the World*, p. 32.

wood.

wood. The people here believe its juice to be so cauſtic as
to erode the ſkin*; but I convinced them, though with
much difficulty, to the contrary, by thruſting my finger into
the plant full of it, without afterwards wiping it off. They
break down the buſhes of *euphorbia*, and ſuffering them to dry,
carry them home for fuel. I met with nothing elſe growing
there, but two or three ſmall ſhrubs, and a few fig-trees
near the bottom of the valley.

The baſis of the hills is a heavy, compact, blueiſh ſtone,
mixed with ſome ſhining particles; and, on the ſurface,
large maſſes of red friable earth, or ſtone, are ſcattered about.
I alſo often found the ſame ſubſtance diſpoſed in thick
ſtrata; and the little earth, ſtrewed here and there, was a
blackiſh mould. There were likewiſe ſome pieces of ſlag;
one of which, from its weight and ſmooth ſurface, ſeemed
almoſt wholly metalline.

The mouldering ſtate of theſe hills is, doubtleſs, owing
to the perpetual action of the ſun, which calcines their
ſurface. This mouldered part being afterwards waſhed
away by the heavy rains, perhaps is the cauſe of their ſides
being ſo uneven. For, as the different ſubſtances of which
they are compoſed, are more or leſs eaſily affected by the
ſun's heat, they will be carried away in the like propor-
tions. Hence, perhaps, the tops of the hills, being of the
hardeſt rock, have ſtood, while the other parts on a decli-
vity have been deſtroyed. As I have uſually obſerved, that
the tops of moſt mountains that are covered with trees
have a more uniform appearance, I am inclined to believe
that this is owing to their being ſhaded.

---

* *Glas*, p. 231, ſpeaking of this plant, ſays, that *he cannot imagine why the natives
of the Canaries do not extract the juice, and uſe it inſtead of pitch, for the bottoms of their
boats.* We now learn from Mr. Anderſon their reaſon for not uſing it.

1775.
August.

Friday 1.

The city of Santa Cruz, though not large, is tolerably well built. The churches are not magnificent without; but within are decent, and indifferently ornamented. They are inferior to some of the churches at Madeira; but, I imagine, this rather arises from the different disposition of the people, than from their inability to support them better. For the private houses, and dress of the Spanish inhabitants of Santa Cruz, are far preferable to those of the Portuguese at Madeira; who, perhaps, are willing to strip themselves, that they may adorn their churches.

Almost facing the stone pier at the landing-place, is a handsome marble column lately put up, ornamented with some human figures, that do no discredit to the artist; with an inscription in Spanish, to commemorate the occasion of the erection; and the date.

In the afternoon of the 2d, four of us hired mules to ride to the city of Laguna *, so called from an adjoining lake, about four miles from Santa Cruz. We arrived there between five and six in the evening; but found a sight of it very unable to compensate for our trouble, as the road was very bad, and the mules but indifferent. The place is, indeed, pretty extensive, but scarcely deserves to be dignified with the name of City. The disposition of its streets is very irregular; yet some of them are of a tolerable breadth, and have some good houses. In general, however, Laguna is inferior in appearance to Santa Cruz, though the latter is but small, if compared with the former. We were informed, likewise, that Laguna is declining fast; there being, at

* Its extended name is St. Christobal de la Laguna; and it used to be reckoned the capital of the island, the gentry and lawyers living there; though the Governor General of the Canary Islands resides at Santa Cruz, as being the center of their trade, both with Europe and America. See Glas's *Hist.* p. 248.

present,

present, some vineyards where houses formerly stood; whereas Santa Cruz is encreasing daily.

The road leading from Santa Cruz to Laguna runs up a steep hill, which is very barren; but, lower down, we saw some fig-trees, and several corn fields. These are but small, and not thrown into ridges, as is practised in England. Nor does it appear that they can raise any corn here without great labour, as the ground is so encumbered with stones, that they are obliged to collect and lay them in broad rows, or walls, at small distances. The large hills that run to the South-west, appeared to be pretty well furnished with trees. Nothing else worth noticing presented itself during this excursion, except a few aloe plants in flower, near the side of the road, and the cheerfulness of our guides, who amused us with songs by the way.

Most of the laborious work in this island is performed by mules; horses being to appearance scarce, and chiefly reserved for the use of the officers. They are of a small size, but well shaped and spirited. Oxen are also employed to drag their casks along upon a large clumsy piece of wood; and they are yoked by the head; though it doth not seem that this has any peculiar advantage over our method of fixing the harness on the shoulders. In my walks and excursions I saw some hawks, parrots, which are natives of the island, the sea swallow or tern, sea gulls, partridges, wagtails, swallows, martins, blackbirds, and Canary-birds in large flocks. There are also lizards of the common, and another sort; some insects, as locusts; and three or four sorts of dragon flies.

I had an opportunity of conversing with a sensible and well-informed gentleman residing here, and whose veracity I have

1776.
August.

I have not the least reason to doubt. From him I learnt some particulars, which, during the short stay of three days, did not fall within my own observation. He informed me, that a shrub is common here, agreeing exactly with the description given by Tournefort and Linnæus, of the *tea shrub*, as growing in China and Japan. It is reckoned a weed, and he roots out thousands of them every year, from his vineyards. The Spaniards, however, of the island, sometimes use it as tea, and ascribe to it all the qualities of that imported from China. They also give it the name of tea; but what is remarkable, they say it was found here when the islands were first discovered.

Another botanical curiosity, mentioned by him, is what they call the *impregnated lemon**. It is a perfect and distinct lemon, inclosed within another, differing from the outer one only in being a little more globular. The leaves of the tree that produces this sort, are much longer than those of the common one; and it was represented to me as being crooked, and not equal in beauty.

From him I learnt also, that a certain sort of grape growing here, is reckoned an excellent remedy in phthisical complaints. And the air and climate, in general, are remarkably healthful, and particularly adapted to give relief in such diseases. This he endeavoured to account for, by its being always in one's power to procure a different temperature of the air, by residing at different heights in the island; and he expressed his surprize that the English physicians should never have thought of sending their consumptive patients to Teneriffe, instead of Nice or Lisbon.

* The Writer of the *Relation of Teneriffe*, in Sprat's *History*, p. 207, takes notice of this lemon as produced here, and calls it *Pregnada*. Probably, *compreynada*, the Spanish word for *impregnated*, is the same it goes by.

How much the temperature of the air varies here, I myself could fenfibly perceive, only in riding from Santa Cruz up to Laguna; and you may afcend till the cold becomes intolerable. I was affured that no perfon can live comfortably within a mile of the perpendicular height of the Pic, after the month of Auguft *.

Although fome fmoke conftantly iffues from near the top of the Pic, they have had no earthquake or eruption of a volcano fince 1704, when the port of Garrachica, where much of their trade was formerly carried on, was deftroyed †.

Their trade, indeed, muft be confidered as very confiderable; for they reckon that forty thoufand pipes of wine are annually made; the greateft part of which is either confumed in the ifland, or made into brandy, and fent to the Spanifh Weft Indies ‡. About fix thoufand pipes were exported every year to North America, while the trade with it

---

* This agrees with Dr. T. Heberden's account, who fays that the fugar-loaf part of the mountain, or le periripfe (as it is called), which is an eighth part of a league (or 1980 feet) to the top, is covered with fnow the greateft part of the year. See Philofophical Tranfactions, as quoted above.

† This port was then filled up by the rivers of burning lava that flowed into it from a volcano; infomuch that houfes are now built where fhips formerly lay at anchor. See Glas's Hift. p. 244.

‡ Glas, p. 342, fays, that they annually export no lefs than fifteen thoufand pipes of wine and brandy. In another place, p. 252, he tells us, that the number of the inhabitants of Tenerific, when the laft account was taken, was no lefs than 96,000. We may reafonably fuppofe that there has been a confiderable increafe of population fince Glas vifited the ifland, which is above thirty years ago. The quantity of wine annually confumed, as the common beverage of at leaft one hundred thoufand perfons, muft amount to feveral thoufand pipes. There muft be a vaft expenditure of it, by converfion into brandy; to produce one pipe of which, five or fix pipes of wine muft be diftilled. An attention to thefe particulars will enable every one to judge, that the account given to Mr. Anderfon, of an annual produce of 40,000 pipes of wine, has a foundation in truth.

1776.
August.

was uninterrupted; at present, they think not above half the quantity. The corn they raise is, in general, insufficient to maintain the inhabitants; but the deficiency used to be supplied by importation from the North Americans, who took their wines in return.

They make a little silk; but unless we reckon the filtering-stones, brought in great numbers from Grand Canary, the wine is the only considerable article of the foreign commerce of Teneriffe.

None of the race of inhabitants found here when the Spaniards discovered the Canaries now remain a distinct people *, having intermarried with the Spanish settlers; but their descendants are known, from their being remarkably tall, large-boned, and strong. The men are, in general, of a tawny colour, and the women have a pale complexion, entirely destitute of that bloom which distinguishes our Northern beauties. The Spanish custom of wearing black clothes continues amongst *them*; but the men seem more indifferent about this, and, in some measure, dress like the French. In other respects, we found the inhabitants of Teneriffe to be a decent and very civil people, retaining that grave cast which distinguishes those of their country from other European nations. Although we do not think that there is a great similarity between our manners and those of the Spaniards, it is worth observing, that Omai did not think there was much difference. He only said, that they seemed not so friendly as the English; and that, in their persons, they approached those of his countrymen."

* It was otherwise in Glas's time, when a few families of the *Guanches* (as they are called) remained still in Teneriffe, not blended with the Spaniards. *Glas*, p. 240.

CHAP.

CHAP. III.

Departure from Teneriffe.—Danger of the Ship near Bonavista.—Isle of Mayo.—Port Praya.—Precautions against the Rain and sultry Weather in the Neighbourhood of the Equator.—Position of the Coast of Brazil.—Arrival at the Cape of Good Hope.—Transactions there.—Junction of the Discovery.—Mr. Anderson's Journey up the Country.—Astronomical Observations.—Nautical Remarks on the Passage from England to the Cape, with regard to the Currents and the Variation.

HAVING completed our water, and got on board every other thing we wanted at Teneriffe, we weighed anchor on the 4th of August, and proceeded on our voyage, with a fine gale at North East.

At nine o'clock in the evening on the 10th [*], we saw the island of Bonavista bearing South, distant little more than a league; though, at this time, we thought ourselves much farther off; but this proved a mistake. For, after hauling to the Eastward till twelve o'clock, to clear the sunken rocks that lie about a league from the South East point of the island, we found ourselves, at that time, close upon them,

---

[*] As a proof of Captain Cook's attention, both to the discipline and to the health of his ship's company, it may be worth while to observe here, that it appears from his log-book, he exercised them at great guns and small arms, and cleared and smoked the ship below deck, twice in the interval between the 4th and the 10th of August.

and did but juſt weather the breakers. Our ſituation, for a few minutes, was very alarming. I did not chuſe to ſound, as that might have heightened the danger, without any poſſibility of leſſening it. I make the North end of the iſland of Bonaviſta to lie in the latitude of 16° 17′ North, and in the longitude of 22° 59′ Weſt.

Sunday 11. As ſoon as we were clear of the rocks, we ſteered South South Weſt, till day-break next morning, and then hauled to the Weſtward, to go between Bonaviſta and the iſle of Mayo, intending to look into Port Praya for the Diſcovery, as I had told Captain Clerke that I ſhould touch there, and did not know how ſoon he might ſail after me. At one in the afternoon, we ſaw the rocks that lie on the South Weſt ſide of Bonaviſta, bearing South Eaſt, diſtant three or four leagues.

Monday 12. Next morning, at ſix o'clock, the iſle of Mayo bore South South Eaſt, diſtant about five leagues. In this ſituation we ſounded, and found ground at ſixty fathoms. At the ſame time the variation, by the mean of ſeveral azimuths taken with three different compaſſes, was 9° 32′ Weſt. At eleven o'clock, one extreme of Mayo bore Eaſt by North, and the other South Eaſt by South. In this poſition, two roundiſh hills appeared near its North Eaſt part; farther on, a large and higher hill; and, at about two-thirds of its length, a ſingle one that is peaked. At the diſtance we now ſaw this iſland, which was three or four miles, there was not the leaſt appearance of vegetation, nor any relief to the eye from that lifeleſs brown which prevails in countries under the Torrid Zone that are unwooded.

Here I cannot help remarking that Mr. Nichelſon, in his Preface to *Sundry Remarks and Obſervations made in a Voyage to*

the

the *East Indies* *, tells us, that " with eight degrees West variation, or any thing above that, you may venture to sail by the Cape de Verde Islands night or day, being well assured, with that variation, that you are to the Eastward of them." Such an assertion might prove of dangerous consequence, were there any that would implicitly trust to it. We also tried the current, and found one setting South West by West, something more than half a mile an hour. We had reason to expect this, from the differences between the longitude given by the watch and dead reckoning, which, since our leaving Teneriffe, amounted to one degree.

While we were amongst these islands we had light breezes of wind, varying from the South East to East, and some calms. This shews that the Cape de Verde Islands are either extensive enough to break the current of the trade wind, or that they are situated just beyond its verge, in that space where the variable winds, found on getting near the line, begin. The first supposition, however, is the most probable, as Dampier † found the wind westerly here in the month of February; at which time the trade wind is supposed to extend farthest towards the equinoctial. The weather was hot and sultry, with some rain; and, for the most part, a dull whiteness prevailed in the sky, that seems a medium between fog and clouds. In general, the tropical regions seldom enjoy that clear atmosphere observable where variable winds blow; nor does the sun shine with such brightness. This circumstance, however, seems an advantage; for otherwise, perhaps, the rays of the sun, being uninterrupted, would render the heat quite unsup-

* On board his Majesty's ship Elizabeth, from 1758 to 1764; by William Nicholson, Master of the said Ship. London, 1773.
† Dampier's Voyages, Vol. iii. p. 10.

portable.

1776.
August.

Tuesday 13.

Wednes. 14
Friday 30.

portable. The nights are, nevertheless, often clear and serene.

At nine o'clock in the morning of the 13th, we arrived before Port Praya, in the island of St. Jago, where we saw two Dutch East India ships, and a small brigantine at anchor. As the Discovery was not there, and we had expended but little water in our passage from Teneriffe, I did not think proper to go in, but stood to the Southward. Some altitudes of the Sun were now taken, to ascertain the true time. The longitude by the watch, deduced therefrom, was 23° 48' West; the little island in the bay bore West North West, distant near three miles, which will make its longitude 23° 51'. The same watch, on my late voyage, made the longitude to be 23° 30' West; and we observed the latitude to be 14° 53' 30" North.

The day after we left the Cape de Verde Islands, we lost the North East trade wind; but did not get that which blows from the South East till the 30th, when we were in the latitude of 2° North, and in the twenty-fifth degree of West longitude.

During this interval [*], the wind was mostly in the South West quarter. Sometimes it blew fresh, and in squalls; but for the most part a gentle breeze. The calms were few, and of short duration. Between the latitude of 12° and of 7° North, the weather was generally dark and gloomy,

[*] On the 18th, I sunk a bucket with a thermometer seventy fathoms below the surface of the sea, where it remained two minutes; and it took three minutes more to haul it up. The mercury in the thermometer was at 66, which before, in the air, stood at 78, and in the surface of the sea at 79. The water which came up in the bucket contained, by Mr. Cavendish's table, $\frac{1}{31}$ part salt; and that at the surface of the sea $\frac{1}{31}$ 4. As this last was taken up after a smart shower of rain, it might be lighter on that account. *Captain Cook's log-book.*

with frequent rains, which enabled us to save as much water as filled most of our empty casks.

These rains, and the close sultry weather accompanying them, too often bring on sickness in this passage. Every bad consequence, at least, is to be apprehended from them; and commanders of ships cannot be too much upon their guard, by purifying the air between decks with fires and smoke, and by obliging the people to dry their clothes at every opportunity. These precautions were constantly observed on board the Resolution* and Discovery; and we certainly profited by them, for we had now fewer sick than on either of my former voyages. We had, however, the mortification to find our ship exceedingly leaky in all her upper works. The hot and sultry weather we had just passed through, had opened her seams, which had been badly caulked at first, so wide, that they admitted the rain water through as it fell. There was hardly a man that could lie dry in his bed; and the officers in the gun-room were all driven out of their cabbins, by the water that came through the sides. The sails in the sail-room got wet; and before we had weather to dry them, many of them were much damaged, and a great expence of canvas and of time became necessary to make them in some degree serviceable. Having experienced the same defect in our sail-rooms on my late voyage, it had been represented to the yard officers, who undertook to remove it. But it did not appear to me that any thing had been done to remedy the complaint.

* The particulars are mentioned in his log-book. On the 14th of August, a fire was made in the well, to air the ship below. On the 15th, the spare sails were aired upon deck, and a fire made to air the sail-room. On the 17th, cleaned and smoked between decks, and the bread-room aired with fires. On the 21st, cleaned and smoked between decks; and on the 22d, the men's bedding was spread on deck to air.

34   A VOYAGE TO

1776.   To repair thefe defects the caulkers were fet to work, as
Auguſt. ſoon as we got into fair ſettled weather, to caulk the decks
         and inſide weather-works of the ſhip; for I would not truſt
         them over the ſides while we were at ſea.

September.   On the firſt of September * we croſſed the Equator, in the
Sunday 1.   longitude of 27° 38′ Weſt, with a fine gale at South Eaſt by
             South; and notwithſtanding my apprehenſions of falling in
             with the coaſt of Brazil in ſtretching to the South Weſt, I
             kept the ſhip a full point from the wind. However, I
             found my fears were ill-grounded; for on drawing near
             that coaſt, we met with the wind more and more eaſterly;
             ſo that, by the time we were in the latitude of 10° South,
             we could make a South Eaſterly courſe good.

Sunday 8.   On the 8th, we were in the latitude of 8° 57′ South; which
             is a little to the Southward of Cape St. Auguſtine, on the
             coaſt of Braſil. Our longitude, deduced from a very great
             number of lunar obſervations, was 34° 16′ Weſt; and by the

---

* The afternoon, as appears from Mr. Anderſon's Journal, was ſpent in performing the old and ridiculous ceremony of ducking thoſe who had not croſſed the Equator before. Though Captain Cook did not ſupport the cuſtom, he thought it too trifling to deſerve the leaſt mention of it in his Journal, or even in his log-book. Pernetty, the Writer of Bougainville's Voyage to the Falkland Iſlands, in 1763 and 1764, thought differently; for his account of the celebration of this childiſh feſtival on board his ſhip, is extended through ſeventeen pages, and makes the ſubject of an entire chapter, under the title of *Baptême de la Ligne*.

It may be worth while to tranſcribe his introduction to the deſcription of it. "C'eſt un uſage qui ne remonte pas plus haut que ce voyage célèbre de Gama, qui a fourni au Camoens le ſujet de la Luſiade. L'Idée qu'on ne ſçauroit être un bon marin, ſans avoir traverſé l'Equateur, l'ennui inſeparable d'une longue navigation, un certain eſprit republicain qui regne dans toutes les petites ſocietés, peut-être toutes ces cauſes reunies, ont pu donner naiſſance à ces eſpeces de ſaturnales. Quoiqu'il en ſoit, elles furent adopréés, en un inſtant, dans toutes les nations, & les hommes les plus eclairés furent obligés de ſe ſoumettre à une coutume dont ils recomnoiſſoient l'abſurdité. Car, partout, dès que le peuple parle, il faut que le ſage ſe mette à l'uniſon." *Hiſtoire d'un Voyage aux Iſles Malouines*, p. 107, 108.

watch,

watch, 34° 47'. The former is 1° 43', and the latter 2° 14' more Wefterly than the ifland of Fernando de Noronha, the fituation of which was pretty well determined during my late voyage *. Hence I concluded that we could not now be farther from the continent than twenty or thirty leagues at moft; and perhaps not much lefs, as we neither had foundings, nor any other figns of land. Dr. Halley, however, in his voyage, publifhed by Mr. Dalrymple, tells us †, that *he made no more than one hundred and two miles, meridian diftance, from the ifland* [Fernando de Noronha] *to the coaft of Brafil*; and feems to think that *currents could not be the whole caufe* of his making fo little. But I rather think that he was miftaken, and that the currents had hurried him far to the Weftward of his intended courfe. This was, in fome meafure, confirmed by our own obfervations; for we had found, during three or four days preceding the 8th, that the currents fet to the Weftward; and, during the laft twenty-four hours, it had fet ftrong to the Northward, as we experienced a difference of twenty-nine miles between our obferved latitude and that by dead reckoning. Upon the whole, till fome better aftronomical obfervations are made on fhore on the Eaftern coaft of Brafil, I fhall conclude that its longitude is thirty-five degrees and a half, or thirty-fix degrees Weft, at moft.

We proceeded on our voyage, without meeting with any thing of note, till the 6th of October. Being then in the latitude of 35° 15' South, longitude 7° 45' Weft, we met with light airs and calms by turns, for three days fucceffively. We had, for fome days before, feen albatroffes, pintadoes, and other petrels; and here we faw three penguins, which

---

* See Cook's Voyage, Vol. II. p. 278. † P. 11.

occafioned

1776.
October.

occasioned us to sound; but we found no ground with a line of one hundred and fifty fathoms. We put a boat in the water, and shot a few birds; one of which was a black petrel, about the size of a crow, and, except as to the bill and feet, very like one. It had a few white feathers under the throat; and the under-side of the quill-feathers were of an ash-colour. All the other feathers were jet black, as also the bill and legs.

Tuesday 8.

On the 8th, in the evening, one of those birds which sailors call noddies, settled on our rigging, and was caught. It was something larger than an English black-bird, and nearly as black, except the upper part of the head, which was white, looking as if it were powdered; the whitest feathers growing out from the base of the upper bill, from which they gradually assumed a darker colour, to about the middle of the upper part of the neck, where the white shade was lost in the black, without being divided by any line. It was web-footed; had black legs and a black bill, which was long, and not unlike that of a curlew. It is said these birds never fly far from land. We knew of none nearer the station we were in, than Gough's or Richmond Island, from which our distance could not be less than one hundred leagues. But it must be observed that the Atlantic Ocean, to the Southward of this latitude, has been but little frequented; so that there may be more islands there than we are acquainted with.

We frequently, in the night, saw those luminous marine animals mentioned and described in my first voyage [*]. Some of them seemed to be considerably larger than any I

[*] See Hawkesworth's Collection of Voyages, Vol. II. p. 15.

had

had before met with; and sometimes they were so numerous, that hundreds were visible at the same moment.

This calm weather was succeeded by a fresh gale from the North West, which lasted two days. Then we had again variable light airs for about twenty-four hours; when the North West wind returned, and blew with such strength, that on the 17th we had sight of the Cape of Good Hope; and the next day anchored in Table Bay, in four fathoms water, with the church bearing South West ½ South, and Green Point North West ¼ West.

As soon as we had received the usual visit from the Master Attendant and the Surgeon, I sent an officer to wait on Baron Plettenberg, the Governor; and, on his return, saluted the garrison with thirteen guns, which compliment was returned with the same number.

We found in the bay two French East India Ships; the one outward, and the other homeward bound. And two or three days before our arrival, another homeward bound ship of the same nation had parted from her cable, and been driven on shore at the head of the bay, where she was lost. The crew were saved; but the greatest part of the cargo shared the same fate with the ship, or (which amounted to the same) was plundered and stolen by the inhabitants, either out of the ship, or as it was driven or carried on shore. This is the account the French officers gave to me; and the Dutch themselves could not deny the fact. But, by way of excusing themselves from being guilty of a crime disgraceful to every civilized state, they endeavoured to lay the whole blame on the French Captain, for not applying in time for a guard.

1776.
October.

As soon as we had saluted, I went on shore, accompanied by some of my officers, and waited on the Governor, the Lieutenant Governor, the Fiscal, and the Commander of the troops. These gentlemen received me with the greatest civility; and the Governor, in particular, promised me every assistance that the place afforded. At the same time I obtained his leave to set up our observatory on any spot I should think most convenient; to pitch tents for the sailmakers and coopers; and to bring the cattle on shore, to graze near our encampment. Before I returned on board, I ordered soft bread, fresh meat, and greens, to be provided, every day, for the ship's company.

Tuesday 22.

On the 22d, we set up the tents and observatory, and began to send the several articles out of the ship which I wanted on shore. This could not be done sooner, as the militia of the place were exercising on, or near, the ground which we were to occupy.

Wednes. 23.

The next day, we began to observe equal altitudes of the Sun, in order to ascertain the rate of the watch, or, which is the same thing, to find whether it had altered its rate. These observations were continued every day, whenever the weather would permit, till the time of our departure drew near. But before this, the caulkers had been set to work to caulk the ship; and I had concerted measures with Messrs. Brandt and Chiron, for supplying both ships with such provisions as I should want. Bakers, likewise, had been ordered, immediately after our arrival, to bake such a quantity of bread as I thought would be requisite. As fast as the several articles destined for the Resolution were got ready, they were carried on board.

THE PACIFIC OCEAN.   39

On the 26th, the French ship sailed for Europe, and by her, we sent letters to England. The next day, the Hampshire East India ship, from Bencoolen, anchored in the bay, and saluted us with thirteen guns, which we returned with eleven.

1776.
October.
Saturday 26.
Sunday 27.

Nothing remarkable happened till the evening of the 31st, when it came on to blow excessively hard at South East, and continued for three days; during which time there was no communication between the ship and the shore. The Resolution was the only ship in the bay that rode out the gale without dragging her anchors. We felt its effects as sensibly on shore. Our tents and observatory were torn to pieces; and our astronomical quadrant narrowly escaped irreparable damage. On the 3d of November the storm ceased, and the next day we resumed our different employments.

Thursday 31.

November.
Sunday 3.

On the 6th, the Hampshire India ship sailed for England. In her I sent home an invalid, whom Captain Trimble was so obliging as to receive on board. I was afterwards sorry that I had not availed myself of this opportunity to part with two or three more of my crew, who were troubled with different complaints; but, at this time, there was some hope of their health being re-established.

Wednesday 6.

In the morning of the 10th, the Discovery arrived in the bay. Captain Clerke informed me that he had sailed from Plymouth on the 1st of August, and should have been with us here a week sooner, if the late gale of wind had not blown him off the coast. Upon the whole, he was seven days longer in his passage from England than we had been. He had the misfortune to lose one of his marines, by falling over-board; but there had been no other mortality amongst his people, and they now arrived well and healthy.

Sunday 10.

Captain

1776.
November.
Monday 11.

Captain Clerke having represented to me that his ship was in want of caulking; that no time might be lost in repairing this defect, next day I sent all my workmen on board her, having already completed this service on board the Resolution. I lent every other assistance to the Captain to expedite his supply of provisions and water, having given him an order to receive on board as much of both articles as he could conveniently stow. I now found that the bakers had failed in baking the bread I had ordered for the Discovery. They pretended a want of flour; but the truth was, they were doubtful of her coming, and did not care to begin, till they saw her at anchor in the bay.

Thursday 14.

I have before made mention of our getting our cattle on shore. The bull and two cows, with their calves, were sent to graze along with some other cattle; but I was advised to keep our sheep, sixteen in number, close to our tents, where they were penned up every night. During the night preceding the 14th, some dogs having got in amongst them, forced them out of the pen, killing four, and dispersing the rest. Six of them were recovered the next day; but the two rams, and two of the finest ewes in the whole flock, were amongst those missing. Baron Plettenberg being now in the country, I applied to the Lieutenant Governor, Mr. Hemmy, and to the Fiscal. Both these Gentlemen promised to use their endeavours for the recovery of the lost sheep. The Dutch, we know, boast that the police at the Cape is so carefully executed, that it is hardly possible for a slave, with all his cunning and knowledge of the country, to effectuate his escape. Yet my sheep evaded all the vigilance of the Fiscal's officers and people. However, after much trouble and expence, by employing some of the meanest and lowest scoundrels in the place (who, to use the phrase of the person who recommended

recommended this method to me, would, for a ducatoon, cut their master's throat, burn the house over his head, and bury him and the whole family in the ashes. I recovered them all but the two ewes. Of these I never could hear the least tidings; and I gave over all enquiry after them, when I was told, that since I had got the two rams, I might think myself very well off. One of these, however, was so much hurt by the dogs, that there was reason to believe he would never recover.

Mr. Hemmy very obligingly offered to make up this loss, by giving me a Spanish ram, out of some that he had sent for from Lisbon. But I declined the offer, under a persuasion that it would answer my purpose full as well, to take with me some of the Cape rams: the event proved, that I was under a mistake. This Gentleman has taken some pains to introduce European sheep at the Cape; but his endeavours, as he told me, have been frustrated by the obstinacy of the country people, who hold their own breed in greater estimation, on account of their large tails, of the fat of which they sometimes make more money than of the whole carcass besides *; and think that the wool of European sheep will, by no means, make up for their deficiency in this respect. Indeed, I have heard some sensible men here make the same observation. And there seems to be foundation for it. For, admitting that European sheep were

---

* " The most remarkable thing in the Cape sheep, is the length and thickness of their tails, which weigh from fifteen to twenty pounds. The fat is not so tallowish as that of European mutton, and the poorer sort use it for butter." *Kolben's Cape of Good Hope* [English translation], Vol. II. p. 65. De la Caille, who finds every thing wrong in Kolben, says, the weight of the tail of the Cape sheep is not above five or six pounds. *Voyage de la Caille*, p. 343. If the information given to Captain Cook may be depended upon, it will prove that, in this instance at least, Kolben is unjustly accused of exaggeration.

1775.
November.

to produce wool of the same quality here as in Europe, which experience has shewn not to be the case, the Dutch have not hands, at the Cape of Good Hope, to spare for the manufacturing even their own clothing. It is certain that, were it not for the continual importation of slaves, this settlement would be thinner of people than any other inhabited part of the world.

While the ships were getting ready for the prosecution of our voyage, some of our officers made an excursion to take a view of the neighbouring country. Mr. Anderson, my Surgeon, who was one of the party, gave me the following relation of their proceedings *:

Saturday 16.

"On the 16th, in the forenoon, I set out in a waggon, with five more, to take a view of some part of the country. We crossed the large plain that lies to the Eastward of the town, which is entirely a white sand, like that commonly found on beaches, and produces only heath, and other small plants of various sorts. At five in the afternoon we passed a large farm-house, with some corn-fields, and pretty considerable vineyards, situated beyond the plain, near the foot of some low hills, where the soil becomes worth cultivating. Between six and seven we arrived at Stellenbosh, the colony next to that of the Cape for its importance.

The village does not consist of more than thirty houses, and stands at the foot of the range of lofty mountains,

* In the Philosophical Transactions, Vol. lxvi. p. 268 to 319, is an Account of Three Journies from the Cape Town into the Southern Parts of Africa, in 1772, 1773, and 1774, by Mr. Francis Masson, who had been sent from England for the discovery of new plants, towards the improvement of the Royal Botanical Garden at Kew. Much curious information is contained in Mr. Masson's account of these journies. M. de Pages, who was at the Cape in 1773, gives some remarks on the state of that settlement, and also the particulars of his journey from False Bay to the Cape Town. *Voyage vers le Pole du Sud*, p. 17 to 32.

above

above twenty miles to the Eastward of the Cape Town. The houses are neat; and, with the advantage of a rivulet which runs near, and the shelter of some large oaks, planted at its first settling, forms what may be called a rural prospect in this desert country. There are some vineyards and orchards about the place, which, from their thriving appearance, seem to indicate an excellent soil; though, perhaps, they owe much to climate, as the air here has an uncommon serenity.

I employed the next day in searching for plants and insects about Stellenbosh, but had little success. Few plants are in flower here at this season, and insects but scarce. I examined the soil in several places, and found it to consist of yellowish clay, mixed with a good deal of sand. The sides of the low hills, which appear brown, seem to be constituted of a sort of stone marle.

We left Stellenbosh next morning, and soon arrived at the house we had passed on Saturday; the owner of which, Mr. Cloeder, had sent us an invitation, the evening before, to visit him. This Gentleman entertained us with the greatest hospitality, and in a manner very different from what we expected. He received us with music; and a band also played while we were at dinner; which, considering the situation of the place, might be reckoned elegant. He shewed us his wine-cellars, his orchards, and vineyards; all which, I must own, inspired me with a wish to know in what manner these industrious people could create such plenty, in a spot where, I believe, no other European nation would have attempted to settle.

In the afternoon we crossed the country, and passed a few plantations, one of which seemed very considerable, and was

A VOYAGE TO

1776.
November.

laid out in a taste somewhat different from any other we saw. In the evening we arrived at a farm-house, which is the first in the cultivated tract called the *Pearl*. We had, at the same time, a view of Drakenstein, the third colony of this country, which lies along by the foot of the lofty hills already mentioned, and contains several farms or plantations, not very extensive.

Tuesday 19.

I went, on the 19th in the forenoon, in quest of plants and insects, which I found almost as scarce as at Stellenbosh; but I met with more shrubs or small trees, naturally produced, in the valleys, than in any part of the country I had hitherto seen.

In the afternoon, we went to see a stone of a remarkable size, called by the inhabitants the Tower of Babylon, or the Pearl Diamond *. It lies, or stands, upon the top of some low hills, at the foot of which our farm-house was situated; and though the road to it is neither very steep nor rugged, we were above an hour and a half in walking to it. It is of an oblong shape, rounded on the top, and lies nearly South and North. The East and West sides are steep, and al-

* In the Philosophical Transactions, Vol. lxviii. Part I. p. 102. we have a Letter from Mr. Anderson to Sir John Pringle, describing this remarkable stone. The account sent home from the Cape, and read before the Royal Society, is much the same with that now published, but rather fuller. In particular, he tells Sir John, that he went to see it at Mr. *Maffin's defire*, who, probably, had not had an opportunity of sufficiently examining it himself. In the account of his journey, above referred to, p. 270, he only says, " there are two large solid rocks on the *Perel Berg*, each of which (he believes) is more than a mile in circumference at the base, and upwards of two hundred feet high. Their surfaces are nearly smooth, without chink or fissures; and they are found to be a species of granite, different from that which composes the neighbouring mountains."

Mr. Anderson having, with his Letter to Sir John Pringle, also sent home a specimen of the rock, it was examined by Sir William Hamilton, whose opinion is, that " this singular, immense fragment of granite, must probably has been raised by a vulcani, explosion, or some such cause." See his Letter to Sir John Pringle, annexed to Mr. Anderson's, in the Philosophical Transactions.

most

moſt perpendicular. The South end is likewiſe ſteep, and its greateſt height is there; from whence it declines gently to the North part, by which we aſcended to its top, and had an extenſive view of the whole country.

Its circumference, I think, muſt be at leaſt half a mile; as it took us above half an hour to walk round it, including every allowance for the bad road, and ſtopping a little. At its higheſt part, which is the South end, comparing it with a known object, it ſeems to equal the dome of St. Paul's church. It is one uninterrupted maſs of ſtone, if we except ſome fiſſures, or rather impreſſions, not above three or four feet deep, and a vein which runs acroſs near its North end. It is of that ſort of ſtone called, by Mineralogiſts, *Saxum conglutinatum*, and conſiſts chiefly of pieces of coarſe *quartz* and *glimmer*, held together by a clayey cement. But the vein which croſſes it, though of the ſame materials, is much compacter. This vein is not above a foot broad or thick; and its ſurface is cut into little ſquares or oblongs, diſpoſed obliquely, which makes it look like the remains of ſome artificial work. But I could not obſerve whether it penetrated far into the large rock, or was only ſuperficial. In deſcending, we found at its foot a very rich black mould; and on the ſides of the hills, ſome trees of a conſiderable ſize, natives of the place, which are a ſpecies of *olea* [*].

In

---

[*] It is ſtrange that neither Kolben nor de la Caille ſhould have thought the *Tower of Bobjſm* worthy of a particular deſcription. The former (Vol. II. p. 52, 53. Engliſh Tranſlation) only mentions it as a *high mountain*. The latter contents himſelf with telling us, that it is a very low hillock, *un très bas monticule*. *Voyage de la Caille*, p. 341. We are much obliged to Mr. Anderſon for his very accurate account of this remarkable rock, which agrees with Mr. Sonnerat's, who was at the Cape of Good Hope ſo late as 1781. His words are, "La Montagne de la *Perle*, merite d'être obſervée. C'eſt un des plus hautes des environs du Cap. Elle n'eſt compoſée que
"d'un

1776.
November.
Wednes. 20.

In the morning on the 20th, we set out from the *Pearl*; and going a different road from that by which we came, passed through a country wholly uncultivated, till we got to the *Tyger* hills, when some tolerable corn-fields appeared. At noon, we stopped in a hollow for refreshment; but, in walking about here, were plagued with a vast number of musquitoes or sand flies, which were the first I saw in the country. In the afternoon we set out again, and in the evening arrived at the Cape Town, tired with the jolting waggon."

Saturday 23.

On the 23d, we got on board the observatory, clock, &c. By a mean of the several results of the equal altitudes of the Sun, taken with the astronomical quadrant, the astronomical clock was found to lose on sidereal time, 1' 8",368 each day. The pendulum was kept at the same length as at Greenwich, where the daily loss of the clock on sidereal time, was 4".

The watch, by the mean of the results of fifteen days observations, was found to be losing 2",261, on mean time, each day; which is 1",652 more than at Greenwich: and on the 21st, at noon, she was too slow for mean time by 1ʰ. 20' 57",66. From this, 6' 48",956, is to be substracted, for what she was too slow on the 11th of June at Greenwich, and her daily rate since; and the remainder, viz. 1ʰ. 14'. 08",704, or 18° 32' 10", will be the longitude of the Cape Town by the watch. Its true longitude, as found by Messrs. Mason and Dixon, is

---

" d'un seul bloc de granit crevassé dans plusieurs endroits." *Voyage aux Indes*, Tom. II. p. 91.

Mr. Sonnerat tells us, that Mr. Gordon, Commander of the troops at the Cape, had lately made three journies up the country, from which, when he publishes his Journal, we may expect much curious information.

18°

18° 23' 15". As our observations were made about half a mile to the East of theirs, the error of the watch, in longitude, is no more than 8' 25". Hence we have reason to conclude, that she had gone well all the way from England, and that the longitude, thus given, may be nearer the truth than any other.

If this be admitted, it will, in a great measure, enable me to find the direction and strength of the currents we met with on this passage from England. For, by comparing the latitude and longitude by dead reckoning, with those by observation and the watch, we shall, from time to time, have, very accurately, the error of the ship's reckoning, be the cause what it will. But as all imaginable care was taken in heaving and keeping the log, and every necessary allowance made for lee-way, heave of the sea, and other such circumstances, I cannot attribute those errors that did happen, to any other cause but currents; but more particularly when the error was constantly the same way, for several days successively.

On the contrary, if we find the ship a-head of the reckoning on one day, and a-stern of it on another, we have reason to believe that such errors are owing to accidental causes, and not to currents. This seems to have been the case in our passage between England and Teneriffe. But, from the time of our leaving that island, till the 15th of August, being then in the latitude of 12° North, and longitude 24° West, the ship was carried 1° 20' of longitude to the Westward of her reckoning. At this station, the currents took a contrary direction, and set to East South East, at the rate of twelve or fourteen miles a day, or twenty-four hours, till we arrived into the latitude of 5° North, and longitude of 20° West; which was our most Easterly situation

1776.
November.

tion after leaving the Cape de Verde Islands, till we got to the Southward. For in this situation the wind came Southerly, and we tacked and stretched to the Westward; and, for two or three days, could not find that our reckoning was affected by any current. So that, I judged, we were between the current that generally, if not constantly, sets to the East upon the coast of Guinea, and that which sets to the West towards the coast of Brasil.

This Westerly current was not considerable till we got into 2° North, and 25° West. From this station, to 3° South and 30° West, the ship, in the space of four days, was carried one hundred and fifteen miles in the direction of South West by West, beyond her reckoning; an error by far too great to have any other cause but a strong current running in the same direction. Nor did its strength abate here; but its course was, afterward, more Westerly, and to the North of West; and off Cape Auguilline, North, as I have already mentioned. But this Northerly current did not exist at twenty or thirty leagues to the Southward of that Cape; nor any other, that I could perceive, in the remaining part of the passage. The little difference we afterward found between the reckoning and observations, might very well happen without the assistance of currents; as will appear by the Table of Days Works.

In the account of my last voyage [*], I remarked, that the currents one meets with in this passage generally balance each other. It happened so then; because we crossed the line about 20° more to the Eastward than we did now; so that we were, of consequence, longer under the influence of the Easterly current, which made up for the Westerly one,

[*] Captain Cook's Voyage, Vol. I. p. 14.

And

And this, I apprehend, will generally be the case, if you cross the line 10° or 15° to the East of the meridian of St. Jago.

From these remarks I shall draw the following conclusion, That, after passing the Cape de Verde Island, if you do not make above 4° or 5° Easting, and cross the line in, or to the Westward of, the meridian of St. Jago, you may expect to find your ship 3° or 4° to the Westward of her reckoning, by the time you get into the latitude of 10° South. If, on the other hand, you keep well to the East, and cross the line 15° or 20° to the East of St. Jago, you will be then as much to the East of your reckoning; and the more you keep to the Eastward, the greater will be your error; as has been experienced by some India ships, whose people have found themselves close upon the coast of Angola, when they thought its distance was above two hundred leagues.

During the whole of our passage from England, no opportunity was omitted of observing, with all the attention and accuracy that circumstances would permit, the variation of the compass, which I have inserted in a Table, with the latitude and longitude of the ship at the time of observation. As the longitude may be depended upon, to a quarter or half a degree at most, this Table will be of use to those navigators who correct their reckoning by the variation. It will also enable Mr. Dun to correct his new Variation Chart, a thing very much wanted.

It seems strange to me, that the advocates for the variation should not agree amongst themselves. We find one * of them telling us, as I have already observed, *that with 8° West variation, or any thing above that, you may venture to sail by the*

* Nicholson.

1776.
November.

Cape de Verde Iflands, by night or day, being well affured, with that variation, that you are to the Eaftward of them. Another, in his Chart *, lays down this variation ninety leagues to the Weftward of them. Such a difagreement as this, is a ftrong proof of the uncertainty of both. However, I have no doubt, the former found here, as well as in other places, the variation he mentions. But he fhould have confidered, that at fea, nay even on land, the refults of the moft accurate obfervations will not always be the fame. Different compaffes will give different variations; and even the fame compafs will differ from itfelf two degrees, without our being able to difcover, much lefs to remove, the caufe.

Whoever imagines he can find the variation within a degree, will very often fee himfelf much deceived. For, befides the imperfection which may be in the conftruction of the inftrument, or in the power of the needle, it is certain that the motion of the fhip, or attraction of the iron-work, or fome other caufe not yet difcovered, will frequently occafion far greater errors than this. That the variation may be found, with a fhare of accuracy more than fufficient to determine the fhip's courfe, is allowed; but that it can be found fo exactly as to fix the longitude within a degree, or fixty miles, I abfolutely deny.

* Mr. Dun.

CHAP.

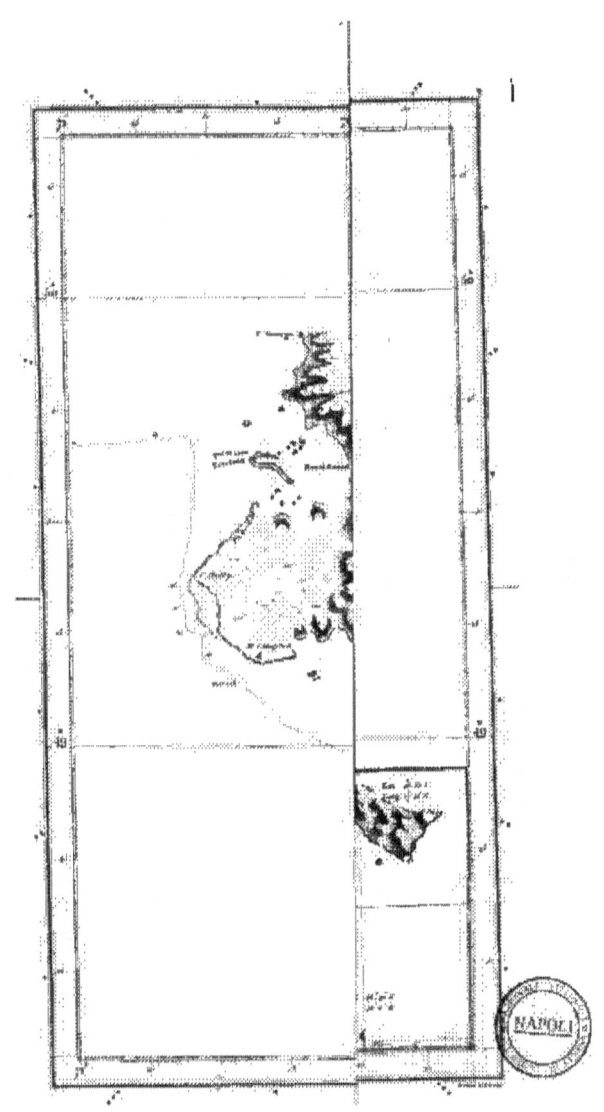

CHAP. IV.

The two Ships leave the Cape of Good Hope.—Two Islands, named Prince Edward's, seen, and their Appearance described.—Kerguelen's Land visited.—Arrival in Christmas Harbour.—Occurrences there.—Description of it.

AFTER the disaster which happened to our sheep, it may be well supposed I did not trust those that remained, long on shore; but got them, and the other cattle, on board as fast as possible. I also added to my original stock, by purchasing two young bulls, two heifers, two young stone-horses, two mares, two rams, several ewes and goats, and some rabbits and poultry. All of them were intended for New Zealand, Otaheite, and the neighbouring islands, or any other places, in the course of our voyage, where there might be a prospect that the leaving any of them would be useful to posterity.

Towards the latter end of November, the caulkers had finished their work on board the Discovery, and she had received all her provisions and water. Of the former, both ships had a supply sufficient for two years and upwards. And every other article we could think of, necessary for such a voyage, that could be had at the Cape, was procured; neither knowing when, nor where, we might come to a place where we could furnish ourselves so well.

1776.
November.

Having

1776.
November.
Saturday 30.

Having given Captain Clerke a copy of my instructions, and an order directing him how to proceed in case of separation; in the morning of the 30th, we repaired on board. At five in the afternoon a breeze sprung up at South East, with which we weighed, and stood out of the bay. At nine it fell calm, and we anchored between Penguin Island and the East shore, where we lay till three o'clock next morning. We then weighed and put to sea, with a light breeze at South; but did not get clear of the land till the morning of the 3d, when, with a fresh gale at West North West, we stood to the South East, to get more into the way of these winds.

December,
Sunday 1.

Tuesday 3.

Thursday 5.

On the 5th, a sudden squall of wind carried away the Resolution's mizen top-mast. Having another to replace it, the loss was not felt; especially as it was a bad stick, and had often complained. On the 6th, in the evening, being then in the latitude of 39° 14' South, and in the longitude of 23° 56' East, we passed through several small spots of water of a reddish colour. Some of this was taken up; and it was found to abound with a small animal, which the microscope discovered to be like a cray-fish, of a reddish hue.

Friday 6.

We continued our course to the South East, with a very strong gale from the Westward, followed by a mountainous sea; which made the ship roll and tumble exceedingly, and gave us a great deal of trouble to preserve the cattle we had on board. Notwithstanding all our care, several goats, especially the males, died; and some sheep. This misfortune was, in a great measure, owing to the cold, which we now began most sensibly to feel.

Thursday 12.

On the 12th, at noon, we saw land extending from South East by South, to South East by East. Upon a nearer approach,

proach, we found it to be two iflands. That which lies moft to the South, and is alfo the largeft, I judged to be about fifteen leagues in circuit; and to be in the latitude of 46° 53′ South, and in the longitude of 37° 46′ Eaft. The moft Northerly one is about nine leagues in circuit; and lies in the latitude of 46° 40′ South, and in 38° 8′ Eaft longitude. The diftance from the one to the other is about five leagues.

We paffed through this channel, at equal diftance from both iflands; and could not difcover, with the affiftance of our beft glaffes, either tree or fhrub on either of them. They feemed to have a rocky and bold fhore; and, excepting the South Eaft parts, where the land is rather low and flat, a furface compofed of barren mountains, which rife to a confiderable height, and whofe fummits and fides were covered with fnow, which in many places feemed to be of a confiderable depth. The South Eaft parts had a much greater quantity on them than the reft; owing, probably, to the Sun acting for a lefs fpace of time on thefe than on the North and North Weft parts. The ground, where it was not hid by the fnow, from the various fhades it exhibited, may be fuppofed to be covered with mofs, or, perhaps, fuch a coarfe grafs as is found in fome parts of Falkland's Iflands. On the North fide of each of the iflands is a detached rock: that near the South ifland is fhaped like a tower, and feemed to be at fome diftance from the fhore. As we paffed along, a quantity of fea-weed was feen, and the colour of the water indicated foundings. But there was no appearance of an inlet, unlefs near the rock juft mentioned; and that, from its fmallnefs, did not promife a good anchoring-place.

Thefe

54   A VOYAGE TO

1776.
December.

These two islands, as also four others which lie from nine to twelve degrees of longitude more to the East, and nearly in the same latitude, were discovered, as I have mentioned in my late Voyage [*], by Captains Marion du Fresne, and Crozet, French Navigators, in January 1772, on their passage in two ships from the Cape of Good Hope to the Philippine Islands. As they have no names in the French chart of the Southern hemisphere, which Captain Crozet communicated to me in 1775 [†], I shall distinguish the two we now saw, by calling them Prince Edward's Islands, after his Majesty's fourth son; and the other four, by the name of Marion's and Crozet's Islands, to commemorate their discoverers.

We had now, for the most part, strong gales between the North and West, and but very indifferent weather; not better, indeed, than we generally have in England in the very depth of Winter, though it was now the middle of Summer in this hemisphere. Not discouraged, however, by this, after leaving Prince Edward's Islands, I shaped our course to pass to the Southward of the others, that I might get into the latitude of the land discovered by Monsieur de Kerguelen.

I had applied to the Chevalier de Borda, whom, as I have mentioned, I found at Teneriffe, requesting, that if he knew any thing of the island discovered by Monsieur de Kerguelen, between the Cape of Good Hope and New Holland, he

---

[*] *Captain Crd's Voyage*, Vol. ii. p. 266. These islands are there said to be in the latitude of 48° South; that is, two degrees farther South, than what here appears to be their real position.

[†] See Cook's Voyage, as above. Dr. Forster, in his *observations made during that voyage*, p. 30, gives us this description of the Chart then communicated by Monsieur Crozet: that it was *published under the patronage of the Duke de Croy, by Robert de Vaugondy*. Captain Cook tells us lower in this Chapter, that it was published in 1773.

would

THE PACIFIC OCEAN.

1776. December.

would be so obliging as to communicate it to me. Accordingly, just before we sailed from Santa Cruz bay, he sent me the following account of it, viz. "That the Pilot of the "Boussole, who was in the voyage with Monsieur de Ker- "guelen, had given him the latitude and longitude of a "little island, which Monsieur de Kerguelen called the "Isle of Rendezvous, and which lies not far from the "great island which he saw. Latitude of the little isle, by "seven observations, 48° 26′ South; longitude, by seven ob- "servations of the distance of the Sun and Moon, 64° 57′ "East from Paris." I was very sorry I had not sooner known that there was on board the frigate at Teneriffe, an officer who had been with Monsieur de Kerguelen, especially the Pilot; because from him I might have obtained more interesting information about this land than the situation alone, of which I was not before entirely ignorant *.

My

---

* Captain Cook's proceedings, as related in the remaining part of this Chapter, and in the next, being upon a coast newly discovered by the French, it could not but be an object of his attention to trace the footsteps of the original explorers. But no superiority of professional skill, nor diligence in exerting it, could possibly qualify him to do this successfully, without possessing, at the same time, full and authentic intelligence of all that had been performed here by his predecessors in the discovery. But that he was not so fortunate as to be thus sufficiently instructed, will appear from the following facts, which the Reader is requested to attend to, before he proceeds to the perusal of this part of the Journal.

How very little was known, with any precision, about the operations of Kerguelen, when Captain Cook sailed in 1776, may be inferred from the following paragraph of his Instructions: "You are to proceed in search of some islands *said to have been lately* "*seen* by the French in the latitude of 48° South, and in the meridian of Mauri- "tius (*a*)." This was, barely, the amount of the very indefinite and imperfect information, which Captain Cook himself had received from Baron Plettenberg at the Cape of Good Hope, in November 1772 (*b*); in the beginning of which year Kerguelen's *first* voyage had taken place.

(*a*) See the Instructions in the Introduction.
(*b*) See Captain Cook's Voyage, Vol. i, p. 16.

The

A VOYAGE TO

My instructions directing me to examine it, with a view to discover a good harbour, I proceeded in the search; and on

The Captain, on his return homeward, in March 1775, heard, a second time, something about this French discovery at the Cape, where he met with Monsieur Crozet, who very obligingly communicated to him a Chart of the Southern Hemisphere, wherein were delineated not only his own discoveries, but also those of Captain Kerguelen (a). But what little information that Chart could convey, was still necessarily confined to the operations of the first voyage; the Chart here referred to, having been published in France in 1773; that is, before any intelligence could possibly be conveyed from the Southern Hemisphere of the result of Kerguelen's second visit to this new land; which, we now know, happened towards the close of the same year.

Of these latter operations, the only account (if that can be called an account, which conveys no particular information) received by Captain Cook from Monsieur Crozet, was, that a later Voyage had been undertaken by the French, under the command of Captain Kerguelen, which had ended much to the disgrace of that commander (b).

What Crozet had not communicated to our Author, and what we are sure, from a variety of circumstances, he had never heard of from any other quarter, he missed an opportunity of learning at Teneriffe. He expresses his being sorry, as we have just read, that he did not know sooner that there was on board the frigate an officer who had been with Kerguelen, as he might have obtained from him more interesting information about this land, than its situation. And, indeed, if he had conversed with that officer, he might have obtained information more interesting than he was aware of; he might have learnt that Kerguelen had actually visited this Southern land a second time, and that the little isle of which he then received the name and position from the Chevalier de Borda, was a discovery of this later voyage. But the account conveyed to him being, as the Reader will observe, unaccompanied with any date, or other distinguishing circumstance, he left Teneriffe, and arrived on the coasts of Kerguelen's Land, under a full persuasion that it had been visited only once before. And even, with regard to the operations of that first voyage, he had nothing to guide him, but the very scanty materials afforded to him by Baron Plettenberg and Monsieur Crozet.

The truth is, the French seem, for some reason or other, not surely founded on the importance of Kerguelen's discovery, to have been very shy of publishing a full and distinct account of it. No such account had been published while Captain Cook lived. Nay, even after the return of his ships in 1780, the Gentleman who obligingly lent his assistance to give a view of the prior observations of the French, and to connect them on the same Chart with those of our Author, though his ability in procuring geographical information can be equalled only by his readiness in communicating it, had not, it should seem, been able to procure any materials for that purpose, but

(a) See Cook's Voyage, Vol. II. p. 264.   (b) Ibid. p. 258.

Such

THE PACIFIC OCEAN.

on the 16th, being then in the latitude of 48° 45′, and in the longitude of 52° East, we saw penguins and divers, and rock-weed floating in the sea. We continued to meet with more or less of these every day, as we proceeded to the Eastward; and on the 21st, in the latitude of 48° 27′ South, and in the longitude of 65° East, a very large seal was seen. We had now much foggy weather, and, as we expected to fall in with the land every hour, our navigation became both tedious and dangerous.

1776.
December.
Monday 16.

Saturday 21.

At length, on the 24th, at six o'clock in the morning, as we were steering to the Eastward, the fog clearing away a little, we saw land *, bearing South South East, which, upon

Tuesday 24.

---

such as mark the operations of the first French voyage; and even for these, he was indebted to a MS. drawing.

But this veil of unnecessary secrecy is at length drawn aside. Kerguelen himself has, very lately, published the Journal of his proceedings in two successive voyages, in the years 1772 and 1773; and has annexed to his Narrative a Chart of the coasts of this land, as far as he had explored them in both voyages. Monsieur de Pagès, also, much about the same time, favoured us with another account of the second voyage, in some respects fuller than Kerguelen's own, on board whose ship he was then an officer.

From these sources of authentic information, we are enabled to draw every necessary material to correct what is erroneous, and to illustrate what, otherwise, would have remained obscure, in this part of Captain Cook's Journal. We shall take occasion to do this in separate Notes on the passages as they occur, and conclude this tedious, but, it is hoped, not unnecessary, detail of facts, with one general remark, fully expressive of the disadvantages our Author laboured under. He never saw that part of the coast upon which the French had been in 1772; and he never knew that they had been upon another part of it in 1773, which was the very scene of his own operations. Consequently, what he knew of the *former* voyage, as *delineated* upon Crozet's Chart, only served to perplex and mislead his judgment; and his total ignorance of the *latter*, put it out of his power to compare his own observations with those then made by Kerguelen; though we, who are better instructed, can do this, by tracing the plainest marks of coincidence and agreement.

* Captain Cook was not the original discoverer of these small islands which he now fell in with. It is certain that they had been seen and named by Kerguelen, on his second voyage, in December 1773. Their position, relatively to each other, and

Vol. I.   I   to

1776.
December.

upon a nearer approach, we found to be an island of considerable height, and about three leagues in circuit *. Soon after, we saw another of the same magnitude, one league to the Eastward †; and between thefe two, in the direction of South East, some smaller ones ‡. In the direction of South by East ; East, from the East end of the first island, a third § high island was seen. At times, as the fog broke away, we had the appearance of land over the small islands; and I had thoughts of steering for it, by running in between them. But, on drawing nearer, I found this would be a dangerous attempt, while the weather continued foggy. For if there should be no passage, or if we should meet with any sudden danger, it would have been impossible for us to get off; the wind being right a-stern, and a prodigious sea running, that broke on all the shores in a frightful surf. At the same time, seeing another island in the North East direction, and not knowing but that there might be more, I judged it prudent to haul off, and wait for clearer weather, lest we should get intangled amongst unknown lands in a thick fog.

We did but just weather the island last mentioned. It is a highround rock, which was named Bligh's Cap. Perhaps

* to the adjoining coasts of the greater land, as represented on the annexed Chart, bears a striking resemblance to Kerguelen's delineation of them; whose Chart, however, the Public may be assured, was unknown in England till after ours had been engraved.
* This is the isle to which Kerguelen gave the name of *Croy* or *Croy*. Besides delineating it upon his Chart, he has added a particular view of it, exactly corresponding with Captain Cook's account of its being of *considerable height*.
† Kerguelen called this *Isle Roland*, after the name of his own ship. There is also a particular view of it on the French Chart.
‡ The observations of the French and English navigators agree exactly, as to the position of these smaller isles.
§ The situation of Kerguelen's *Isle de Clugny*, as marked on his Chart, shews it to be the *third high island* seen by Captain Cook.

this

this is the same that Monsieur de Kerguelen called the Isle of Rendezvous*; but I know nothing that can rendezvous at it, but fowls of the air; for it is certainly inaccessible to every other animal.

At eleven o'clock the weather began to clear up, and we immediately tacked, and steered in for the land. At noon, we had a pretty good observation, which enabled us to determine the latitude of Bligh's Cap, which is the northernmost island, to be 48° 29′ South, and its longitude 68° 40′ East †. We passed it at three o'clock, standing to the South South East, with a fresh gale at West.

Soon after we saw the land, of which we had a faint view in the morning; and at four o'clock it extended from South East ; East, to South West by South, distant about four miles. The left extreme, which I judged to be the Northern point of this land called, in the French Chart of the Southern

---

* This isle, or rock, was the single point about which Captain Cook had received the least information at Teneriffe; and we may observe how sagacious he was in tracing it. What he could only speak of as probable, a comparison of his Chart with that lately published by Kerguelen, proves to be certain; and if he had even read and copied what his predecessor in the discovery says of it, he could scarcely have varied his account of its shape. Kerguelen's words are, "Isle de Rendzin, qui n'est qu'une "Roche, nous servoit de Rendezvous, ou de point de ralliement, et ressemble à un "coin de mire."

† The French and English agree very nearly (as might be expected) in their accounts of the latitude of this island; but the observations by which they fix its longitude, vary considerably.

The Pilot at Teneriffe made it only 64° 57′ East from Paris, which is about 67° 16′ East from London, or 1° 24′ more Westerly than Captain Cook's observations fix it.

Monsieur de Pagès says it is 66° 47′ East from Paris, that is 69° 6′ East from London, or twenty-six miles more Easterly than it is placed by Captain Cook.

Kerguelen himself only says that it is about 68° of East longitude, per 68° de longitude.

60 · A VOYAGE TO

1774.
December.

Hemisphere, Cape St. Louis *, terminated in a perpendicular rock of a confiderable height; and the right one (near which is a detached rock) in a high indented point †. From this point the coaſt ſeemed to turn ſhort round to the Southward; for we could ſee no land to the Weſtward of the direction in which it now bore to us, but the iſlands we had obſerved in the morning; the moſt Southerly ‡ of them lying nearly Weſt from the point, about two or three leagues diſtant.

About the middle of the land there appeared to be an inlet, for which we ſteered; but, on approaching, found it was only a bending in the coaſt, and therefore bore up, to go round Cape St. Louis §. Soon after, land opened off the

---

* Hitherto, we have only had occaſion to ſupply defects, owing to Captain Cook's entire ignorance of Kerguelen's ſecond voyage in 1773; we muſt now correct errors, owing to his very limited knowledge of the operations of the firſt voyage in 1772: The Chart of the Southern Hemiſphere, his only guide, having given him, as he tells us, the name of Cape St. Louis (or Cape Louis) as the moſt Northerly promontory then ſeen by the French; and his own obſervations now ſatisfying him that no part of the main land ſtretched farther North than the left extreme now before him; from this ſuppoſed ſimilarity of ſituation, he judged that his own perpendicular rock muſt be the Cape Louis of the firſt diſcoverers. By looking upon our Chart, we ſhall find Cape Louis lying upon a very different part of the coaſt; and by comparing this Chart with that lately publiſhed by Kerguelen, it will appear, in the cleareſt manner, that the Northern point now deſcribed by Captain Cook, is the very ſame to which the French have given the name of Cape François.

† This right extreme of the coaſt, as it now ſhewed itſelf to Captain Cook, ſeems to be what is repreſented on Kerguelen's Chart under the name of Cape Aubert. It may be proper to obſerve here, that all that extent of coaſt lying between Cape Louis and Cape François, of which the French ſaw very little during their firſt viſit in 1772, and may be called the North Weſt ſide of this land, they had it in their power to trace the poſition of in 1773, and have aſſigned names to ſome of its bays, rivers, and promontories, upon their Chart.

‡ Kerguelen's Iſle de Clugny.

§ Cape François, as already obſerved.

9
Cape,

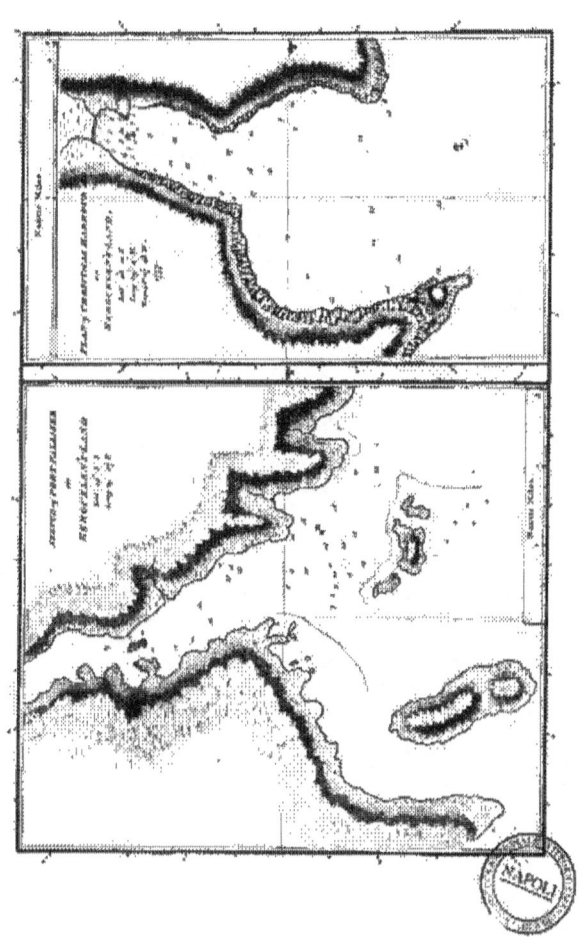

Cape, in the direction of South 53° East, and appeared to be a point at a considerable distance; for the trending of the coast from the Cape was more Southerly. We also saw several rocks and islands to the Eastward of the above directions, the most distant of which was about seven leagues from the Cape, bearing South 88° East [*].

We had no sooner got off the Cape, than we observed the coast, to the Southward, to be much indented by projecting points and bays; so that we now made sure of soon finding a good harbour. Accordingly, we had not run a mile farther, before we discovered one behind the Cape, into which we began to ply; but after making one board, it fell calm, and we anchored at the entrance in forty-five fathoms water, the bottom black sand; as did the Discovery soon after. I immediately dispatched Mr. Bligh, the Master, in a boat to sound the harbour; who, on his return, reported it to be safe and commodious, with good anchorage in every part; and great plenty of fresh water, seals, penguins, and other birds on the shore; but not a stick of wood. While we lay at anchor, we observed that the flood tide came from the South East, running two knots, at least, in an hour.

At day-break, in the morning of the 25th, we weighed with a gentle breeze at West; and having wrought into the harbour, to within a quarter of a mile of the sandy beach at its head, we anchored in eight fathoms water, the bottom a fine dark sand. The Discovery did not get in till two o'clock in the afternoon; when Captain Clerke informed me, that he had narrowly escaped being driven on the South

---

[*] The observations of the French, round Cape François, remarkably coincide with Captain Cook's in this paragraph; and the rocks and islands here mentioned by him, also appear upon their Chart.

1776.
December.

point of the harbour, his anchor having ſtarted before they had time to ſhorten in the cable. This obliged them to ſet ſail, and drag the anchor after them, till they had room to heave it up; and then they found one of its palms was broken off.

As ſoon as we had anchored, I ordered all the boats to be hoiſted out; the ſhip to be moored with a kedge anchor; and the water-caſks to be got ready to ſend on ſhore. In the mean time I landed, to look for the moſt convenient ſpot where they might be filled, and to ſee what elſe the place afforded.

I found the ſhore, in a manner, covered with penguins and other birds, and ſeals. Theſe latter were not numerous, but ſo inſenſible of fear (which plainly indicated that they were unaccuſtomed to ſuch viſiters), that we killed as many as we choſe, for the ſake of their fat or blubber, to make oil for our lamps, and other uſes. Freſh water was in no leſs plenty than were birds; for every gully afforded a large ſtream. But not a ſingle tree or ſhrub, nor the leaſt ſign of any, was to be diſcovered, and but very little herbage of any ſort. The appearances, as we ſailed into the harbour, had flattered us with the hope of meeting with ſomething conſiderable growing here, as we obſerved the ſides of many of the hills to be of a lively green. But I now found that this was occaſioned by a ſingle plant, which, with the other natural productions, ſhall be deſcribed in another place. Before I returned to my ſhip, I aſcended the firſt ridge of rocks, which riſe in a kind of amphitheatre above one another. I was in hopes, by this means, of obtaining a view of the country; but before I reached the top, there came on ſo thick a fog, that I could hardly find my way down again. In the evening, we hauled the feine at the head of the harbour, but caught only half a dozen fmall fifh. We had no better fuccefs next day, when we tried with hook and line. So that our only refource here, for frefh provifions, were birds, of which there was an inexhauftible ftore.

The morning of the 26th proved foggy, with rain. However, we went to work to fill water, and to cut grafs for our cattle, which we found in fmall fpots near the head of the harbour. The rain which fell, fwelled all the rivulets to fuch a degree, that the fides of the hills, bounding the harbour, feemed to be covered with a fheet of water. For the rain, as it fell, run into the fiffures and crags of the rocks that compofed the interior parts of the hills, and was precipitated down their fides in prodigious torrents.

The people having wrought hard the two preceding days, and nearly completed our water, which we filled from a brook at the left corner of the beach, I allowed them the 27th as a day of reft, to celebrate Chriftmas. Upon this indulgence, many of them went on fhore, and made excurfions, in different directions, into the country, which they found barren and defolate in the higheft degree. In the evening, one of them brought to me a quart bottle which he had found, faftened with fome wire to a projecting rock on the North fide of the harbour. This bottle contained a piece of parchment, on which was written the following infcription:

Ludovico

A VOYAGE TO

*Ludovico XV Galliarum
rege, at d.* de Boynes
regi a Secretis ad res
maritimas annis* 1772 *et*
1773.

From this inscription, it is clear, that we were not the first Europeans who had been in this harbour. I supposed it to be left by Monsieur de Boisguehenneu, who went on shore in a boat on the 13th of February 1772, the same day that Monsieur de Kerguelen discovered this land; as appears by a Note in the French Chart of the Southern Hemisphere, published the following year †.

As

---

* The *(d)*, no doubt is a contraction of the word *Domino*. The French Secretary of the Marine was then Monsieur de Boynes.

† On perusing this paragraph of the Journal, it will be natural to ask, How could Monsieur de Boisguehenneu, in the beginning of 1772, leave an inscription, which, upon the very face of it, commemorates a transaction of the following year? Captain Cook's manner of expressing himself here, strongly marks, that he made this supposition, only for want of information to enable him to make any other. He had no idea that the French had visited this land a second time; and, reduced to the necessity of trying to accommodate what he saw himself, to what little he had heard of their proceedings, he confounds a transaction which we, who have been better instructed, know, for a certainty, belongs to the second Voyage, with a similar one, which his Chart of the Southern Hemisphere has recorded, and which happened in a different year, and at a different place.

The bay, indeed, in which Monsieur de Boisguehenneu landed, is upon the West side of this land, considerably to the South of Cape Louis, and not far from another more Southerly promontory, called Cape Bourbon; a part of the coast which our ships were not upon. Its situation is marked upon our Chart; and a particular view of the bay *du Lion Marin* (for so Boisguehenneu called it), with the soundings, is preserved by Kerguelen.

But if the bottle and inscription found by Captain Cook's people, were not left here by Boisguehenneu, by whom and when were they left? This we learn most satisfactorily, from the account of Kerguelen's second Voyage, as published by himself and Monsieur de Pages, which present us with the following particulars: That they arrived on the West side of this land on the 14th of December 1773; that, steering to the
North

As a memorial of our having been in this harbour, I wrote on the other side of the parchment.

North East, they discovered, on the 16th, the *Isle de Reunion*, and the other small islands as mentioned above; that, on the 17th, they had before them the principal land (which they were sure was connected with that seen by them on the 14th), and a high point of that land, named by them Cape François; that beyond this Cape, the coast took a South Easterly direction, and behind it they found a bay, called by them *Baie de l'Oiseau*, from the name of their frigate; that they then endeavoured to enter it, but were prevented by contrary winds and blowing weather, which drove them off the coast Eastward; but that, at last, on the 6th of January, Monsieur de Rosnevet, Captain of the Oiseau, was able to send his boat on shore into this bay, under the command of Monsieur de Rochegude, one of his officers, "*who took possession of that bay, and of all the country, in the name of the King of France, with all the requisite formalities.*"

Here then we trace, by the most unexceptionable evidence, the history of the bottle and inscription; the leaving of which was, no doubt, one of the requisite formalities observed by Monsieur de Rochegude on this occasion. And though he did not land till the 6th of January 1774, yet, as Kerguelen's ships arrived upon the coast on the 14th of December 1773, and had discovered and looked into this very bay on the 17th of of that month, it was with the strictest propriety and truth that 1773, and not 1774, was mentioned as the date of the discovery.

We need only look at Kerguelen's and Cook's Charts, to judge that the *Baie de l'Oiseau*, and the harbour where the French inscription was found, is one and the same place. But besides this agreement as to the general position, the same conclusion results more decisively still, from another circumstance worth mentioning: The French, as well as the English visiters of this bay and harbour, have given us a particular Plan of it; and whoever compares ours, published in this Volume, with that to be met with in Kerguelen's and de Pagès's Voyages, must be struck with a resemblance that could only be produced by copying one common original with fidelity. Nay, even the soundings are the same upon the same spots in both Plans, being forty-five fathoms between the two Capes, before the entrance of the bay; sixteen fathoms farther in, where the shores begin to contract; and eight fathoms up, near the bottom of the harbour.

To these particulars, which throw abundant light on this part of our Author's Journal, I shall only add, that the distance of our harbour from that where Boisguehenneu landed in 1772, is forty leagues. For this we have the authority of Kerguelen, in the following passage: " Monsieur de Boisguehenneu descendit le 13 de " Fevrier 1772, dans un baie, qu'il nomma Baie du Lion Marin, & prit possession " de cette terre au nom de Roi; il n'y vit aucune trace d'habitants. Monsieur de " Rochegude, en 1774 a descendu dans un autre baie, que nous avons nommé á " Baie de l'Oiseau, & cette seconde rade est à quarantes lieues de la premiere. " Il en a également pris possession, & il n'y trouva également aucune trace d'habitants." *Kerguelen*, p. 92.

A VOYAGE TO

*Naves Resolution
et Discovery
de Rege Magnæ Britanniæ,
Decembris* 1776.

I then put it again into a bottle, together with a silver two-penny piece of 1772; and having covered the mouth of the bottle with a leaden cap, I placed it, the next morning, in a pile of stones erected for the purpose, upon a little eminence on the North shore of the harbour, and near to the place where it was first found; in which position it cannot escape the notice of any European, whom chance or design may bring into this port. Here I displayed the British flag, and named the place *Christmas Harbour*, from our having arrived in it on that festival.

It is the first, or northernmost inlet that we meet with on the South East side of Cape St. Louis*, which forms the North side of the harbour, and is also the Northern point of this land. The situation alone is sufficient to distinguish it from any of the other inlets; and, to make it more remarkable, its South point terminates in a high rock, which is perforated quite through, so as to appear like the arch of a bridge. We saw none like this upon the whole coast †. The harbour has another distinguishing mark within, from a
single

---

* Cape François, for reasons already assigned.

† If there could be the least doubt remaining of the identity of the Baie de l'Oiseau, and Christmas harbour, the circumstance of the perforated rock, which divides it from another bay to the South, would amount to a strict demonstration. For Monsieur de Pagès had observed this discriminating mark before Captain Cook. His words are as follows: " L'on vit que la côte de l'est, voisine du Cap François, avoit deux baies ; " elles étoient séparées par une p ... te très reconnoissable par sa forme, qui représentoit " une porte cochere, ou maniere de ... qu'ils l'on aperçoit le jour." Voyages de M. de Pagès, Vol. ii. p. 67. Every one knows how exactly the form of a *porte cochere*, or arched
gateway,

single stone or rock, of a vast size, which lies on the top of a hill on the South side, near its bottom; and opposite this, on the North side, there is another hill, much like it, but smaller. There is a small beach at its bottom, where we commonly landed; and, behind it, some gently rising ground, on the top of which is a large pool of fresh water. The land on both sides of the inlet is high, and it runs in West, and West North West, about two miles. Its breadth is one mile and a quarter, for more than half its length; above which, it is only half a mile. The depth of water, which is forty-five fathoms at the entrance, varies, as we proceed farther in, from thirty, to five and four fathoms, as marked upon the Plan. The shores are steep; and the bottom is every where a fine dark sand, except in some places close to the shore, where there are beds of sea-weed, which always grows on rocky ground. The head of the harbour lies open only to two points of the compass; and even these are covered by islands in the offing, so that no sea can fall in to hurt a ship. The appearances on shore confirmed this; for we found grass growing close to high-water mark, which is a sure sign of a pacific harbour [*].

It

---

gateway, corresponds with that of the arch of a bridge. It is very satisfactory to find the two navigators, neither of whom knew any thing of the other's description, adopting the same idea; which both proves that they had the same uncommon object before their eyes, and that they made an accurate report.

[*] In the last Note, we saw how remarkably Monsieur de Pagés and Captain Cook agree about the appearance of the South Point of the harbour; I shall here subjoin another quotation from the former, containing his account of the harbour itself, in which the Reader may trace the same distinguishing features observed by Captain Cook in the foregoing paragraph.

"Le 6, l'on mit à terre dans la premiere baie à l'Est du Cap François, & l'on prit
"possession de ces contrées. Ce mouillage consiste en un petite rade, qui a environ
"quatre encablures, ou quatre cents toiles de profondeur, sur un tiers ou sur de lar-
"geur.

1773.
December.

It is high-water here, at the full and change days, about ten o'clock; and the tide rises and falls about four feet.

After I had finished this business of the inscription, I went in my boat round the harbour, and landed in several places, to examine what the shore afforded; and, particularly, to look for drift wood. For, although the land here was totally destitute of trees, this might not be the case in other parts; and if there were any, the torrents would force some, or, at least, some branches, into the sea, which would afterward throw them upon the shores; as in all other countries where there is wood, and in many where there is none: but, throughout the whole extent of the harbour, I found not a single piece.

In the afternoon, I went upon Cape St. Louis*, accompanied by Mr. King, my Second Lieutenant. I was in hopes, from this elevation, to have had a view of the sea-coast, and of the islands lying off it. But, when I got up, I found every distant object below me hid in a thick fog. The land on the same plain, or of a greater height, was visible enough, and appeared naked and desolate in the highest

" gour. En dedans de cette rade est un petit port, dont l'entrée, de quatre encen-
" blures de largeur, presente au Sud-Est. La sonde de la petite rade est depuis qua-
" rante-cinq jusqu'à trente brasses; et celle du port depuis seize jusqu'à huit. Le
" fond des deux est de sable noir et vaseux. La côte des deux bords est haute, & par
" une pente très rude; elle est couverte de verdure, & il y a une quantité prodigieuse
" d'Outardes. Le fond du port est occupé par un monticule qui laisse entre lui, et
" la mer une plage de sable. Une petite rivière, de très bonne eau, coule à la mer
" dans cet endroit; & elle est fournie par un lac qui est un peu au loin, au dessus du
" monticule. Il y avoit sur la plage beaucoup de pinguoins & de lions marins. Ces
" deux especes d'animaux ne fuyoient pas, & l'on augura que le pays n'étoit point
" habité; la terre rapportoit de l'herbe large, noire, & bien nourrie, qui n'avoit ce-
" pendant que cinque pouces ou plus de hauteur. L'on ne vit aucun arbre, ni signe
" d'habitation." *Voyage de Monsieur de Pagés,* Tom. ii. p. 69, 70.

* Cape François.

degree;

degree; except some hills to the Southward, which were covered with snow.

When I got on board, I found the launch hoisted in, the ships unmoored, and ready to put to sea; but our sailing was deferred till five o'clock the next morning, when we weighed anchor.

CHAP.

CHAP. V.

Departure from Christmas Harbour.—Range along the Coast, to discover its Position and Extent.—Several Promontories and Bays, and a Peninsula, described and named.—Danger from Shoals.—Another Harbour and a Sound.—Mr. Anderson's Observations on the natural Productions, Animals, Soil, &c. of Kerguelen's Land.

1776.
December.
Sunday 29.

AS soon as the ships were out of Christmas Harbour, we steered South East ¼ South, along the coast, with a fine breeze at North North West, and clear weather. This we thought the more fortunate, as, for some time past, fogs had prevailed, more or less, every day; and the continuance of them would have defeated our plan of extending Kerguelen's discovery. We kept the lead constantly going; but seldom struck ground with a line of fifty or sixty fathoms.

About seven or eight o'clock, we were off a promontory, which I called Cape Cumberland. It lies a league and a half from the South point of Christmas Harbour, in the direction of South East ¼ South. Between them is a bay with two arms, both of which seemed to afford good shelter for shipping. Off Cape Cumberland is a small but pretty high island, on the summit of which is a rock like a sentry-box, which occasioned our giving that name to the island. Two miles further to the Eastward, lies a groupe of
small

small islands and rocks, with broken ground about them: we sailed between these and Sentry-Box Island, the channel being a full mile broad, and more than forty fathoms deep; for we found no bottom with that length of line.

Being through this channel, we discovered, on the South side of Cape Cumberland, a bay, running in three leagues to the Westward. It is formed by this Cape to the North, and by a promontory to the South, which I named Point Pringle, after my good friend Sir John Pringle, President of the Royal Society. The bottom of this bay was called Cumberland Bay; and it seemed to be disjoined from the sea, which washes the North West coast of this country, by a narrow neck of land. Appearances, at least, favoured such a conjecture.

To the Southward of Point Pringle, the coast is formed into a fifth bay, of which this point is the Northern extreme; and from it, to the Southern extreme, is about four miles in the direction of South South East ½ East. In this bay, which obtained the Name of White Bay, on account of some white spots of land or rocks in the bottom of it, are several lesser bays or coves, which seemed to be sheltered from all winds. Off the South point, are several rocks which raise their heads above water; and, probably, many more that do not.

Thus far our course was in a direction parallel to the coast, and not more than two miles from it. Thither our glasses were continually pointed; and we could easily see that, except the bottoms of the bays and coves, which, for the most part, terminated in sandy beaches, the shores were rocky, and, in many places, swarmed with birds; but the

country

country had the same barren and naked appearance as in the neighbourhood of Christmas Harbour.

We had kept on our larboard bow, the land which first opened off Cape St. Louis *, in the direction of South 53° East, thinking that it was an island, and that we should find a passage between it and the main. We now discovered this to be a mistake; and found that it was a peninsula, joined to the rest of the coast by a low isthmus. I called the bay, formed by this peninsula, Repulse Bay; and a branch of it seemed to run a good way inland towards the South South West. Leaving this, we steered for the Northern point of the peninsula, which we named Howe's Foreland, in honour of Admiral Lord Howe.

As we drew near it, we perceived some rocks and breakers near the North West part; and two islands a league and a half to the Eastward of it, which, at first, appeared as one. I steered between them and the Foreland †, and was in the middle of the channel by noon. At that time our latitude, by observation, was 48° 51′ South; and we had made twenty-six miles of East longitude from Cape St. Louis ‡.

From this situation, the most advanced land to the Southward bore South East; but the trending of the coast from the Foreland was more Southerly. The islands which lie

---

* Cape François.

† Though Kerguelen's ships, in 1773, did not venture to explore this part of the coast, Monsieur de Pagés's account of it answers well to Captain Cook's. "Du 17 au 23, l'on ne prit d'autre connoissance que celle de la figure de la côte, qui, courant d'abord au Sud-Est, & revenant ensuite au Nord-Est, formoit un grand golfe. Il etoit occupé par des brisans & des rochers; il avoit aussi une isle basse, & assez etendue, & l'on usa d'une bien soigneuse precaution, pour ne pas s'affaler dans ce golfe." *Voyage de M. de Pagés*, Tom. ii. p. 67.

‡ Cape François.

off Chriſtmas Harbour bore North; and the North point of the Foreland, North 60° Weſt, diſtant three miles. The land of this Peninſula, or Foreland, is of a moderate height, and of a hilly and rocky ſubſtance. The coaſt is low, with rocky points ſhooting out from it; between which points are little coves, with ſandy beaches; and theſe, at this time, were moſtly covered with ſea birds. We alſo ſaw upon them ſome ſeals.

As ſoon as we were clear of the rocks and iſlands before mentioned, I gave orders to ſteer South Eaſt by South, along the coaſt. But before theſe orders could be carried into execution, we diſcovered the whole ſea before us to be chequered with large beds of rock-weed, which we knew to be faſt to the bottom, and to grow on rocky ſhoals. I had often found a great depth of water on ſuch ſhoals; and I had, as often, found rocks that have raiſed their heads nearly to the ſurface of the water. It is always dangerous, therefore, to ſail over them before they are well examined; but more eſpecially, when there is no ſurge of the ſea to diſcover the danger. This was the caſe at preſent, for the ſea was as ſmooth as a mill-pond. Conſequently we endeavoured to avoid them, by ſteering through the winding channels by which they were ſeparated. We kept the lead continually going; but never ſtruck ground with a line of ſixty fathoms. This circumſtance increaſed the danger, as we could not anchor, whatever neceſſity there might be for it. After running in this manner above an hour, we diſcovered a lurking rock, juſt even with the ſurface of the ſea. It bore North Eaſt ¼ Eaſt, diſtant three or four miles, and lay in the middle of one of theſe large beds of weeds. This was a ſufficient warning to make us uſe every precaution to prevent our coming upon them.

1778.
December.

We were now cross the mouth of a large bay, that lies about eight miles to the Southward of Howe's Foreland. In and before the entrance of this bay are several low islands, rocks, and those beds of sea-weed. But there seemed to be winding channels between them. After continuing our course half an hour longer, we were so much embarrassed with these shoals, that I resolved to haul off to the Eastward, as the likeliest means of extricating ourselves from the danger that threatened us. But so far was this from answering the intended purpose, that it brought us into more. I therefore found it absolutely necessary to secure the ships, if possible, in some place before night; especially as the weather had now become hazy, and a fog was apprehended. And seeing some inlets to the South West of us, I ordered Captain Clerke, as the Discovery drew less water than the Resolution, to lead in for the shore; which was accordingly done.

In standing in, it was not possible to avoid running over the edges of some of the shoals, on which we found from ten to twenty fathoms water; and the moment we were over, had no ground at the depth of fifty fathoms. After making a few boards to weather a spit that run out from an island on our lee, Captain Clerke made the signal for having discovered an harbour; in which, about five o'clock, we anchored in fifteen fathoms water, over a bottom of fine dark sand, about three quarters of a mile from the shore; the North point of the harbour bearing North by East ½ East, one mile distant; and the small islands in the entrance, within which we anchored, extending from East to South East.

Scarcely were the ships secured, when it began to blow very strong; so that we thought it prudent to strike top-
gallant

gallant yards. The weather, however, continued fair; and the wind difperfing the fog that had fettled on the hills, it was tolerably clear alfo. The moment, therefore, we had anchored, I hoifted out two boats; in one of which I fent Mr. Bligh, the Mafter, to furvey the upper-part of the harbour, and look for wood; for not a fhrub was to be feen from the fhip. I alfo defired Captain Clerke to fend his Mafter to found the channel that is on the South fide of the fmall ifles, between them and a pretty large ifland which lies near the South point of the harbour. Having given thefe directions, I went myfelf, in my other boat, accompanied by Mr. Gore, my firft Lieutenant, and Mr. Baily, and landed on the North point, to fee what I could difcover from thence.

From the higheft hill over the point, we had a pretty good view of the fea-coaft, as far as Howe's Foreland. It is much indented, and feveral rocky points feemed to fhoot out from it, with coves and inlets of unequal extent. One of the latter, the end of which I could not fee, was disjoined from that in which the fhips were at anchor, by the point we then ftood upon. A great many fmall iflands, rocks, and breakers appeared fcattered along the coaft, as well to the Southward as Northward; and I faw no better channel to get out of the harbour, than by the one through which we had entered it.

While Mr. Baily and I were making the obfervations, Mr. Gore encompaffed the hill, and joined us by a different route, at the place where I had ordered the boat to wait for us. Except the craggy precipices, we met with nothing to obftruct our walk. For the country was, if poffible, more barren and defolate than about Chriftmas Harbour. And yet,

yet, if there be the least fertility in any part of this land, we ought to have found it in this, which is completely sheltered from the predominating bleak Southerly and Westerly winds. I observed, with regret, that there was neither food nor covering for cattle of any sort; and that, if I left any, they must inevitably perish. In the little cove where the boat waited for us (which I called Penguin Cove, as the beach was covered with these birds), is a fine rivulet of fresh water, that may be easily come at. Here were also some large seals, shags, and a few ducks; and Mr. Baily had a transient sight of a very small land bird; but it flew amongst the rocks, and we lost it. About nine o'clock we got on board.

Soon after, Mr. Bligh returned, and reported, that he had been four miles up the harbour, and, as he judged, not far from the head of it. He found that its direction was West South West; and that its breadth, a little above the ships, did not exceed a mile; but grew narrower towards the head. The soundings were very irregular, being from thirty-seven to ten fathoms; and, except under the beds of sea-weed, which in many places extended from the shore near half channel over, the bottom was a fine sand. He landed on both shores, which he found barren and rocky, without the least signs of tree or shrub, and with very little verdure of any kind. Penguins, and other oceanic birds and seals, occupied part of the coast; but not in such numbers as at Christmas Harbour.

Finding no encouragement to continue our researches, and the next morning, both wind and weather being favourable, I weighed anchor and put to sea. To this harbour I gave the name of Port Pallifer, in honour of my worthy friend

friend Admiral Sir Hugh Pallifer. It is fituated in the latitude of 49° 3′ South, in the longitude of 63° 37′ Eaſt, and five leagues from Howe's Foreland, in the direction of South 25° Eaſt. There are ſeveral iſlands, rocks, and breakers lying in and without the entrance, for which the annexed Chart of the coaſt, and ſketch of the harbour, may be conſulted. We went in and out between them and the North head; but I have no doubt that there are other channels.

As we were ſtanding out of Port Pallifer, we diſcovered a round hill, like a fugar-loaf, in the direction of South 72° Eaſt, about nine leagues diſtant. It had the appearance of an iſland lying at ſome diſtance from the coaſt; but we afterwards found it was upon the main land. In getting out to ſea, we had to ſteer through the winding channels amongſt the ſhoals. However, we ventured to run over ſome of them, on which we never found leſs than eighteen fathoms, and often did not ſtrike ground with twenty-four; ſo that, had it not been for the ſea-weed growing upon all of them, they would not have been diſcovered.

After we had got about three or four leagues from the coaſt, we found a clear ſea, and then ſteered Eaſt till nine o'clock, when the Sugar Loaf hill, above mentioned, which I named Mount Campbell, bore South Eaſt, and a ſmall iſland that lies to the Northward of it, South South Eaſt, diſtant four leagues. I now ſteered more Southerly, in order to get in with the land. At noon, the latitude by double altitudes was 49° 0′ South; and we had made eighty miles of Eaſt longitude from Cape St. Louis*. Mount Campbell bore South 47° Weſt, diſtant about four leagues; a low point, beyond which no land was to be ſeen, bore South

* Cape François.

South.

1776.
December.

South East, at the distance of about twenty miles; and we were about two leagues from the shore.

The land here is low and level [*]. The mountains ending about five leagues from the low point, a great extent of low land is left, on which Mount Campbell is situated, about four miles from the foot of the mountains, and one from the sea coast. These mountains have a considerable elevation, as also most of the inland ones. They seemed to be composed of naked rocks, whose summits were capt with snow. Nor did the valleys appear to greater advantage. To whatever quarter we directed our glasses, nothing but sterility was to be seen.

We had scarcely finished taking the bearings at noon, before we observed low land opening off the low point just mentioned, in the direction of South South East, and eight miles beyond it. This new point proved to be the very Eastern extremity of this land, and it was named Cape Digby. It is situated in the latitude of 49° 23′ South, and in the longitude of 70° 34′ East.

Between Howe's Foreland and Cape Digby, the shore forms (besides the several lesser bays and harbours) one great bay that extends several leagues to the South West, where it seemed to lose itself in various arms running in between the mountains. A prodigious quantity of sea-weed grows all over it, which seemed to be the same sort of weed that Mr. Banks distinguished by the name of *fucus*

---

[*] This part of the coast seems to be what the French saw on the 5th of January 1774. Monsieur de Pages speaks of it thus: "Nous reconnumes une nouvelle cote etendue de toute veu dans l'Est, & dans le Ouest. Les terres de cette cote etoient moins elevées que celles que nous avions veues jusques ici; elles étoient aussi d'un aspect moins rude." *De Pagis*, Tom. ii. p. 68.

giganteus.

giganteus *. Some of this weed is of a most enormous length, though the stem is not much thicker than a man's thumb. I have mentioned, that on some of the shoals upon which it grows, we did not strike ground with a line of twenty-four fathoms. The depth of water, therefore, must have been greater. And as this weed does not grow in a perpendicular direction, but makes a very acute angle with the bottom, and much of it afterwards spreads many fathoms on the surface of the sea, I am well warranted to say, that some of it grows to the length of sixty fathoms and upward.

At one o'clock (having run two leagues upon a South East ½ East course, from noon) we sounded, and found eighteen fathoms water, and a bottom of fine sand. Seeing a small bending in the coast, on the North side of Cape Digby, I steered for it. It was my intention to anchor there, if I should find it might be done with safety, and to land on the Cape, to examine what the low land within it produced. After running in one league, we sounded again, and found thirteen fathoms; and immediately after, saw a shoal right before us, that seemed to extend off from the shore, from which we were distant about two miles. This discovery obliged us to haul off, East by South, one league, where our depth of water encreased to twenty-five fathoms. We then steered along shore, and continued in the same depth, over a bottom of fine sand, till Cape Digby bore West, two leagues distant, when we found twenty-six fathoms.

After this we did not strike ground, though we tried several times; but the ship having a good deal of way, ran

* See Hawkesworth's Collection of Voyages, Vol. ii. p. 42.

1776.
December.

the line out before the lead could reach the bottom; and being disappointed in my views both of anchoring and of landing, I would not shorten sail, but pushed forward, in order to see as much of the coast as possible before night. From Cape Digby, it trends nearly South West by South for about four or five leagues, or to a low point, to which, in honour of her Majesty, I gave the name of Point Charlotte, and it is the Southernmost on the low coast.

Six leagues from Cape Digby, in the direction of South South West ¼ West, is a pretty high projecting point, which was called Prince of Wales's Foreland; and six leagues beyond that, in the same direction, and in the latitude of 49° 54' South, and the longitude of 70° 13' East, is the most Southerly point of the whole coast, which I distinguished by the name of Cape George, in honour of his Majesty.

Between Point Charlotte and Prince of Wales's Foreland, where the country to the South West began again to be hilly, is a deep inlet, which was called Royal Sound. It runs in West, quite to the foot of the mountains which bound it on the South West, as the low land before-mentioned does on the North. There are islands lying in the entrance, and others higher up, as far as we could distinguish. As we advanced to the South, we observed, on the South West side of Prince of Wales's Foreland, another inlet into Royal Sound; and it then appeared, that the Foreland was the East point of a large island lying in the mouth of it. There are several small islands in this inlet; and one about a league to the Southward of Prince of Wales's Foreland.

All the land on the South West side of Royal Sound, quite to Cape George, is composed of elevated hills, that rise directly from the sea, one behind another, to a considerable height.

height. Most of the summits were capt with snow, and they appeared as naked and barren as any we had seen. The smallest vestige of a tree or shrub was not discoverable, either inland or on the coast, and, I think, I may venture to pronounce that the country produces none. The low land about Cape Digby, when examined through our glasses, resembled the rest of the low land we had before met with; that is, it appeared to be partly naked and partly covered with a green turf; a description of which shall be given in its proper place. The shore is composed of sandy beaches, on which were many penguins, and other oceanic birds; and an immense number of shags kept perpetually flying about the ships as we sailed along.

Being desirous of getting the length of Cape George, to be assured whether or no it was the most Southerly point of the whole land, I continued to stretch to the South, under all the sail we could carry, till half an hour past seven o'clock; when, seeing no likelihood of accomplishing my design, as the wind had, by this time, shifted to West South West, the very direction in which we wanted to go, I took the advantage of the shifting of the wind, and stood away from the coast.

At this time Cape George bore South 53° West, distant about seven leagues. A small island that lies off the pitch of the Cape, was the only land we could see to the South of it; and we were farther confirmed that there was no more in that quarter, by a South West swell which we met as soon as we brought the Cape to bear in this direction.

But we have still a stronger proof that no part of this land can extend much, if at all, to the Southward of Cape George; and that is, Captain Furneaux's track in February

1773, after his separation from me during my late voyage. His log-book is now lying before me; and I find from it, that he crossed the meridian of this land only about seventeen leagues to the Southward of Cape George; a distance at which it may very well be seen in clear weather. This seems to have been the case when Captain Furneaux passed it. For his log-book makes no mention of fogs or hazy weather; on the contrary, it expressly tells us, that, when in this situation, they had it in their power to make observations, both for latitude and longitude, on board his ship; so that, if this land extends farther South than Cape George, it would have been scarcely possible that he should have passed without seeing it.

From these circumstances we are able to determine, within a very few miles, the quantity of latitude that this land occupies; which does not much exceed one degree and a quarter. As to its extent from East to West, that still remains undecided. We only know, that no part of it can reach so far to the West as the meridian of 63°; because, in 1773, under that meridian, I searched for it in vain *.

The French discoverers, with some reason, imagined Cape St. Louis † to be the projecting point of a Southern continent.

---

* If the French observations, as marked upon Captain Cook's Chart, and still more authentically upon that published by their own discoverers, may be depended upon, this land doth not reach so far to the West as the meridian of 68°; Cape Louis, which is represented as its most Westerly point, being laid down by them to the East of that meridian.

† The idea of Cape Louis being this projecting point of a Southern continent, must have soon vanished, as Cape François, within a year after, was found, by the same discoverer, to lie above one third of a degree farther North upon the same land. But if Kerguelen entertained any such imagination at first, we are sure that, at present, he thinks very differently. This appears from the following explicit declaration of his sentiments, which deserves to be transcribed from his last publication, as it does equal h:.r.out

nent. The English have since proved that no such continent exists; and that the land in question is an island of no great extent*; which, from its sterility, I should, with great propriety, call the Island of Desolation, but that I would not rob Monsieur de Kerguelen of the honour of its bearing his name †.

honour to his candour, and to Captain Cook's abilities. "La terre que j'ai decou-
"verte est certainement une *Isle*; puisque le célèbre Capitaine Cook a passé au Sud,
"lors de son premiere voyage, sans rien rencontrer. Je juge même, que cette iste n'est
"pas bien grande. Il y a nulle apparence, d'apres le Voyage de Monsieur Cook,
"que toute cette étendue de Mers Meridionales, est semée d'Isles ou de rochers;
"mais qu'il n'y a ni *continent ni grande terre.*" Kerguelen, p. 92.

* Kerguelen, as we see in the last Note, concurs with Captain Cook as to this. However, he tells us, that he has reason to believe that it is about two hundred leagues in circuit; and that he was acquainted with about fourscore leagues of its coast. "J'en connois environs quatre-vingt lieues des cotes; & j'ai lieu de croire, qu'elle "a environs deux cents lieues de circuit." *Kerguelen, ibid.*

† Some of Monsieur de Kerguelen's own countrymen seem more desirous than we are, to rob him of this honour. It is very remarkable that Monsieur de Pagès never once mentions the name of his commander. And, though he takes occasion to enumerate the several French explorers of the Southern Hemisphere, from Gonneville down to Crozet, he affects to preserve an entire silence about Kerguelen, whose first voyage, in which the discovery of this considerable tract of land was made, is kept as much out of sight, as if it never had taken place. Nay, not satisfied with refusing to acknowledge the right of another, he almost assumes it to himself. For upon a Map of the World, annexed to his book, at the spot where the new land is delineated, we read this inscription: *Isles nouvelles Australes vues par Monsieur de Pagès, en 1774.* He could scarcely have expressed himself in stronger terms, if he had meant to convey an idea that he was the conductor of the discovery. And yet we know, that he was only a Lieutenant [Enseigne de vaisseau] on board one of the three ships commanded by Kerguelen; and that the discovery had been already made in a former voyage, undertaken while he was actually engaged in his singular journey round the world.

After all, it cannot but be remarked, that Kerguelen was peculiarly unfortunate, in having done so little to complete what he had begun. He discovered a new land indeed; but, in two expeditions to it, he could not once bring his ships to an anchor upon any part of its coasts. Captain Cook, as we have seen in this, and in the foregoing Chapter, had either fewer difficulties to struggle with, or was more successful in surmounting them.

M 2

1776.
December.

Mr. Anderson, my Surgeon, who, as I have already mentioned, had made Natural History a part of his studies, lost no opportunity, during the short time we lay in Christmas Harbour, of searching the country in every direction. He afterwards communicated to me the observations he made on its natural productions; and I shall insert them here in his own words.

"Perhaps no place, hitherto discovered in either hemisphere, under the same parallel of latitude, affords so scanty a field for the naturalist as this barren spot. The verdure which appears, when at a little distance from the shore, would flatter one with the expectation of meeting with some herbage; but in this we were much deceived. For on landing, we saw that this lively colour was occasioned only by one small plant, not much unlike some sorts of *saxifrage*, which grows in large spreading tufts, to a considerable way up the hills. It forms a surface of a pretty large texture, and grows on a kind of rotten turf, into which one sinks a foot or two at every step. This turf, dried, might, in cases of necessity, serve for fuel, and is the only thing we met with here that could possibly be applied to this use.

There is another plant, plentifully enough scattered about the boggy declivities, which grows to near the height of two feet, and not much unlike a small cabbage, when it has shot into seeds. The leaves about the root are numerous, large, and rounded; narrower at the base, and ending in a small point. Those on the stalks are much smaller, oblong, and pointed. The stalks, which are often three or four, all rise separately from the root, and run into long cylindrical heads, composed of small flowers. It has not only

only the appearance, but the watery acrid taste of the anti-
scorbutic plants, and yet differs materially from the whole
tribe; so that we looked upon it as a production entirely
peculiar to the place. We eat it frequently raw, and
found it almost like the New Zealand scurvy-grass. But it
seemed to acquire a rank flavour by being boiled; which,
however, some of our people did not perceive, and esteemed
it good. If it could be introduced into our kitchen gardens,
it would, in all probability, improve so far by cultivation,
as to be an excellent pot-herb. At this time, none of its
seeds were ripe enough to be preserved, and brought home
to try the experiment.

Two other small plants were found near the brooks and
boggy places, which were eaten as sallad; the one almost
like garden cresses, and very fiery; and the other very mild.
This last, though but small, is in itself a curiosity, having not only male and female, but what the botanists call
androgynous plants.

A coarse grass, which we cut down for the cattle, grows
pretty plentifully in a few small spots about the sides of the
harbour, with a smaller sort which is rarer; and, upon
the flat ground, a sort of goose-grass, and another small
plant much like it. In short, the whole catalogue of plants
does not exceed sixteen or eighteen, including some sorts of
moss, and a beautiful species of *lichen*, which grows upon
the rocks, higher up than the rest of the vegetable productions. Nor is there even the least appearance of a shrub in
the whole country.

Nature has rather been more bountiful in furnishing it
with animals; though, strictly speaking, they are not inhabitants of the place, being all of the marine kind; and, in
general,

1776．
December．

general, only using the land for breeding, and for a resting-place. The most considerable are seals, or (as we used to call them) sea bears; being that sort called the ursine seal. These come ashore to rest or breed; but they were not very numerous, which is not to be wondered at, as it is known that these animals rather frequent out-rocks, and little islands lying off coasts, than bays or inlets. They were, at this time, shedding their hair, and so tame, that we killed what number we chose.

No other quadruped, either of the sea or of the land kind, was seen; but a great number of birds, viz. ducks, petrels, albatrosses, shags, gulls, and sea-swallows.

The ducks are about the size of a teal or widgeon; but somewhat different in colour from either. They were in tolerable plenty about the sides of the hills, or even lower; and we killed a considerable number, which were good, and without the least fishy taste. We met with some of the same sort at the island of Georgia, in our late voyage.

The Cape petrel, or Pintado bird; the small blue one, which is always seen at sea; and the small black one, or Mother Carey's Chicken, are not here in great numbers. But we found a nest of the first with an egg in it, about the size of a pullet's; and the second, though scarce, was met with in some holes like rabbit-burrows.

Another sort, which is the largest of all the petrels, and called by the seamen Mother Carey's Goose, is in greater numbers; and so tame, that at first we could kill them with a stick upon the beach. They are not inferior in size to an albatross, and are carnivorous, feeding on the dead carcases of seals or birds, that were thrown into the sea.

Their

Their colour is a futty brown, with a greenish bill and feet; and, doubtless, they are the same that the Spaniards call *quebrantahuessos*, whose head is figured in Pernetty's Voyage to Falkland Islands [*].

1776. December.

Of the albatrosses, none were found on shore except the grey one, which is commonly met with at sea in the higher Southern latitudes. Once I saw one of these sitting in the cliff of a rock, but they were frequently flying about the harbour; and the common large sort, as well as a smaller with a black face, were seen farther out.

Penguins form, by far, the greatest number of birds here; and are of three sorts. The first, or largest, I have seen formerly at the island of Georgia [†]. It is also mentioned by Bougainville [‡]; but it does not seem to be so solitary as he represents it, for we found considerable numbers flocking together. The head is black, the upper part of the body a leaden grey, and the under part white, with black feet. It has two broad stripes of fine yellow, that begin on the sides of the head, and descending by each side of the neck, meet above its breast. The bill is partly reddish, and longer than in the other sorts.

The second sort of penguin scarcely exceeds half the size of the former. The upper part of the body is a blackish grey, with a white spot on the upper part of the head, growing broader at each side. The bill and feet are yellowish. A very accurate figure and description, both of this and of the preceding, is given by Mr. Sonnerat [§].

---

[*] Fig. 3. Plate VIII.
[†] Pennant's Patagonian penguin. See his *Genera of Birds*. Tab. 14. p. 66.
[‡] *Voyage autour du Monde*, p. 69.
[§] *Voyage à la Nouvelle Guinée*, p. 181, 182. Tab. 113. 115.

The

1776.
December.

The third sort of penguin met with here, had never been seen by any of us before. Its length is twenty-four inches, and its breadth twenty. The upper part of the body and throat are black; the rest white, except the upper part of the head, which has a fine yellow arch, looking backward, and ending on each side in long soft feathers, which it can erect as two crests.

The two first sorts were found together on the beach; the large ones keeping by themselves, and walking in small flocks amongst the others, which were more numerous, and were sometimes seen a considerable way up the sides of the hills. The third sort were only found by themselves, but in great numbers, on the outer shores of the harbour. They were breeding at this time; and they lay, on the bare stones, only one white egg, larger than that of a duck. All the three sorts of penguins were so tame, that we took as many as we pleased with our hands.

The shags of this place are of two sorts; the lesser corvorant or water crow, and another, which is black above, with a white belly; the same that is found in New Zealand, Terra del Fuego, and the island of Georgia.

We also met with here the common sea-gull, sea-swallow, tern, and Port Egmont hen; the last of which were tame and numerous.

Another sort of white bird, flocks of which flew about the bay, is very singular; having the base of the bill covered with a horny crust *. It is larger than a pigeon, with the bill black and the feet white, made like those of a cur-

* The Sheath-bill. See *Pennant's Genera of Birds*, p. 43.

lew.

few. Some of our people put it in competition with the duck, as food.

The seine was hauled once; but we found only a few fish about the size of a small haddock, though quite different from any we knew. The snout is lengthened; the head armed with some strong spines; the rays of the back-fin long, and very strong; the belly is large; and the body without scales. The only shell fish are a few limpets and muscles; and, amongst the stones, a few small star-fish, and sea-anemonies, were found.

The hills are of a moderate height; yet many of their tops were covered with snow at this time, though answering to our June. Some of them have large quantities of stones, irregularly heaped together at their foot, or on their sides. The sides of others, which form steep cliffs towards the sea, are rent from the top downward, and seem ready to fall off, having stones of a considerable size lying in the fissures. Some were of opinion that frost might be the cause of these fissures, which I shall not dispute; but how others of the appearances could be effected, but by earthquakes, or some such severe shocks, I cannot say.

It appears that rain must be almost constant here, not only from the marks of large torrents having rushed down, but from the disposition of the country, which, even on the hills, is almost an entire bog or swamp, the ground sinking at every step.

The rocks, or foundations of the hills, are composed chiefly of a dark blue, and very hard, stone, intermixed with small particles of glimmer or quartz. This seems to be one of the most universal productions of Nature, as it constitutes whole mountains in Sweden, in Scotland, at the

1776.
December.

Canary Iflands, the Cape of Good Hope, and at this place. Another brownifh brittle ftone forms here fome confiderable rocks; and one which is blacker, and found in detached pieces, inclofes bits of coarfe quartz: A red, a dull yellow, and a purplifh fand-ftone, are alfo found in fmall pieces; and pretty large lumps of femi-tranfparent quartz, difpofed irregularly in polyedral pyramidal cryftals of long fhining fibres. Some fmall pieces of the common fort are met with in the brooks, made round by attrition; but none hard enough to refift a file. Nor were any of the other ftones acted on by aqua fortis, or attracted by the magnet.

Nothing, that had the leaft appearance of an ore or metal, was feen."

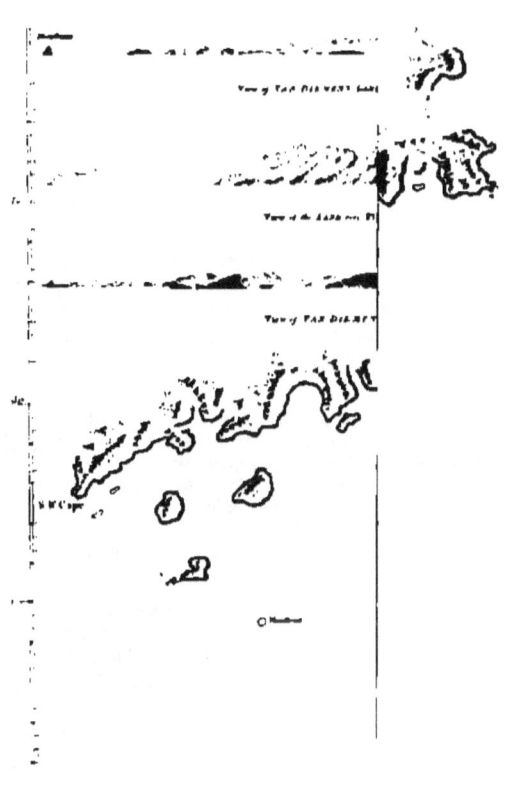

CHAP. VI.

Passage from Kerguelen's to Van Diemen's Land.—Arrival in Adventure Bay.—Incidents there.—Interviews with the Natives.—Their Persons and Dress described.—Account of their Behaviour.—Table of the Longitude, Latitude, and Variation.—Mr. Anderson's Observations on the natural Productions of the Country, on the Inhabitants, and their Language.

AFTER leaving Kerguelen's Land, I steered East by North, intending, in obedience to my instructions, to touch next at New Zealand; to recruit our water, to take in wood, and to make hay for the cattle. Their number, by this time, had been considerably diminished; two young bulls, one of the heifers, two rams, and several of the goats having of late died, while we were employed in exploring this desolate coast.

1776. December.

The 31st, in the morning, being the day after we stood out to sea, we had several observations of the sun and moon. Their results gave the longitude 72° 33' 36" East. The timekeeper, in this situation, gave 72° 38' 15". These observations were the more useful, as we had not been able to get any for some time before, and they now served to assure us that no material error had crept into the time keeper.

Tuesday 31.

On the 1st of January, being then in the latitude of 48° 41' South, longitude 76° 50' East, the variation was 30° 30' West;

1777. January. Wednes. 1.

1777.
January.
Thursday 2.

Friday 3.

West; and the next day, in the latitude of 48° 22' South, longitude 80° 22' East, it was 30° 47' 18" West. This was the greatest variation we found in this passage; for afterward it began to decrease, but so flowly, that on the 3d, in the evening, being then in the latitude of 48° 16' South, longitude 85° East, it was 29° 38' West.

Tuesday 7.

Thus far we had fresh gales from the West and South West, and tolerably clear weather. But now the wind veered to the North, where it continued eight days, and was attended with a thick fog. During this time, we ran above three hundred leagues in the dark. Now and then the weather would clear up, and give us a sight of the sun; but this happened very seldom, and was always of short continuance. On the 7th, I hoisted out a boat, and sent an order to Captain Clerke, appointing Adventure Bay, in Van Diemen's Land, as our place of rendezvous, in case of separation before we arrived in the meridian of that land. But we were fortunate enough, amidst all this foggy weather, by frequently firing guns as signals, though we seldom saw each other, not to lose company.

Sunday 12.

On the 12th, being in the latitude of 48° 40' South, longitude 110° 26' East, the Northerly winds ended in a calm; which, after a few hours, was succeeded by a wind from the Southward. This, with rain, continued for twenty-four hours; when it freshened, and veered to the West and North West, and brought on fair and clear weather.

Sunday 19.

We continued our course to the Eastward, without meeting with any thing worthy of notice, till four o'clock in the morning of the 19th; when, in a sudden squall of wind, though the Discovery received no damage, our fore-top-mast went by the board, and carried the main-top-gallant-mast with

THE PACIFIC OCEAN.

with it. This occasioned some delay, as it took us up the whole day to clear the wreck, and to fit another top-mast. The former was accomplished without losing any part of it, except a few fathoms of small rope. Not having a spare main-top-gallant-mast on board, the fore-top-gallant-mast was converted into one for our immediate use.

The wind continued Westerly, blew a fresh gale, and was attended with clear weather; so that scarcely a day passed without being able to get observations for fixing the longitude, and the variation of the compass. The latter decreased in such a manner, that in the latitude of 44° 18′ South, longitude 132° 2′ East, it was no more than 5° 34′ 18″ West; and on the 22d, being then in the latitude of 45° 27′ South, longitude 141° 50′ East, it was 1° 24′ 15″ East. So that we had crossed the line where the compass has no variation.

On the 24th, at three o'clock in the morning, we discovered the coast of Van Diemen's Land, bearing North ½ West. At four o'clock, the South West Cape bore North North West ½ West; and the Mewstone, North East by East, three leagues distant. There are several islands and high rocks lying scattered along this part of the coast. the Southernmost of which is the Mewstone. It is a round elevated rock, five or six leagues distant from the South West Cape, in the direction of South 55° East.

At noon, our latitude was 43° 47′ South, longitude 147° East; and the situation of the lands round us as follows: An elevated round-topped hill bore North 17° West; the South West Cape North 74° West; the Mewstone West ½ North; Swilly Isle or Rock South 40° East; and the South East or South Cape North 40° East, distant near three leagues. The land

land between the South West and the South Cape is broken and hilly, the coast winding, with points shooting out from it; but we were too far off, to be able to judge whether the bays formed by these points were sheltered from the sea-winds. The bay which appeared to be the largest and deepest, lies to the Westward of the peaked hill above-mentioned. The variation of the compass here, was 5° 15' East.

At six o'clock in the afternoon we sounded, and found sixty fathoms water, over a bottom of broken coral and shells. The South Cape then bore North 75° West, two or three leagues distant; Tasman's Head North East; and Swilly Rock South by West ¼ West. About a league to the Eastward of Swilly, is another elevated rock, that is not taken notice of by Captain Furneaux. I called it the Eddystone, from its very great resemblance to that light-house. Nature seems to have left these two rocks here, for the same purpose that the Eddystone light-house was built by man, viz. to give navigators notice of the dangers around them. For they are the conspicuous summits of a ledge of rocks under water, on which the sea, in many places, breaks very high. Their surface is white with the dung of sea-fowls; so that they may be seen at some distance, even in the night. On the North East side of Storm Bay, which lies between the South Cape and Tasman's Head, there are some coves or creeks, that seemed to be sheltered from the sea-winds; and I am of opinion that, were this coast examined, there would be found some good harbours.

Soon after we had sight of land the Westerly winds left us, and were succeeded by variable light airs and alternate calms, till the 26th at noon. At that time a breeze sprung up up and freshened at South East, which put it in my power to carry into execution the design I had, upon due consideration, formed, of carrying the ships into Adventure Bay, where I might expect to get a supply of wood and of grass for the cattle; of both which articles we should, as I now found, have been in great want, if I had waited till our arrival in New Zealand. We therefore stood for the bay, and anchored in it at four o'clock in the afternoon, in twelve fathoms water, over a bottom of sand and ouse. Penguin Island, which lies close to the East point of the bay, bore North 84° East; the Southernmost point of Maria's Islands bore North 76° ½ East; and Cape Frederic Henry, or the North point of the bay, bore North 33° East. Our distance from the nearest shore was about three quarters of a mile.

As soon as we had anchored, I ordered the boats to be hoisted out. In one of them I went myself, to look for the most commodious place for furnishing ourselves with the necessary supplies; and Captain Clerke went in his boat upon the same service. Wood and water we found in plenty, and in situations convenient enough, especially the first. But grass, of which we stood most in need, was scarce, and also very coarse. Necessity, however, obliged us to take such as we could get.

Next morning early, I sent Lieutenant King to the East side of the bay with two parties; one to cut wood, and the other to cut grass, under the protection of the marines, whom I judged it prudent to land as a guard. For although, as yet, none of the natives had appeared, there could be no doubt that some were in our neighbourhood, as we had seen columns of smoke, from the time of our approaching the coast; and some now was observed, at no great distance

up

1777.
January.

up in the woods. I also sent the launch for water; and afterwards visited all the parties myself. In the evening, we drew the seine at the head of the bay, and, at one haul, caught a great quantity of fish. We should have got many more, had not the net broken in drawing it ashore. Most of them were of that sort known to seamen by the name of elephant fish. After this, every one repaired on board with what wood and grafs we had cut, that we might be ready to fail whenever the wind should serve.

Tuesday 21.

This not happening next morning, the people were sent on shore again, on the same duty as the day before. I also employed the carpenter, with part of his crew, to cut some spars for the use of the ship; and dispatched Mr. Roberts, one of the mates, in a small boat to survey the bay.

In the afternoon, we were agreeably surprised, at the place where we were cutting wood, with a visit from some of the natives; eight men and a boy. They approached us from the woods, without betraying any marks of fear, or rather with the greatest confidence imaginable; for none of them had any weapons, except one, who held in his hand a stick about two feet long, and pointed at one end.

They were quite naked, and wore no ornaments; unless we consider as such, and as a proof of their love of finery, some large punctures or ridges raised on different parts of their bodies, some in straight, and others in curved lines.

They were of the common stature, but rather slender. Their skin was black, and also their hair, which was as woolly as that of any native of Guinea; but they were not distinguished by remarkably thick lips, nor flat noses. On the contrary, their features were far from being disagreeable.

able. They had pretty good eyes, and their teeth were tolerably even, but very dirty. Most of them had their hair and beards smeared with a red ointment; and some had their faces also painted with the same composition.

They received every present we made to them, without the least appearance of satisfaction. When some bread was given, as soon as they understood that it was to be eaten, they either returned it, or threw it away, without even tasting it. They also refused some elephant fish, both raw and dressed, which we offered to them. But upon giving some birds to them, they did not return these, and easily made us comprehend that they were fond of such food. I had brought two pigs ashore, with a view to leave them in the woods. The instant these came within their reach, they seized them, as a dog would have done, by the ears, and were for carrying them off immediately; with no other intention, as we could perceive, but to kill them.

Being desirous of knowing the use of the stick which one of our visiters carried in his hand, I made signs to them to shew me; and so far succeeded, that one of them set up a piece of wood as a mark, and threw at it, at the distance of about twenty yards. But we had little reason to commend his dexterity; for, after repeated trials, he was still very wide from the object. Omai, to shew them how much superior our weapons were to theirs, then fired his musquet at it; which alarmed them so much, that notwithstanding all we could do or say, they ran instantly into the woods. One of them was so frightened, that he let drop an axe and two knives, that had been given to him. From us, however, they went to the place, where some of the Discovery's people were employed in taking water into their boat. The officer

1777.
January.

of that party, not knowing that they had paid us fo friendly a vifit, nor what their intent might be, fired a mufquet in the air, which fent them off with the greateſt precipitation.

Thus ended our firſt interview with the natives. Immediately after their final retreat, judging that their fears would prevent their remaining near enough to obferve what was paſſing, I ordered the two pigs, being a boar and fow, to be carried about a mile within the woods, at the head of the bay. I faw them left there, by the fide of a freſh-water brook. A young bull and a cow, and fome fheep and goats, were alfo, at firſt, intended to have been left by me, as an additional prefent to Van Diemen's Land. But I foon laid afide all thought of this, from a perfuafion that the natives, incapable of entering into my views of improving their country, would deſtroy them. If ever they ſhould meet with the pigs, I have no doubt this will be their fate. But as that race of animals foon becomes wild, and is fond of the thickeſt cover of the woods, there is great probability of their being preferved. An open place muſt have been chofen for the accommodation of the other cattle; and in fuch a fituation, they could not poſſibly have remained concealed many days.

Wednef. 29.

The morning of the 29th was uſhered in with a dead calm, which continued all day, and effectually prevented our failing. I therefore fent a party over to the Eaſt point of the bay to cut grafs; having been informed that fome of a fuperior quality grew there. Another party, to cut wood, was ordered to go to the ufual place, and I accompanied them myfelf. We had obferved feveral of the natives, this morning, fauntering along the ſhore, which aſſured us, that
though

though their consternation had made them leave us so abruptly the day before, they were convinced that we intended them no mischief, and were desirous of renewing the intercourse. It was natural that I should wish to be present on the occasion.

We had not been long landed, before about twenty of them, men and boys, joined us, without expressing the least sign of fear or distrust. There was one of this company conspicuously deformed; and who was not more distinguishable by the hump upon his back, than by the drollery of his gestures, and the seeming humour of his speeches; which he was very fond of exhibiting, as we supposed, for our entertainment. But, unfortunately, we could not understand him; the language spoken here being wholly unintelligible to us. It appeared to me, to be different from that spoken by the inhabitants of the more northern parts of this country, whom I met with in my first voyage; which is not extraordinary, since those we now saw, and those we then visited, differ in many other respects*. Nor did they seem to be

---

* The most striking difference seems to be with regard to the texture of the hair. The natives whom Captain Cook met with at Endeavour River in 1769, are said, by him, to have *naturally long and thick hair, though it be universally cropped short. In general it is frizzled, but sometimes it has a slight curl. We saw none that was not matted and filthy. Their beards were of the same colour with the hair, and busky and thick.* See Hawkesworth's Collection, Vol. iii. chap. 8. p. 632.

It may be necessary to mention here, on the authority of Captain King, that Captain Cook was very unwilling to allow that the hair of the natives now met with in Adventure Bay was *woolly*, fancying that his people, who first observed this, had been deceived, from its being clotted with grease and red ochre. But Captain King prevailed upon him afterward, to examine carefully the hair of the boys, which was generally, as well as that of the women, free from this dirt; and then he owned himself satisfied that it was *naturally woolly*. Perhaps we may suppose it possible, that he himself had been deceived when he was in Endeavour River, from this very circumstance; as he expressly says, that *they saw none that was not matted and filthy*.

such miserable wretches as the natives whom Dampier mentions to have seen on its western coast *.

Some of our present groupe wore, loose, round their necks, three or four folds of small cord, made of the fur of some animal; and others of them had a narrow slip of the kangooroo skin tied round their ancles. I gave to each of them a string of beads, and a medal; which I thought they received with some satisfaction. They seemed to set no value on iron, or on iron tools. They were even ignorant of the use of fish-hooks, if we might judge from their manner of looking at some of ours which we shewed to them.

We cannot, however, suppose it to be possible that a people who inhabit a sea-coast, and who seem to derive no part of their sustenance from the productions of the ground, should not be acquainted with some mode of catching fish, though we did not happen to see any of them thus employed; nor observe any canoe or vessel, in which they could go upon the water. Though they absolutely rejected the sort of fish that we offered to them, it was evident that shell-

---

* And yet Dampier's New Hollanders, on the Western coast, bear a striking resemblance to Captain Cook's at Van Diemen's Land, in many remarkable instances: 1st, As to their becoming familiar with the strangers.

2dly, As to their persons; being straight-bodied, and thin; their skin black; and black, short, curled hair, like the Negroes of Guinea; with wide mouths.

3dly, As to their wretched condition; having no houses, no garment, no canoes, no instrument to catch large fish; feeding on broiled muscles, cockles, and periwinckles; having no fruits of the earth; their weapons a straight pole, sharpened and hardened at the end, &c. &c.

The chief peculiarities of Dampier's *miserable wretches* are, 1st, Their eye-lids being always half closed, to keep the flies out, which were excessively troublesome there: and, 2dly, Their wanting the two fore-teeth of the upper jaw, and their having no beards. See *Dampier's Voyages*, Vol. i. p. 464, &c. There seems to be no reason for supposing that Dampier was mistaken in the above account of what he saw.

fish,

fish, at least, made a part of their food, from the many heaps of muscle-shells we saw in different parts near the shore, and about some deserted habitations near the head of the bay. These were little sheds or hovels built of sticks, and covered with bark. We could also perceive evident signs of their sometimes taking up their abode in the trunks of large trees, which had been hollowed out by fire, most probably for this very purpose. In or near all these habitations, and wherever there was a heap of shells, there remained the marks of fire; an indubitable proof that they do not eat their food raw.

After staying about an hour with the wooding party and the natives, as I could now be pretty confident that the latter were not likely to give the former any disturbance, I left them, and went over to the grass-cutters on the East point of the bay, and found that they had met with a fine patch. Having seen the boats loaded, I left that party, and returned on board to dinner; where, some time after, Lieutenant King arrived.

From him I learnt, that I had but just left the shore, when several women and children made their appearance, and were introduced to him by some of the men who attended them. He gave presents to all of them, of such trifles as he had about him. These females wore a *kangooroo* skin (in the same shape as it came from the animal) tied over the shoulders, and round the waist. But its only use seemed to be, to support their children when carried on their backs; for it did not cover those parts which most nations conceal; being, in all other respects, as naked as the men, and as black, and their bodies marked with scars in the same manner. But in this they differed from the men, that though their hair was of the same colour and texture, some of them had their heads completely shorn or shaved; in others this operation had been performed only on one side, while the rest of them had all the upper part of the head shorn close, leaving a circle of hair all round; somewhat like the tonsure of the Romish Ecclesiastics *. Many of the children had fine features, and were thought pretty; but of the persons of the women, especially those advanced in years, a less favourable report was made. However, some of the Gentlemen belonging to the Discovery, I was told, paid their addresses, and made liberal offers of presents, which were rejected with great disdain; whether from a sense of virtue, or the fear of displeasing their men, I shall not pretend to determine. That this gallantry was not very agreeable to the latter, is certain: for an elderly man, as soon as he observed it, ordered all the women and children to retire, which they obeyed, though some of them shewed a little reluctance.

This conduct of Europeans amongst Savages, to their women, is highly blameable; as it creates a jealousy in their men, that may be attended with consequences fatal to the success of the common enterprize, and to the whole body

---

* Captain Cook's account of the natives of Van Diemen's Land, in this Chapter, no doubt proves that they differ, in many respects, as he says, from the inhabitants of the more northerly parts of the East coast of New Holland, whom he met with in his first voyage. It seems very remarkable, however, that the only woman any of his people came close to, in Botany Bay, should have *her hair cropped short*; while the man who was with her, is said to have had *the hair of his head bushy, and his beard long and rough*. Hawkesworth's Collection, Vol. iii. p. 502. Could the natives of Van Diemen's Land be more accurately described, than by saying that the hair of the men's heads is *bushy, and their beards long and rough, and that the women's hair is cropped short?* So far North, therefore, as Botany Bay, the natives of the East coast of New Holland seem to resemble those of Van Diemen's Land, in this circumstance.

of

of adventurers, without advancing the private purpose of the individual, or enabling him to gain the object of his wishes. I believe it has been generally found amongst uncivilized people, that where the women are easy of access, the men are the first to offer them to strangers; and that, where this is not the case, neither the allurement of presents, nor the opportunity of privacy, will be likely to have the desired effect. This observation, I am sure, will hold good, throughout all the parts of the South Sea where I have been. Why then should men act so absurd a part, as to risk their own safety, and that of all their companions, in pursuit of a gratification which they have no probability of obtaining?

In the afternoon I went again to the grass-cutters, to forward their work. I found them then upon Penguin Island, where they had met with a plentiful crop of excellent grass. We laboured hard till sun-set, and then repaired on board, satisfied with the quantity we had collected, and which I judged sufficient to last till our arrival in New Zealand.

During our whole stay, we had either calms or light airs from the Eastward. Little or no time, therefore, was lost by my putting in at this place. For if I had kept the sea, we should not have been twenty leagues advanced farther on our voyage. And, short as our continuance was here, it has enabled me to add somewhat to the imperfect acquaintance that hath hitherto been acquired, with this part of the globe.

Van Diemen's Land has been twice visited before. It was so named by Tasman, who discovered it in November 1642. From that time it had escaped all further notice by European navigators, till Captain Furneaux touched at it in March

March 1773. I hardly need say, that it is the Southern point of New Holland, which, if it doth not deserve the name of a continent, is by far the largest island in the world.

The land is, for the most part, of a good height, diversified with hills and valleys, and every where of a greenish hue. It is well wooded; and, if one may judge from appearances, and from what we met with in Adventure Bay, is not ill supplied with water. We found plenty of it in three or four places in this bay. The best, or what is most convenient for ships that touch here, is a rivulet, which is one of several that fall into a pond, that lies behind the beach at the head of the bay. It there mixes with the sea-water; so that it must be taken up above this pond, which may be done without any great trouble. Fire-wood is to be got, with great ease, in several places.

The only wind to which this bay is exposed, is the North East. But as this wind blows from Maria's islands, it can bring no very great sea along with it; and therefore, upon the whole, this may be accounted a very safe road. The bottom is clean, good holding ground; and the depth of water from twelve, to five and four fathoms. But the annexed Chart will convey a better idea of every thing necessary to be known about Adventure Bay, than any description.

Captain Furneaux's sketch of Van Diemen's Land, published with the Narrative of my last Voyage*, appears to me to be without any material error, except with regard to Maria's Islands, which have a different situation from what is there represented. What my idea of them is, will be seen

* Vol. i. p. 115.

in the sketch of that coast here inserted; and I insert it, not as the result of a more faithful, but merely of a second examination. The longitude was determined by a great number of lunar observations, which we had before we made the land, while we were in sight of it, and after we had left it; and reduced to Adventure Bay, and the several principal points, by the time-keeper. The following Table will exhibit both the longitude and latitude at one view:

	Latitude South.	Longitude East.
Adventure Bay,	43° 21′ 20″	147° 29′ 0″
Tasman's Head,	43 33 0	147 28 0
South Cape,	43 42 0	146 56 0
South West Cape,	43 37 0	146 7 0
Swilly Isle,	43 55 0	147 6 0

Adventure Bay, { Variation of the compass 5° 15′ East.
{ Dip of the South End of the Needle 70° 15½″.

We had high-water on the 29th, being two days before the last quarter of the moon, at nine in the morning. The perpendicular rise then was eighteen inches; and there was no appearance of its having ever exceeded two feet and a half. These are all the memorials useful to navigation, which my short stay has enabled me to preserve, with respect to Van Diemen's Land.

Mr. Anderson, my Surgeon, with his usual diligence, spent the few days we remained in Adventure Bay, in examining the country. His account of its natural productions, with which he favoured me, will more than compensate for my silence about them: some of his remarks on the inhabitants will supply what I may have omitted or represented imperfectly; and his specimen of their language, however.

however short, will be thought worth attending to, by those who wish to collect materials for tracing the origin of nations. I shall only premise, that the tall straight forest trees, which Mr. Anderson describes in the following account, are of a different sort from those which are found in the more Northern parts of this coast. The wood is very long and close-grained; extremely tough; fit for spars, oars, and many other uses; and would, on occasion, make good masts (perhaps none better), if a method could be found to lighten it.

"At the bottom of Adventure Bay is a beautiful sandy beach, which seems to be wholly formed by the particles washed by the sea from a very fine white sand-stone, that in many places bounds the shore, and of which Fluted Cape, in the neighbourhood, from its appearance, seems to be composed. This beach is about two miles long, and is excellently adapted for hauling a seine, which both ships did repeatedly with success. Behind this, is a plain or flat, with a salt, or rather brackish lake (running in length parallel with the beach), out of which we caught, with angling rods, many whitish bream, and some small trout. The other parts of the country adjoining the bay are quite hilly; and both those and the flat are an entire forest of very tall trees, rendered almost impassable by shrubs, brakes of fern, and fallen trees; except on the sides of some of the hills, where the trees are but thin, and a coarse grass is the only interruption.

"To the Northward of the bay there is low land, stretching farther than the eye can reach, which is only covered with wood in certain spots; but we had no opportunity to examine in what respects it differed from the hilly country.

The soil on the flat land is either sandy, or consists of a yellowish mould, and, in some places, of a reddish clay. The same is found on the lower part of the hills; but farther up, especially where there are few trees, it is of a grey tough cast, to appearance very poor.

In the valleys between the hills, the water drains down from their sides; and at last, in some places, forms small brooks; such indeed as were sufficient to supply us with water, but by no means of that size we might expect in so extensive a country, especially as it is both hilly and well wooded. Upon the whole, it has many marks of being naturally a very dry country; and perhaps might (independent of its wood) be compared to Africa, about the Cape of Good Hope, though that lies ten degrees farther Northward, rather than to New Zealand, on its other side, in the same latitude, where we find every valley, however small, furnished with a considerable stream of water. The heat too appears to be great, as the thermometer stood at 64, 70, and once at 74. And it was remarked, that birds were seldom killed an hour or two, before they were almost covered with small maggots, which I would rather attribute merely to the heat; as we had not any reason to suppose there is a peculiar disposition in the climate to render substances soon putrid.

No mineral bodies, nor indeed stones of any other sort, but the white sand one already mentioned, were observed.

Amongst the vegetable productions, there is not one, that we could find, which afforded the smallest subsistence for man.

The forest trees are all of one sort, growing to a great height, and in general quite straight, branching but little,

1777.
January.

till towards the top. The bark is white, which makes them appear, at a distance, as if they had been peeled; it is also thick; and within it are sometimes collected, pieces of a reddish transparent gum or resin, which has an astringent taste. The leaves of this tree are long, narrow, and pointed; and it bears clusters of small white flowers, whose cups were, at this time, plentifully scattered about the ground, with another sort resembling them somewhat in shape, but much larger; which makes it probable that there are two *species* of this tree. The bark of the smaller branches, fruit, and leaves, have an agreeable pungent taste, and aromatic smell, not unlike peppermint; and in its nature, it has some affinity to the *myrtus* of botanists.

The most common tree, next to this, is a small one about ten feet high, branching pretty much, with narrow leaves, and a large, yellow, cylindrical flower, consisting only of a vast number of filaments; which, being shed, leave a fruit like a pine top. Both the above-mentioned trees are unknown in Europe.

The underwood consists chiefly of a shrub somewhat resembling a myrtle, and which seems to be the *leptospermum scoparium*, mentioned in Dr. Forster's *Char. Gen. Plant.*; and, in some places, of another, rather smaller, which is a new *species* of the *melaleuca* of Linnæus.

Of other plants, which are by no means numerous, there is a *species* of *gladiolus*, rush, bell-flower, samphire, a small sort of wood-sorrel, milk-wort, cudweed, and Job's tears; with a few others, peculiar to the place. There are several kinds of fern, as polypody, spleenwort, female fern, and some mosses; but the *species* are either common, or at least found in some other countries, especially New Zealand.

The

The only animal of the quadruped kind we got, was a sort of *opossum*, about twice the size of a large rat; and is, most probably, the male of that *species* found at Endeavour River, as mentioned in Hawkesworth's Collection of Voyages *. It is of a dusky colour above, tinged with a brown or rusty cast, and whitish below. About a third of the tail, towards its tip, is white, and bare underneath; by which it probably hangs on the branches of trees, as it climbs these, and lives on berries. Mr. Webber's drawing will give a better idea of it than any description. The *kangooroo*, another animal found farther Northward in New Holland, as described in the same Voyage †, without all doubt also inhabits here, as the natives we met with had some pieces of their skins; and we several times saw animals, though indistinctly, run from the thickets when we walked in the woods, which, from the size, could be no other. It should seem also, that they are in considerable numbers, from the dung we saw almost every where, and from the narrow tracks or paths they have made amongst the shrubbery.

There are several sorts of birds, but all so scarce and shy, that they are evidently harassed by the natives, who, perhaps, draw much of their subsistence from them. In the woods, the principal sorts are large brown hawks or eagles; crows, nearly the same as ours in England; yellowish paroquets; and large pigeons. There are also three or four small birds, one of which is of the thrush kind; and another small one, with a pretty long tail, has part of the head and neck of a most beautiful azure colour; from whence we named it *motacilla cyanea*. On the shore were several com-

* Vol. iii. p. 586.   † Ibid. p. 577.

mon and sea gulls; a few black oyster catchers, or sea-pies; and a pretty plover of a stone colour, with a black hood. About the pond or lake behind the beach, a few wild ducks were seen; and some shags used to perch upon the high leafless trees near the shore.

Some pretty large blackish snakes were seen in the woods; and we killed a large, hitherto unknown, lizard, fifteen inches long and six round, elegantly clouded with black and yellow; besides a small sort, of a brown gilded colour above, and rusty below.

The sea affords a much greater plenty, and at least as great a variety as the land. Of these the elephant fish, or *pejegallo*, mentioned in Frezier's Voyage *, are the most numerous; and though inferior to many other fish, were very palatable food. Several large rays, nurses, and small leather-jackets were caught; with some small white bream, which were firmer and better than those caught in the lake. We likewise got a few soles and flounders; two sorts of gurnards, one of them a new *species*; some small spotted mullet; and, very unexpectedly, the small fish with a silver band on its side, called *atherina hepsetus* by Hasselquist †.

But that next in number, and superior in goodness, to the elephant fish, was a sort none of us recollected to have seen before. It partakes of the nature both of a round and of a flat fish, having the eyes placed very near each other; the fore-part of the body much flattened or depressed, and the rest rounded. It is of a brownish sandy colour, with rusty spots on the upper part, and whitish below. From the

* Tom. ii. p. 211. 11mo. Planche XVII.   † *Iter Palæstinum*.

quantity

quantity of flime it was always covered with, it seems to live after the manner of flat fish, at the bottom.

Upon the rocks are plenty of muscles, and some other small shell-fish. There are also great numbers of sea-stars; some small limpets; and large quantities of sponge; one sort of which, that is thrown on shore by the sea, but not very common, has a most delicate texture; and another, is the *spongia dichotoma*.

Many pretty *Medusa's heads* were found upon the beach; and the stinking *laplysia* or sea-hare, which, as mentioned by some authors, has the property of taking off the hair by the acrimony of its juice; but this sort was deficient in this respect.

Insects, though not numerous, are here in considerable variety. Amongst them are grashoppers, butterflies, and several sorts of small moths, finely variegated. There are two sorts of dragon-flies, gad-flies, camel-flies; several sorts of spiders; and some *scorpions*; but the last are rather rare. The most troublesome, though not very numerous tribe of insects, are the musquitoes; and a large black ant, the pain of whose bite is almost intolerable, during the short time it lasts. The musquitoes, also, make up the deficiency of their number, by the severity of their venomous *proboscis*.

The inhabitants whom we met with here, had little of that fierce or wild appearance common to people in their situation; but, on the contrary, seemed mild and cheerful, without reserve or jealousy of strangers. This, however, may arise from their having little to lose or care for.

With.

1777.
January.

With respect to personal activity or genius, we can say but little of either. They do not seem to possess the first in any remarkable degree; and as for the last, they have, to appearance, less than even the half-animated inhabitants of Terra del Fuego, who have not invention sufficient to make clothing for defending themselves from the rigor of their climate, though furnished with the materials. The small stick, rudely pointed, which one of them carried in his hand, was the only thing we saw that required any mechanical exertion, if we except the fixing on the feet of some of them pieces of *kangooroo* skin, tied with thongs; though it could not be learnt whether these were in use as shoes, or only to defend some sore. It must be owned, however, they are masters of some contrivance, in the manner of cutting their arms and bodies in lines of different lengths and directions, which are raised considerably above the surface of the skin, so that it is difficult to guess the method they use in executing this embroidery of their persons. Their not expressing that surprize which one might have expected from their seeing men so much unlike themselves, and things, to which, we were well assured, they had been hitherto utter strangers; their indifference for our presents; and their general inattention; were sufficient proofs of their not possessing any acuteness of understanding.

Their colour is a dull black, and not quite so deep as that of the African Negroes. It should seem also, that they sometimes heightened their black colour, by smutting their bodies; as a mark was left behind on any clean substance, such as white paper, when they handled it. Their hair, however, is perfectly woolly, and it is clotted or divided into small parcels, like that of the Hottentots, with the use of of some sort of greafe, mixed with a red paint or ochre, which they smear in great abundance over their heads. This practice, as some might imagine, has not the effect of changing their hair into the frizzling texture we obferved; for, on examining the head of a boy, which appeared never to have been smeared, I found the hair to be of the same kind. Their noses, though not flat, are broad and full. The lower part of the face projects a good deal, as is the cafe of moft Indians I have feen; fo that a line let fall from the forehead, would cut off a much larger portion than it would in Europeans. Their eyes are of a middling fize, with the white lefs clear than in us; and though not remarkably quick or piercing, fuch as give a frank cheerful caft to the whole countenance. Their teeth are broad, but not equal, nor well fet; and, either from nature or from dirt, not of fo true a white as is ufual among people of a black colour. Their mouths are rather wide; but this appearance feems heightened by wearing their beards long, and clotted with paint, in the fame manner as the hair on their heads. In other refpects, they are well-proportioned; though the belly feems rather projecting. This may be owing to the want of compreffion there, which few nations do not ufe, more or lefs. The pofture of which they feem fondeft, is to ftand with one fide forward, or the upper part of the body gently reclined, and one hand grafping (acrofs the back) the oppofite arm, which hangs down by the projecting fide.

What the ancient Poets tell us of *Fauns* and *Satyrs* living in hollow trees, is here realized. Some wretched conftructions of flicks, covered with bark, which do not even deferve the name of huts, were indeed found near the fhore in the bay; but thefe feemed only to have been erected for temporary

porary purposes; and many of their largest trees were converted into more comfortable habitations. These had their trunks hollowed out by fire, to the height of six or seven feet; and that they take up their abode in them sometimes, was evident from the hearths, made of clay, to contain the fire in the middle, leaving room for four or five persons to sit round it *. At the same time, these places of shelter are durable; for they take care to leave one side of the tree found, which is sufficient to keep it growing as luxuriantly as those which remain untouched.

The inhabitants of this place are, doubtless, from the same stock with those of the Northern parts of New Holland. Though some of the circumstances mentioned by Dampier, relative to those he met with on the Western coast of this country, such as their defective sight, and want of fore-teeth, are not found here; and though Hawkesworth's account of those met with by Captain Cook on the East side, shews also that they differ in many respects; yet still, upon the whole, I am persuaded that distance of place, entire separation, diversity of climate, and length of time, all concurring to operate, will account for greater differences, both as to their persons and as to their customs, than really exist between our Van Diemen's Land natives, and those described by Dampier, and in Captain Cook's first voyage. This is certain, that the figure of one of those seen in Endeavour River, and represented in Sidney Parkinson's Journal of that voyage, very much resembles our visiters in Adventure Bay. That there is not the like resemblance in their language, is a circumstance that need not create any difficulty. For though

* Tasman, when in the bay of Frederick Henry, adjoining to Adventure Bay, found two trees, one of which was two fathoms, and the other two fathoms and a half in girth, and sixty or sixty-five feet high, from the root to the branches. See his *Voyage*, in *Harris's Collection*, *Campbell's Edition*, Vol. i. p. 326.

the

the agreement of the languages of people living distant from
each other, may be assumed as a strong argument for their
having sprung from one common source; disagreement of
language is by no means a proof of the contrary*.

However, we must have a far more intimate acquaintance
with the languages spoken here and in the more Northern
parts of New Holland, before we can be warranted to pronounce that they are totally different. Nay, we have good
grounds for the opposite opinion; for we found that the
animal called *kanguroo* at Endeavour river, was known under the same name here; and I need not observe, that it is
scarcely possible to suppose that this was not transmitted
from one another, but accidentally adopted by two nations,
differing in language and extraction. Besides, as it seems
very improbable that the Van Diemen's Land inhabitants
should have ever lost the use of canoes or sailing vessels, if
they had been originally conveyed thither by sea, we must
necessarily admit that they, as well as the *kangooroo* itself,
have been stragglers by land from the more Northern parts

* The ingenious Author of *Recherches sur les Américains*, illustrates the grounds of
this assertion in the following satisfactory manner: " C'est quelque chose de surpre-
" nant, que la foule des idiomes, tous variés entr'eux, que parlent les naturels de
" l'Amérique Septentrionale. Qu'on réduise ces idiomes à des racines, qu'on les sim-
" plifie, qu'on en sépare les dialectes & les jargons derivés, il en résulte toujours cinq
" ou six langues-meres, respectivement incomprehensibles. On a observé la même
" singularité dans la Siberie & la Tartarie, où le nombre des idiomes, & des dialectes,
" est également multiplié; & rien n'est plus commun, que d'y voir deux hordes voi-
" sines qui ne se comprennent point. On retrouve cette même multiplicité de jar-
" gons dans toutes les Provinces de l'Amérique Meridionale." [He might also have
included Africa.] " Il y a beaucoup d'apparence que la vie sauvage, en diffusant les
" hommes par petites troupes isolées dans des bois épais, occasione necessairement cette grande
" diversité des langues, dont le nombre diminue à mesure que la société, en rassemblant
" les barbares vagabonds, en forme un corps de nation. Alors l'idiome le plus
" riche, ou le moins pauvre en mots, devient dominant, & absorbe les autres."
Tom. i. p. 159, 160.

of the country. And if there be any force in this observation, while it traces the origin of the people, it will, at the same time, serve to fix another point, if Captain Cook and Captain Fourneaux have not already decided it, that New Holland is no where totally divided by the sea into islands, as some have imagined [*].

As the New Hollanders seem all to be of the same extraction, so neither do I think there is any thing peculiar in them. On the contrary, they much resemble many of the inhabitants whom I have seen at the islands Tanna and Manicola. Nay, there is even some foundation for hazarding a supposition, that they may have originally come from the same place with all the inhabitants of the South Sea. For, of only about ten words which we could get from them, that which expresses *cold*, differs little from that of New Zealand and Otaheite; the first being *Mallareede*, the second *Makka'reede*, and the third *Ma'reede*. The rest of our very scanty Van Diemen's Land Vocabulary is as follows:

Quadne,	*A woman.*
Eve'rai,	*The eye.*
Muidje,	*The nose.*
Ka'my,	*The teeth, mouth, or tongue.*
Lae'renne,	*A small bird, a native of the woods here.*
Koy'gee,	*The ear.*
No'onga,	*Elevated scars on the body.*
Teegera,	*To eat.*
Toga'rago,	*I must be gone*, or, *I will go.*

Their pronunciation is not disagreeable, but rather quick; though not more so than is that of other nations of the

[*] Dampier seems to be of this opinion. Vol. iii. p. 104. 125.

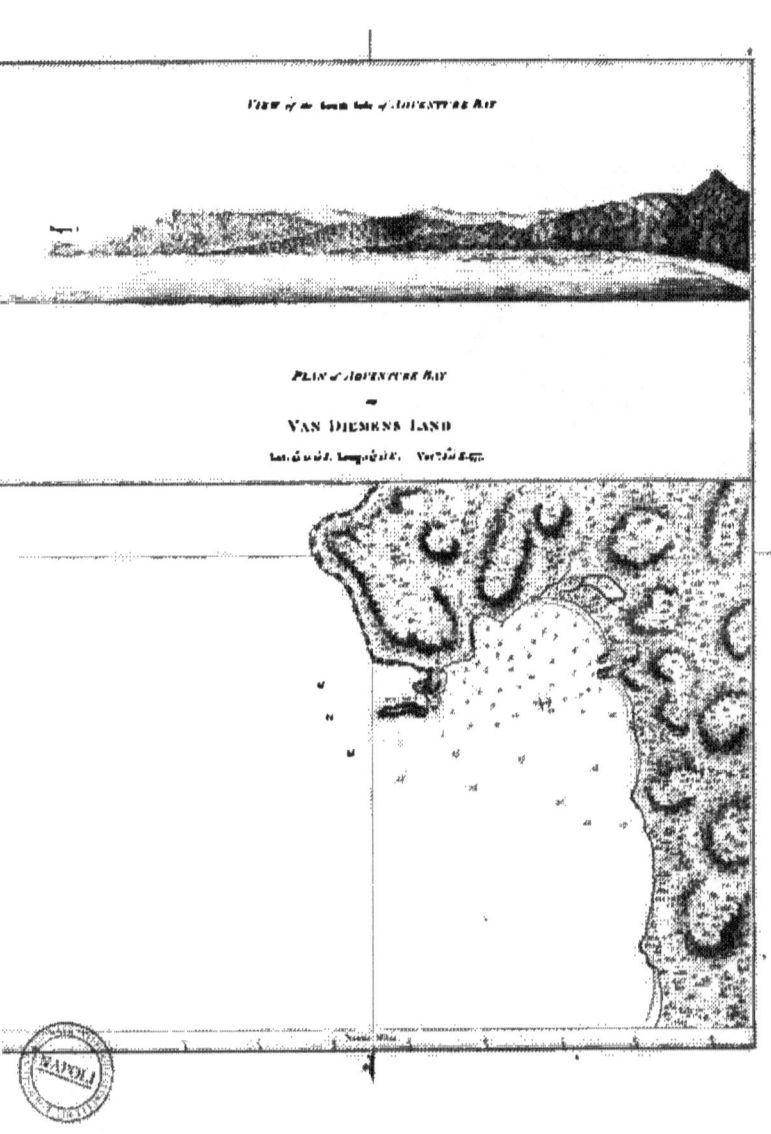

THE PACIFIC OCEAN.

1777.
January.

South Sea; and, if we may depend upon the affinity of languages as a clue to guide us in discovering the origin of nations, I have no doubt but we shall find, on a diligent inquiry, and when opportunities offer to collect accurately a sufficient number of these words, and to compare them, that all the people from New Holland, Eastward to Easter Island, have been derived from the same common root*."

* We find Mr. Anderson's notions on this subject conformable to those of Mr. Marsden, who has remarked, "that one general language prevailed (however mutilated and changed in the course of time) throughout all this portion of the world, from Madagascar to the most distant discoveries Eastward; of which the Malay is a dialect, much corrupted or refined by a mixture of other tongues. This very extensive similarity of language indicates a common origin of the inhabitants; but the circumstances and progress of their separation are wrapped in the darkest veil of obscurity.". *History of Sumatra*, p. 35.

See also his very curious paper, read before the Society of Antiquaries, and published in their *Archæologia*, Vol. vi. p. 155; where his sentiments on this subject are explained more at large, and illustrated by two Tables of corresponding Words.

CHAP.

CHAP. VII.

The Passage from Van Diemen's Land to New Zealand.—Employments in Queen Charlotte's Sound.—Transactions with the Natives there.—Intelligence about the Massacre of the Adventure's Boat's Crew.—Account of the Chief who headed the Party on that Occasion.—Of the two young Men who embark to attend Omai.—Various Remarks on the Inhabitants.—Astronomical and Nautical Observations.

1777.
January.
Thursday 30.

AT eight o'clock in the morning of the 30th of January, a light breeze springing up at West, we weighed anchor, and put to sea from Adventure Bay. Soon after, the wind veered to the Southward, and increased to a perfect storm. Its fury abated in the evening, when it veered to the East and North East.

This gale was indicated by the barometer, for the wind no sooner began to blow, than the mercury in the tube began to fall. Another remarkable thing attended the coming on of this wind, which was very faint at first. It brought with it a degree of heat that was almost intolerable. The mercury in the thermometer rose, as it were instantaneously, from about 70° to near 90°. This heat was of so short a continuance, that it seemed to be wafted away before the breeze that brought it; so that some on board did not perceive it.

We

We pursued our course to the Eastward, without meeting with any thing worthy of note, till the night between the 6th and 7th of February, when a marine belonging to the Discovery fell over-board, and was never seen afterward. This was the second misfortune of the kind that had happened to Captain Clerke since he left England.

1777.
February.

Friday 7.

On the 10th, at four in the afternoon, we discovered the land of New Zealand. The part we saw proved to be Rock's Point, and bore South East by South, about eight or nine leagues distant. During this run from Van Diemen's Land, the wind, for the first four or five days, was at North East, North, and North North West, and blew, for the most part, a gentle breeze. It afterward veered to South East, where it remained twenty-four hours. It then came to West and South West; in which points it continued, with very little deviation, till we reached New Zealand.

Monday 10.

After making the land, I steered for Cape Farewell, which at day-break, the next morning, bore South by West, distant about four leagues. At eight o'clock, it bore South West by South, about five leagues distant; and, in this situation, we had forty-five fathoms water over a sandy bottom. In rounding the Cape we had fifty fathoms, and the same sort of bottom.

Tuesday 11.

I now steered for Stephens's Island, which we came up with at nine o'clock at night; and at ten, next morning, anchored in our old station, in Queen Charlotte's Sound*. Unwilling to lose any time, our operations commenced that very afternoon, when we landed a number of empty water-casks, and began to clear a place where we might set up

Wednes. 12.

* See the Chart of Queen Charlotte's Sound, in Hawkesworth's Collection, Vol. ii. p. 385.

S

the

the two observatories, and tents for the reception of a guard, and of such of our people whose business might make it necessary for them to remain on shore.

We had not been long at anchor before several canoes, filled with natives, came along-side of the ships; but very few of them would venture on board; which appeared the more extraordinary, as I was well known to them all. There was one man in particular amongst them, whom I had treated with remarkable kindness, during the whole of my stay when I was last here. Yet now, neither professions of friendship, nor presents, could prevail upon him to come into the ship. This shyness was to be accounted for only upon this supposition, that they were apprehensive we had revisited their country, in order to revenge the death of Captain Furneaux's people. Seeing Omai on board my ship now, whom they must have remembered to have seen on board the Adventure when the melancholy affair happened, and whose first conversation with them, as they approached, generally turned on that subject, they must be well assured that I was no longer a stranger to it. I thought it necessary, therefore, to use every endeavour to assure them of the continuance of my friendship, and that I should not disturb them on that account. I do not know whether this had any weight with them; but certain it is, that they very soon laid aside all manner of restraint and distrust.

Thursday 13. On the 13th we set up two tents, one from each ship, on the same spot where we had pitched them formerly. The observatories were at the same time erected; and Messrs. King and Bayly began their operations immediately, to find the rate of the time-keeper, and to make other observations. The remainder of the empty water-casks were also sent on shore,

shore, with the cooper to trim, and a sufficient number of sailors to fill them. Two men were appointed to brew spruce beer; and the carpenter and his crew were ordered to cut wood. A boat, with a party of men, under the direction of one of the mates, was sent to collect grafs for our cattle; and the people that remained on board were employed in refitting the ship, and arranging the provisions. In this manner, we were all profitably busied during our stay. For the protection of the party on shore, I appointed a guard of ten marines, and ordered arms for all the workmen; and Mr. King, and two or three petty officers, constantly remained with them. A boat was never sent to any considerable distance from the ships without being armed, and under the direction of such officers as I could depend upon, and who were well acquainted with the natives. During my former visits to this country, I had never taken some of these precautions; nor were they, I firmly believe, more necessary now than they had been formerly. But after the tragical fate of the Adventure's boat's crew in this sound, and of Captain Marion du Fresne, and of some of his people, in the Bay of Islands[*], it was impossible totally to divest ourselves of all apprehension of experiencing a similar calamity.

If the natives entertained any suspicion of our revenging these acts of barbarity, they very soon laid it aside. For, during the course of this day, a great number of families came from different parts of the coast, and took up their residence close to us; so that there was not a spot in the cove where a hut could be put up, that was not occupied by them, except the place where we had fixed our little encampment.

[*] In 1773.

campment. This they left us in quiet poſſeſſion of; but they came and took away the ruins of ſome old huts that were there, as materials for their new erections.

It is curious to obſerve with what facility they build theſe occaſional places of abode. I have ſeen above twenty of them erected on a ſpot of ground, that, not an hour before, was covered with ſhrubs and plants. They generally bring ſome part of the materials with them; the reſt they find upon the premiſes. I was preſent when a number of people landed, and built one of theſe villages. The moment the canoes reached the ſhore, the men leaped out, and at once took poſſeſſion of a piece of ground, by tearing up the plants and ſhrubs, or ſticking up ſome part of the framing of a hut. They then returned to their canoes, and ſecured their weapons, by ſetting them up againſt a tree, or placing them in ſuch a poſition, that they could be laid hold of in an inſtant. I took particular notice that no one neglected this precaution. While the men were employed in raiſing the huts, the women were not idle. Some were ſtationed to take care of the canoes; others to ſecure the proviſions, and the few utenſils in their poſſeſſion; and the reſt went to gather dry ſticks, that a fire might be prepared for dreſſing their victuals. As to the children, I kept them, as alſo ſome of the more aged, ſufficiently occupied in ſcrambling for beads, till I had emptied my pockets, and then I left them.

Theſe temporary habitations are abundantly ſufficient to afford ſhelter from the wind and rain, which is the only purpoſe they are meant to anſwer. I obſerved that, generally, if not always, the ſame tribe or family, though it were ever ſo large, aſſociated and built together; ſo that we frequently

quently saw a village, as well as their larger towns, divided into different districts, by low pallisades, or some similar mode of separation.

The advantage we received from the natives coming to live with us, was not inconsiderable. For, every day, when the weather would permit, some of them went out to catch fish; and we generally got, by exchanges, a good share of the produce of their labours. This supply, and what our own nets and lines afforded us, was so ample, that we seldom were in want of fish. Nor was there any deficiency of other refreshments. Celery, scurvy-grass, and portable soup were boiled with the pease and wheat, for both ships companies, every day during our whole stay; and they had spruce-beer for their drink. So that, if any of our people had contracted the seeds of the scurvy, such a regimen soon removed them. But the truth is, when we arrived here, there were only two invalids (and these on board the Resolution) upon the sick lists in both ships.

Besides the natives who took up their abode close to us, we were occasionally visited by others of them, whose residence was not far off; and by some who lived more remote. Their articles of commerce were, curiosities, fish, and women. The two first always came to a good market; which the latter did not. The seamen had taken a kind of dislike to these people, and were either unwilling, or afraid, to associate with them; which produced this good effect, that I knew no instance of a man's quitting his station, to go to their habitations.

A connection with women I allow, because I cannot prevent it; but never encourage, because I always dread its consequences. I know, indeed, that many men are of opinion, that such an intercourse is one of our greatest securities amongst savages; and perhaps they who, either from necessity or choice, are to remain and settle with them, may find it so. But with travellers and transient visiters, such as we were, it is generally otherwise; and, in our situation, a connection with their women betrays more men than it saves. What else can be reasonably expected, since all their views are selfish, without the least mixture of regard or attachment? My own experience, at least, which hath been pretty extensive, hath not pointed out to me one instance to the contrary.

Amongst our occasional visiters, was a chief named Kahoora, who, as I was informed, headed the party that cut off Captain Furneaux's people, and himself killed Mr. Rowe, the officer who commanded. To judge of the character of Kahoora, by what I heard from many of his countrymen, he seemed to be more feared than beloved amongst them. Not satisfied with telling me that he was a very bad man, some of them even importuned me to kill him: and, I believe, they were not a little surprised that I did not listen to them; for, according to their ideas of equity, this ought to have been done. But if I had followed the advice of all our pretended friends, I might have extirpated the whole race; for the people of each hamlet or village, by turns, applied to me to destroy the other. One would have almost thought it impossible, that so striking a proof of the divided state in which this miserable people live, could have been assigned. And yet I was sure that I did not misconceive the meaning of those who made these strange applications to me; for Omai, whose language was a dialect of their own, and perfectly understood all that they said, was our interpreter.

On the 15th, I made an excursion in my boat to look for grass, and visited the Hippah, or fortified village at the South West point of Motuara, and the places where our gardens had been planted on that island. There were no people at the former; but the houses and pallisades had been rebuilt, and were now in a state of good repair; and there were other evident marks of its having been inhabited not long before. It would be unnecessary, at present, to give a particular account of this Hippah, sufficient notice having been taken of it in the Account of my first Voyage, to which I refer [*]; and to the annexed drawing, which represents part of the inside of the village, and will convey a better idea of it, than any written description.

When the Adventure arrived first at Queen Charlotte's Sound, in 1773 [†], Mr. Bayly fixed upon this place for making his observations; and he, and the people with him, at their leisure hours, planted several spots with English garden seeds. Not the least vestige of these now remained. It is probable that they had been all rooted out to make room for buildings, when the village was reinhabited: for, at all the other gardens then planted by Captain Furneaux, although now wholly over-run with the weeds of the country, we found cabbages, onions, leeks, purslain, radishes, mustard, &c. and a few potatoes. These potatoes, which were first brought from the Cape of Good Hope, had been greatly improved by change of soil; and, with proper cultivation, would be superior to those produced in most other countries. Though the New Zealanders are fond of this root, it was evident that they had not taken the trouble to plant a single one (much less any other of the articles which we had in-

[*] Hawkesworth's Collection, Vol. ii. p. 395, &c.
[†] Cook's Voyage, Vol. i. p. 120.

troduced);

1777.
February.

troduced); and if it were not for the difficulty of clearing ground where potatoes had been once planted, there would not have been any now remaining.

Sunday 16.

On the 16th, at day-break, I set out with a party of men, in five boats, to collect food for our cattle. Captain Clerke, and several of the officers, Omai, and two of the natives, accompanied me. We proceeded about three leagues up the sound, and then landed on the East side, at a place where I had formerly been. Here we cut as much grass as loaded the two launches.

As we returned down the sound, we visited Grass Cove, the memorable scene of the Massacre of Captain Furneaux's people. Here I met with my old friend Pedro, who was almost continually with me the last time I was in this sound, and is mentioned in my History of that Voyage*. He, and another of his countrymen, received us on the beach, armed with the pa-too and spear. Whether this form of reception was a mark of their courtesy or of their fear, I cannot say; but I thought they betrayed manifest signs of the latter. However, if they had any apprehensions, a few presents soon removed them, and brought down to the beach two or three more of the family; but the greatest part of them remained out of sight.

Whilst we were at this place, our curiosity prompted us to inquire into the circumstances attending the melancholy fate of our countrymen; and Omai was made use of as our interpreter for this purpose. Pedro, and the rest of the natives present, answered all the questions that were put to them on the subject, without reserve, and like men who

* Captain Cook's Voyage, Vol. ii. p. 158, 159.

are

are under no dread of punishment for a crime of which they are not guilty. For we already knew that none of them had been concerned in the unhappy transaction. They told us, that while our people were sitting at dinner, surrounded by several of the natives, some of the latter stole, or snatched from them, some bread and fish, for which they were beat. This being resented, a quarrel ensued, and two New Zealanders were shot dead, by the only two musquets that were fired. For before our people had time to discharge a third, or to load again those that had been fired, the natives rushed in upon them, overpowered them with their numbers, and put them all to death. Pedro and his companions, besides relating the history of the massacre, made us acquainted with the very spot that was the scene of it. It is at the corner of the cove on the right-hand. They pointed to the place of the sun, to mark to us at what hour of the day it happened; and, according to this, it must have been late in the afternoon. They also shewed us the place where the boat lay; and it appeared to be about two hundred yards distant from that where the crew were seated. One of their number, a black servant of Captain Furneaux, was left in the boat to take care of her.

We were afterward told that this black was the cause of the quarrel, which was said to have happened thus: One of the natives stealing something out of the boat, the Negro gave him a severe blow with a stick. The cries of the fellow being heard by his countrymen at a distance, they imagined he was killed, and immediately began the attack on our people; who, before they had time to reach the boat, or to arm themselves against the unexpected impending danger, fell a sacrifice to the fury of their savage assailants.

The

1777.
February.

The first of these accounts, was confirmed by the testimony of many of the natives, whom we conversed with, at different times, and who, I think, could have no interest in deceiving us. The second manner of relating the transaction, rests upon the authority of the young New Zealander, who chose to abandon his country and go away with us, and who, consequently, could have no possible view in disguising the truth. All agreeing that the quarrel happened when the boat's crew were sitting at their meal, it is highly probable that both the accounts are true, as they perfectly coincide. For we may very naturally suppose, that while some of the natives were stealing from the man who had been left in the boat, others of them might take the same liberties with the property of our people who were on shore.

Be this as it will, all agree, that the quarrel first took its rise from some thefts, in the commission of which the natives were detected. All agree, also, that there was no premeditated plan of bloodshed, and that, if these thefts had not been, unfortunately, too hastily resented, no mischief would have happened. For Kahoora's greatest enemies, those who solicited his destruction most earnestly, at the same time confessed that he had no intention to quarrel, much less to kill, till the fray had actually commenced. It also appears that the unhappy victims were under no sort of apprehension of their fate; otherwise they never would have ventured to sit down to a repast at so considerable a distance from their boat, amongst people who were the next moment to be their murderers. What became of the boat I never could learn. Some said she was pulled to pieces and burnt; others told us that she was carried, they knew not whither, by a party of strangers.

We

We stayed here till the evening, when, having loaded the rest of the boats with grafs, celery, scurvy-grafs, &c. we embarked to return to the ships. We had prevailed upon Pedro to launch his canoe, and accompany us; but we had scarcely put off from the shore, when the wind began to blow very hard at North West, which obliged him to put back. We proceeded ourselves, but it was with a good deal of difficulty that we could reach the ships; where some of the boats did not arrive till one o'clock the next morning; and it was fortunate that they got on board then, for it afterward blew a perfect storm, with abundance of rain, so that no manner of work could go forward that day. In the evening the gale ceased, and the wind having veered to the East, brought with it fair weather.

1777.
February.

Monday 17.

The next day we resumed our works; the natives ventured out to catch fish; and Pedro, with all his family, came and took up his abode near us. This Chief's proper name is Matahouah; the other being given him by some of my people during my last Voyage, which I did not know till now. He was, however, equally well known amongst his countrymen by both names.

Tuesday 18.

On the 20th, in the forenoon, we had another storm from the North West. Though this was not of so long continuance as the former, the gusts of wind from the hills were far more violent, insomuch that we were obliged to strike the yards and top-masts to the very utmost; and, even with all this precaution, it was with difficulty that we rode it out. These storms are very frequent here, and sometimes violent and troublesome. The neighbouring mountains, which at these times are always loaded with vapours, not only increase the force of the wind, but alter its direction in

Thursday 20.

Vol. I.   S   such

1777.
February.

such a manner, that no two blasts follow each other from the same quarter; and the nearer the shore, the more their effects are felt.

The next day we were visited by a tribe or family, consisting of about thirty persons, men, women, and children, who came from the upper part of the Sound. I had never seen them before. The name of their Chief was Tomatongeauooranuc; a man of about forty-five years of age, with a cheerful open countenance. And, indeed, the rest of his tribe were, in general, the handsomest of the New Zealand race I had ever met with.

By this time more than two-thirds of the inhabitants of the Sound had settled themselves about us. Great numbers of them daily frequented the ships, and the encampment on shore: but the latter became, by far, the most favourite place of resort, while our people there were melting some seal blubber. No Greenlander was ever fonder of train-oil, than our friends here seemed to be. They relished the very skimmings of the kettle, and dregs of the casks; but a little of the pure stinking oil was a delicious feast, so eagerly desired, that I suppose it is seldom enjoyed.

Sunday 23.
Monday 24.

Having got on board as much hay and grass as we judged sufficient to serve the cattle till our arrival at Otaheite, and having completed the wood and water of both ships, on the 23d we struck our tents, and carried every thing off from the shore; and next morning we weighed anchor, and stood out of the Cove. But the wind not being very fair, and finding that the tide of ebb would be spent before we could get out of the Sound, we cast anchor again a little without the island Motuara, to wait for a more favourable opportunity of putting into the strait.

While

While we were unmooring and getting under fail, Tomatongeauooranuc, Matahouah, and many more of the natives, came to take their leave of us, or rather to obtain, if they could, some additional presents from us before we left them. These two Chiefs became suitors to me for some goats and hogs. Accordingly, I gave to Matahouah two goats, a male and female with kid; and to Tomatongeauooranuc two pigs, a boar and a sow. They made me a promise not to kill them; though I must own I put no great faith in this. The animals, which Captain Furneaux sent on shore here, and which soon after fell into the hands of the natives, I was now told were all dead; but I could get no intelligence about the fate of those I had left in West Bay, and in Cannibal Cove, when I was here in the course of my last Voyage. However, all the natives, whom I conversed with, agreed, that poultry are now to be met with wild in the woods behind Ship Cove; and I was afterward informed, by the two youths who went away with us, that Tiratou, a popular Chief amongst them, had a great many cocks and hens in his separate possession, and one of the sows.

On my present arrival at this place, I fully intended to have left not only goats and hogs, but sheep, and a young bull, with two heifers, if I could have found either a Chief powerful enough to protect and keep them, or a place where there might be a probability of their being concealed from those who would ignorantly attempt to destroy them. But neither the one nor the other presented itself to me. Tiratou was now absent; and Tringoboohee, whom I had met with during my last Voyage [*], and who seemed to be a person of much consequence at that time, had been killed five

[*] See Cook's Voyage, Vol. ii. p. 157.

months ago, with about seventy persons of his tribe; and I could not learn that there now remained in our neighbourhood any tribe, whose numbers could secure to them a superiority of power over the rest of their countrymen. To have given the animals to any of the natives who possessed no such power, would not have answered the intention. For in a country like this, where no man's property is secure, they would soon have fallen a prey to different parties, and been either separated or killed; but most likely both. This was so evident, from what we had observed since our arrival, that I had resolved to leave no kind of animal, till Matahouah and the other Chief solicited me for the hogs and goats. As I could spare them, I let them go, to take their chance. I have, at different times, left in New Zealand, not less than ten or a dozen hogs, besides those put on shore by Captain Furneaux. It will be a little extraordinary, therefore, if this race should not increase and be preserved here, either in a wild or in a domestic state, or in both.

We had not been long at anchor near Motuara, before three or four canoes, filled with natives, came off to us from the South East side of the Sound; and a brisk trade was carried on with them for the curiosities of this place. In one of these canoes was Kahoora, whom I have already mentioned as the leader of the party who cut off the crew of the Adventure's boat. This was the third time he had visited us, without betraying the smallest appearance of fear. I was ashore when he now arrived, but had got on board just as he was going away. Omai, who had returned with me, presently pointed him out, and solicited me to shoot him. Not satisfied with this, he addressed himself to Kahoora,

threatening

threatening to be his executioner, if ever he presumed to visit us again.

The New Zealander paid so little regard to these threats, that he returned, the next morning, with his whole family, men, women, and children, to the number of twenty and upwards. Omai was the first who acquainted me with his being along-side the ship, and desired to know if he should ask him to come on board. I told him he might; and accordingly he introduced the Chief into the cabin, saying, " There is Kahoora; kill him!" But, as if he had forgot his former threats, or were afraid that I should call upon him to perform them, he immediately retired. In a short time, however, he returned; and seeing the Chief unhurt, he expostulated with me very earnestly, saying, " Why do " you not kill him! You tell me, if a man kills another in " England, that he is hanged for it. This man has killed " ten, and yet you will not kill him; though many of his " countrymen desire it, and it would be very good." Omai's arguments, though specious enough, having no weight with me, I desired him to ask the Chief, why he had killed Captain Furneaux's people? At this question, Kahoora folded his arms, hung down his head, and looked like one caught in a trap: And, I firmly believe, he expected instant death. But no sooner was he assured of his safety, than he became cheerful. He did not, however, seem willing to give me an answer to the question that had been put to him, till I had, again and again, repeated my promise that he should not be hurt. Then he ventured to tell us, That one of his countrymen having brought a stone hatchet to barter, the man, to whom it was offered, took it, and would neither return it, nor give any thing for it; on which the owner of it snatched up the bread as an equivalent; and then the quarrel began.

The remainder of Kahoora's account of this unhappy affair, differed very little from what we had before learnt, from the rest of his countrymen. He mentioned the narrow escape he had, during the fray; a musquet being levelled at him, which he avoided by skulking behind the boat; and another man, who stood close to him, was shot dead. As soon as the musquet was discharged, he instantly seized the opportunity to attack Mr. Rowe, who commanded the party, and who defended himself with his hanger (with which he wounded Kahoora in the arm), till he was overpowered by numbers.

Mr. Burney, who was sent by Captain Furneaux the next day *, with an armed party, to look for his missing people, upon discovering the horrid proofs of their shocking fate, had fired several vollies amongst the crowds of natives who still remained assembled on the spot, and were, probably, partaking of the detestable banquet. It was natural to suppose that he had not fired in vain; and that, therefore, some of the murderers and devourers of our unhappy countrymen had suffered under our just resentment. Upon inquiry, however, into this matter, not only from Kahoora, but from others who had opportunities of knowing, it appeared that our supposition was groundless, and that not one of the shot fired by Mr. Burney's people had taken effect, so as to kill, or even to hurt, a single person.

It was evident, that most of the natives we had met with since our arrival, as they knew I was fully acquainted with

* See his Narrative. Cook's Voyage, Vol. II. p. 255-259.

the

the history of the massacre, expected I should avenge it with the death of Kahoora. And many of them seemed not only to wish it, but expressed their surprize at my forbearance. As he could not be ignorant of this, it was a matter of wonder to me, that he put himself so often in my power. When he visited us while the ships lay in the Cove, confiding in the number of his friends that accompanied him, he might think himself safe. But his two last visits had been made under such circumstances, that he could no longer rely upon this. We were then at anchor in the entrance of the Sound, and at some distance from any shore; so that he could not have any assistance from thence, nor flatter himself he could have the means of making his escape, had I determined to detain him. And yet, after his first fears, on being interrogated, were over, he was so far from entertaining any uneasy sensations, that, on seeing a portrait of one of his countrymen hanging up in the cabin, he desired to have his own portrait drawn; and sat till Mr. Webber had finished it, without marking the least impatience. I must confess, I admired his courage, and was not a little pleased to observe the extent of the confidence he put in me. For he placed his whole safety in the declarations I had uniformly made to those who solicited his death, That I had always been a friend to them all, and would continue so, unless they gave me cause to act otherwise: that as to their inhuman treatment of our people, I should think no more of it, the transaction having happened long ago, and when I was not present; but that, if ever they made a second attempt of that kind, they might rest assured of feeling the weight of my resentment.

For some time before we arrived at New Zealand, Omai had expressed a desire to take one of the natives with him to

his

his own country. We had not been there many days, before he had an opportunity of being gratified in this; for a youth about seventeen or eighteen years of age, named Taweiharooa, offered to accompany him; and took up his residence on board. I paid little attention to this at first, imagining that he would leave us when we were about to depart, and after he had got what he could from Omai. At length, finding that he was fixed in his resolution to go with us, and having learnt that he was the only son of a deceased Chief, and that his mother, still living, was a woman much respected here, I was apprehensive that Omai had deceived him and his friends, by giving them hopes and assurances of his being sent back. I therefore caused it to be made known to them all, that if the young man went away with us, he would never return. But this declaration seemed to make no sort of impression. The afternoon before we left the Cove, Tiratoutou, his mother, came on board, to receive her last present from Omai. The same evening, she and Taweiharooa parted, with all the marks of tender affection that might be expected between a parent and a child, who were never to meet again. But she said she would cry no more; and, sure enough, she kept her word. For when she returned the next morning, to take her last farewell of him, all the time she was on board she remained quite cheerful, and went away wholly unconcerned.

That Taweiharooa might be sent away in a manner becoming his birth, another youth was to have gone with him as his servant; and, with this view, as we supposed, he remained on board till we were about to sail, when his friends took him ashore. However, his place was supplied, next morning, by another, a boy of about nine or ten years of age,

age, named Kokoa. He was presented to me by his own father, who, I believe, would have parted with his dog with far less indifference. The very little clothing the boy had, he stript him of, and left him as naked as he was born. It was to no purpose that I endeavoured to convince these people of the improbability, or rather of the impossibility, of these youths ever returning home. Not one, not even their nearest relations, seemed to trouble themselves about their future fate. Since this was the case, and I was well satisfied that the boys would be no losers by exchange of place, I the more readily gave my consent to their going.

From my own observations, and from the information of Taweiharooa and others, it appears to me that the New Zealanders must live under perpetual apprehensions of being destroyed by each other; there being few of their tribes that have not, as they think, sustained wrongs from some other tribe, which they are continually upon the watch to revenge. And, perhaps, the desire of a good meal may be no small incitement. I am told that many years will sometimes elapse, before a favourable opportunity happens, and that the son never loses sight of an injury that has been done to his father. Their method of executing their horrible designs, is by stealing upon the adverse party in the night; and if they find them unguarded (which, however, I believe, is very seldom the case), they kill every one indiscriminately; not even sparing the women and children. When the massacre is completed, they either feast and gorge themselves on the spot, or carry off as many of the dead bodies as they can, and devour them at home, with acts of brutality too shocking to be described. If they are discovered before they can execute their bloody purpose, they generally steal off again; and sometimes are pursued and attacked

attacked by the other party, in their turn. To give quarter, or to take prisoners, makes no part of their military law; so that the vanquished can only save their lives by flight. This perpetual state of war, and destructive method of conducting it, operates so strongly in producing habitual circumspection, that one hardly ever finds a New Zealander off his guard, either by night or by day. Indeed, no other man can have such powerful motives to be vigilant, as the preservation both of body and of soul depends upon it. For, according to their system of belief, the soul of the man whose flesh is devoured by the enemy, is doomed to a perpetual fire, while the soul of the man whose body has been rescued from those who killed him, as well as the souls of all who die a natural death, ascend to the habitations of the Gods. I asked, Whether they eat the flesh of such of their friends as had been killed in war, but whose bodies were saved from falling into the enemy's hands? They seemed surprised at the question, which they answered in the negative, expressing some abhorrence at the very idea. Their common method of disposing of their dead, is by depositing their bodies in the earth; but if they have more of their slaughtered enemies than they can eat, they throw them into the sea.

They have no such thing as *morais*, or other places of public worship; nor do they ever assemble together with this view. But they have Priests, who alone address the Gods in prayers, for the prosperity of their temporal affairs; such as an enterprise against a hostile tribe, a fishing party, or the like.

Whatever the principles of their religion may be, of which we remain very ignorant, its instructions are very strongly inculcated

inculcated into them from their very infancy. Of this I saw a remarkable inflance, in the youth who was firft deftined to accompany Taweiharooa. He refrained from eating the greateft part of the day, on account of his hair being cut; though every method was tried to induce him to break his refolution; and he was tempted with the offer of fuch victuals as he was known to efteem the moft. He faid, if he eat any thing that day, the *Eatoua* would kill him. However, towards evening, the cravings of nature got the better of the precepts of his religion, and he eat, though but fparingly. I had often conjectured, before this, that they had fome fuperftitious notions about their hair, having frequently obferved quantities of it tied to the branches of trees near fome of their habitations; but what thefe notions are, I never could learn.

Notwithftanding the divided and hoftile ftate in which the New Zealanders live, travelling ftrangers, who come with no ill defign, are well received and entertained during their ftay; which, however, it is expected, will be no longer than is requifite to tranfact the bufinefs they come upon. Thus it is that a trade for *poenammoo*, or green talc, is carried on throughout the whole northern ifland. For they tell us, that there is none of this ftone to be found, but at a place which bears its name, fomewhere about the head of Queen Charlotte's Sound, and not above one or two days journey, at moft, from the ftation of our fhips. I regretted much that I could not fpare time fufficient for paying a vifit to the place; as we were told a hundred fabulous ftories about this ftone, not one of which carried with it the leaft probability of truth, though fome of their moft fenfible men would have us believe them. One of thefe ftories is, that this ftone is originally a fifh, which they ftrike with a gig in the water, tie a rope to it, and drag it to the shore, to which they fasten it, and it afterward becomes stone. As they all agree, that it is fished out of a large lake, or collection of waters, the most probable conjecture is, that it is brought from the mountains, and deposited in the water, by the torrents. This lake is called by the natives *Tavai Poenammoo*; that is, the water of Green Talc; and it is only the adjoining part of the country, and not the whole Southern island of New Zealand, that is known to them by the name which hath been given to it on my chart [*].

Polygamy is allowed amongst these people; and it is not uncommon for a man to have two or three wives. The women are marriageable at a very early age; and it should seem, that one who is unmarried, is but in a forlorn state. She can with difficulty get a subsistence; at least, she is, in a great measure, without a protector, though, in constant want of a powerful one.

The New Zealanders seem to be a people perfectly satisfied with the little knowledge they are masters of, without attempting, in the least, to improve it. Nor are they remarkably curious, either in their observations, or their inquiries. New objects do not strike them with such a degree of surprize as one would naturally expect; nor do they even fix their attention for a moment. Omai, indeed, who was a great favourite with them, would sometimes attract a circle about him; but they seemed to listen to his speeches, like persons who neither understood, nor wished to understand, what they heard.

One day, on our inquiring of Taweiharooa, how many ships, such as ours, had ever arrived in Queen Charlotte's

[*] See Captain Cook's chart of New Zealand, in Hawkes. Coll. vol. ii. p. 281.

Sound, or in any part of its neighbourhood? He began with giving an account of one absolutely unknown to us. This, he said, had put into a port on the North West coast of Teerawitte, but a very few years before I arrived in the Sound in the Endeavour, which the New Zealanders distinguish, by calling Tupia's ship. At first, I thought he might have been mistaken as to the time and place; and that the ship in question might be either Monsieur Surville's, who is said to have touched upon the North East coast of Eaheinomauwe, the same year I was there in the Endeavour; or else Monsieur Marion du Fresne's, who was in the Bay of Islands, on the same coast, a few years after. But he assured us, that he was not mistaken, either as to the time, or as to the place of this ship's arrival; and that it was well known to every body about Queen Charlotte's Sound and Teerawitte. He said, that the Captain of her, during his stay here, cohabited with a woman of the country; and that she had a son by him still living, and about the age of Kokoa; who, though not born then, seemed to be equally well acquainted with the story. We were also informed by Taweiharooa, that this ship first introduced the venereal disease amongst the New Zealanders. I wish that subsequent visiters from Europe may not have their share of guilt, in leaving so dreadful a remembrance of them amongst this unhappy race. The disorder now is but too common here; though they do not seem to regard it; saying, that its effects are not near so pernicious at present, as they were at its first appearance. The only method, as far as I ever heard, that they make use of as a remedy, is by giving the patient the use of a sort of hot bath, which they produce by the steam of certain green plants laid over hot stones.

I regretted

1777.
February.

I regretted much that we did not hear of this ship while we were in the Sound; as, by means of Omai, we might have had full and correct information about her from eye-witnesses. For Taweiharooa's account was only from what he had been told, and therefore liable to many mistakes. I have not the least doubt, however, that his testimony may so far be depended upon, as to induce us to believe, that a ship really had been at Teerawitte prior to my arrival in the Endeavour, as it corresponds with what I had formerly heard. For in the latter end of 1773, the second time I visited New Zealand, during my last voyage, when we were continually making inquiries about the Adventure, after our separation, some of the natives informed us of a ship's having been in a port on the coast of Teerawitte. But, at that time, we thought we must have misunderstood them, and took no notice of the intelligence.

The arrival of this unknown ship has been marked by the New Zealanders with more causes of remembrance, than the unhappy one just mentioned. Taweiharooa told us, their country was indebted to her people for the present of an animal, which they left behind them. But as he had not seen it himself, no sort of judgment could be formed from his description, of what kind it was.

We had another piece of intelligence from him, more correctly given, though not confirmed by our own observations, that there are snakes and lizards there of an enormous size. He described the latter as being eight feet in length, and as big round as a man's body. He said, they sometimes seize and devour men; that they burrow in the ground; and that they are killed by making fires at the mouths of the holes. We could not be mistaken as to the animal; for,

with

THE PACIFIC OCEAN.

with his own hand, he drew a very good reprefentation of a lizard on a piece of paper; as alfo of a fnake, in order to fhew what he meant.

Though much has been faid, in the Narratives of my Two former Voyages, about this country and its inhabitants, Mr. Anderfon's Remarks, as ferving either to confirm or to correct our former accounts, may not be fuperfluous. He had been three times with me in Queen Charlotte's Sound, during my laft Voyage; and, after this fourth vifit, what he thought proper to record, may be confidered as the refult of fufficient obfervation. The Reader will find it in the next Chapter; and I have nothing farther to add, before I quit New Zealand, but to give fome account of the aftronomical and nautical obfervations made during our ftay there.

The Longitude of the Obfervatory in Ship Cove, by a mean of 103 fets of obfervations, each fet confifting of fix or more obferved diftances, was - - - 174° 25' 15" Eaft.
By the time-keeper, at Greenwich rate, it was - - - - - - 175 26 30
By ditto, at the Cape rate, it was - 174 56 12
Variation of the compafs, being the mean of fix needles, obferved on board the fhip 12 40 0 Eaft.
By the fame needles on fhore, it was - 13 53 0
The dip of the South end, obferved on fhore, was - - - - - 63 42 0

By a mean of the refults of eleven days obfervations, the time-keeper was too flow for mean time, on February 22 at noon, by 11° 50' 37",396; and fhe was found to be lofing

on

on mean time, at the rate of 2",913 *per* day. From this rate the longitude will be computed, till some other opportunity offers to ascertain her rate anew. The astronomical clock, with the same length of pendulum as at Greenwich, was found to be losing on sidereal time 40",239 *per* day.

It will not be amiss to mention, that the longitude, by lunar observations, as above, differs only 6' 45" from what Mr. Wales made it during my last Voyage; his being so much more to the West, or 174° 18' 30".

The latitude of Ship Cove is 41° 6' 0", as found by Mr. Wales.

CHAP.

CHAP. VIII.

Mr. Anderson's Remarks on the Country near Queen Charlotte's Sound.—The Soil.—Climate.—Weather.—Winds.—Trees.—Plants.—Birds.—Fish.—Other Animals.—Of the Inhabitants.—Description of their Persons.—Their Dress.—Ornaments.—Habitations.—Boats.—Food and Cookery.—Arts.—Weapons.—Cruelty to Prisoners.—Various Customs.—Specimen of their Language.

THE land every where about Queen Charlotte's Sound is uncommonly mountainous, rising immediately from the sea into large hills with blunted tops. At considerable distances are valleys, or rather impressions on the sides of the hills, which are not deep; each terminating toward the sea in a small cove, with a pebbly or sandy beach; behind which are small flats, where the natives generally build their huts, at the same time hauling their canoes upon the beaches. This situation is the more convenient, as in every cove a brook of very fine water (in which are some small trout) empties itself into the sea.

The bases of these mountains, at least toward the shore, are constituted of a brittle, yellowish sand-stone, which acquires a bluish cast, where the sea washes it. It runs, at some places, in horizontal, and, at other places, in oblique *strata*; being frequently divided, at small distances, by thin

1777.
February.

veins

veins of coarse *quartz*, which commonly follow the direction of the other; though they sometimes intersect it. The mould, or soil, which covers this, is also of a yellowish cast, not unlike marl; and is commonly from a foot to two, or more, in thickness.

The quality of this soil is best indicated by the luxuriant growth of its productions. For the hills (except a few toward the sea, which are covered with smaller bushes) are one continued forest of lofty trees, flourishing with a vigour almost superior to any thing that imagination can conceive, and affording an august prospect to those who are delighted with the grand and beautiful works of nature.

The agreeable temperature of the climate, no doubt, contributes much to this uncommon strength in vegetation. For, at this time, though answering to our month of August, the weather was never disagreeably warm; nor did it raise the thermometer higher than 66°. The winter, also, seems equally mild with respect to cold: for in June 1773, which corresponds to our December, the mercury never fell lower than 40°; and the trees, at that time, retained their verdure, as if in the Summer season; so that, I believe, their foliage is never shed, till pushed off by the succeeding leaves in spring.

The weather, in general, is good; but sometimes windy, with heavy rain; which, however, never lasts above a day; nor does it appear that it is ever excessive. For there are no marks of torrents rushing down the hills, as in many countries; and the brooks, if we may judge from their channels, seem never to be greatly increated. I have observed, in the four different times of my being here, that the winds

from

from the South Eaſtward are commonly moderate, but attended with cloudy weather, or rain. The South Weſt winds blow very ſtrong, and are alſo attended with rain; but they ſeldom laſt long. The North Weſt winds are the moſt prevailing; and though often pretty ſtrong, are almoſt conſtantly connected with fine weather. In ſhort, the only obſtacle to this being one of the fineſt countries upon earth, is its great hillineſs; which, allowing the woods to be cleared away, would leave it leſs proper for paſturage than flat land; and ſtill more improper for cultivation, which could never be effected here by the plough.

The large trees which cover the hills are chiefly of two ſorts. One of them, of the ſize of our largeſt firs, grows much after their manner; but the leaves, and ſmall berries on their points, are much liker the yew. It was this which ſupplied the place of ſpruce in making beer; which we did with a ſtrong decoction of its leaves, fermented with treacle or ſugar. And this liquor, when well prepared, was acknowledged to be little inferior to the American ſpruce beer, by thoſe who had experience of both. The other ſort of tree is not unlike a maple; and grows often to a great ſize; but it only ſerved for fuel, as the wood, both of this and of the preceding, was found to be rather too heavy for maſts, yards, and other ſimilar repairs.

There is a greater variety of trees on the ſmall flat ſpots behind the beaches. Amongſt theſe are two that bear a kind of plum of the ſize of prunes; the one yellow, called *karraca*; and the other black, called *maitao*; but neither of them of a very agreeable taſte; though the natives eat both, and our people did the ſame. Thoſe of the firſt ſort grow

1777.
February.

on small trees, always facing the sea; but the others belong to larger trees that stand farther within the wood, and which we frequently cut down for fuel.

A species of *Philadelphus* grows on the eminences which jut out into the sea; and also a tree bearing flowers almost like myrtle, with roundish spotted leaves of a disagreeable smell. We drank the leaves of the *Philadelphus* as tea; and found that they had a pleasant taste and smell, and might make an excellent substitute for the oriental sort *.

Among other plants that were useful to us, may be reckoned wild celery, which grows plentifully in almost every cove; especially if the natives have ever resided there before; and one that we used to call scurvy-grass, though entirely different from the plant to which we give that name. This, however, is far preferable to ours for common use; and may be known by its jagged leaves, and small clusters of white flowers on the top. Both sorts were boiled every morning, with wheat ground in a mill, and with portable soup, for the people's breakfast; and also amongst their pease-soup, for dinner. Sometimes they were used as sallad, or dressed as greens. In all which ways they are good; and, together with the fish, with which we were constantly supplied, they formed a sort of refreshment, perhaps little inferior to what is to be met with in places most noted by navigators for plentiful supplies of animal and vegetable food.

Amongst the known kinds of plants met with here, are common and rough bindweed; night-shade and nettles, both

* See a representation of this, *Plate* N° XXII. in Captain Cook's *Account of his Second Voyage*, Vol. i. p. 100.

which

which grow to the fize of fmall trees; a fhrubby fpeedwell, found near all the beaches; fow-thiftles, virgin's bower, vanelloe, French willow, euphorbia, and crane's-bill: alfo eudweed, rufhes, bull-rufhes, flax, all-heal, American nightfhade, knot-grafs, brambles, eye-bright, and groundfel; but the *fpecies* of each are different from any we have in Europe. There is alfo polypody, fpleenwort, and about twenty other different forts of ferns, entirely peculiar to the place; with feveral forts of moffes, either rare, or produced only here; befides a great number of other plants, whofe ufes are not yet known, and fubjects fit only for botanical books.

Of thefe, however, there is one which deferves particular notice here, as the natives make their garments of it, and it produces a fine filky flax, fuperior in appearance to any thing we have; and probably, at leaft, as ftrong. It grows every where near the fea, and in fome places a confiderable way up the hills, in bunches or tufts, with fedge-like leaves, bearing, on a long ftalk, yellowifh flowers, which are fucceeded by a long roundifh pod, filled with very thin fhining black feeds. A fpecies of long pepper is found in great plenty; but it has little of the aromatic flavour that makes fpices valuable; and a tree much like a palm at a diftance, is pretty frequent in the woods, though the deceit appears as you come near it. It is remarkable that, as the greateft part of the trees and plants had, at this time, loft their flowers, we perceived they were generally of the berry-bearing kind; of which, and other feeds, I brought away about thirty different forts. Of thefe, one in particular, which bears a red berry, is much like the fupple-jack, and grows about the trees, ftretching from one to another, in fuch a manner as to render the woods almoft wholly impaffable.

The

The birds, of which there is a tolerable flock, as well as the vegetable productions, are almost entirely peculiar to the place. And though it be difficult to follow them, on account of the quantity of underwood, and the climbing plants, that render travelling, for pleasure alone, uncommonly fatiguing, yet a person, by remaining in one place, may shoot as many in a day as would serve six or eight others. The principal sorts are, large brown parrots, with white or greyish heads; green parroquets, with red foreheads; large wood pigeons, brown above, with white bellies, the rest green, and the bill and feet red. Two sorts of cuckoos, one as large as our common sort, of a brown colour, variegated with black; the other not larger than a sparrow, of a splendid green cast above, and elegantly varied with waves of golden, green, brown, and white colours below. Both these are scarce; but several others are in greater plenty; one of which, of a black colour, with a greenish cast, is remarkable for having a tuft of white curled feathers hanging under the throat, and was called the *Poy* bird [*] by our people. Another sort, rather smaller, is black, with a brown back and wings, and two small gills under the root of the bill. This we called the small wattle bird, to distinguish it from another, which we called the large one, of the size of a common pigeon, with two large yellow and purple membranes also, at the root of the bill. It is black, or rather blue, and has no resemblance of the other but in name; for the bill is thick, short, and crooked, and has altogether an uncommon appearance. A grosbeak, about the size of a thrush, of a brown colour, with a reddish tail, is frequent; as is also a small greenish bird, which

[*] See a drawing of this bird, Plate N° LII. *in Captain Cook's Account of his Second Voyage*, Vol. I. p. 97. It had this name from its tuft of feathers, resembling the white flowers used as ornaments in the ears at Otaheite, and called there *Poora*.

is almost the only musical one here, but is sufficient by itself to fill the woods with a melody, that is not only sweet, but so varied, that one would imagine he was surrounded by a hundred different sorts of birds, when the little warbler is near. From this circumstance we named it the mocking bird. There are likewise three or four sorts of smaller birds; one of which, in figure and tameness, exactly resembles our robin, but is black where that is brown, and white where that is red. Another differs but little from this, except in being smaller; and a third sort has a long tail, which it expands as a fan on coming near, and makes a chirping noise when it perches. King-fishers are seen, though rare, and are about the size of our English ones, but with an inferior plumage.

About the rocks are seen black sea-pies with red bills; and crested shags of a leaden colour, with small black spots on the wings and shoulders, and the rest of the upper part, of a velvet black tinged with green. We frequently shot both these, and also a more common sort of shags, black above and white underneath, that build their nests upon trees, on which sometimes a dozen or more sit at once. There are also, about the shore, a few sea-gulls; some blue herons; and sometimes, though very rarely, wild ducks; a small sandy coloured plover, and some sand larks. And small penguins black above, with a white belly, as well as numbers of little black divers, swim often about the Sound. We likewise killed two or three rails of a brown or yellowish colour, variegated with black, which feed about the small brooks, and are nearly as large as a common fowl. No other sort of game was seen, except a single snipe, which was shot, and differs but little from that of Europe.

The

The principal fish we caught by the Seine were mullets and elephant fish, with a few soles and flounders; but those that the natives mostly supplied us with, were a sort of sea-bream of a silver colour with a black spot on the neck, large Conger eels, and a fish in shape much like the bream, but so large as to weigh five, six, or seven pounds. It is blackish with thick lips, and called *Mogge* by the natives. With hook and line we caught chiefly a blackish fish of the size of a haddock, called cole-fish by the seamen, but differing much from that known by the same name in Europe; and another of the same size, of a reddish colour with a little beard, which we called night walkers, from the greatest number being caught in the night. Sometimes we got a sort of small salmon, gurnards, skate, and nurses; and the natives, now and then, brought hake, paracutas, a small sort of mackerel, parrot-fish, and leather-jackets; besides another fish which is very rare, shaped almost like a dolphin, of a black colour, with strong bony jaws, and the back-fin, as well as those opposite to it, much lengthened at the end. All these sorts, except the last, which we did not try, are excellent to eat; but the *Mogge*, small salmon, and cole-fish are superior to the rest.

The rocks are abundantly furnished with great quantities of excellent muscles; one sort of which, that is not very common, measures above a foot in length. There are also cockles buried in the sand of the small beaches; and in some places oysters, which, though very small, are well tasted. Of other shell-fish there are ten or twelve sorts, such as periwinckles, wilks, limpets, and some very beautiful sea-ears; also another sort which stick to the weeds; with some other things, as sea-eggs, star-fish, &c. several of which are peculiar

culiar to the place. The natives likewise sometimes brought us very fine cray-fish, equal to our largest lobsters, and cuttle fish, which they eat themselves.

Insects are very rare. Of these, we only saw two sorts of dragon-flies, some butterflies, small grashoppers, several sorts of spiders, some small black ants, and vast numbers of scorpion flies, with whose chirping the woods resound. The only noxious one is the sand-fly, very numerous here, and almost as troublesome as the musquitoe; for we found no reptile here, except two or three sorts of small harmless lizards [*].

It is remarkable, that, in this extensive land, there should not even be the traces of any quadruped, only excepting a few rats, and a sort of fox-dog, which is a domestic animal with the natives.

Neither is there any mineral worth notice, but a green jasper or serpent-stone, of which the New Zealanders make their tools and ornaments. This is esteemed a precious article by them; and they have some superstitious notions about the method of its generation, which we could not perfectly understand. It is plain, however, that wherever it may be found (which, they say, is in the channel of a large river far to the Southward), it is disposed in the earth in thin layers, or, perhaps, in detached pieces, like our flints; for the edges of those pieces, which have not been cut, are covered with a whitish crust like these. A piece of this sort was purchased, about eighteen inches long, a foot broad, and near two inches thick; which yet seemed to be only the fragment of a larger piece.

---

[*] In a separate memorandum-book, Mr. Anderson mentions the monstrous animal of the lizard kind, described by the two boys after they left the island.

1727.
February.

The natives do not exceed the common stature of Europeans; and, in general, are not so well made, especially about the limbs. This is, perhaps, the effect of sitting, for the most part, on their hams; and of being confined, by the hilly disposition of the country, from using that sort of exercise which contributes to render the body straight and well-proportioned. There are, however, several exceptions to this; and some are remarkable for their large bones and muscles; but few that I have seen are corpulent.

Their colour is of different casts, from a pretty deep black to a yellowish or olive tinge; and their features also are various, some resembling Europeans. But, in general, their faces are round, with their lips full, and also their noses toward the point; though the first are not uncommonly thick, nor the last flat. I do not, however, recollect to have seen an instance of the true aquiline nose amongst them. Their teeth are commonly broad, white, and well set; and their eyes large, with a very free motion, which seems the effect of habit. Their hair is black, straight, and strong, commonly cut short on the hind part, with the rest tied on the crown of the head: but some have it of a curling disposition, or of a brown colour. In the young, the countenance is generally free or open; but in many of the men it has a serious cast, and sometimes a sullenness or reserve, especially if they are strangers. The women are, in general, smaller than the men; but have few peculiar graces, either in form or features, to distinguish them.

The dress of both sexes is alike; and consists of an oblong garment about five feet long, and four broad, made from the silky flax already mentioned. This seems to be their most material and complex manufacture, which is executed by by knotting; and their work is often ornamented with pieces of dog-skin, or chequered at the corners. They bring two corners of this garment over the shoulders, and fasten it on the breast with the other part, which covers the body; and about the belly, it is again tied with a girdle made of mat. Sometimes they cover it with large feathers of birds (which seem to be wrought into the piece of cloth when it is made), or with dog-skin; and that alone we have seen worn as a covering. Over this garment many of them wear mats, which reach from the shoulders to near the heels. But the most common outer-covering is a quantity of the above sedgy plant, badly dressed, which they fasten on a string to a considerable length, and, throwing it about the shoulders, let it fall down on all sides, as far as the middle of the thighs. When they sit down with this upon them, either in their boats, or upon the shore, it would be difficult to distinguish them from large grey stones, if their black heads, projecting beyond their coverings, did not engage one to a stricter examination.

By way of ornament, they fix in their heads feathers, or combs of bone, or wood, adorned with pearl shell, or the thin inner skin of some leaf. And in the ears, both of men and women, which are pierced, or rather slit, are hung small pieces of jasper, bits of cloth, or beads when they can get them. A few also have the *septum* of the nose bored in its lower part; but no ornament was worn there that we saw; though one man passed a twig through it, to shew us that it was sometimes used for that purpose. They wear long beards, but are fond of having them shaved.

Some are punctured or stained in the face with curious spiral and other figures, of a black or deep blue colour;

1777.
February.

but it is doubtful whether this be ornamental, or intended as a mark of particular diſtinction; and the women, who are marked ſo, have the puncture only on their lips, or a ſmall ſpot on their chins. Both ſexes often beſmear their faces and heads with a red paint, which ſeems to be a martial ochre mixed with greaſe; and the women ſometimes wear necklaces of ſhark's teeth, or bunches of long beads, which ſeem to be made of the leg-bones of ſmall birds, or a particular ſhell. A few alſo have ſmall triangular aprons adorned with the feathers of parrots, or bits of pearl ſhells, furniſhed with a double or treble ſet of cords to faſten them about the waiſt. I have ſometimes ſeen caps or bonnets made of the feathers of birds, which may be reckoned as ornaments; for it is not their cuſtom to wear any covering on their heads.

They live in the ſmall coves formerly deſcribed, in companies of forty or fifty, or more; and ſometimes in ſingle families, building their huts contiguous to each other; which, in general, are miſerable lodging-places. The beſt I ever ſaw was about thirty feet long, fifteen broad, and ſix high, built exactly in the manner of one of our country barns. The inſide was both ſtrong and regularly made of ſupporters at the ſides, alternately large and ſmall, well faſtened by means of withes, and painted red and black. The ridge pole was ſtrong; and the large bull-ruſhes, which compoſed the inner part of the thatching, were laid with great exactneſs parallel to each other. At one end was a ſmall ſquare hole, which ſerved as a door to creep in at; and near it another much ſmaller, ſeemingly for letting out the ſmoke, as no other vent for it could be ſeen. This, however, ought to be conſidered as one of the beſt, and the reſidence of ſome principal perſon; for the greateſt part of them

them are not half the above size, and seldom exceed four
feet in height; being, besides, indifferently built, though
proof against wind and rain.

1777.
February.

No other furniture is to be seen in them, than a few small
baskets or bags, in which they put their fishing-hooks, and
other trifles; and they sit down in the middle round a small
fire, where they also probably sleep, without any other covering than what they wear in the day, or perhaps without
that; as such confined places must be very warm, though
inhabited but by a few persons.

They live chiefly by fishing, making use either of nets of
different kinds, or of wooden fish-hooks pointed with bone;
but so oddly made, that a stranger is at a loss to know how
they can answer such a purpose. It also appears, that they
remove their habitations from one place to another when
the fish grow scarce, or for some other reason; for we found
houses now built in several parts, where there had been
none when we were here during our last voyage, and even
these have been already deserted.

Their boats are well built, of planks raised upon each
other, and fastened with strong withes, which also bind a
long narrow piece on the outside of the seams to prevent
their leaking. Some are fifty feet long, and so broad as to
be able to sail without an outrigger; but the smaller sort
commonly have one; and they often fasten two together by
rafters, which we then call a double canoe. They carry
from five to thirty men or more; and have often a large
head ingeniously carved, and painted with a figure at the
point, which seems intended to represent a man, with his
features distorted by rage. Their paddles are about four
or five feet long, narrow, and pointed; with which, when
they

they keep time, the boat is pushed along pretty swiftly. Their sail, which is seldom used, is made of a mat of a triangular shape, having the broadest part above.

The only method of dressing their fish, is by roasting, or rather baking; for they are intirely ignorant of the art of boiling. In the same manner they dress the root, and part of the stalk, of the large fern-tree, in a great hole dug for that purpose, which serves as an oven. After which they split it, and find, within, a fine gelatinous substance, like boiled sago powder, but firmer. They also use another smaller fern root, which seems to be their substitute for bread, as it is dried and carried about with them, together with dried fish in great quantities, when they remove their families, or go far from home. This they beat with a stick till it becomes pretty soft, when they chew it sufficiently, and spit out the hard fibrous part, the other having a sweetish mealy taste not at all disagreeable.

When they dare not venture to sea, or perhaps from choice, they supply the place of other fish with muscles and sea-ears; great quantities of the shells of which lie in heaps near their houses. And they sometimes, though rarely, find means to kill rails, penguins, and shags, which help to vary their diet. They also breed considerable numbers of the dogs, mentioned before, for food; but these cannot be considered as a principal article of diet. From whence we may conclude, that, as there is not the least sign of cultivation of land, they depend principally for their subsistence on the sea, which, indeed, is very bountiful in its supply.

Their method of feeding corresponds with the nastiness of their persons, which often smell disagreeably from the

quantity

quantity of greafe about them, and their clothes never being wafhed. We have feen them eat the vermin, with which their heads are fufficiently ftocked.

They alfo ufed to devour, with the greateft eagernefs, large quantities of ftinking train oil, and blubber of feals, which we were melting at the tent, and had kept near two months; and, on board the ships, they were not fatisfied with emptying the lamps, but actually fwallowed the cotton, and fragrant wick, with equal voracity. It is worthy of notice, that though the inhabitants of Van Diemen's land appear to have but a fcanty fubfiftence, they would not even tafte our bread, though they faw us eat it; whereas thefe people devoured it greedily, when both mouldy and rotten. But this muft not be imputed to any defect in their fenfations; for I have obferved them throw away things which we eat, with evident difguft, after only fmelling to them.

They fhew as much ingenuity, both in invention and execution, as any uncivilized nations under fimilar circumftances. For, without the ufe of any metal tools, they make every thing by which they procure their fubfiftence, clothing, and warlike weapons, with a degree of neatnefs, ftrength, and convenience for accomplifhing their feveral purpofes. Their chief mechanical tool is formed exactly after the manner of our adzes; and is made, as are alfo the chiffel and goudge, of the green ferpent-ftone or jafper, already mentioned; though fometimes they are compofed of a black, fmooth, and very folid ftone. But their mafter-piece feems to be carving, which is found upon the moft trifling things; and, in particular, the heads of their canoes are fometimes ornamented with it in fuch a manner, as not only fhews much defign, but is alfo an example of
their

1777.
February.

their great labour and patience in execution. Their cordage for fishing-lines is equal, in strength and evenness, to that made by us; and their nets not at all inferior. But what must cost them more labour than any other article, is the making the tools we have mentioned; for the stone is exceedingly hard, and the only method of fashioning it, we can guess at, is by rubbing one stone upon another, which can have but a slow effect. Their substitute for a knife is a shell, a bit of flint, or jasper. And, as an auger, to bore holes, they fix a shark's tooth in the end of a small piece of wood. It is true, they have a small saw made of some jagged fishes teeth, fixed on the convex edge of a piece of wood nicely carved. But this, they say, is only used to cut up the bodies of their enemies whom they kill in battle.

No people can have a quicker sense of an injury done to them, and none are more ready to resent it. But, at the same time, they will take an opportunity of being insolent when they think there is no danger of punishment; which is so contrary to the spirit of genuine bravery, that, perhaps, their eagerness to resent injuries is to be looked upon rather as an effect of a furious disposition than of great courage. They also appear to be of a suspicious or mistrustful temper (which, however, may rather be acquired than natural), for strangers never came to our ships immediately, but lay in their boats at a small distance, either to observe our motions, or consult whether or no they should risk their safety with us. To this they join a great degree of dishonesty; for they steal every thing they can lay their hands on, if there be the least hope of not being detected; and, in trading, I have little doubt but they would take advantages, if they thought it could be done with safety; as they not only refuse

to

to trust a thing in one's hand for examination, but exult if they think they have tricked you in the bargain.

Such conduct, however, is, in some measure, to be expected where there appears to be but little subordination, and consequently few, if any, laws, to punish transgressions. For no man's authority seems to extend farther than his own family; and when, at any time, they join for mutual defence, or any other purpose, those amongst them who are eminent for courage or prudence, are directors. How their private quarrels are terminated is uncertain; but, in the few we saw, which were of little consequence, the parties concerned were clamorous and disorderly.

Their public contentions are frequent, or rather perpetual; for it appears, from their number of weapons, and dexterity in using them, that war is their principal profession. These weapons are spears, *patoos* and halberts, or sometimes stones. The first are made of hard wood pointed, of different lengths, from five, to twenty, or even thirty feet long. The short ones are used for throwing as darts. The *patoo* or *emette* is of an elliptical shape, about eighteen inches long, with a handle made of wood, stone, the bone of some sea animal, or green jasper, and seems to be their principal dependence in battle. The halbert, or long club, is about five or six feet long, tapering at one end with a carved head, and at the other, broad or flat, with sharp edges.

Before they begin the onset, they join in a war-song, to which they all keep the exactest time, and soon raise their passion to a degree of frantic fury, attended with the most horrid distortion of their eyes, mouths, and tongues, to strike terror into their enemies; which, to those who have not been accustomed to such a practice, makes them ap-

1777.
February.

pear more like demons than men, and would almost chill the boldest with fear. To this succeeds a circumstance, almost foretold in their fierce demeanor, horrid, cruel, and disgraceful to human nature; which is, cutting in pieces, even before being perfectly dead, the bodies of their enemies, and, after dressing them on a fire, devouring the flesh, not only without reluctance, but with peculiar satisfaction.

One might be apt to suppose, that people, capable of such excess of cruelty, must be destitute of every humane feeling, even amongst their own party. And yet we find them lamenting the loss of their friends, with a violence of expression which argues the most tender remembrance of them. For both men and women, upon the death of those connected with them, whether in battle or otherwise, bewail them with the most doleful cries; at the same time cutting their foreheads and cheeks, with shells or pieces of flint, in large gashes, until the blood flows plentifully and mixes with their tears. They also carve pieces of their green stone, rudely shaped, as human figures, which they ornament with bright eyes of pearl-shell, and hang them about their necks, as memorials of those whom they held most dear; and their affections of this kind are so strong, that they even perform the ceremony of cutting, and lamenting for joy, at the return of any of their friends, who have been absent but for a short time.

The children are initiated, at a very early age, into all the practices, good or bad, of their fathers; so that you find a boy or girl, nine or ten years old, able to perform all the motions, and to imitate the frightful gestures, by which the more aged use to inspire their enemies with terror, keeping the strictest time in their song. They likewise sing, with some degree of melody, the traditions of their forefathers, their actions in war, and other indifferent subjects; of all which they are immoderately fond, and spend much of their time, in these amusements, and in playing on a sort of flute.

Their language is far from being harsh or disagreeable, though the pronunciation is frequently guttural; and whatever qualities are requisite in any other language to make it musical, certainly obtain to a considerable degree here, if we may judge from the melody of some sorts of their songs. It is also sufficiently comprehensive, though, in many respects, deficient, if compared with our European languages, which owe their perfection to long improvement. But a small specimen is here subjoined, from which some judgment may be formed. I collected a great many of their words, both now and in the course of our former voyage; and being equally attentive, in my inquiries, about the languages of the other islands throughout the South Sea, I have the amplest proof of their wonderful agreement, or rather identity. This general observation has, indeed, been already made in the accounts of the former voyages [*]. I shall be enabled, however, to confirm and strengthen it, by a fresh list of words, selected from a large vocabulary in my possession; and by placing, in the opposite column, the corresponding words as used at Otaheite, the curious reader will, at one view, be furnished with sufficient materials for judging by what subordinate changes the difference of dialect has been effected.

[*] See Hawkesworth's Collection, Vol. III. p. 474, 475. and Captain Cook's Voyage, Vol. II. p. 364.

English.	New Zealand.	Otaheite.
Water,	Ewy,	Evy.
A tail of a dog,	Wyeroo,	Ero.
Death, dead,	Kaoo, matte,	Matte, roa.
To fly,	Ererre,	Eraire.
A house,	Ewharre,	Ewharre.
To sleep,	Moea,	Moe.
A fish-hook,	Makoee,	Matou.
Shut,	Opanee,	Opanee.
A bed,	Moenga,	Moera.
A butterfly,	Epaipe,	Pepe.
To chew, or eat,	Hekaee,	Ey.
Cold,	Makkareede,	Mareede.
To-day,	Agooanai,	Aooanai.
The hand,	Reenga,	Ereema.
Large,	Keerahoi,	Erahoi.
Red,	Whairo,	Oora, oora.
We,	Taooa,	Taooa.
Where is it?	Kahaia,	Tehaia.
A stone,	Powhy,	Owhy.
A man,	Tangata,	Taata.
Black,	Purra, purra	Ere, ere.
White,	Ema,	Ooama.
To reside, or dwell,	Nohoanna,	Nohonoa.
Out, not within,	Woho,	Woho.
Male kind (of any animal),	Toa,	Etoa.
Female,	Eoowha,	Eooha.
A shark,	Mango,	Mao.
To understand,	Geetaia,	Eetea.
Forget,	Warre,	Ooaro.
Yesterday,	Taeninnahoi,	Ninnahoi.
One,	Tahaee,	Atahay.

English.	New Zealand.	Otaheite.
Two,	Rooa,	Erooa.
Three,	Toroo,	Toroo.
Four,	Faa,	Ahaa.
Five,	Reema,	Ereema.
Six,	Ono,	Aono.
Seven,	Heetoo,	Aheitoo.
Eight,	Waroo,	Awaroo.
Nine,	Eeva,	Aeeva.
Ten,	Angahoora,	Ahooroo.

The New Zealanders to these numerals prefix *Ma*; as,

Eleven,	Matahee.
Twelve, &c. &c.	Marooa, &c. &c.
Twenty,	Mangahoora.

A VOYAGE TO THE PACIFIC OCEAN.

BOOK II.

From leaving New Zealand, to our Arrival at Otaheite, or the Society Iſlands.

CHAP. I.

Proſecution of the Voyage.—Behaviour of the Two New Zealanders on board.—Unfavourable Winds.—An Iſland called Mangeea diſcovered.—The Coaſt of it examined.—Tranſactions with the Natives.—An Account of their Perſons, Dreſs, and Canoes.—Deſcription of the Iſland.—A Specimen of the Language.—Diſpoſition of the Inhabitants.

ON the 25th, at ten o'clock in the morning, a light breeze ſpringing up at North Weſt by Weſt, we weighed, ſtood out of the Sound, and made ſail through the ſtrait, with the Diſcovery in company. We had hardly got the length of Cape Tierawhitte, when the wind took us aback at South Eaſt. It continued in this quarter till

1777.
February.
Tueſday 25.

two

1777.
February.
Wednesd. 26.
Thursday 27.

two o'clock the next morning, when we had a few hours calm. After which we had a breeze at North; but here it fixed not long, before it veered to the East, and after that to the South. At length, on the 27th, at eight o'clock in the morning, we took our departure from Cape Pallifer, which, at this time, bore West, seven or eight leagues distant. We had a fine gale, and I steered East by North.

We had no sooner lost sight of the land than our two New Zealand adventurers, the sea sickness they now experienced giving a turn to their reflections, repented heartily of the step they had taken. All the soothing encouragement we could think of, availed but little. They wept, both in public and in private; and made their lamentations in a kind of song, which, as far as we could comprehend the meaning of the words, was expressive of their praises of their country and people, from which they were to be separated for ever. Thus they continued for many days, till their sea sickness wore off, and the tumult of their minds began to subside. Then these fits of lamentation became less and less frequent, and at length entirely ceased. Their native country and their friends were, by degrees, forgot, and they appeared to be as firmly attached to us, as if they had been born amongst us.

Friday 28.

The wind had not remained many hours at South, before it veered to South East and East; and, with this, we stood to the North, till the 28th at noon. Being then in the latitude of 41° 17′, and in the longitude of 177° 17′ East, we tacked and stood to the South East, with a gentle breeze at East North East. It afterward freshened, and came about to North East; in which quarter it continued two days, and sometimes blew a fresh gale with squalls, accompanied with showers of rain.

On

THE PACIFIC OCEAN.

On the 2d of March at noon, being in the latitude of 42° 35' 30", longitude 180° 8' East, the wind shifted to North West; afterward to South West; and between this point and North it continued to blow, sometimes a strong gale with hard squalls, and at other times very moderate. With this wind we steered North East by East and East, under all the sail we could carry, till the 11th at noon, at which time we were in the latitude of 39° 29', longitude 196° 4' East.

The wind now veered to North East and South East, and I stood to the North, and to the North East, as the wind would admit, till one o'clock in the morning on the 16th, when having a more favourable gale from the North, I tacked and stood to the East; the latitude being 33° 40', and the longitude 198° 50' East. We had light airs and calms by turns, till noon the next day, when the wind began to freshen at East South East, and I again stood to the North East. But as the wind often veered to East and East North East, we frequently made no better than a northerly course; nay, sometimes to the Westward of North. But the hopes of the wind coming more Southerly, or of meeting with it from the Westward, a little without the Tropic, as I had experienced in my former visits to this ocean, encouraged me to continue this course. Indeed it was necessary that I should run all risks, as my proceeding to the North this year, in prosecution of the principal object of the voyage, depended entirely on my making a quick passage to Otaheite, or the Society Islands.

The wind continued invariably fixed at East South East, or seldom shifting above two points on either side. It also blew very faint, so that it was the 27th before we crossed the Tropic, and then we were only in the longitude of 201° 23' East, which was nine degrees to the Westward of our intended port. In all this run we saw nothing, except now and then a Tropic bird, that could induce us to think we had failed near any land. In the latitude of 34° 20', longitude 199°, we passed the trunk of a large tree, which was covered with barnacles; a sign that it had been long at sea.

Saturday 29. On the 29th, at ten in the morning, as we were standing to the North East, the Discovery made the signal of seeing land. We saw it from the mast-head almost the same moment, bearing North East by East by compass. We soon discovered it to be an island of no great extent, and stood for it till sunset, when it bore North North East, distant about two or three leagues.

Sunday 30. The night was spent in standing off and on, and at day-break the next morning, I bore up for the lee or West side of the island, as neither anchorage nor landing appeared to be practicable on the South side, on account of a great surf*, which broke every where with violence against the shore, or against the reef that surrounded it.

We presently found that the island was inhabited, and saw several people, on a point of the land we had passed, wading to the reef, where, as they found the ship leaving them quickly, they remained. But others, who soon appeared in different parts, followed her course; and sometimes several of them collected into small bodies, who made a shouting noise all together, nearly after the manner of the inhabitants of New Zealand.

Between seven and eight o'clock, we were at the West North West part of the island, and, being near the shore, we

---

* A very ingenious and satisfactory account of the cause of the surf, is to be met with in Marsden's History of Sumatra, p. 19. 32.

could

could perceive with our glasses, that several of the natives, who appeared upon a sandy beach, were all armed with long spears and clubs, which they brandished in the air with signs of threatening, or, as some on board interpreted their attitudes, with invitations to land. Most of them appeared naked, except having a sort of girdle, which, being brought up between the thighs, covered that part of the body. But some of them had pieces of cloth of different colours, white, striped, or chequered, which they wore as a garment, thrown about their shoulders. And almost all of them had a white wrapper about their heads, not much unlike a turban; or, in some instances, like a high conical cap. We could also perceive that they were of a tawny colour, and in general of a middling stature, but robust, and inclining to corpulence.

At this time, a small canoe was launched in a great hurry from the further end of the beach, and a man getting into it, put off, as with a view to reach the ship. On perceiving this, I brought to, that we might receive the visit; but the man's resolution failing, he soon returned toward the beach, where, after some time, another man joined him in the canoe; and then they both paddled toward us. They stopt short, however, as if afraid to approach, until Omai, who addressed them in the Otaheite language, in some measure quieted their apprehensions. They then came near enough to take some beads and nails, which were tied to a piece of wood, and thrown into the canoe. They seemed afraid to touch these things, and put the piece of wood aside without untying them. This, however, might arise from superstition; for Omai told us, that when they saw us offering them presents, they asked something for their *Eatoa*, or god. He also, perhaps improperly,

1777.
March.

perly, put the question to them, Whether they ever eat human flesh? which they answered in the negative, with a mixture of indignation and abhorrence. One of them, whose name was Mouroa, being asked how he came by a scar on his forehead, told us that it was the consequence of a wound he had got in fighting with the people of an island, which lies to the North Eastward, who sometimes came to invade them. They afterward took hold of a rope. Still, however, they would not venture on board; but told Omai, who understood them pretty well, that their countrymen on shore had given them this caution, at the same time directing them to inquire, from whence our ship came, and to learn the name of the Captain. On our part, we inquired the name of the island, which they called *Mangya* or *Mangeea*; and sometimes added to it *Now, nei, naivua*. The name of their Chief, they said, was Orooaeeka.

Mouroa was lusty and well made, but not very tall. His features were agreeable, and his disposition seemingly no less so; for he made several droll gesticulations, which indicated both good-nature and a share of humour. He also made others which seemed of a serious kind, and repeated some words with a devout air, before he ventured to lay hold of the rope at the ship's stern; which was probably to recommend himself to the protection of some Divinity. His colour was nearly of the same cast with that common to the most southern Europeans. The other man was not so handsome. Both of them had strong, straight hair, of a jet colour, tied together on the crown of the head with a bit of cloth. They wore such girdles as we had perceived about those on shore, and we found they were a substance made from the *Morus papyrifera*, in the same manner as at the other islands of this ocean. It was

glazed

glazed like the fort ufed by the natives of the Friendly Iflands; but the cloth on their heads was white, like that which is found at Otaheite. They had on, a kind of fandals, made of a graffy fubftance interwoven, which we alfo obferved were worn by thofe who ftood upon the beach; and, as we fuppofed, intended to defend their feet againft the rough coral rock. Their beards were long; and the infide of their arms, from the fhoulder to the elbow, and fome other parts, were punctured or *tatooed*, after the manner of the inhabitants of almoft all the other iflands in the South Sea. The lobe of their ears was pierced, or rather flit, and to fuch a length, that one of them ftuck there a knife and fome beads, which he had received from us; and the fame perfon had two polifhed pearl-fhells, and a bunch of human hair, loofely twifted, hanging about his neck, which was the only ornament we obferved. The canoe they came in (which was the only one we faw), was not above ten feet long, and very narrow; but both ftrong and neatly made. The forepart had a flat board faftened over it, and projecting out, to prevent the fea getting in on plunging, like the fmall *Evaas* at Otaheite; but it had an upright ftern, about five feet high, like fome in New Zealand; and the upper end of this ftern-poft was forked. The lower part of the canoe was of white wood; but the upper was black, and their paddles, made of wood of the fame colour, not above three feet long, broad at one end, and blunted. They paddled either end of the canoe forward indifferently; and only turned about their faces to paddle the contrary way.

We now ftood off and on; and as foon as the fhips were in a proper ftation, about ten o'clock I ordered two boats, one of them from the Difcovery, to found the coaft; and to

endeavour

endeavour to find a landing-place. With this view, I went in one of them myself, taking with me such articles to give the natives, as I thought might serve to gain their good-will. I had no sooner put off from the ship, than the canoe, with the two men, which had left us not long; before, paddled towards my boat; and, having come alongside, Mourooa stept into her, without being asked, and without a moment's hesitation.

Omai, who was with me, was ordered to inquire of him, where we could land; and he directed us to two different places. But I saw, with regret, that the attempt could not be made at either place, unless at the risk of having our boats filled with water, or even staved to pieces. Nor were we more fortunate in our search for anchorage; for we could find no bottom, till within a cable's length of the breakers. There we met with from forty to twenty fathoms depth, over sharp coral rocks; so that anchoring would have been attended with much more danger than landing.

While we were thus employed in reconnoitring the shore, great numbers of the natives thronged down upon the reef, all armed as above mentioned. Mourooa, who was now in my boat, probably thinking that this warlike appearance hindered us from landing, ordered them to retire back. As many of them complied, I judged he must be a person of some consequence among them. Indeed, if we understood him right, he was the king's brother. So great was the curiosity of several of them, that they took to the water, and, swimming off to the boats, came on board them without reserve. Nay, we found it difficult to keep them out; and still more difficult to prevent their carrying off every thing they could lay their hands upon.

upon. At length, when they perceived that we were returning to the ships, they all left us, except our original visiter Mourooa. He, though not without evident signs of fear, kept his place in my boat, and accompanied me on board the ship.

The cattle and other new objects, that presented themselves to him there, did not strike him with so much surprise as one might have expected. Perhaps his mind was too much taken up about his own safety, to allow him to attend to other things. It is certain, that he seemed very uneasy; and the ship, on our getting on board, happening to be standing off shore, this circumstance made him the more so. I could get but little new information from him; and therefore, after he had made a short stay, I ordered a boat to carry him in toward the land. As soon as he got out of the cabin, he happened to stumble over one of the goats. His curiosity now overcoming his fear, he stopped, looked at it, and asked Omai, what bird this was! and not receiving an immediate answer from him, he repeated the question to some of the people upon deck. The boat having conveyed him pretty near to the surf, he leaped into the sea, and swam ashore. He had no sooner landed, than the multitude of his countrymen gathered round him, as if with an eager curiosity to learn from him what he had seen; and in this situation they remained, when we lost sight of them. As soon as the boat returned, we hoisted her in, and made sail from the land to the Northward.

Thus were we obliged to leave, unvisited, this fine island, which seemed capable of supplying all our wants. It lies in the latitude of 21° 57′ South; and in the longitude of 201° 53′ East. Such parts of the coast, as fell under our

observation,

observation, are guarded by a reef of coral rock, on the outside of which the sea is of an unfathomable depth. It is full five leagues in circuit, and of a moderate and pretty equal height; though, in clear weather, it may be certainly seen at the distance of ten leagues; for we had not lost sight of it at night, when we had run above seven leagues, and the weather was cloudy. In the middle, it rises into little hills, from whence there is a gentle descent to the shore, which, at the South West part, is steep, though not above ten or twelve feet high; and has several excavations made by the beating of the waves against a brownish sand-stone of which it is composed. The descent here is covered with trees of a deep green colour, very thick, but not high, which seem all of one sort, unless nearest the shore, where there are great numbers of that species of *dracena* found in the woods of New Zealand, which are also scattered in some other places. On the North West part, the shore, as we mentioned above, ends in a sandy beech; beyond which the land is broken down into small chasms or gullies, and has a broad border of trees resembling tall willows; which, from its regularity, might be supposed a work of art, did not its extent forbid us to think so. Farther up on the ascent, the trees were of the deep green mentioned before. Some of us supposed these to be the *rima*, intermixed with low cocoa palms; and a few of some other sorts. They seemed not so thick as on the South West part, and higher; which appearance might be owing to our nearer approach to the shore. On the little hills, were some trees of a taller sort, thinly scattered; but the other parts of them were either bare, and of a reddish colour, or covered with something like fern. Upon the whole, the island has a pretty aspect, and might be made a beautiful spot by cultivation.

As the inhabitants seemed to be both numerous and well fed, such articles of provision as the island produces must be in great plenty. It might, however, be a matter of curiosity to know, particularly, their method of subsistence; for our friend Mourooa told us, that they had no animals, as hogs and dogs, both which, however, they had heard of; but acknowledged they had plantains, bread fruit, and taro. The only birds we saw, were some white egg-birds, terns, and noddies; and one white heron, on the shore.

The language of the inhabitants of Mangeea is a dialect of that spoken at Otaheite; though their pronunciation, as that of the New Zealanders, be more guttural. Some of their words, of which two or three are perhaps peculiar to this island, are here subjoined, as taken, by Mr. Anderson, from Omai, who had learnt them in his conversations with Mourooa. The Otaheite words, where there is any resemblance, are placed opposite.

English.	Mangeea.	Otaheite.
A cocoa nut,	Eakkaree,	Aree.
Bread-fruit,	Kooroo,	Ooroo.
A canoe,	Ewakka,	Evaa.
Friend,	Naoo, mou.	
A man,	Taata, or Tangata,	Taata.
Cloth, or cloth plant,	Taia, taia aoutee,	Eoute.
Good,	Mata,	Myty.
A club,	Pooroohee,	
Yes,	Aee,	Ai.
No,	Aoure,	Aoure.
A spear,	Heyhey,	
A fight, or battle,	Etamagee,	Tamaee.
A woman,	Waheine,	Waheine.

English.	Mangeea.	Otaheite.
A daughter,	Maheine,	Maheine.
The sun,	Heetaia matooa.	
I,	Ou,	Wou.
The shore,	Eata,	Futa.
What is that?	Ebataiece?	Owytaiecoa!
There,	Oo.	
A chief,	Ereckoe,	Eree.
Great, or powerful,	Manna (*an adjunct to the last*).	
To kiss,	Ooma.	

The natives of Mangeea seem to resemble those of Otaheite and the Marquesas in the beauty of their persons, more than any other nation I have seen in these seas; having a smooth skin, and not being muscular. Their general disposition also corresponds, as far as we had opportunities of judging, with that which distinguishes the first mentioned people. For they are not only cheerful, but, as Mourooa shewed us, are acquainted with all the lascivious gesticulations which the Otaheiteans practise in their dances. It may also be supposed, that their method of living is similar. For, though the nature of the country prevented our seeing many of their habitations, we observed one house near the beach, which much resembled, in its mode of construction, those of Otaheite. It was pleasantly situated in a grove of trees, and appeared to be about thirty feet long, and seven or eight high, with an open end, which represented an ellipse divided transversely. Before it, was spread something white on a few bushes; which we conjectured to be a fishing net, and, to appearance, of a very delicate texture.

THE PACIFIC OCEAN. 179

1777. March.

They falute ſtrangers much after the manner of the New Zealanders, by joining noſes; adding, however, the additional ceremony of taking the hand of the perſon to whom they are paying civilities, and rubbing it with a degree of force upon their noſe and mouth *.

* The inhabitants of the Palaos, New Philippines, or rather Caroline Iſlands, at the diſtance of almoſt fifteen hundred leagues from Mangeea, have the ſame mode of ſalutation. " Leur civilité, & la marque de leur reſpect, conſiſte à prendre la main " de le pied de celui à qui ils veulent faire honneur, & s'en frotter doucement tout " le viſage." Lettres Edifiantes & Curieuſes, Tom. xv. p. 208. Edit. 1781.

A a 2   CHAP.

CHAP. II.

The Discovery of an Island called Wateeoo.—Its Coasts examined.—Visits from the Natives on board the Ships. —Messrs. Gore, Burney, and Anderson, with Omai, sent on Shore.—Mr. Anderson's Narrative of their Reception.—Omai's Expedient to prevent their being detained.—His meeting with some of his Countrymen, and their distressful Voyage.—Farther Account of Wateeoo, and of its Inhabitants.

1777.
March.
Sunday 30.
Monday 31.

AFTER leaving Mangeea, on the afternoon of the 30th, we continued our course Northward all that night, and till noon on the 31st; when we again saw land, in the direction of North East by North, distant eight or ten leagues.

April
Tuesday 1.

Next morning, at eight o'clock, we had got abreast of its North end, within four leagues of it, but to leeward; and could now pronounce it to be an island, nearly of the same appearance and extent with that we had so lately left. At the same time, another island, but much smaller, was seen right ahead. We could have soon reached this; but the largest one had the preference, as most likely to furnish a supply of food for the cattle, of which we began to be in great want.

With this view I determined to work up to it; but as there was but little wind, and that little was unfavourable,

we

THE PACIFIC OCEAN.   181

1777.
April.
Wednef. 2.

we were still two leagues to leeward at eight o'clock the
following morning. Soon after, I sent two armed boats
from the Resolution, and one from the Discovery, under
the command of Lieutenant Gore, to look for anchoring-
ground, and a landing-place. In the mean time, we plyed
up under the island with the ships.

Just as the boats were putting off, we observed several
single canoes coming from the shore. They went first to
the Discovery, she being the nearest ship. It was not long
after, when three of these canoes came along-side of the
Resolution, each conducted by one man. They are long
and narrow, and supported by outriggers. The stern is
elevated about three or four feet, something like a ship's
stern-post. The head is flat above, but prow-like below, and
turns down at the extremity, like the end of a violin. Some
knives, beads, and other trifles were conveyed to our visiters; and they gave us a few cocoa-nuts, upon our asking
for them. But they did not part with them by way of exchange for what they had received from us. For they
seemed to have no idea of bartering; nor did they appear
to estimate any of our presents at a high rate.

With a little persuasion, one of them made his canoe fast
to the ship, and came on board; and the other two, encouraged by his example, soon followed him. Their whole
behaviour marked that they were quite at their ease, and
felt no sort of apprehension of our detaining, or using
them ill.

After their departure, another canoe arrived, conducted by a man who brought a bunch of plantains as a
present to me; asking for me by name, having learnt it
from Omai, who was sent before us in the boat with Mr.

8   Gore.

Gore. In return for this civility, I gave him an axe, and a piece of red cloth; and he paddled back to the shore well satisfied. I afterward understood from Omai, that this present had been sent from the king, or principal Chief of the island.

Not long after, a double canoe, in which were twelve men, came toward us. As they drew near the ship, they recited some words in concert, by way of chorus*, one of their number first standing up, and giving the word before each repetition. When they had finished their solemn chant, they came along-side, and asked for the Chief. As soon as I shewed myself, a pig and a few cocoa-nuts were conveyed up into the ship; and the principal person in the canoe made me an additional present of a piece of matting, as soon as he and his companions got on board.

Our visiters were conducted into the cabin, and to other parts of the ship. Some objects seemed to strike them with a degree of surprize; but nothing fixed their attention for a moment. They were afraid to come near the cows and horses; nor did they form the least conception of their nature. But the sheep and goats did not surpass the limits of their ideas; for they gave us to understand, that they knew them to be birds. It will appear rather incredible, that human ignorance could ever make so

---

* Something like this ceremony was performed by the inhabitants of the Marquesas, when Captain Cook visited them in 1774. See his Voyage, Vol. i. p. 301. It is curious to observe, at what immense distances this mode of receiving strangers prevails. Padillo, who sailed from Manilla in 1710, on a voyage to discover the Palaos Islands, was thus received there. The writer of the relation of his voyage says, " Aussitot qu'ils approcherent de notre bord, ils se mirent à chanter. Ils " regloient la cadence, en frappant des mains sur leurs cuisses."
Lettres Edifiantes & Curieuses, Tom. xv. p. 313.

strange

strange a mistake; there not being the most distant similitude between a sheep or goat, and any winged animal. But these people seemed to know nothing of the existence of any other land-animals, besides hogs, dogs, and birds. Our sheep and goats, they could see, were very different creatures from the two first, and therefore they inferred, that they must belong to the latter class, in which they knew there is a considerable variety of species. I made a present to my new friend of what I thought might be most acceptable to him; but, on his going away, he seemed rather disappointed than pleased. I afterward understood that he was very desirous of obtaining a dog, of which animal this island could not boast, though its inhabitants knew that the race existed in other islands of their ocean. Captain Clerke had received the like present, with the same view, from another man, who met with from him the like disappointment.

The people in these canoes were in general of a middling size, and not unlike those of Mangeea; though several were of a blacker cast than any we saw there. Their hair was tied on the crown of the head, or flowing loose about the shoulders; and though in some it was of a frizzling disposition, yet, for the most part, that, as well as the straight sort, was long. Their features were various, and some of the young men rather handsome. Like those of Mangeea, they had girdles of glazed cloth, or fine matting, the ends of which, being brought betwixt their thighs, covered the adjoining parts. Ornaments, composed of a sort of broad grass, stained with red, and strung with berries of the night-shade, were worn about their necks. Their ears were bored, but not slit; and they were punctured upon the legs, from the knee to the heel, which made them appear

pear as if they wore a kind of boots. They also resembled the inhabitants of Mangeea in the length of their beards, and, like them, wore a sort of sandals upon their feet. Their behaviour was frank and cheerful, with a great deal of good-nature.

At three o'clock in the afternoon, Mr. Gore returned with the boat, and informed me, that he had examined all the West side of the island, without finding a place where a boat could land, or the ships could anchor, the shore being every where bounded by a steep coral rock, against which the sea broke in a dreadful surf. But as the natives seemed very friendly, and to express a degree of disappointment when they saw that our people failed in their attempts to land, Mr. Gore was of opinion, that by means of Omai, who could best explain our request, they might be prevailed upon to bring off to the boats, beyond the surf, such articles as we most wanted; in particular, the stems of plantain trees, which make good food for the cattle. Having little or no wind, the delay of a day or two was not of any moment; and therefore I determined to try the experiment, and got every thing ready against the next morning.

Soon after day-break, we observed some canoes coming off to the ships, and one of them directed its course to the Resolution. In it was a hog, with some plantains and cocoa nuts, for which the people, who brought them, demanded a dog from us, and refused every other thing that we offered in exchange. One of our gentlemen on board, happened to have a dog and a bitch, which were great nuisances in the ship, and might have been disposed of on this occasion for a purpose of real utility, by propagating a race of so useful an animal in this island. But their owner had no such views, in making them the companions of his voyage.

voyage. However, to gratify thefe people, Omai parted
with a favourite dog he had brought from England; and
with this acquifition they departed highly fatisfied.

About ten o'clock, I difpatched Mr. Gore with three
boats, two from the Refolution, and one from the Difcovery, to try the experiment he had propofed. And, as I
could confide in his diligence and ability, I left it entirely
to himfelf, to act as, from circumftances, he fhould judge to
be moft proper. Two of the natives, who had been on
board, accompanied him, and Omai went with him in his
boat as an interpreter. The fhips being a full league from
the ifland when the boats put off, and having but little
wind, it was noon before we could work up to it. We then
faw our three boats riding at their grapplings, juft without
the furf, and a prodigious number of the natives on the
fhore, abreaft of them. By this we concluded, that Mr.
Gore, and others of our people, had landed, and our impatience to know the event may be eafily conceived. In order
to obferve their motions, and to be ready to give them fuch
affiftance as they might want, and our refpective fituations
would admit of, I kept as near the fhore as was prudent. I
was fenfible, however, that the reef was as effectual a barrier
between us and our friends who had landed, and put them
as much beyond the reach of our protection, as if half the
circumference of the globe had intervened. But the
iflanders, it was probable, did not know this fo well as we
did. Some of them, now and then, came off to the fhips in
their canoes, with a few cocoa nuts, which they exchanged
for whatever was offered to them, without feeming to give
the preference to any particular article.

Thefe occafional vifits ferved to leffen my folicitude about
our people who had landed. Though we could get no in-
VOL. I. D b formation

1777.
March.

formation from our vifiters; yet their ventuiing on board feemed to imply, at leaft, that their countrymen on fhore had not made an improper ufe of the confidence put in them. At length, a little before fun-fet, we had the fatisfaction of feeing the boats put off. When they got on board, I found that Mr. Gore himfelf, Omai, Mr. Anderfon, and Mr. Burney, were the only perfons who had landed. The tranfactions of the day were now fully reported to me by Mr. Gore; but Mr. Anderfon's account of them being very particular, and including fome remarks on the ifland and its inhabitants, I fhall give it a place here, nearly in his own words.

"We rowed toward a fmall fandy beach, upon which, and upon the adjacent rocks, a great number of the natives had affembled; and came to an anchor within a hundred yards of the reef, which extends about as far, or a little farther, from the fhore. Several of the natives fwam off, bringing cocoa nuts; and Omai, with their countrymen, whom we had with us in the boats, made them fenfible of our wifh to land. But their attention was taken up, for a little time, by the dog, which had been carried from the fhip, and was juft brought on fhore, round whom they flocked with great eagernefs. Soon after, two canoes came off; and, to create a greater confidence in the iflanders, we determined to go unarmed, and run the hazard of being treated well or ill.

Mr. Burney, the firft Lieutenant of the Difcovery, and I, went in one canoe, a little time before the other; and our conductors, watching attentively the motions of the furf, landed us fafely upon the reef. An iflander took hold of each of us, obvioufly with an intention to fupport us in walking,

7   over

over the rugged rocks, to the beach, where several of the others met us, holding the green boughs, of a species of *Mimosa*, in their hands, and saluted us by applying their noses to ours.

We were conducted from the beach by our guides, amidst a great crowd of people, who flocked with very eager curiosity to look at us; and would have prevented our proceeding, had not some men, who seemed to have authority, dealt blows, with little distinction, amongst them, to keep them off. We were then led up an avenue of cocoa-palms; and soon came to a number of men, arranged in two rows, armed with clubs, which they held on their shoulders, much in the manner we rest a musquet. After walking a little way amongst these, we found a person who seemed a Chief, sitting on the ground crofs-legged, cooling himself with a fort of triangular fan, made from a leaf of the cocoa-palm, with a polished handle, of black wood, fixed to one corner. In his ears were large bunches of beautiful red feathers, which pointed forward. But he had no other mark, or ornament, to distinguish him from the rest of the people; though they all obeyed him with the greatest alacrity. He either naturally had, or at this time put on, a serious, but not severe countenance; and we were desired to salute him as he sat, by some people who seemed of consequence.

We proceeded still amongst the men armed with clubs, and came to a second Chief, who sat fanning himself, and ornamented as the first. He was remarkable for his size, and uncommon corpulence, though, to appearance, not above thirty years of age. In the same manner, we were conducted to a third Chief, who seemed older than the two former,

former, and, though not so far as the second, was of a large size. He also was sitting, and adorned with red feathers; and after saluting him as we had done the others, he desired us both to sit down. Which we were very willing to do, being pretty well fatigued with walking up, and with the excessive heat we felt amongst the vast crowd that surrounded us.

In a few minutes, the people were ordered to separate; and we saw, at the distance of thirty yards, about twenty young women, ornamented as the Chiefs, with red feathers, engaged in a dance, which they performed to a slow and serious air, sung by them all. We got up, and went forward to see them; and though we must have been strange objects to them, they continued their dance, without paying the least attention to us. They seemed to be directed by a man who served as a prompter, and mentioned each motion they were to make. But they never changed the spot, as we do in dancing, and though their feet were not at rest, this exercise consisted more in moving the fingers very nimbly, at the same time holding the hands in a prone position near the face, and now and then also clapping them together[*]. Their motions and song were performed in such exact concert, that it should seem they had been taught with great care; and probably they were selected for this ceremony, as few of those whom we saw in the crowd equalled them in beauty. In general, they were rather stout than slender, with black hair flowing in ringlets down the neck, and of an olive complexion. Their features were,

[*] The dances of the inhabitants of the Caroline Islands, have a great resemblance to those here described. See *Lettres Edif. et Curieuses*, Tom. xv. p. 315. See also, in the same volume, p. 207. what is said of the singing and dancing of the inhabitants of the Palaos Islands, which belong to the same group.

rather,

rather, fuller than what we allow to perfect beauties, and much alike; but their eyes were of a deep black, and each countenance expressed a degree of complacency and modesty, peculiar to the sex in every part of the world; but perhaps more conspicuous here, where Nature presented us with her productions in the fullest perfection, unbiassed in sentiment by custom, or unrestrained in manner by art. Their shape and limbs were elegantly formed. For, as their dress consisted only of a piece of glazed cloth fastened about the waist, and scarcely reaching so low as the knees, in many we had an opportunity of observing every part. This dance was not finished, when we heard a noise, as if some horses had been galloping toward us; and, on looking aside, we saw the people armed with clubs, who had been desired, as we supposed, to entertain us with the sight of their manner of fighting. This they now did, one party pursuing another who fled.

As we supposed the ceremony of being introduced to the Chiefs was at an end, we began to look about for Mr. Gore and Omai; and, though the crowd would hardly suffer us to move, we at length found them coming up, as much incommoded by the number of people as we had been, and introduced in the same manner to the three Chiefs, whose names were Otteroo, Taroa, and Fatouweera. Each of these expected a present; and Mr. Gore gave them such things as he had brought with him from the ship, for that purpose. After this, making use of Omai as his interpreter, he informed the Chiefs with what intention we had come on shore; but was given to understand, that he must wait till the next day, and then he should have what was wanted.

They

They now seemed to take some pains to separate us from each other; and every one of us had his circle, to surround and gaze at him. For my own part, I was, at one time, above an hour apart from my friends; and when I told the Chief, with whom I sat, that I wanted to speak to Omai, he peremptorily refused my request. At the same time, I found the people began to steal several trifling things which I had in my pocket; and when I took the liberty of complaining to the Chief of this treatment, he justified it. From these circumstances, I now entertained apprehensions, that they might have formed the design of detaining us amongst them. They did not, indeed, seem to be of a disposition so savage, as to make us anxious for the safety of our persons; but it was, nevertheless, vexing to think, we had hazarded being detained by their curiosity. In this situation, I asked for something to eat; and they readily brought to me some cocoa-nuts, bread-fruit, and a sort of sour pudding, which was presented by a woman. And on my complaining much of the heat, occasioned by the crowd, the Chief himself condescended to fan me, and gave me a small piece of cloth, which he had round his waist.

Mr. Burney happening to come to the place where I was, I mentioned my suspicions to him; and, to put it to the test, whether they were well-founded, we attempted to get to the beach. But we were stopped, when about half-way, by some men, who told us, that we must go back to the place which we had left. On coming up, we found Omai entertaining the same apprehensions. But he had, as he fancied, an additional reason for being afraid; for he had observed, that they had dug a hole in the ground for an oven, which they were now heating; and he could assign no other reason for this, than that they meant to roast, and eat

us,

us, as is practised by the inhabitants of New Zealand. Nay, he went so far as to ask them the question; at which they were greatly surprised, asking, in return, whether that was a custom with us? Mr. Burney and I were rather angry that they should be thus suspected by him; there having, as yet, been no appearances, in their conduct toward us, of their being capable of such brutality.

In this manner we were detained the greatest part of the day, being sometimes together, and sometimes separated; but always in a crowd, who, not satisfied with gazing at us, frequently desired us to uncover parts of our skin; the sight of which commonly produced a general murmur of admiration. At the same time, they did not omit these opportunities of rifling our pockets; and, at last, one of them snatched a small bayonet from Mr. Gore, which hung in its sheath by his side. This was represented to the Chief, who pretended to send some person in search of it. But, in all probability, he countenanced the theft; for, soon after, Omai had a dagger stolen from his side, in the same manner; though he did not miss it immediately.

Whether they observed any signs of uneasiness in us, or that they voluntarily repeated their emblems of friendship when we expressed a desire to go, I cannot tell; but, at this time, they brought some green boughs, and, sticking their ends in the ground, desired we might hold them as we sat. Upon our urging again the business we came upon, they gave us to understand, that we must stay and eat with them; and a pig which we saw, soon after, lying near the oven, which they had prepared and heated, removed Omai's apprehension of being put into it himself; and made us think it might be intended for our repast. The Chief also
promised

promised to send some people to procure food for the cattle; but it was not till pretty late in the afternoon, that we saw them return with a few plantain-trees, which they carried to our boats.

In the mean time, Mr. Burney and I attempted again to go to the beach; but when we arrived, found ourselves watched by people, who, to appearance, had been placed there for this purpose. For when I tried to wade in upon the reef, one of them took hold of my clothes, and dragged me back. I picked up some small pieces of coral, which they required me to throw down again; and, on my refusal, they made no scruple to take them forcibly from me. I had gathered some small plants; but these also I could not be permitted to retain. And they took a fan from Mr. Burney, which he had received as a present on coming ashore. Omai said, we had done wrong in taking up any thing; for it was not the custom here to permit freedoms of that kind to strangers, till they had, in some measure, naturalized them to the country, by entertaining them with festivity for two or three days.

Finding that the only method of procuring better treatment was to yield implicit obedience to their will, we went up again to the place we had left; and they now promised, that we should have a canoe to carry us off to our boats, after we had eaten a repast which had been prepared for us.

Accordingly, the second Chief, to whom we had been introduced in the morning, having seated himself upon a low broad stool of blackish hard wood, tolerably polished, and directing the multitude to make a pretty large ring, made us sit down by him. A considerable number of cocoa-nuts were

were now brought; and, shortly after, a long green basket, with a sufficient quantity of baked plantains to have served a dozen persons. A piece of the young hog, that had been dressed, was then set before each of us, of which we were desired to eat. Our appetites, however, had failed, from the fatigue of the day; and though we did eat a little to please them, it was without satisfaction to ourselves.

It being now near sun-set, we told them it was time to go on board. This they allowed; and sent down to the beach the remainder of the victuals that had been dressed, to be carried with us to the ships. But, before we set out, Omai was treated with a drink he had been used to in his own country; which, we observed, was made here, as at other islands in the South Sea, by chewing the root of a sort of pepper. We found a canoe ready to put us off to our boats; which the natives did, with the same caution as when we landed. But, even here, their thievish disposition did not leave them. For a person of some consequence among them, who came with us, took an opportunity, just as they were pushing the canoe into the surf, to snatch a bag out of her, which I had, with the greatest difficulty, preserved all the day; there being in it a small pocket-pistol, which I was unwilling to part with. Perceiving him, I called out, expressing as much displeasure as I could. On which he thought proper to return, and swim with the bag to the canoe; but denied he had stolen it, though detected in the very act. They put us on board our boats, with the cocoa-nuts, plantains, and other provisions, which they had brought; and we rowed to the ships, very well pleased that we had at last got out of the hands of our troublesome masters.

1777.
April.

We regretted much, that our restrained situation gave us so little opportunity of making observations on the country. For, during the whole day, we were seldom a hundred yards from the place where we were introduced to the Chiefs on landing; and, consequently, were confined to the surrounding objects. The first thing that presented itself, worthy of our notice, was the number of people; which must have been at least, two thousand. For those who welcomed us on the shore, bore no proportion to the multitude we found amongst the trees, on proceeding a little way up.

We could also observe, that, except a few, those we had hitherto seen on board, were of the lower class. For a great number of those we now met with, had a superior dignity in their air, and were of a much whiter cast. In general, they had the hair tied on the crown of the head, long, black, and of a most luxuriant growth. Many of the young men were perfect models in shape, of a complexion as delicate as that of the women, and, to appearance, of a disposition as amiable. Others, who were more advanced in years, were corpulent; and all had a remarkable smoothness of the skin. Their general dress was a piece of cloth, or mat, wrapped about the waist, and covering the parts which modesty conceals. But some had pieces of mats, most curiously varied with black and white, made into a sort of jacket without sleeves; and others wore conical caps of cocoa-nut core, neatly interwoven with small beads, made of a shelly substance. Their ears were pierced; and in them they hung bits of the membraneous part of some plant, or stuck there an odoriferous flower, which seemed to be a species of *gardenia*. Some, who were of a superior class, and also the Chiefs, had two little balls, with a common base,

made

made from the bone of some animal, which was hung round the neck, with a great many folds of small cord. And after the ceremony of introduction to the Chiefs was over, they then appeared without their red feathers; which are certainly considered here as a particular mark of distinction; for none but themselves, and the young women who danced, assumed them.

Some of the men were punctured all over the sides and back, in an uncommon manner; and some of the women had the same ornament on their legs. But this method was confined to those who seemed to be of a superior rank; and the men, in that case, were also generally distinguished by their size and corpulence, unless very young. The women of an advanced age had their hair cropped short; and many were cut, in oblique lines, all over the fore-part of the body; and some of the wounds, which formed rhomboidal figures, had been so lately inflicted, that the coagulated blood still remained in them.

The wife of one of the Chiefs appeared with her child, laid in a piece of red cloth, which had been presented to her husband; and seemed to carry it with great tenderness, suckling it much after the manner of our women. Another Chief introduced his daughter, who was young and beautiful; but appeared with all the timidity natural to the sex; though she gazed on us with a kind of anxious concern, that seemed to struggle with her fear, and to express her astonishment at so unusual a sight. Others advanced with more firmness, and, indeed, were less reserved than we expected; but behaved with a becoming modesty. We did not observe any personal deformities amongst either sex; except in a few who had scars of broad superficial ulcers, remaining

remaining on the face and other parts. In proportion to the number of people assembled, there appeared not many old men or women; which may easily be accounted for, by supposing that such as were in an advanced period of life, might neither have the inclination, nor the ability, to come from the more distant parts of the island. On the other hand, the children were numerous; and both these, and the men, climbed the trees to look at us, when we were hid by the surrounding crowd.

About a third part of the men were armed with clubs and spears; and, probably, these were only the persons who had come from a distance, as many of them had small baskets, mats, and other things, fastened to the ends of their weapons. The clubs were generally about six feet long, made of a hard black wood, lance-shaped at the end, but much broader, with the edge nicely scolloped, and the whole nearly polished. Others of them were narrower at the point, much shorter, and plain; and some were even so small, as to be used with one hand. The spears were made of the same wood, simply pointed; and, in general, above twelve feet long; though some were so short, that they seemed intended to be thrown as darts.

The place where we were all the day, was under the shade of various trees; in which they preserved their canoes from the sun. About eight or ten of them were here, all double ones; that is, two single ones fastened together (as is usual, throughout the whole extent of the Pacific Ocean), by rafters lashed across. They were about twenty feet long, about four feet deep, and the sides rounded with a plank raised upon them, which was fastened strongly by means of withes. Two of these canoes were most curiously ftained, or painted, all over with black, in numberless small figures; as squares, triangles, &c. and excelled, by far, any thing of that kind I had ever seen at any other island in this ocean. Our friends here, indeed, seemed to have exerted more skill in doing this, than in puncturing their own bodies. The paddles were about four feet long, nearly elliptical; but broader at the upper end than the middle. Near the same place was a hut or shed, about thirty feet long, and nine or ten high; in which, perhaps, these boats are built; but, at this time, it was empty.

The greatest number of the trees around us were *cocoa-palms*; some sorts of *hibiscus*; a species of *euphorbia*; and, toward the sea, abundance of the same kind of trees we had seen at Mangeea Nooe Nainaiwa; and which seemed to surround the shores of this island in the same manner. They are tall and slender, not much unlike a cypress; but with bunches of long, round, articulated leaves. The natives call them *etoa*. On the ground we saw some grass; a species of *convolvulus*; and a good deal of *treacle-mustard*. There are also, doubtless, other fruit-trees and useful plants which we did not see. For, besides several sorts of *plantains*, they brought, at different times, roots which they call *taro* (the *coccos* of other countries); a bread-fruit; and a basket of roasted nuts, of a kidney-shape, in taste like a chesnut, but coarser.

What the soil of the island may be, farther inland, we could not tell. But, toward the sea, it is nothing more than a bank of coral, ten or twelve feet high, steep, and rugged; except where there are small sandy beaches, at some clefts where the ascent is gradual. The coral, though it has, probably, been exposed to the weather for many centuries, has undergone no farther change than becoming black on the surface; which, from its irregularity, is not much unlike large masses of a burnt substance. But, on breaking some pieces off, we found, that, at the depth of two or three inches, it was just as fresh as the pieces that had been lately thrown upon the beach by the waves. The reef or rock, that lines the shore entirely, runs to different breadths into the sea, where it ends, all at once, and becomes like a high, steep wall. It is, nearly, even with the surface of the water, and of a brown or brick colour; but the texture is rather porous, yet sufficient to withstand the washing of the surf which continually breaks upon it."

Though the landing of our Gentlemen proved the means of enriching my Journal with the foregoing particulars, the principal object I had in view was, in a great measure, unattained; for the day was spent without getting any one thing from the island worth mentioning. The natives, however, were gratified with a sight they never before had; and, probably, will never have again. And mere curiosity seems to have been their chief motive for keeping the gentlemen under such restraint, and for using every art to prolong their continuance amongst them.

It has been mentioned, that Omai was sent upon this expedition; and, perhaps, his being Mr. Gore's interpreter was not the only service he performed this day. He was asked, by the natives, a great many questions concerning us, our ships, our country, and the sort of arms we used; and, according to the account he gave me, his answers were not a little upon the marvellous. As, for instance, he told them, that our country had ships as large as their island; on board which were instruments of war (describing our guns), of such dimensions, that several people might sit within them;

and

and that one of them was sufficient to crush the whole island at one shot. This led them to inquire of him, what sort of guns we actually had in our two ships. He said, that though they were but small, in comparison with those he had just described, yet, with such as they were, we could, with the greatest ease, and at the distance the ships were from the shore, destroy the island, and kill every soul in it. They persevered in their inquiries, to know by what means this could be done; and Omai explained the matter as well as he could. He happened luckily to have a few cartridges in his pocket. These he produced; the balls, and the gunpowder which was to set them in motion, were submitted to inspection; and, to supply the defects of his description, an appeal was made to the senses of the spectators. It has been mentioned above, that one of the Chiefs had ordered the multitude to form themselves into a circle. This furnished Omai with a convenient stage for his exhibition. In the center of this amphitheatre, the inconsiderable quantity of gunpowder, collected from his cartridges, was properly disposed upon the ground, and, by means of a bit of burning wood from the oven, where dinner was dressing, set on fire. The sudden blast, and loud report, the mingled flame and smoke, that instantly succeeded, now filled the whole assembly with astonishment; they no longer doubted the tremendous power of our weapons, and gave full credit to all that Omai had said.

If it had not been for the terrible ideas they conceived of the guns of our ships, from this specimen of their mode of operation, it was thought that they would have detained the gentlemen all night. For Omai assured them, that, if he and his companions did not return on board the same day, they might expect that I would fire upon the island.

And

1777.
April.

And as we stood in nearer the land in the evening, than we had done any time before, of which position of the ships they were observed to take great notice, they, probably, thought we were meditating this formidable attack; and, therefore, suffered their guests to depart; under the expectation, however, of seeing them again on shore next morning. But I was too sensible of the risk they had already run, to think of a repetition of the experiment.

This day, it seems, was destined to give Omai more occasions than one, of being brought forward to bear a principal part in its transactions. The island, though never before visited by Europeans, actually happened to have other strangers residing in it; and it was entirely owing to Omai's being one of Mr. Gore's attendants, that this curious circumstance came to our knowledge.

Scarcely had he been landed upon the beach, when he found, amongst the crowd there assembled, three of his own countrymen, natives of the Society Islands. At the distance of about two hundred leagues from those islands, an immense, unknown ocean intervening, with such wretched sea-boats as their inhabitants are known to make use of, and fit only for a passage where sight of land is scarcely ever lost, such a meeting, at such a place, so accidentally visited by us, may well be looked upon as one of those unexpected situations, with which the writers of feigned adventures love to surprise their readers, and which, when they really happen in common life, deserve to be recorded for their singularity.

It may easily be guessed, with what mutual surprise and satisfaction Omai and his countrymen engaged in conversation. Their story, as related by them, is an affecting one.
About

About twenty persons in number, of both sexes, had embarked on board a canoe at Otaheite, to cross over to the neighbouring island Ulietea. A violent contrary wind arising, they could neither reach the latter, nor get back to the former. Their intended passage being a very short one, their stock of provisions was scanty, and soon exhausted. The hardships they suffered, while driven along by the storm, they knew not whither, are not to be conceived. They passed many days without having any thing to eat or drink. Their numbers gradually diminished, worn out by famine and fatigue. Four men only survived, when the canoe overset; and then the perdition of this small remnant seemed inevitable. However, they kept hanging by the side of their vessel, during some of the last days, till Providence brought them in sight of the people of this island, who immediately sent out canoes, took them off their wreck, and brought them ashore. Of the four who were thus saved, one was since dead. The other three, who lived to have this opportunity of giving an account of their almost miraculous transplantation, spoke highly of the kind treatment they here met with. And so well satisfied were they with their situation, that they refused the offer made to them by our gentlemen, at Omai's request, of giving them a passage on board our ships, to restore them to their native islands. The similarity of manners and language, had more than naturalized them to this spot; and the fresh connexions which they had here formed, and which it would have been painful to have broken off, after such a length of time, sufficiently account for their declining to revisit the places of their birth. They had arrived upon this island at least twelve years ago. For I learnt from Mr. Anderson, that he found they knew nothing of Captain Wallis's visit to Otaheite in 1765; nor of several other memorable occurrences, such as the conquest of Ulietea by those of Bolabola, which had preceded the arrival of the Europeans. To Mr. Anderson I am also indebted for their names, Orououle, Otirreroa, and Tavee; the first, born at Matavai in Otaheite; the second, at Ulietea; and the third at Huaheine.

The landing of our gentlemen on this island, though they failed in the object of it, cannot but be considered as a very fortunate circumstance. It has proved, as we have seen, the means of bringing to our knowledge a matter of fact, not only very curious, but very instructive. The application of the above narrative is obvious. It will serve to explain, better than a thousand conjectures of speculative reasoners, how the detached parts of the earth, and, in particular, how the islands of the South Sea, may have been first peopled; especially those that lie remote from any inhabited continent, or from each other*.

* Such accidents as this here related, probably happen frequently in the Pacific Ocean. In 1696, two canoes, having on board thirty persons of both sexes, were driven, by contrary winds and tempestuous weather, on the isle of Samal, one of the Philippines, after being tost about at sea seventy days, and having performed a voyage, from an island called by them Amorsot, 300 leagues to the East of Samal. Five of the number who had embarked, died of the hardships suffered during this extraordinary passage. See a particular account of them, and of the islands they belonged to, in *Lettres Edifiantes & Curieuses*, Tom. xv. from p. 196. to p. 215. In the same Volume, from p. 282. to p. 320. we have the relation of a similar adventure, in 1721, when two canoes, one containing twenty-four, and the other six persons, men, women, and children, were driven, from an island they called Farroilep, Northward to the isle of Guam, or Guahan, one of the Ladrones or Marianes. But these had not failed so far as their countrymen, who reached Samal as above, and they had been at sea only twenty days. There seems to be no reason to doubt the general authenticity of these two relations. The information contained in the letters of the Jesuits, about their islands, now known under the name of the Carolines, and discovered to the Spaniards by the arrival of the canoes at Samal and Guam, has been adopted by all our later writers. See President de Brosse's *Voyages aux Terres Australes*, Tom. ii. from p. 443. to p. 493. See also the *Modern Universal History*.

This

This island is called Wateeoo by the natives. It lies in the latitude of 20° 1' South, and in the longitude 201° 45' East, and is about six leagues in circumference. It is a beautiful spot, with a surface composed of hills and plains, and covered with verdure of many hues. Our gentlemen found the soil, where they passed the day, to be light and sandy. But farther up the country, a different sort, perhaps, prevails; as we saw from the ship, by the help of our glasses, a reddish cast upon the rising grounds. There the inhabitants have their houses; for we could perceive two or three, which were long and spacious. Its produce, with the addition of hogs, we found to be the same as at the last island we had visited, which the people of this, to whom we pointed out its position, called Owhavarouah; a name so different from Mangeea Nooe Nainaiwa, which we learnt from its own inhabitants, that it is highly probable Owhavarouah is another island.

From the circumstances already mentioned, it appears, that Wateeoo can be of little use to any ship that wants refreshment, unless in a case of the most absolute necessity. The natives, knowing now the value of some of our commodities, might be induced to bring off fruits and hogs, to a ship standing off and on, or to boats lying off the reef, as ours did. It is doubtful, however, if any fresh water could be procured. For, though some was brought, in cocoa nut shells, to the gentlemen, they were told, that it was at a considerable distance; and, probably, it is only to be met with in some stagnant pool, as no running stream was any where seen.

According to Omai's report of what he learnt in conversation with his three countrymen, the manners of these islanders,

islanders, their method of treating strangers, and their general habits of life, are much like those that prevail at Otaheite, and its neighbouring isles. Their religious ceremonies and opinions are also nearly the same. For, upon seeing one man, who was painted all over of a deep black colour, and inquiring the reason, our gentlemen were told, that he had lately been paying the last good offices to a deceased friend; and they found, that it was upon similar occasions, the women cut themselves, as already mentioned. From every circumstance, indeed, it is indubitable, that the natives of Wateeoo sprung, originally, from the same stock, which hath spread itself so wonderfully all over the immense extent of the South Sea. One would suppose, however, that they put in their claim to a more illustrious extraction; for Omai assured us, that they dignified their island with the appellation of *W'enooa no te Eatooa*, that is, A land of gods; esteeming themselves a sort of divinities, and possessed with the spirit of the Eatooa. This wild enthusiastic notion Omai seemed much to approve of, telling us there were instances of its being entertained at Otaheite; but that it was universally prevalent amongst the inhabitants of Mataia, or Osnaburg Island.

The language spoken at Wateeoo was equally well understood by Omai, and by our two New Zealanders. What its peculiarities may be, when compared with the other dialects, I am not able to point out; for, though Mr. Anderson had taken care to note down a specimen of it, the natives, who made no distinction of the objects of their theft, stole the memorandum book.

CHAP.

CHAP. III.

Wenooa-ette, or Otakootaia, visited.—Account of that Island, and of its Produce.—Hervey's Island, or Terougge mou Attooa, found to be inhabited.—Transactions with the Natives.—Their Persons, Dress, Language, Canoes.—Fruitless Attempt to land there.—Reasons for bearing away for the Friendly Islands.—Palmerston's Island touched at.—Description of the two Places where the Boats landed.—Refreshments obtained there.—Conjectures on the Formation of such low Islands. —Arrival at the Friendly Islands.

LIGHT airs and calms having prevailed, by turns, all the night of the 3d, the Easterly swell had carried the ships some distance from Wateeoo, before day-break. But as I had failed in my object of procuring, at that place, some effectual supply, I saw no reason for staying there any longer. I, therefore, quitted it, without regret, and steered for the neighbouring island, which, as has been mentioned, we discovered three days before.

With a gentle breeze at East, we got up with it, before ten o'clock in the morning, and I immediately dispatched Mr. Gore, with two boats, to endeavour to land, and get some food for our cattle. As there seemed to be no inhabitants here to obstruct our taking away whatever we might think proper, I was confident of his being able to make amends for our late disappointment, if the landing could

be

be effected. There was a reef here surrounding the land, as at Wateeoo, and a confiderable furf breaking againſt the rocks. Notwithſtanding which, our boats no fooner reached the lee, or Weſt fide of the iſland, but they ventured in, and Mr. Gore and his party got fafe on ſhore. I could, from the ſhip, fee that they had fucceeded fo far; and I immediately fent a fmall boat to know what farther affiſtance was wanting. She did not return till three o'clock in the afternoon, having waited to take in a lading of what uſeful produce the iſland afforded. As foon as ſhe was cleared, ſhe was fent again for another cargo; the Jolly boat was alfo difpatched, and Mr. Gore was ordered to be on board, with all the boats, before night; which was complied with.

The fupply obtained here, confiſted of about a hundred cocoa nuts for each ſhip; and befides this refreſhment for ourſelves, we got for our cattle fome graſs, and a quantity of the leaves and branches of young cocoa trees, and of the *wharra* tree, as it is called at Otaheite, the *pandanus* of the Faſt Indies. This latter being of a foft, fpungy, juicy nature, the cattle eat it very well, when cut into fmall pieces; fo that it might be faid, without any deviation from truth, that we fed them upon billet wood.

This iſland lies in the latitude of 19° 15' South, and the longitude of 201° 37' Eaſt, about three or four leagues from Wateeoo, the inhabitants of which called it *Otakootaia*; and fometimes they ſpoke of it under the appellation of *Wenooaette*, which fignifies little iſland. Mr. Anderfon, who was on ſhore with our party, and walked round it, gueſſed that it could not be much more than three miles in circuit. From him I alfo learned the following particulars. The beach,

beach, within the reef, is composed of a white coral fand; above which, the land within does not rise above six or seven feet, and is covered with a light reddish soil; but is entirely destitute of water.

The only common trees found there were cocoa-palms, of which there were several clusters; and vast numbers of the *wharra*. There were, likewise, the *callophyllum*, *fariana*, *guettarda*, a species of *tournefortia*, and *taberne montane*, with a few other shrubs; and some of the *etoa* tree seen at Wateeoo. A sort of *bind weed* over-ran the vacant spaces; except in some places, where was found a considerable quantity of *treacle-mustard*, a species of *spurge*, with a few other small plants, and the *morinda citrifolia*; the fruit of which is eaten by the natives of Otaheite in times of scarcity. Omai, who had landed with the party, dressed some of it for their dinner; but it proved very indifferent.

The only bird seen amongst the trees, was a beautiful cuckoo, of a chesnut brown, variegated with black, which was shot. But, upon the shore, were some egg-birds; a small sort of curlew; blue and white herons; and great numbers of noddies; which last, at this time, laid their eggs, a little farther up, on the ground, and often rested on the *wharra* tree.

One of our people caught a lizard, of a most forbidding aspect, though small, running up a tree; and many, of another sort, were seen. The bushes toward the sea, were frequented by infinite numbers of a sort of moth, elegantly speckled with red, black, and white. There were also several other sorts of moths, as well as some pretty butterflies; and a few other insects.

Though

1777.
April.

Though there were, at this time, no fixed inhabitants upon the island, indubitable marks remained of its being, at least, occasionally frequented. In particular, a few empty huts were found. There were also several large stones erected, like monuments, under the shade of some trees; and several spaces inclosed with smaller ones; where, probably, the dead had been buried. And, in one place, a great many cockle-shells, of a particular sort, finely grooved, and larger than the fist, were to be seen; from which it was reasonable to conjecture, that the island had been visited by persons who feed, partly, on shell-fish. In one of the huts, Mr. Gore left a hatchet, and some nails, to the full value of what we took away.

Sunday 6.

As soon as the boats were hoisted in, I made sail again to the northward, with a light air of wind Easterly; intending to try our fortune at Hervey's Island, which was discovered in 1773, during my last voyage*. Although it was not above fifteen leagues distant, yet we did not get sight of it till day-break in the morning of the 6th, when it bore West South West, at the distance of about three leagues. As we drew near it, at eight o'clock, we observed several canoes put off from the shore; and they came directly toward the ships. This was a sight that, indeed, surprized me, as no signs of inhabitants were seen when the island was first discovered; which might be owing to a pretty brisk wind that then blew, and prevented their canoes venturing out, as the ships passed to leeward; whereas now we were to windward.

* See Captain Cook's Voyage, Vol. i. p. 190, where this island is said to be about six leagues in circuit.

As we still kept on toward the island, six or seven of the canoes, all double ones, soon came near us. There were, from three to six men, in each of them. They stopped at the distance of about a stone's throw from the ship; and it was some time before Omai could prevail upon them to come along-side; but no intreaties could induce any of them to venture on board. Indeed their disorderly and clamorous behaviour, by no means indicated a disposition to trust us, or treat us well. We afterward learnt that they had attempted to take some oars out of the Discovery's boat, that lay along-side, and struck a man who endeavoured to prevent them. They also cut away, with a shell, a net with meat, which hung over that ship's stern, and absolutely refused to restore it; though we, afterward, purchased it from them. Those who were about our ship, behaved in the same daring manner; for they made a sort of hook, of a long stick, with which they endeavoured, openly, to rob us of several things; and, at last, actually got a frock belonging to one of our people, that was rowing over-board. At the same time, they immediately shewed a knowledge of bartering, and sold some fish they had (amongst which was an extraordinary flounder, spotted like porphyry; and a cream-coloured eel, spotted with black), for small nails, of which they were immoderately fond, and called them *goure*. But, indeed, they caught, with the greatest avidity, bits of paper, or any thing else that was thrown to them; and if what was thrown fell into the sea, they made no scruple to swim after it.

These people seemed to differ as much in person, as in disposition, from the natives of Wateeoo; though the distance between the two islands is not very great. Their colour was of a deeper cast; and several had a fierce, rugged aspect, resembling the natives of New Zealand; but some were fairer. They had strong black hair, which, in general, they wore either hanging loose about the shoulders, or tied in a bunch on the crown of the head. Some, however, had it cropped pretty short; and, in two or three of them, it was of a brown, or reddish colour. Their only covering was a narrow piece of mat, wrapt several times round the lower part of the body, and which passed between the thighs; but a fine cap of red feathers was seen lying in one of the canoes. The shell of a pearl-oyster polished, and hung about the neck, was the only ornamental fashion that we observed amongst them; for not one of them had adopted that mode of ornament, so generally prevalent amongst the natives of this Ocean, of puncturing, or *tatooing* their bodies.

Though singular in this, we had the most unequivocal proofs of their being of the same common race. Their language approached still nearer to the dialect of Otaheite, than that of Wateeoo, or Mangeea. Like the inhabitants of these two islands, they inquired from whence our ships came; and whither bound; who was our Chief; the number of our men on board; and even the ship's name. And they very readily answered such questions as we proposed to them. Amongst other things, they told us, they had seen two great ships, like ours, before; but that they had not spoken with them as they sailed past. There can be no doubt, that these were the Resolution and Adventure. We learnt from them, that the name of their island is Te-rouggemou Atooa; and that they were subject to Teere-varooeah, king of Wateeoo[*]. According to the account

[*] The reader will observe, that this name bears little affinity to any one of the names of the three Chiefs of Wateeoo, as preserved by Mr. Anderson.

that

that they gave, their articles of food are cocoa-nuts, fish, and turtle; the island not producing plantains, or bread-fruit; and being destitute of hogs and dogs. Their canoes, of which near thirty were, at one time, in sight, are pretty large, and well built. In the construction of the stern, they bear some resemblance to those of Watceoo; and the head projects out nearly in the same manner; but the extremity is turned up instead of down.

Having but very little wind, it was one o'clock before we drew near the North West part of the island; the only part where there seemed to be any probability of finding anchorage for our ships, or a landing-place for our boats. In this position, I sent Lieutenant King, with two armed boats, to sound and reconnoitre the coast, while we stood off and on with the ships. The instant the boats were hoisted out, our visiters in the canoes, who had remained along-side all the while, bartering their little trifles, suspended their traffic, and, pushing for the shore as fast as they could, came near us no more.

At three o'clock, the boats returned; and Mr. King informed me, " That there was no anchorage for the ships; and that the boats could only land on the outer edge of the reef, which lay about a quarter of a mile from the dry land. He said, that a number of the natives came down upon the reef, armed with long pikes and clubs, as if they intended to oppose his landing. And yet, when he drew near enough, they threw some cocoa-nuts to our people, and invited them to come on shore; though, at the very same time, he observed that the women were very busy bringing down a fresh supply of spears and darts. But, as he

1777.
April

he had no motive to land, he did not give them an opportunity to ufe them."

Having received this report, I confidered, that, as the fhips could not be brought to an anchor, we fhould find that the attempt to procure grafs here, would occafion much delay, as well as be attended with fome danger. Befides, we were equally in want of water; and though the inhabitants had told us, that there was water on their ifland, yet we neither knew in what quantity, nor from what diftance, we might be obliged to fetch it. And, after all, fuppofing no other obftruction, we were fure, that to get over the reef, would be an operation equally difficult and tedious.

Being thus difappointed at all the iflands we had met with, fince our leaving New Zealand, and the unfavourable winds, and other unforefeen circumftances, having unavoidably retarded our progrefs fo much, it was now impoffible to think of doing any thing this year, in the high latitudes of the Northern hemifphere, from which we were ftill at fo great a diftance, though the feafon for our operations there was already begun. In this fituation, it was abfolutely neceffary to purfue fuch meafures as were moft likely to preferve the cattle we had on board, in the firft place; and, in the next place (which was ftill a more capital object), to fave the ftores and provifions of the fhips, that we might be better enabled to profecute our Northern difcoveries, which could not now commence till a year later than was orginally intended.

If I had been fo fortunate as to have procured a fupply of water, and of grafs, at any of the iflands we had lately vifited, it was my purpofe to have ftood back to the South, till I had

had met with a Westerly wind. But the certain consequence of doing this, without such a supply, would have been the loss of all the cattle, before we could possibly reach Otaheite, without gaining any one advantage, with regard to the great object of our voyage.

I, therefore, determined to bear away for the Friendly Islands, where I was sure of meeting with abundance of every thing I wanted: and it being necessary to run in the night, as well as in the day, I ordered Captain Clerke to keep about a league ahead of the Resolution. I used this precaution, because his ship could best claw off the land; and it was very possible we might fall in with some, in our passage.

The longitude of Hervey's Island, when first discovered, deduced from Otaheite, by the time-keeper, was found to be 201° 6' East, and now, by the same time-keeper, deduced from Queen Charlotte's Sound, 200° 56' East. Hence I conclude, that the error of the time-keeper, at this time, did not exceed twelve miles in longitude.

When we bore away, I steered West by South, with a fine breeze Easterly. I proposed to proceed first to Middleburgh, or Eooa; thinking, if the wind continued favourable, that we had food enough on board, for the cattle, to last till we should reach that island. But, about noon, next day, those faint breezes, that had attended and retarded us so long, again returned; and I found it necessary to haul more to the North, to get into the latitude of Palmerston's and Savage Islands, discovered in 1774, during my last voyage*; that, if necessity required it, we might have recourse to them.

* See Cook's Voyage, Vol. II. p. 2, 3.

1777.
April.

Monday 7.

This

1777.
April.

This day, in order to save our water, I ordered the still to be kept at work, from six o'clock in the morning to four in the afternoon; during which time, we procured from thirteen to sixteen gallons of fresh water. There has been lately made some improvement, as they are pleased to call it, of this machine, which, in my opinion, is much for the worse.

Thursday 10.

These light breezes continued till the 10th, when we had, for some hours, the wind blowing fresh from the North, and North North West; being then in the latitude of 18° 38', and longitude 196° 24' East. In the afternoon, we had some thunder squalls from the South, attended with heavy rain; of which water, we collected enough to fill five puncheons. After these squalls had blown over, the wind came round to the North East, and North West; being very unsettled both in strength and in position, till about noon the next day, when it fixed at North West, and North North West, and blew a fresh breeze, with fair weather.

Friday 11.

Thus were we persecuted with a wind in our teeth, whichever way we directed our course; and we had the additional mortification to find here, those very winds, which we had reason to expect 8° or 10° farther South. They came too late; for I durst not trust their continuance; and the event proved that I judged right.

Sunday 13.

At length, at day-break, in the morning of the 13th, we saw Palmerston Island, bearing West by South, distant about five leagues. However, we did not get up with it, till eight o'clock the next morning. I then sent four boats, three from the Resolution, and one from the Discovery, with an officer in each, to search the coast for the most convenient landing-place. For, now, we were under an absolute necessity

Monday 14.

fity of procuring, from this island, some food for the cattle; otherwise we must have lost them.

What is comprehended under the name of Palmerston's Island, is a group of small islots, of which there are, in the whole, nine or ten, lying in a circular direction, and connected together by a reef of coral rocks. The boats first examined the South Easternmost of the islots which compose this group; and, failing there, ran down to the second, where we had the satisfaction to see them land. I then bore down with the ships, till abreast of the place, and there we kept standing off and on. For no bottom was to be found to anchor upon; which was not of much consequence, as the party who had landed from our boats, were the only human beings upon the island.

About one o'clock, one of the boats came on board, laden with scurvy-grass and young cocoa-nut trees; which, at this time, was a feast for the cattle. The same boat brought a message from Mr. Gore, who commanded the party, informing me, that there was plenty of such produce upon the island, as also of the *wharra* tree, and some cocoa-nuts. This determined me to get a good supply of these articles, before I quitted this station; and, before evening, I went ashore in a small boat, accompanied by Captain Clerke.

We found every body hard at work, and the landing place to be in a small creek, formed by the reef, of something more than a boat's length in every direction, and covered from the force of the sea, by rocks projecting out on each side of it. The island is scarcely a mile in circuit; and not above three feet higher than the level of the sea. It appeared to be composed entirely of a coral sand, with a small mixture of blackish mould, produced from rotten vegetables.

1777.
April.

tables. Notwithstanding this poor soil, it is covered with trees and bushes of the same kind as at Wenooa-ette, though with less variety; and amongst these are some cocoa-palms. Upon the trees or bushes that front the sea, or even farther in, we found a great number of men of war birds, Tropic birds, and two sorts of boobies, which, at this time, were laying their eggs, and so tame, that they suffered us to take them off with our hands. Their nests were only a few sticks loosely put together; and the Tropic birds laid their eggs on the ground, under the trees. These differ much from the common sort, being entirely of a most splendid white, slightly tinged with red, and having the two long tail-feathers of a deep crimson or blood colour. Of each sort, our people killed a considerable number; and, though not the most delicate food, they were acceptable enough to us who had been long confined to a salt diet, and who, consequently, could not but be glad of the most indifferent variety. We met with vast numbers of red crabs, creeping about, every where amongst the trees; and we caught several fish that had been left in holes upon the reef, when the sea retired.

At one part of the reef, which looks into, or bounds, the lake that is within, there was a large bed of coral, almost even with the surface, which afforded, perhaps, one of the most enchanting prospects, that Nature has, any where, produced. Its base was fixed to the shore, but reached so far in, that it could not be seen; so that it seemed to be suspended in the water, which deepened so suddenly, that, at the distance of a few yards, there might be seven or eight fathoms. The sea was, at this time, quite unruffled; and the sun, shining bright, exposed the various sorts of coral, in the most beautiful order; some parts branching into the

water

water with great luxuriance; others, lying collected in round balls, and in various other figures; all which were greatly heightened by spangles of the richest colours, that glowed from a number of large clams, which were every where interspersed. But the appearance of these was still inferior to that of the multitude of fishes, that glided gently along, seemingly with the most perfect security. The colours of the different sorts were the most beautiful that can be imagined; the yellow, blue, red, black, &c. far exceeding any thing that art can produce. Their various forms, also, contributed to increase the richness of this submarine grotto, which could not be surveyed without a pleasing transport, mixed, however, with regret, that a work, so stupendously elegant, should be concealed, in a place where mankind could seldom have an opportunity of rendering the praises justly due to so enchanting a scene.

There were no traces of inhabitants having ever been here; if we except a small piece of a canoe that was found upon the beach; which, probably, may have drifted from some other island. But, what is pretty extraordinary, we saw several small brown rats on this spot; a circumstance, perhaps, difficult to account for, unless we allow that they were imported in the canoe of which we saw the remains.

After the boats were laden, I returned on board, leaving Mr. Gore, with a party, to pass the night on shore, in order to be ready to go to work early the next morning.

That day, being the 15th, was accordingly spent, as the preceding one had been, in collecting, and bringing on board, food for the cattle, consisting chiefly of palm-cabbage, young cocoa-nut trees, and the tender branches of the *wharra* tree. Having got a sufficient supply of these,

1777.
April.

by sunset, I ordered every body on board. But having little or no wind, I determined to wait, and to employ the next day, by endeavouring to get some cocoa-nuts for our people, from the next island to leeward, where we could observe that those trees were in much greater abundance, than upon that where we had already landed, and where only the wants of our cattle had been relieved.

Wednes. 16.

With this view, I kept standing off and on, all night; and, in the morning, between eight and nine o'clock, I went with the boats to the West side of the island, and landed with little difficulty. I immediately set the people with me to work, to gather cocoa-nuts, which we found in great abundance. But to get them to our boats was a tedious operation; for we were obliged to carry them at least half a mile over the reef, up to the middle in water. Omai, who was with me, caught, with a scoop net, in a very short time, as much fish as served the whole party on shore for dinner, besides sending some to both ships. Here were also great abundance of birds, particularly men-of-war and Tropic birds; so that we fared sumptuously. And it is but doing justice to Omai to say, that, in these excursions to the uninhabited islands, he was of the greatest use. For he not only caught the fish, but dressed these, and the birds we killed, in an oven, with heated stones, after the fashion of his country, with a dexterity and good-humour that did him great credit. The boats made two trips, before night, well laden; with the last, I returned on board, leaving Mr. Williamson, my third Lieutenant, with a party of men, to prepare another lading for the boats which I proposed to send next morning.

Thursday 17.

I, accordingly, dispatched them at seven o'clock, and they returned laden by noon. No time was lost in sending them back

back for another cargo; and they carried orders for every body to be on board by sunset. This being complied with, we hoisted in the boats and made sail to the Westward, with a light air of wind from the North.

We found this islot near a half larger than the other, and almost entirely covered with cocoa-palms; the greatest part of which abounded with excellent nuts, having, often, both old and young on the same tree. They were, indeed, too thick, in many places, to grow with freedom. The other productions were, in general, the same as at the first islot. Two pieces of board, one of which was rudely carved, with an elliptical paddle, were found on the beach. Probably, these had belonged to the same canoe, the remains of which were seen on the other beach, as the two islots are not above half a mile apart. A young turtle had also been lately thrown ashore here, as it was still full of maggots. There were fewer crabs than at the last place; but we found some scorpions, a few other insects, and a greater number of fish upon the reefs. Amongst these were some large eels, beautifully spotted, which, when followed, would raise themselves out of the water, and endeavour, with an open mouth, to bite their pursuers. The other sorts were, chiefly, parrot-fish, snappers, and a brown spotted rock-fish, about the size of a haddock, so tame, that, instead of swimming away, it would remain fixed, and gaze at us. Had we been in absolute want, a sufficient supply might have been had; for thousands of the clams, already mentioned, stuck upon the reef, some of which weighed two or three pounds. There were, besides, some other sorts of shell-fish; particularly, the large periwinkle. When the tide flowed, several sharks came in, over the reef, some of which our people killed;

but

but they rendered it rather dangerous to walk in the water at that time.

The party who were left on shore with Mr. Williamson, were a good deal pestered (as Mr. Gore's had been) with musquitoes, in the night. Some of them, in their excursions, shot two curlews, exactly like those of England; and saw some plovers, or sand-pipers, upon the shore; but, in the wood, no other bird, besides one or two of the cuckoos that were seen at Wenooa-ette.

Upon the whole, we did not spend our time unprofitably at this last islot; for we got there about twelve hundred cocoa-nuts, which were equally divided amongst the whole crew; and were, doubtless, of great use to them, both on account of the juice and of the kernel. A ship, therefore, passing this way, if the weather be moderate, may expect to succeed as we did. But there is no water upon either of the islots where we landed. Were that article to be had, and a passage could be got into the lake, as we may call it, surrounded by the reef, where a ship could anchor, I should prefer this to any of the inhabited islands, if the only want were refreshment. For the quantity of fish that might be procured, would be sufficient; and the people might roam about, unmolested by the petulance of any inhabitants.

The nine or ten low islots, comprehended under the name of Palmerston's Island, may be reckoned the heads or summits of the reef of coral rock, that connects them together, covered only with a thin coat of sand, yet clothed, as already observed, with trees and plants, most of which are of the same sorts that are found on the low grounds of the high Islands of this ocean.

There

There are different opinions, amongst ingenious theorists, concerning the formation of such low islands as Palmerston's. Some will have it, that, in remote times, these little separate heads or islots were joined, and formed one continued and more elevated tract of land, which the sea, in the revolution of ages, has washed away, leaving only the higher grounds; which, in time, also, will, according to this theory, share the same fate. Another conjecture is, that they have been thrown up by earthquakes, and are the effect of internal convulsions of the globe. A third opinion, and which appears to me as the most probable one, maintains, that they are formed from shoals, or coral banks, and, of consequence, increasing. Without mentioning the several arguments made use of in support of each of these systems, I shall only describe such parts of Palmerston's Island, as fell under my own observation when I landed upon it.

The foundation is, every where, a coral rock; the soil is coral sand, with which the decayed vegetables have, but in a few places, intermixed, so as to form any thing like mould. From this, a very strong presumption may be drawn, that these little spots of land, are not of very ancient date, nor the remains of larger islands now buried in the ocean. For, upon either of these suppositions, more mould must have been formed, or some part of the original soil would have remained. Another circumstance confirmed this doctrine of the increase of these islots. We found upon them, far beyond the present reach of the sea, even in the most violent storms, elevated coral rocks, which, on examination, appeared to have been perforated, in the same manner that the rocks are, that now compose the outer edge of the reef. This evidently shews, that the

sea

1777.
April.

sea had formerly reached so far; and some of these perforated rocks were almost in the centre of the land.

But the strongest proof of the increase, and from the cause we have assigned, was the gentle gradation observable in the plants round the skirts of the islands; from within a few inches of high-water mark, to the edge of the wood. In many places, the divisions of the plants, of different growths, were very distinguishable, especially on the lee, or west-side. This, I apprehend, to have been the operation of extraordinary high tides, occasioned by violent, accidental gales from the Westward; which have heaped up the sand beyond the reach of common tides. The regular and gentle operation of these latter, again, throw up sand enough to form a barrier against the next extraordinary high tide, or storm, so as to prevent its reaching as far as the former had done, and destroying the plants that may have begun to vegetate from cocoa-nuts, roots, and seed brought thither by birds, or thrown up by the sea. This, doubtless, happens very frequently; for we found many cocoa-nuts, and some other things, just sprouting up, only a few inches beyond where the sea reaches at present, in places where, it was evident, they could not have had their origin from those farther in, already arrived at their full growth. At the same time, the increase of vegetables will add fast to the height of this new-created land; as the fallen leaves, and broken branches, are, in such a climate, soon converted into a true black mould, or soil [*].

Perhaps

[*] Mr. Anderson, in his Journal, mentions the following particulars, relative to Palmerston's Island, which strongly confirm Captain Cook's opinion about its formation. "On the last of the two islets, where we landed, the trees, being in
"great

Perhaps there is another caufe, which, if allowed, will accelerate the increafe of thefe iflands as much as any other; and will alfo account for the fea having receded from thofe elevated rocks before-mentioned. This is, the fpreading of the coral bank, or reef, into the fea; which, in my opinion, is continually, though imperceptibly, affected. The waves receding, as the reef grows in breadth and height, leave a dry rock behind, ready for the reception of the broken coral and fand, and every other depofit neceffary for the formation of land fit for the vegetation of plants.

In this manner, there is little doubt, that, in time, the whole reef will become one ifland; and, I think, it will extend gradually inward, either from the increafe of the iflots already formed; or from the formation of new ones, upon the beds of coral, within the inclofed lake, if once they increafe fo as to rife above the level of the fea.

After leaving Palmerfton's Ifland, I fteered Weft, with a view to make the beft of my way to Annamooka. We ftill continued to have variable winds, frequently between the North and Weft, with fqualls, fome thunder, and much rain. During thefe fhowers, which were, generally, very copious, we faved a confiderable quantity of water; and finding that we could get a greater fupply by the rain, in

" great numbers, had already formed, by their rotten parts, little rifings or eminences,
" which, in time, from the fame caufe, may become fmall hills. Whereas, on the firft
" iflot, the trees being left numerous, no fuch thing had, as yet, happened. Neverthe-
" lefs, on that little fpot, the manner of formation was more plainly pointed out,
" For, adjoining to it, was a fmall ifle, which had, doubtlefs, been very lately formed;
" as it was not, as yet, covered with any trees, but had a great many fhrubs, fome
" of which were growing among pieces of coral that the fea had thrown up. There
" was ftill a more fure proof of this method of formation a little farther on, where
" two patches of fand, about fifty yards long, and a foot or eighteen inches high,
" lay upon the reef, but not, as yet, furnifhed with a fingle bufh, or tree."

one hour, than we could get by distillation in a month, I laid aside the still, as a thing attended with more trouble than profit.

The heat, which had been great for about a month, became now much more disagreeable in this close rainy weather; and, from the moisture attending it, threatened soon to be noxious; as the ships could not be kept dry, nor the scuttles open, for the sea. However, it is remarkable enough, that though the only refreshment we had received since leaving the Cape of Good Hope, was that at New Zealand; there was not, as yet, a single person, on board, sick, from the constant use of salt food, or vicissitude of climate.

Thursday 24.
Friday 25.
Monday 28.

In the night between the 24th and 25th we passed Savage Island, which I had discovered in 1774*; and on the 28th, at ten o'clock in the morning, we got sight of the islands which lie to the Eastward of Annamooka, bearing North by West, about four or five leagues distant. I steered to the South of these islands, and then hauled up for Annamooka; which, at four in the afternoon, bore North West by North, Fallafajeea South West by South, and Komango North by West, distant about five miles. The weather being squally, with rain, I anchored, at the approach of night, in fifteen fathoms deep water, over a bottom of coral-sand, and shells; Komango bearing North West, about two leagues distant.

* For an account of the discovery of Savage Island; a description of it; and the behaviour of its inhabitants, on Captain Cook's landing, see his Voyage, Vol. II. p. 3. to p. 7.

CHAP.

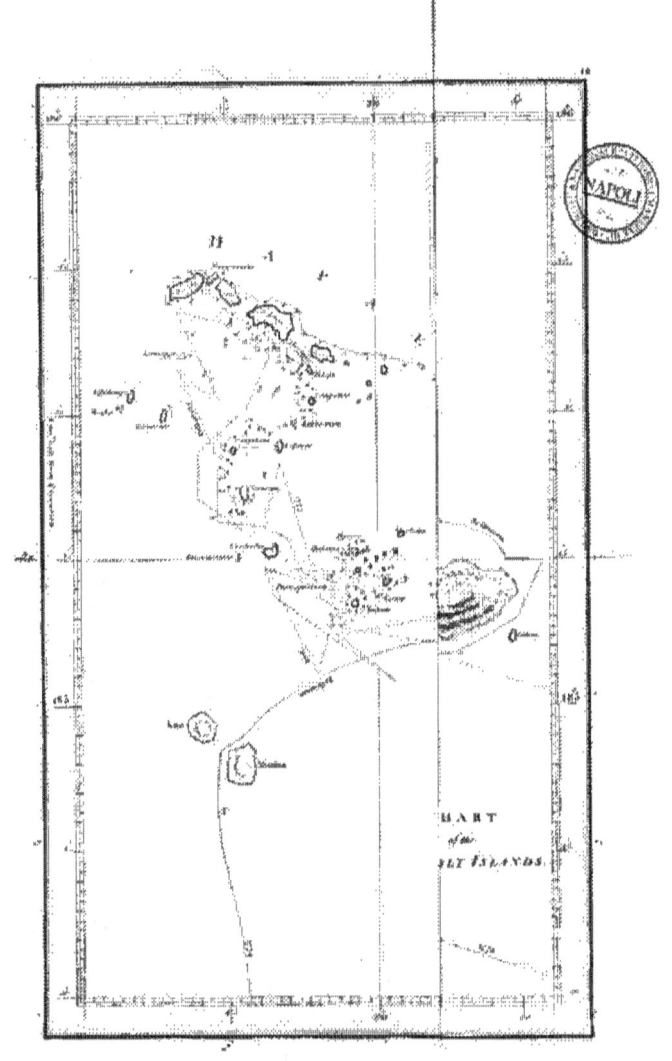

CHAP. IV.

Intercourse with the Natives of Komango, and other Islands.—Arrival at Annamooka—Transactions there.—Feenou, a principal Chief, from Tongataboo, comes on a Visit.—The Manner of his Reception in the Island, and on board.—Instances of the pilfering Disposition of the Natives.—Some Account of Annamooka.—The Passage from it to Hapaee.

SOON after we had anchored, two canoes, the one with four, and the other with three men, paddled toward us, and came along-side without the least hesitation. They brought some cocoa-nuts, bread-fruit, plantains, and sugarcane, which they bartered with us for nails. One of the men came on board; and when these canoes had left us, another visited us; but did not stay long, as night was approaching. Komango, the island nearest to us, was, at least, five miles off; which shews the hazard these people would run, in order to possess a few of our most trifling articles. Besides this supply from the shore, we caught, this evening, with hooks and lines, a considerable quantity of fish.

1777. April. Monday 28.

Next morning, at four o'clock, I sent Lieutenant King, with two boats, to Komango, to procure refreshments; and, at five, made the signal to weigh, in order to ply up to Annamooka, the wind being unfavourable at North West.

Tuesday 29.

It was no sooner day-light, than we were visited by six or seven canoes from different islands, bringing with them, besides fruits and roots, two pigs, several fowls, some large wood-pigeons, small rails, and large violet-coloured coots. All these they exchanged with us for beads, nails, hatchets, &c. They had also other articles of commerce; such as pieces of their cloth, fish-hooks, small baskets, musical reeds, and some clubs, spears, and bows. But I ordered, that no curiosities should be purchased, till the ships should be supplied with provisions, and leave given for that purpose. Knowing, also, from experience, that, if all our people might trade with the natives, according to their own caprice, perpetual quarrels would ensue, I ordered that particular persons should manage the traffic both on board and on shore, prohibiting all others to interfere. Before mid-day, Mr. King's boat returned with seven hogs, some fowls, a quantity of fruit and roots for ourselves, and some grass for the cattle. His party was very civilly treated at Komango. The inhabitants did not seem to be numerous; and their huts, which stood close to each other, within a plantain walk, were but indifferent. Not far from them, was a pretty large pond of fresh water, tolerably good; but there was not any appearance of a stream. With Mr. King, came on board the Chief of the island, named Tooboulangee; and another, whose name was Taipa. They brought with them a hog, as a present to me, and promised more the next day.

As soon as the boats were aboard, I stood for Annamooka; and the wind being scant, I intended to go between Annamooka-ette *, and the breakers to the South East of it. But,

* That is, Little Annamooka.

on drawing near, we met with very irregular soundings, varying, every cast, ten or twelve fathoms. This obliged me to give up the design, and to go to the Southward of all; which carried us to leeward, and made it neceſſary to spend the night under sail. It was very dark; and we had the wind, from every direction, accompanied with heavy showers of rain. So that, at day-light the next morning, we found ourselves much farther off than we had been the evening before; and the little wind that now blew, was right in our teeth.

We continued to ply, all day, to very little purpose; and, in the evening, anchored in thirty-nine fathoms water; the bottom coral rocks, and broken shells; the West point of Annamooka bearing East North East, four miles distant. Tooboulangee and Taipa kept their promise, and brought off to me some hogs. Several others were also procured by bartering, from different canoes that followed us; and as much fruit as we could well manage. It was remarkable, that, during the whole day, our visiters from the islands would hardly part with any of their commodities to any body but me. Captain Clerke did not get above one or two hogs.

At four o'clock next morning, I ordered a boat to be hoisted out, and sent the Master to sound the South West side of Annamooka; where there appeared to be a harbour, formed by the island on the North East, and by small islots, and shoals, to the South West and South East. In the mean time, the ships were got under sail, and wrought up to the island.

When the Master returned, he reported, that he had sounded between Great and Little Annamooka, where he found ten and twelve fathoms depth of water, the bottom coral sand; that the place was very well sheltered from all winds; but that there was no fresh water to be found, except at some distance inland; and that, even there, little of it was to be got, and that little not good. For this reason only, and it was a very sufficient one, I determined to anchor on the North side of the island, where, during my last voyage, I had found a place fit both for watering and landing.

It was not above a league distant; and yet we did not reach it till five o'clock in the afternoon, being considerably retarded by the great number of canoes that continually crowded round the ships, bringing to us abundant supplies of the produce of their island. Amongst these canoes, there were some double ones, with a large sail, that carried between forty and fifty men each. These sailed round us, apparently, with the same ease, as if we had been at anchor. There were several women in the canoes, who were, perhaps, incited by curiosity to visit us; though, at the same time, they bartered as eagerly as the men, and used the paddle with equal labour and dexterity. I came to an anchor in eighteen fathoms water, the bottom coarse coral sand; the island extending from East to South West; and the West point of the Westernmost cove South East, about three quarters of a mile distant. Thus I resumed the very same station which I had occupied when I visited Annamooka three years before *; and, probably, almost in the same place where Tasman, the first discoverer of this, and some of the neighbouring islands, anchored in 1643 †.

* See Captain Cook's last Voyage, Vol. ii. p. 9.
† See Tasman's account of this island, in Mr. Dalrymple's valuable Collection of Voyages to the Pacific Ocean, Vol. ii. p. 79, 80. The few particulars mentioned by Tasman, agree remarkably with Captain Cook's more extended relation.

The

The following day, while preparations were making for watering, I went ashore, in the forenoon, accompanied by Captain Clerke, and some of the Officers, to fix on a place where the observatories might be set up, and a guard be stationed; the natives having readily given us leave. They also accommodated us with a boat-house, to serve as a tent, and shewed us every other mark of civility. Toobou, the Chief of the island, conducted me and Omai to his house. We found it situated on a pleasant spot, in the centre of his plantation. A fine grass-plot surrounded it, which, he gave us to understand, was for the purpose of cleaning their feet, before they went within doors. I had not, before, observed such an instance of attention to cleanliness at any of the places I had visited in this ocean; but, afterward, found that it was very common at the Friendly Islands. The floor of Toobou's house was covered with mats; and no carpet, in the most elegant English drawing-room, could be kept neater. While we were on shore, we procured a few hogs, and some fruit, by bartering; and, before we got on board again, the ships were crowded with the natives. Few of them coming empty-handed, every necessary refreshment was now in the greatest plenty.

I landed again in the afternoon, with a party of marines; and, at the same time, the horses, and such of the cattle as were in a weakly state, were sent on shore. Every thing being settled to my satisfaction, I returned to the ship at sunset, leaving the command upon the island to Mr. King. Taipa, who was now become our fast friend, and who seemed to be the only active person about us, in order to be near our party in the night, as well as the day, had a house brought, on men's shoulders, a full quarter of a mile, and placed close to the shed which our party occupied.

Next

1777.
May.
Saturday 3.

Next day, our various operations on shore began. Some were employed in making hay for the cattle; others in filling our water casks at the neighbouring stagnant pool; and a third party in cutting wood. The greatest plenty of this last article being abreast of the ships, and in a situation the most convenient for getting it on board, it was natural to make choice of this. But the trees here, which our people erroneously supposed to be manchineel, but were a species of pepper, called *faitanoo* by the natives, yielded a juice of a milky colour, of so corrosive a nature, that it raised blisters on the skin, and injured the eyes of our workmen. They were, therefore, obliged to desist at this place, and remove to the cove, in which our guard was stationed, and where we embarked our water. Other wood, more suitable to our purposes, was there furnished to us by the natives. These were not the only employments we were engaged in, for Messrs. King and Bayly began, this day, to observe equal altitudes of the sun, in order to get the rate of the time-keepers. In the evening, before the natives retired from our post, Taipa harangued them for some time. We could only guess at the subject; and judged, that he was instructing them how to behave toward us, and encouraging them to bring the produce of the island to market. We experienced the good effects of his eloquence, in the plentiful supply of provisions which, next day, we received.

Sunday 4.
Monday 5.

Nothing worth notice happened on the 4th and 5th, except that, on the former of these days, the Discovery lost her small-bower anchor, the cable being cut in two by the rocks. This misfortune made it necessary to examine the cables of the Resolution, which were found to be unhurt.

On the 6th, we were visited by a great Chief from Tongataboo, whose name was Feenou, and whom Taipa was pleased to introduce to us as King of all the Friendly Isles. I was now told, that, on my arrival, a canoe had been dispatched to Tongataboo with the news; in consequence of which, this Chief immediately passed over to Annamooka. The Officer on shore informed me, that when he first arrived, all the natives were ordered out to meet him, and paid their obeisance by bowing their heads as low as his feet, the soles of which they also touched with each hand, first with the palm, and then with the back part. There could be little room to suspect that a person, received with so much respect, could be any thing less than the King.

In the afternoon, I went to pay this great man a visit, having first received a present of two fish from him, brought on board by one of his servants. As soon as I landed, he came up to me. He appeared to be about thirty years of age, tall, but thin, and had more of the European features, than any I had yet seen here. When the first salutation was over, I asked if he was the King. For, notwithstanding what I had been told, finding he was not the man whom I remembered to have seen under that character during my former voyage, I began to entertain doubts. Taipa officiously answered for him, and enumerated no less than one hundred and fifty-three islands, of which, he said, Feenou was the Sovereign. After a short stay, our new visiter, and five or six of his attendants, accompanied me on board. I gave suitable presents to them all, and entertained them in such a manner, as I thought would be most agreeable.

In the evening, I attended them on shore in my boat, into which the Chief ordered three hogs to be put, as a return

for

for the presents he had received from me. I was now informed of an accident which had just happened, the relation of which will convey some idea of the extent of the authority exercised here over the common people. While Feenou was on board my ship, an inferior Chief, for what reason our people on shore did not know, ordered all the natives to retire from the post we occupied. Some of them having ventured to return, he took up a large stick, and beat them most unmercifully. He struck one man, on the side of the face, with so much violence, that the blood gushed out of his mouth and nostrils; and, after lying some time motionless, he was, at last, removed from the place, in convulsions. The person who had inflicted the blow, being told that he had killed the man, only laughed at it; and, it was evident, that he was not in the least sorry for what had happened. We heard, afterward, that the poor sufferer recovered.

The Discovery having found again her small bower anchor, shifted her birth on the 7th; but not before her best bower cable had shared the fate of the other. This day, I had the company of Feenou at dinner; and also the next day, when he was attended by Taipa, Toobou, and some other Chiefs. It was remarkable, that none but Taipa was allowed to sit at table with him, or even to eat in his presence. I own that I considered Feenou as a very convenient guest, on account of this etiquette. For, before his arrival, I had, generally, a larger company than I could well find room for, and my table overflowed with crowds of both sexes. For it is not the custom at the Friendly Islands, as it is at Otaheite, to deny to their females the privilege of eating in company with the men.

The

The first day of our arrival at Annamooka, one of the natives had stolen, out of the ship, a large junk axe. I now applied to Feenou to exert his authority to get it restored to me; and so implicitly was he obeyed, that it was brought on board while we were at dinner. These people gave us very frequent opportunities of remarking what expert thieves they were. Even some of their Chiefs did not think this profession beneath them. On the 9th, one of them was detected carrying out of the ship, concealed under his clothes, the bolt belonging to the spun yarn winch; for which I sentenced him to receive a dozen lashes, and kept him confined till he paid a hog for his liberty. After this, we were not troubled with thieves of rank. Their servants, or slaves, however, were still employed in this dirty work, and upon them a flogging seemed to make no greater impression, than it would have done upon the main-mast. When any of them happened to be caught in the act, their masters, far from interceding for them, would often advise us to kill them. As this was a punishment we did not choose to inflict, they generally escaped without any punishment at all; for they appeared to us to be equally insensible of the shame, and of the pain of corporal chastisement. Captain Clerke, at last, hit upon a mode of treatment, which, we thought, had some effect. He put them under the hands of the barber, and completely shaved their heads; thus pointing them out as objects of ridicule to their countrymen, and enabling our people to deprive them of future opportunities for a repetition of their rogueries, by keeping them at a distance.

Feenou was so fond of associating with us, that he dined on board every day; though, sometimes, he did not partake of our fare. On the 10th, some of his servants brought a mess,

mess, which had been dressed for him on shore. It consisted of fish, soup, and yams. Instead of common water to make the soup, cocoa-nut liquor had been made use of, in which the fish had been boiled or stewed; probably in a wooden vessel, with hot stones; but it was carried on board in a plantain leaf. I tasted of the mess, and found it so good, that I, afterward, had some fish dressed in the same way. Though my cook succeeded tolerably well, he could produce nothing equal to the dish he imitated.

Finding that we had quite exhausted the island, of almost every article of food that it afforded, I employed the 11th in moving off, from the shore, the horses, observatories, and other things that we had landed, as also the party of marines who had mounted guard at our station, intending to sail, as soon as the Discovery should have recovered her best bower anchor. Feenou, understanding that I meant to proceed directly to Tongataboo, importuned me strongly to alter this plan, to which he expressed as much aversion, as if he had some particular interest to promote by diverting me from it. In preference to it, he warmly recommended an island, or rather a group of islands, called Hapaee, lying to the North East. There, he assured us, we could be supplied plentifully with every refreshment, in the easiest manner; and, to add weight to his advice, he engaged to attend us thither in person. He carried his point with me; and Hapaee was made choice of for our next station. As it had never been visited by any European ships, the examination of it became an object with me.

The 12th, and the 13th, were spent in attempting the recovery of Captain Clerke's anchor, which, after much trouble, was happily accomplished; and on the 14th, in the morning, we got under sail, and left Annamooka.

This island is somewhat higher than the other small isles that surround it; but, still, it cannot be admitted to the rank of those of a moderate height, such as Mangeea and Watecoo. The shore, at that part where our ships lay, is composed of a steep, rugged coral rock, nine or ten feet high, except where there are two sandy beaches, which have a reef of the same sort of rock extending cross their entrance to the shore, and defending them from the sea. The salt water lake that is in the centre of the island, is about a mile and a half broad; and round it, the land rises like a bank, with a gradual ascent. But we could not trace its having any communication with the sea. And yet, the land that runs across to it, from the largest sandy beach, being flat and low, and the soil sandy, it is most likely that it may have, formerly, communicated that way. The soil, on the rising parts of the island, and especially toward the sea, is either of a reddish clayey disposition, or a black, loose mould; but there is, no where, any stream of fresh water.

The island is very well cultivated, except in a few places; and there are some others, which, though they appear to lie waste, are only left to recover the strength exhausted by constant culture; for we frequently saw the natives at work upon these spots, to plant them again. The plantations consist chiefly of yams and plantains. Many of them are very extensive, and often inclosed with neat fences of reed, disposed obliquely across each other, about six feet high. Within these, we often saw other fences of less compass, surrounding the houses of the principal people. The bread-fruit, and cocoa-nut trees, are interspersed with little order; but chiefly near the habitations of the natives; and the other parts of the island, especially toward the sea, and about the sides of the lake, are covered with trees and bushes of a most luxuriant growth; the last place having a

great

great many mangroves, and the first a vast number of the *faitanoo* trees already mentioned. There seem to be no rocks, or stones, of any kind, about the island, that are not coral; except in one place, to the right of the sandy beach, where there is a rock twenty or thirty feet high, of a calcareous stone, of a yellowish colour, and a very close texture. But even about that place, which is the highest part of the land, are large pieces of the same coral rock that compofes the shore.

Besides walking frequently up into the country, which we were permitted to do without interruption, we sometimes amused ourselves in shooting wild ducks, not unlike the widgeon, which are very numerous upon the salt lake, and the pool where we got our water. In thefe excursions, we found the inhabitants had often deserted their houses to come down to the trading place, without entertaining any suspicion, that strangers, rambling about, would take away, or destroy, any thing that belonged to them. But though, from this circumstance, it might be suppofed that the greater part of the natives were sometimes collected at the beach, it was impossible to form any accurate computation of their number; as the continual resort of visiters from other islands, mixing with them, might easily mislead one: However, as there was never, to appearance, above a thousand persons collected at one time, it would, perhaps, be sufficient to allow double that number for the whole island. The place where such numbers assembled daily, and the bay where our boats landed, are faithfully reprefented in a drawing by Mr. Webber.

To the North and North East of Annamooka, and in the direct track to Hapaee, whither we were now bound, the sea is sprinkled with a great number of small isles. Amidst the shoals and rocks adjoining to this group, I could not be assured

assured that there was a free or safe passage for such large ships as ours; though the natives sailed through the intervals in their canoes. For this substantial reason, when we weighed anchor from Annamooka, I thought it necessary to go to the Westward of the above islands, and steered North North West, toward Kao* and Toofoa, the two most Westerly islands in sight, and remarkable for their great height. Feenou, and his attendants, remained on board the Resolution till near noon, when he went into the large sailing canoe, which had brought him from Tongataboo, and stood in amongst the cluster of islands above mentioned, of which we were now almost abreast; and a tide or current from the Westward had set us, since our sailing in the morning, much over toward them.

They lie scattered, at unequal distances, and are, in general, nearly as high as Annamooka; but only from two or three miles, to half a mile in length, and some of them scarcely so much. They have either steep rocky shores like Annamooka, or reddish cliffs; but some have sandy beaches extending almost their whole length. Most of them are entirely clothed with trees, amongst which are many cocoa palms, and each forms a prospect like a beautiful garden placed in the sea. To heighten this, the serene weather we now had, contributed very much; and the whole might supply the imagination with an idea of some fairy land

---

* As a proof of the great difficulty of knowing accurately the exact names of the South Sea Islands, as procured from the natives, I observe that what Captain Cook calls *Aghao*, Mr. Anderson calls *Kao*; and Tasman's drawing, as I find it in Mr. Dalrymple's Collection of Voyages, gives the name of *Emhoy* to the same island. Tasman's and Captain Cook's *Amattafoa*, is, with Mr. Anderson, *Tofoa*. Captain Cook's *Komango*, is Tasman's *Amango*. There is scarcely an instance, in which such variations are not observable. Mr. Anderson's great attention to matters of this sort being, as we learn from Captain King, well known to every body on board, and admitted always by Captain Cook himself, his mode of spelling has been adopted on the engraved chart of the Friendly Islands; which has made it necessary to adopt it also, in printing the journal.

realized;

realized. It should seem, that some of them, at least, may have been formed, as we supposed Palmerston's Island to have been; for there is one, which, as yet, is entirely sand, and another, on which there is only one bush, or tree.

At four o'clock in the afternoon being the length of Kotoo, the Westernmost of the above cluster of small islands, we steered to the North, leaving Toofoa and Kao on our larboard, keeping along the West side of a reef of rocks, which lie to the Westward of Kotoo, till we came to their Northern extremity, round which we hauled in for the island. It was our intention to have anchored for the night; but it came upon us before we could find a place in less than fifty-five fathoms water; and rather than come to in this depth, I chose to spend the night under sail.

We had, in the afternoon, been within two leagues of Toofoa, the smoke of which we saw several times in the day. The Friendly Islanders have some superstitious notions about the volcano upon it, which they call *Kollofeea*, and say it is an *Otooa*, or divinity. According to their account, it sometimes throws up very large stones; and they compare the *crater*, to the size of a small islot, which has never ceased smoking in their memory; nor have they any tradition that it ever did. We sometimes saw the smoke rising from the centre of the island, while we were at Annamooka, though at the distance of at least ten leagues. Toofoa, we were told, is but thinly inhabited, but the water upon it is good.

At day-break the next morning, being then not far from Kao, which is a vast rock of a conic figure, we steered to the East, for the passage between the islands Footooha and Hafaiva, with a gentle breeze at South East. About ten o'clock, Feenou came on board, and remained with us all day.

day. He brought with him two hogs, and a quantity of fruit; and, in the course of the day, several canoes, from the different islands round us, came to barter quantities of the latter article, which was very acceptable, as our stock was nearly expended. At noon, our latitude was 19° 49' 45" South, and we had made seven miles of longitude from Annamooka; Toofoa bore North, 88° West; Kao North, 71° West; Footooha North, 89° West; and Hafaiva South, 12° West.

After passing Footooha, we met with a reef of rocks; and, as there was but little wind, it cost us some trouble to keep clear of them. This reef lies between Footooha and Neeneeva, which is a small low isle, in the direction of East North East from Footooha, at the distance of seven or eight miles. Footooha is a small island, of middling height, and bounded all round by a steep rock. It lies South 67° East, distant six leagues from Kao, and three leagues from Kotoo, in the direction of North 33° East. Being past the reef of rocks just mentioned, we hauled up for Neeneeva, in hopes of finding anchorage; but were again disappointed, and obliged to spend the night, making short boards. For, although we had land in every direction, the sea was unfathomable.

In the course of this night, we could plainly see flames issuing from the volcano upon Toofoa, though to no great height.

At day-break in the morning of the 16th, with a gentle breeze at South East, we steered North East for Hapaee, which was now in sight; and we could judge it to be low land, from the trees only appearing above the water. About nine o'clock, we could see it plainly forming three islands, nearly of an equal size; and soon after, a fourth to the
Southward

1777. May.

Southward of thefe, as large as the others. Each feemed to be about fix or feven miles long, and of a fimilar height and appearance. The Northernmoft of them is called Haanno, the next Foa, the third Lefooga, and the Southernmoft Hoolaiva; but all four are included, by the natives, under the general name Hapaee.

The wind fcanting upon us, we could not fetch the land; fo that we were forced to ply to windward. In doing this, we once paffed over fome coral rocks, on which we had only fix fathoms water; but the moment we were over them, found no ground with eighty fathoms of line. At this time, the ifles of Hapaee bore, from North, 50° Eaft, to South, 9° Weft. We got up with the Northernmoft of thefe ifles by funfet; and there found ourfelves in the very fame diftrefs, for want of anchorage, that we had experienced the two preceding evenings; fo that we had another night to fpend under fail, with land and breakers in every direction. Toward the evening, Feenou, who had been on board all day, went forward to Hapaee, and took Omai in the canoe with him. He did not forget our difagreeable fituation; and kept up a good fire, all night, by way of a land-mark.

Saturday 17. As foon as the day-light returned, being then clofe in with Foa, we faw it was joined to Haanno, by a reef running even with the furface of the fea, from the one ifland to the other. I now difpatched a boat to look for anchorage. A proper place was foon found; and we came to, abreaft of a reef, being that which joins Lefooga to Foa (in the fame manner that Foa is joined to Haanno), having twenty-four fathoms depth of water; the bottom coral fand. In this ftation, the northern point of Hapaee, or the North end of Haanno, bore North, 16° Eaft. The Southern point

of

of Hapaee, or the South end of Foolaiva, South, 29° West; and the North end of Lefooga, South, 65° East. Two ledges of rocks lay without us; the one bearing South, 50° West; and the other West by North ¼ North, distant two or three miles. We lay before a creek in the reef, which made it convenient landing at all times; and we were not above three quarters of a mile from the shore.

CHAP. V.

Arrival of the Ships at Hapaee, and friendly Reception there.—Presents and Solemnities on the Occasion.—Single Combats with Clubs.—Wrestling and Boxing Matches.—Female Combatants.—Marines exercised.—A Dance performed by Men.—Fireworks exhibited.—The Night-entertainments of singing and dancing particularly described.

1777.
May.
Saturday 17.

BY the time we had anchored, the ships were filled with the natives, and surrounded by a multitude of canoes, filled also with them. They brought, from the shore, hogs, fowls, fruit, and roots, which they exchanged for hatchets, knives, nails, beads, and cloth. Feenou and Omai having come on board, after it was light, in order to introduce me to the people of the island, I soon accompanied them on shore, for that purpose, landing at the North part of Lefooga, a little to the right of the ship's station.

The Chief conducted me to a house, or rather a hut, situated close to the sea-beach, which I had seen brought thither, but a few minutes before, for our reception. In this Feenou, Omai, and myself, were seated. The other Chiefs, and the multitude, composed a circle, on the outside, fronting us; and they also sat down. I was then asked, How long I intended to stay? On my saying, Five days, Taipa was ordered to come and sit by me, and proclaim

claim this to the people. He then harangued them, in a speech mostly dictated by Feenou. The purport of it, as I learnt from Omai, was, that they were all, both old and young, to look upon me as a friend, who intended to remain with them a few days; that, during my stay, they must not steal any thing, nor molest me any other way; and that it was expected, they should bring hogs, fowls, fruit, &c. to the ships, where they would receive, in exchange for them, such and such things, which he enumerated. Soon after Taipa had finished this address to the assembly, Feenou left us. Taipa then took occasion to signify to me, that it was necessary I should make a present to the Chief of the island, whose name was Earoupa. I was not unprepared for this; and gave him such articles as far exceeded his expectation. My liberality to him brought upon me demands, of the same kind, from two Chiefs of other isles who were present; and from Taipa himself. When Feenou returned, which was immediately after I had made the last of these presents, he pretended to be angry with Taipa for suffering me to give away so much; but I looked upon this as a mere finesse; being confident that he acted in concert with the others. He now took his seat again, and ordered Earoupa to sit by him, and to harangue the people as Taipa had done, and to the same purpose; dictating, as before, the heads of the speech.

These ceremonies being performed, the Chief, at my request, conducted me to three stagnant pools of fresh water, as he was pleased to call it; and, indeed, in one of these the water was tolerable, and the situation not inconvenient for filling our casks. After viewing the watering-place, we returned to our former station, where I found a baked hog, and some yams, smoking hot, ready to be carried on board

board for my dinner. I invited Feenou, and his friends, to partake of it; and we embarked for the ship; but none but himself sat down with us at the table. After dinner I conducted them on shore; and, before I returned on board, the Chief gave me a fine large turtle, and a quantity of yams. Our supply of provisions was copious; for, in the course of the day, we got, by barter, along-side the ship, about twenty small hogs, beside fruit and roots. I was told, that, on my first landing in the morning, a man came off to the ships, and ordered every one of the natives to go on shore. Probably, this was done with a view to have the whole body of inhabitants prefent at the ceremony of my reception; for when that was over, multitudes of them returned again to the ships.

Next morning early, Feenou, and Omai, who scarcely ever quitted the Chief, and now slept on shore, came on board. The object of the visit, was to require my presence upon the island. After some time, I accompanied them; and, upon landing, was conducted to the same place where I had been seated the day before; and where I saw a large concourse of people already assembled. I guessed that something more than ordinary was in agitation; but could not tell what, nor could Omai inform me.

I had not been long seated, before near a hundred of the natives appeared in sight, and advanced, laden with yams, bread-fruit, plantains, cocoa-nuts, and sugar-canes. They deposited their burdens, in two heaps, or piles, upon our left, being the side they came from. Soon after, arrived a number of others from the right, bearing the same kind of articles; which were collected into two piles upon that side. To these were tied two pigs, and six fowls; and to those,

those, upon the left, six pigs, and two turtles. Earoupa seated himself before the several articles upon the left; and another Chief before those upon the right; they being, as I judged, the two Chiefs who had collected them, by order of Feenou, who seemed to be as implicitly obeyed here, as he had been at Annamooka; and, in consequence of his commanding superiority over the Chiefs of Hapaee, had laid this tax upon them for the present occasion.

As soon as this munificent collection of provisions was laid down in order, and disposed to the best advantage, the bearers of it joined the multitude, who formed a large circle round the whole. Presently after, a number of men entered this circle, or area, before us, armed with clubs, made of the green branches of the cocoa-nut tree. These paraded about, for a few minutes, and then retired; the one half to one side, and the other half to the other side; seating themselves before the spectators. Soon after, they successively entered the lists, and entertained us with single combats. One champion, rising up and stepping forward from one side, challenged those of the other side, by expressive gestures, more than by words, to send one of their body to oppose him. If the challenge was accepted, which was generally the case, the two combatants put themselves in proper attitudes, and then began the engagement, which continued till one or other owned himself conquered, or till their weapons were broken. As soon as each combat was over, the victor squatted himself down facing the Chief, then rose up, and retired. At the same time, some old men, who seemed to sit as judges, gave their plaudit in a few words; and the multitude, especially those on the side to which the victor belonged, celebrated the glory he had acquired, in two or three huzzas.

This

This entertainment was, now and then, suspended for a few minutes. During these intervals there were both wrestling and boxing matches. The first were performed in the same manner as at Otaheite; and the second differed very little from the method practised in England. But what struck us with most surprise, was, to see a couple of lusty wenches step forth, and begin boxing, without the least ceremony, and with as much art as the men. This contest, however, did not last above half a minute, before one of them gave it up. The conquering heroine received the same applause from the spectators, which they bestowed upon the successful combatants of the other sex. We expressed some dislike at this part of the entertainment; which, however, did not prevent two other females from entering the lists. They seemed to be girls of spirit, and would certainly have given each other a good drubbing, if two old women had not interposed to part them. All these combats were exhibited in the midst of, at least, three thousand people; and were conducted with the greatest good humour on all sides; though some of the champions, women as well as men, received blows, which, doubtless, they must have felt for some time after.

As soon as these diversions were ended, the Chief told me, that the heaps of provisions, on our right-hand, were a present to Omai; and that those, on our left-hand, being about two-thirds of the whole quantity, were given to me. He added, that I might take them on board whenever it was convenient; but that there would be no occasion to set any of our people as guards over them, as I might be assured, that not a single cocoa-nut would be taken away by the natives. So it proved; for I left every thing behind, and returned to the ship to dinner, carrying the Chief with me;
and

and when the provisions were removed on board, in the afternoon, not a single article was missing. There was as much as loaded four boats; and I could not but be struck with the munificence of Feenou; for this present far exceeded any I had ever received from any of the Sovereigns of the various islands I had visited in the Pacific Ocean. I lost no time in convincing my friend, that I was not insensible of his liberality; for, before he quitted my ship, I bestowed upon him such of our commodities, as, I guessed, were most valuable in his estimation. And the return I made was so much to his satisfaction, that, as soon as he got on shore, he left me still indebted to him, by sending me a fresh present, consisting of two large hogs, a considerable quantity of cloth, and some yams.

Feenou had expressed a desire to see the marines go through their military exercise. As I was desirous to gratify his curiosity, I ordered them all ashore, from both ships, in the morning of the 20th. After they had performed various evolutions, and fired several vollies, with which the numerous body of spectators seemed well pleased, the Chief entertained us, in his turn, with an exhibition, which, as was acknowledged by us all, was performed with a dexterity and exactness, far surpassing the specimen we had given of our military manœuvres. It was a kind of a dance, so entirely different from any thing I had ever seen, that, I fear, I can give no description that will convey any tolerable idea of it, to my readers. It was performed by men; and one hundred and five persons bore their parts in it. Each of them had in his hand an instrument neatly made, shaped somewhat like a paddle, of two feet and a half in length, with a small handle, and a thin blade; so that they were very light. With these instruments they made many and

various

various flourishes, each of which was accompanied with a different attitude of the body, or a different movement. At first, the performers ranged themselves in three lines; and, by various evolutions, each man changed his station in such a manner, that those who had been in the rear, came into the front. Nor did they remain long in the same position; but these changes were made by pretty quick transitions. At one time, they extended themselves in one line; they, then, formed into a semicircle; and, lastly, into two square columns. While this last movement was executing, one of them advanced, and performed an antic dance before me; with which the whole ended.

The musical instruments consisted of two drums, or rather two hollow logs of wood, from which some varied notes were produced, by beating on them with two sticks. It did not, however, appear to me, that the dancers were much assisted or directed by these sounds, but by a chorus of vocal music, in which all the performers joined at the same time. Their song was not destitute of pleasing melody; and all their corresponding motions were executed with so much skill, that the numerous body of dancers seemed to act, as if they were one great machine. It was the opinion of every one of us, that such a performance would have met with universal applause on a European theatre; and it so far exceeded any attempt we had made to entertain them, that they seemed to picque themselves upon the superiority they had over us. As to our musical instruments, they held none of them in the least esteem, except the drum; and even that they did not think equal to their own. Our French horns, in particular, seemed to be held in great contempt; for neither here, nor at any other of the islands, would they pay the smallest attention to them.

In order to give them a more favourable opinion of Eng- 1777.
lish amusements, and to leave their minds fully impressed May.
with the deepest sense of our superior attainments, I directed
some fireworks to be got ready; and, after it was dark,
played them off in the presence of Feenou, the other
Chiefs, and a vast concourse of their people. Some of the
preparations we found damaged; but others of them were
in excellent order, and succeeded so perfectly, as to answer
the end I had in view. Our water and sky-rockets, in particular, pleased and astonished them beyond all conception;
and the scale was now turned in our favour.

This, however, seemed only to furnish them with an
additional motive to proceed to fresh exertions of their very
singular dexterity; and our fireworks were no sooner ended,
than a succession of dances, which Feenou had got ready
for our entertainment, began. As [*] a prelude to them, a
band of music, or chorus of eighteen men, seated themselves before us, in the centre of the circle, composed by
the numerous spectators, the area of which was to be the
scene of the exhibitions. Four or five of this band, had
pieces of large bamboo, from three to five or six feet long,
each managed by one man, who held it nearly in a vertical
position, the upper end open, but the other end closed by
one of the joints. With this close end, the performers kept
constantly striking the ground, though slowly, thus producing different notes, according to the different lengths of
the instruments, but all of them of the hollow or base sort;
to counteract which, a person kept striking quickly, and
with two sticks, a piece of the same substance, split, and

[*] Mr. Anderson's account of the night dances being much fuller than Captain
Cook's, the reader will not be displeased that it has been adopted.

laid

laid along the ground, and, by that means, furnishing a tone as acute, as those produced by the others were grave. The rest of the band, as well as those who performed upon the bamboos, sung a slow and soft air, which so tempered the harsher notes of the above instruments, that no bye-stander, however accustomed to hear the most perfect and varied modulation of sweet sounds, could avoid confessing the vast power, and pleasing effect, of this simple harmony.

The concert having continued about a quarter of an hour, twenty women entered the circle. Most of them had, upon their heads, garlands of the crimson flowers of the China rose, or others; and many of them had ornamented their persons with leaves of trees, cut with a great deal of nicety about the edges. They made a circle round the chorus, turning their faces toward it, and began by singing a soft air, to which responses were made by the chorus in the same tone; and these were repeated alternately. All this while, the women accompanied their song with several very graceful motions of their hands toward their faces, and in other directions at the same time, making constantly a step forward, and then back again, with one foot, while the other was fixed. They then turned their faces to the assembly, sung some time, and retreated slowly in a body, to that part of the circle which was opposite the hut where the principal spectators sat. After this, one of them advanced from each side, meeting and passing each other in the front, and continuing their progress round, till they came to the rest. On which, two advanced from each side, two of whom also passed each other, and returned as the former; but the other two remained, and to these came one, from each side,

side, by intervals, till the whole number had again formed a circle about the chorus.

Their manner of dancing was now changed to a quicker measure, in which they made a kind of half turn by leaping, and clapped their hands, and snapped their fingers, repeating some words in conjunction with the chorus. Toward the end, as the quickness of the music increased, their gestures and attitudes were varied with wonderful vigour and dexterity; and some of their motions, perhaps, would, with us, be reckoned rather indecent. Though this part of the performance, most probably, was not meant to convey any wanton ideas, but merely to display the astonishing variety of their movements.

To this grand female ballet, succeeded one performed by fifteen men. Some of them were old; but their age seemed to have abated little of their agility or ardour for the dance. They were disposed in a sort of circle, divided at the front, with their faces not turned out toward the assembly, nor inward to the chorus; but one half of their circle faced forward as they had advanced, and the other half in a contrary direction. They, sometimes, sung slowly, in concert with the chorus; and, while thus employed, they also made several very fine motions with their hands, but different from those made by the women, at the same time inclining the body to either side alternately, by raising one leg, which was stretched outward, and resting on the other; the arm of the same side being also stretched fully upward. At other times, they recited sentences in a musical tone, which were answered by the chorus; and, at intervals, increased the measure of the dance, by clapping the hands, and quickening the motions of the feet, which, however, were never varied. At the end, the rapidity of the music, and of the dancing, increased so much, that it was scarcely possible to distinguish the different movements; though one might suppose the actors were now almost tired, as their performance had lasted near half an hour.

After a considerable interval, another act, as we may call it, began. Twelve men now advanced, who placed themselves in double rows fronting each other, but on opposite sides of the circle; and, on one side, a man was stationed, who, as if he had been a prompter, repeated several sentences, to which the twelve new performers, and the chorus, replied. They then sung slowly; and afterward danced and sung more quickly, for about a quarter of an hour, after the manner of the dancers whom they had succeeded.

Soon after they had finished, nine women exhibited themselves, and sat down fronting the hut where the Chief was. A man then rose, and struck the first of these women on the back, with both fists joined. He proceeded, in the same manner, to the second and third; but when he came to the fourth, whether from accident or design I cannot tell, instead of the back, he struck her on the breast. Upon this, a person rose instantly from the crowd, who brought him to the ground with a blow on the head; and he was carried off without the least noise or disorder. But this did not save the other five women from so odd a discipline, or perhaps necessary ceremony; for a person succeeded him, who treated them in the same manner. Their disgrace did not end here; for when they danced, they had the mortification to find their performance twice disapproved of, and were obliged to repeat it. This dance did not differ much from that of the first women, except in this one circumstance, that the present set, sometimes raised the body upon one leg,

by

by a fort of double motion, and then upon the other alternately, in which attitude they kept snapping their fingers; and, at the end, they repeated, with great agility, the brisk movements, in which the former group of female dancers had shewn themselves so expert.

In a little time, a person entered unexpectedly, and said something in a ludicrous way, about the fireworks that had been exhibited, which extorted a burst of laughter from the multitude. After this, we had a dance composed of the men who attended, or had followed, Feenou. They formed a double circle (i. e. one within another) of twenty-four each, round the chorus, and began a gentle soothing song, with corresponding motions of the hands and head. This lasted a considerable time, and then changed to a much quicker measure, during which they repeated sentences, either in conjunction with the chorus, or in answer to some spoken by that band. They then retreated to the back part of the circle, as the women had done, and again advanced, on each side, in a triple row, till they formed a semicircle, which was done very slowly, by inclining the body on one leg, and advancing the other a little way, as they put it down. They accompanied this, with such a soft air as they had sung at the beginning; but soon changed it to repeat sentences in a harsher tone, at the same time quickening the dance very much, till they finished with a general shout and clap of the hands. The same was repeated several times; but, at last, they formed a double circle, as at the beginning, danced, and repeated very quickly, and finally closed with several very dexterous transpositions of the two circles.

The entertainments of this memorable night concluded with a dance, in which the principal people present exhibited.

exhibited. It resembled the immediately preceding one, in some respects, having the same number of performers, who began nearly in the same way; but their ending, at each interval, was different. For they increased their motions to a prodigious quickness, shaking their heads from shoulder to shoulder, with such force, that a spectator, unaccustomed to the sight, would suppose, that they ran a risk of dislocating their necks. This was attended with a smart clapping of the hands, and a kind of savage holla! or shriek, not unlike what is sometimes practised in the comic dances on our European theatres. They formed the triple semicircle, as the preceding dancers had done; and a person, who advanced at the head on one side of the semicircle, began by repeating something in a truly musical recitative, which was delivered with an air so graceful, as might put to the blush our most applauded performers. He was answered in the same manner, by the person at the head of the opposite party. This being repeated several times, the whole body, on one side, joined in the responses to the whole corresponding body on the opposite side, as the semicircle advanced to the front; and they finished, by singing and dancing as they had begun.

These two last dances were performed with so much spirit, and so great exactness, that they met with universal approbation. The native spectators, who, no doubt, were perfect judges whether the several performances were properly executed, could not withhold their applauses at some particular parts; and even a stranger, who never saw the diversion before, felt similar satisfaction, at the same instant. For though, through the whole, the most strict concert was observed, some of the gestures were so expressive, that it might be said, they spoke the language that accompanied them; if we allow that there is any connection be-

tween

tween motion and sound. At the same time, it should be observed, that though the music of the chorus, and that of the dancers, corresponded, constant practice in these favourite amusements of our friends, seems to have a great share in effecting the exact time they keep in their performances. For we observed, that if any of them happened accidentally to be interrupted, they never found the smallest difficulty in recovering the proper place of the dance or song. And their perfect discipline was, in no instance, more remarkable, than in the sudden transitions they so dexterously made from the ruder exertions, and harsh sounds, to the softest airs, and gentlest movements*.

The place where the dances were performed, was an open space amongst the trees, just by the sea, with lights, at small intervals, placed round the inside of the circle. The concourse of people was pretty large, though not equal to the number assembled in the forenoon, when the marines exercised. At that time, some of our gentlemen guessed there might be present about five thousand persons; others thought there were more; but they who reckoned that there were fewer, probably, came nearer to the truth.

---

* In a former note, at p. 188. it was observed, that the songs and dances of the Caroline Islanders, in the North Pacific, bear a great resemblance to those of the inhabitants of Wateeoo. The remark may be now extended to those of the Friendly Islanders, described at large in this chapter. That the reader may judge for himself, I have selected the following particulars from Father Cantova's account. "Pendant la nuit, au clair de la lune, ils s'assemblent, de temps en temps, pour chanter & danser devant la maison de leur Tamole. Leurs danses se font au son de la voix, car ils n'ont point d'instrument de musique. La beauté de la danse, consiste dans l'exacte uniformité des mouvemens du corps. Les hommes, separés des femmes, se placent vis-à-vis les uns des autres; après quoi, ils remuent la tête, les bras, les mains, les pieds, en cadence.—Leur tête est couverte de plumes, ou de fleurs;—et l'on voit, attachées à leurs oreilles, des feuilles de palmier tissues avec assez d'art.—Les femmes, de leur coté,—se regardant les unes les autres, commencent un chant pathétique & langoureux, accompagnant le son de leur voix de mouvemens cadencés de la tête & des bras." *Lettres Edifiantes & Curieuses*, Tom. xv. p. 314, 315.

CHAP.

CHAP. VI.

Description of Lefooga.—Its cultivated State.—Its Extent.—Transactions there.—A Female Oculist.—Singular Expedients for shaving off the Hair.—The Ships change their Station.—A remarkable Mount and Stone. —Description of Hoolaiva.—Account of Poulaho, King of the Friendly Islands —Respectful Manner in which he is treated by his People.—Departure from the Hapaee Islands.—Some Account of Kotoo.—Return of the Ships to Annamooka.—Poulaho and Feenou meet.— Arrival at Tongataboo.

1777.
May.

Wednes. 21.

CURIOSITY, on both sides, being now sufficiently gratified, by the exhibition of the various entertainments I have described, I began to have time to look about me. Accordingly, next day, I took a walk into the island of Lefooga, of which I was desirous to obtain some knowledge. I found it to be, in several respects, superior to Annamooka. The plantations were both more numerous, and more extensive. In many places, indeed, toward the sea, especially on the East side, the country is still waste; owing, perhaps, to the sandy soil; as it is much lower than Annamooka, and its surrounding isles. But, toward the middle of the island, the soil is better; and the marks of considerable population, and of improved cultivation, were very conspicuous. For we met here with very large plantations,

inclosed

inclofed in fuch a manner, that the fences running parallel to each other, form fine fpacious public roads, that would appear ornamental in countries where rural conveniences have been carried to the greateſt perfection. We obferved large fpots covered with the paper mulberry-trees; and the plantations, in general, were well ſtocked with fuch roots and fruits as are the natural produce of the iſland. To thefe I made fome addition, by fowing the feeds of Indian corn, melons, pumpkins, and the like. At one place was a houſe, four or five times as large as thoſe of the common fort, with a large area of grafs before it; and, I take it for granted, the people refort thither on certain public ocaſions. Near the landing-place, we faw a mount, two or three feet high, covered with gravel; and on it ſtood four or five fmall huts, in which, the natives told us, the bodies of fome of their principal people had been interred.

The iſland is not above feven miles long; and, in fome places, not above two or three broad. The Eaſt fide of it, which is expofed to the trade-wind, has a reef, running to a confiderable breadth from it, on which the fea breaks with great violence. It is a continuation of this reef that joins Lefooga to Foa, which is not above half a mile diſtant; and, at low water, the natives can walk upon this reef, which is then partly dry, from the one iſland to the other. The ſhore itfelf is either a coral rock, fix or feven feet high, or a fandy beach; but higher than the Weſt fide; which, in general, is not more than three or four feet from the level of the fea, with a fandy beach its whole length.

When I returned from my excurſion into the country, and went on board to dinner, I found a large failing canoe faſt to the ſhip's ſtern. In this canoe was Latooliboula, whom I had

1777.
May.

I had seen at Tongataboo, during my last voyage; and who was then supposed by us to be the King of that island. He sat in the canoe, with all that gravity, by which, as I have mentioned in my Journal*, he was so remarkably distinguished at that time; nor could I, by any intreaties, prevail upon him now to come into the ship. Many of the islanders were present; and they all called him *Areekee*, which signifies King. I had never heard any one of them give this title to Feenou, however extensive his authority over them, both here, and at Annamooka, had appeared to be; which had, all along, inclined me to suspect, that he was not the King; though his friend Taipa had taken pains to make me believe he was. Latooliboula remained under the stern till the evening, when he retired in his canoe to one of the islands. Feenou was on-board my ship at the same time; but neither of these great men took the least notice of the other.

Thursday 22.

Nothing material happened the next day, except that some of the natives stole a tarpaulin, and other things, from off the deck. They were soon missed, and the thieves pursued;

* See *Captain Cook's Voyage*, Vol. I. p. 206, 207. The name of this extraordinary personage is there said to be *Kohagee-too Fallangou*; which cannot, by the most skilful etymologist, be tortured into the least most distant resemblance of *Latooliboula*. It is remarkable, that Captain Cook should not take any notice of his having called the same person by two names so very different. Perhaps we may account for this by supposing one to be the name of the person, and the other the description of his title or rank. This supposition seems well founded, when we consider, that *Latoo*, in the language of these people, is sometimes used to signify a Great Chief; and Dr. Foster, in his *Observations*, p. 378, 379. and elsewhere, speaks of the Sovereign of Tongatabou, under the title of their *Latoo*. This very person is called, by Dr. Foster, p. 370. *Latoo-Nipooroo*; which furnishes a very striking instance of the variations of our people in writing down the same word as pronounced by the natives. However, we can easily trace the affinity between *Nipooroo* and *Liboula*, as the changes of the consonants are such as are perpetually made, upon hearing a word pronounced, to which our ears have not been accustomed. Mr. Anderson here agrees with Captain Cook in writing Latooliboula.

but

but a little too late. I applied, therefore, to Feenou, who, if he was not king, was at least vested with the highest authority here, to exert it, in order to have my things restored. He referred me to Earoupa; who put me off, from time to time; and, at last, nothing was done.

In the morning of the 23d, as we were going to unmoor, in order to leave the island, Feenou, and his prime-minister Taipa, came along-side in a sailing canoe, and informed me, that they were setting out for Vavaoo, an island, which, they said, lies about two days sail to the Northward of Hapaee. The object of their voyage, they would have me believe, was to get for me an additional supply of hogs, and some red-feathered caps for Omai, to carry to Otaheite, where they are in high esteem. Feenou assured me, that he should be back in four or five days; and desired me not to sail till his return, when, he promised, he would accompany me to Tongataboo. I thought this a good opportunity to get some knowledge of Vavaoo, and proposed to him to go thither with the ships. But he seemed not to approve of the plan; and, by way of diverting me from it, told me, that there was neither harbour, nor anchorage about it. I, therefore, consented to wait, in my present station, for his return; and he immediately set out.

The next day, our attention was, for some time, taken up with a report, industriously spread about by some of the natives, that a ship, like ours, had arrived at Annamooka since we left it; and was now at anchor there. The propagators of the report were pleased to add, that Toobou, the Chief of that island, was hastening thither to receive these new-comers; and as we knew that he had actually left us, we were the more ready to believe there might be

some

some foundation for the story of this unexpected arrival. However, to gain some farther information, I went on shore with Omai, in quest of the man who, it was said, had brought the first account of this event from Annamooka. We found him at the house of Earoupa; where Omai put such questions to him as I thought necessary; and the answers he gave, were so clear and satisfactory, that I had not a doubt remaining. But, just about this time, a Chief, of some note, whom we well knew, arrived from Annamooka; and declared, that no ship was, at that island, nor had been, since our leaving it. The propagator of the report, finding himself detected in a falsehood, instantly withdrew, and we saw no more of him. What end the invention of this tale could answer, was not easy to conjecture; unless we suppose it to have been artfully contrived, to get us removed from the one island to the other.

Sunday 25. In my walk, on the 25th, I happened to step into a house, where a woman was dressing the eyes of a young child, who seemed blind; the eyes being much inflamed, and a thin film spread over them. The instruments she used were two slender wooden probes, with which she had brushed the eyes so as to make them bleed. It seems worth mentioning, that the natives of these islands should attempt an operation of this sort; though I entered the house too late, to describe exactly how this female oculist employed the wretched tools she had to work with.

I was fortunate enough to see a different operation going on in the same house, of which I can give a tolerable account. I found there another woman shaving a child's head, with a shark's tooth, stuck into the end of a piece of stick. I observed, that she first wet the hair with a rag dipped

dipped in water, applying her inftrument to that part which fhe had previoufly foaked. The operation feemed to give no pain to the child; although the hair was taken off as clofe as if one of our razors had been employed. Encouraged by what I now faw, I, foon after, tried one of thefe fingular inftruments upon myfelf, and found it to be an excellent *fuccedaneum*. However, the men of thefe iflands have recourfe to another contrivance when they fhave their beards. The operation is performed with two fhells; one of which they place under a fmall part of the beard, and with the other, applied above, they fcrape that part off. In this manner they are able to fhave very clofe. The procefs is, indeed, rather tedious, but not painful; and there are men amongft them who feem to profefs this trade. It was as common, while we were here, to fee our failors go afhore to have their beards fcraped off, after the fafhion of Hapaee, as it was to fee their Chiefs come on board to be fhaved by our barbers.

Finding that little or nothing of the produce of the ifland was now brought to the fhips, I refolved to change our ftation, and to wait Feenou's return from Vavaoo, in fome other convenient anchoring-place, where refrefhments might ftill be met with. Accordingly, in the forenoon of the 26th, we got under fail, and ftood to the Southward along the reef of the ifland; having fourteen and thirteen fathoms water, with a fandy bottom. However, we met with feveral detached fhoals. Some of them were difcovered by breakers; fome, by the water upon them appearing difcoloured; and others, by the lead. At half paft two in the afternoon, having already paffed feveral of thefe fhoals, and feeing more of them before us, I hauled into a bay, that lies between the South end of Lefooga, and the North end of Hoolaiva,

laiva, and there anchored in seventeen fathoms water; the bottom a coral-sand; the point of Lefooga bearing South East by East, a mile and a half distant. The Discovery did not get to an anchor till sunset. She had touched upon one of the shoals; but backed off again, without receiving any damage.

As soon as we had anchored, I sent Mr. Bligh to sound the bay where we were now stationed; and myself, accompanied by Mr. Gore, landed on the Southern part of Lefooga, to examine the country, and to look for fresh water. Not that we now wanted a supply of this article, having filled all the casks at our late station; but I had been told, that this part of the island could afford us some, preferable to any we had got at the former watering-place. This will not be the only time I shall have occasion to remark, that these people do not know what good water is. We were conducted to two wells; but the water in both of them proved to be execrable; and the natives, our guides, assured us that they had none better.

Near the South end of the island, and on the West side, we met with an artificial mount. From the size of some trees that were growing upon it, and from other appearances, I guessed that it had been raised in remote times. I judged it to be about forty feet high; and the diameter of its summit measured fifty feet. At the bottom of this mount, stood a stone, which must have been hewn out of coral rock. It was four feet broad, two and a half thick, and fourteen high; and we were told by the natives present, that not above half its length appeared above ground. They called it *Tangata Arekee* *; and said, that it had been set up, and the

* *Tangata*, in their language, is man; *Arekee*, king.

mount

mount raifed, by fome of their forefathers, in memory of one of their kings; but how long fince, they could not tell.

Night coming on, Mr. Gore and I returned on board; and, at the fame time, Mr. Bligh got back from founding the bay, in which he found from fourteen to twenty fathoms water; the bottom, for the moft part, fand, but not without fome coral rocks. The place where we now anchored is much better fheltered than that which we had lately come from; but between the two is another anchoring flation, much better than either. Lefooga and Hoolaiva are divided from each other by a reef of coral rocks, which is dry at low water; fo that one may walk, at that time, from the one to the other, without wetting a foot. Some of our Gentlemen, who landed in the latter ifland, did not find the leaft mark of cultivation, or habitation, upon it; except a fingle hut, the refidence of a man employed to catch fifh and turtle. It is rather extraordinary, that it fhould be in this deferted ftate, communicating fo immediately with Lefooga, which is fo perfectly cultivated. For, though the foil is quite fandy, all the trees and plants found, in a natural ftate, on the neighbouring iflands, are produced here with the greateft vigour. The Eaft fide of it has a reef like Lefooga; and the Weft fide has a bending, at the North part, where there feems to be good anchorage. Uninhabited as Hoolaiva is, an artificial mount, like that at the adjoining ifland, has been raifed upon it, as high as fome of the furrounding trees.

At day-break, next morning, I made the fignal to weigh; and, as I intended to attempt a paffage to Annamooka, in my way to Tongataboo, by the South Weft, amongft the intervening iflands, I fent the Mafter in a boat to found before the fhips. But before we could get under sail, the wind became unsettled; which made it unsafe to attempt a passage this way, till we were better acquainted with it. I, therefore, lay fast, and made the signal for the Master to return; and afterward sent him and the Master of the Discovery, each in a boat, with instructions to examine the channels, as far as they could, allowing themselves time to get back to the ships before the close of the day.

About noon, a large sailing canoe came under our stern, in which was a person named Funafaihe, or Poulaho, or both; who, as the natives then on board told us, was King of Tongataboo, and of all the neighbouring islands that we had seen or heard of. It was a matter of surprize to me, to have a stranger introduced under this character, which I had so much reason to believe really belonged to another. But they persisted in their account of the supreme dignity of this new visiter; and now, for the first time, they owned to me, that Feenou was not the King, but only a subordinate Chief, though of great power; as he was often sent from Tongataboo to the other islands, on warlike expeditions, or to decide differences. It being my interest, as well as my inclination, to pay court to all the great men, without making inquiry into the validity of their assumed titles, I invited Poulaho on board; as I understood he was very desirous to come. He could not be an unwelcome guest; for he brought with him, as a present to me, two good fat hogs; though not so fat as himself. If weight of body could give weight in rank or power, he was certainly the most eminent man in that respect, we had seen; for, though not very tall, he was very unwieldy, and almost shapeless with corpulence. He seemed to be about forty years of age, had straight hair, and his features differed a

good

good deal from those of the bulk of his people. I found him to be a sedate, sensible man. He viewed the ship, and the several new objects, with uncommon attention; and asked many pertinent questions; one of which was, What could induce us to visit these islands? After he had satisfied his curiosity in looking at the cattle, and other novelties which he met with upon deck, I desired him to walk down into the cabin. To this, some of his attendants objected, saying, that, if he were to accept of that invitation, it must happen, that people would walk over his head; which could not be permitted. I directed my interpreter Omai, to tell them, that I would obviate their objection, by giving orders, that no one should presume to walk upon that part of the deck which was over the cabin. Whether this expedient would have satisfied them, was far from appearing; but the Chief himself, less scrupulous, in this respect, than his attendants, waved all ceremony, and walked down without any stipulation. He now appeared to be as solicitous himself, as his people were, to convince us that he was king, and not Feenou, who had passed with us as such. For he soon perceived, that we had some doubts about it; which doubts Omai was not very desirous of removing. The closest connection had been formed between him and Feenou, in testimony of which, they had exchanged names; and, therefore, he was not a little chagrined, that another person now put in his claim to the honours which his friend had hitherto enjoyed.

Poulaho sat down with us to dinner; but he eat little, and drank less. When we rose from the table, he desired me to accompany him ashore. Omai was asked to be of the party; but he was too faithfully attached to Feenou, to shew any attention to his competitor; and, therefore, excused himself.

self. I attended the Chief in my own boat, having first made presents to him, of such articles as, I could observe, he valued much, and were even beyond his expectation to receive. I was not disappointed in my view of thus securing his friendship; for the moment the boat reached the beach, and, before he quitted her, he ordered two more hogs to be brought, and delivered to my people to be conveyed on board. He was then carried out of the boat, by some of his own people, upon a board resembling a handbarrow, and went and seated himself in a small house near the shore; which seemed to have been erected there for his accommodation. He placed me at his side; and his attendants, who were not numerous, seated themselves in a semicircle before us, on the outside of the house. Behind the Chief, or rather on one side, sat an old woman, with a sort of fan in her hand, whose office it was to prevent his being pestered with the flies.

The several articles which his people had got, by trading on board the ships, were now displayed before him. He looked over them all, with attention, inquired what they had given in exchange, and seemed pleased with the bargains they had made. At length, he ordered every thing to be restored to the respective owners, except a glass bowl, with which he was so much pleased, that he reserved it for himself. The persons who brought these things to him, first squatted themselves down before him, then they deposited their several purchases, and immediately rose up and retired. The same respectful ceremony was observed in taking them away; and not one of them presumed to speak to him standing. I stayed till several of his attendants left him, first paying him obeisance, by bowing the head down to the sole of his foot, and touching or tapping the same, with the upper and under side of the fingers of both hands. Others, who were not in the circle, came, as it seemed, on purpose, and paid him this mark of respect, and then retired, without speaking a word. I was quite charmed with the decorum that was observed. I had, no where, seen the like, not even amongst more civilized nations.

I found the master returned from his expedition, when I got on board. He informed me, that, as far as he had proceeded, there was anchorage, and a passage for the ships; but that, toward the South and South East, he saw a number of small isles, shoals, and breakers. Judging, from this report, that my attempting a passage that way would be attended with some risk, I now dropped all thoughts of it; thinking it better to return toward Annamooka by the same route, which we had so lately experienced to be a safe one.

Having come to this resolution, I should have sailed next morning, if the wind had not been too far Southerly, and, at the same time, very unsettled. Poulaho, the king, as I shall now call him, came on board betimes; and brought, as a present to me, one of their caps, made, or, at least, covered, with red feathers. These caps were much sought after by us; for we knew they would be highly valued at Otaheite. But, though very large prices were offered, not one was ever brought for sale; which shewed, that they were no less valuable in the estimation of the people here; nor was there a person in either ship, that could make himself the proprietor of one, except myself, Captain Clerke, and Omai. These caps, or rather bonnets, are composed of the tail feathers of the Tropic bird, with the red feathers of the parroquets wrought upon them, or jointly with them. They are made

1777.
May.

made so as to tie upon the forehead without any crown, and have the form of a semicircle, whose *radius* is eighteen or twenty inches. But a drawing which Mr. Webber has made of Poulaho, dressed in one of these bonnets, will convey the best idea of them. The Chief stayed on board till the evening, when he left us; but his brother, whose name was also Futafaihe, and one or two, or more, of his attendants, continued in the ship all night.

Thursday 29.

At day-break, the next morning, I weighed with a fine breeze, at East North East, and stood to the Westward, with a view to return to Annamooka, by the track we had already experienced. We were followed by several sailing canoes, in one of which was the king. As soon as he got on board the Resolution, he inquired for his brother, and the others who had remained with us all night. It now appeared, that they had stayed without his leave; for he gave them, in a very few words, such a reprimand as brought tears from their eyes; and yet they were men not less than thirty years of age. He was, however, soon reconciled to their making a longer stay; for, on quitting us, he left his brother, and five of his attendants, on board. We had also the company of a Chief, just then arrived from Tongataboo, whose name was Tooboueitoa. The moment he arrived, he sent his canoe away, and declared, that he and five more, who came with him, would sleep on board; so that I had now my cabin filled with visiters. This, indeed, was some inconvenience; but I bore with it more willingly, as they brought plenty of provisions with them, as presents to me; for which they always had suitable returns.

About

About one o'clock in the afternoon, the Easterly wind was succeeded by a fresh breeze at South South East. Our course, now being South South West, or more Southerly, we were obliged to ply to windward, and did but just fetch the North Side of Footooha by eight o'clock, where we spent the night, making short boards.

The next morning, we plyed up to Lofanga, where, according to the information of our friends, there was anchorage. It was one o'clock, in the afternoon, before we got soundings, under the lee or North West side, in forty fathoms water, near half a mile from the shore; but the bank was steep, and the bottom rocky, and a chain of breakers lay to leeward. All these circumstances being against us, I stretched away for Kotoo, with the expectation of finding better anchoring ground under that island. But so much time had been spent in plying up to Lofanga, that it was dark before we reached the other; and, finding no place to anchor in, the night was spent as the preceding one.

At day-break, on the 31st, I stood for the channel which is between Kotoo, and the reef of rocks that lie to the Westward of it; but, on drawing near, I found the wind too scant to lead us through. I, therefore, bore up on the outside of the reef, and stretched to the South West, till near noon, when, perceiving that we made no progress to windward, and being apprehensive of losing the islands, with so many of the natives on board, I tacked and stood back, intending to wait till some more favourable opportunity. We did but just fetch in with Footooha, between which and Kotoo we spent the night, under reefed topsails and foresail. The wind blew fresh, and by squalls, with rain; and we

were

1777.
May.

were not without apprehensions of danger. I kept the deck till midnight, when I left it to the Master, with such directions as, I thought, would keep the ships clear of the shoals and rocks, that lay round us. But, after making a trip to the North, and standing back again to the South, our ship, by a small shift of the wind, fetched farther to the windward than was expected. By this means she was very near running full upon a low sandy isle, called Pootoo Pootooa, surrounded with breakers. It happened, very fortunately, that the people had just been ordered upon the deck, to put the ship about, and the most of them were at their stations; so that the necessary movements were not only executed with judgment, but also with alertness; and this alone saved us from destruction. The Discovery being astern, was out of danger. Such hazardous situations are the unavoidable companions of the man, who goes upon a voyage of discovery.

June.
Sunday 1.

This circumstance frightened our passengers so much, that they expressed a strong desire to get ashore. Accordingly, as soon as day-light returned, I hoisted out a boat, and ordered the Officer who commanded her, after landing them at Kotoo, to sound along the reef that spits off from that island, for anchorage. For I was full as much tired as they could be, with beating about amongst the surrounding isles and shoals, and determined to get to an anchor, somewhere or other, if possible. While the boat was absent, we attempted to turn the ships through the channel, between the sandy isle and the reef of Kotoo, in expectation of finding a moderate depth of water behind them to anchor in. But, meeting with a tide or current against us, we were obliged to desist, and anchor in fifty fathoms water, with the sandy isle bearing East by North, one mile distant.

We

We lay here till the 4th. While in this station we were, several times, visited by the king, by Tooboueitoa, and by people from the neighbouring islands, who came off to trade with us, though the wind blew very fresh most of the time. The master was now sent to sound the channels between the islands that lie to the Eastward; and I landed on Kotoo, to examine it, in the forenoon of the 2d.

This island is scarcely accessible by boats, on account of coral reefs that surround it. It is not more than a mile and half, or two miles, long; and not so broad. The North West end of it is low, like the islands of Hapaee; but it rises suddenly in the middle, and terminates in reddish clayey cliffs, at the South East end, about thirty feet high. The soil, in that quarter, is of the same sort as in the cliffs; but, in the other parts, it is a loose, black mould. It produces the same fruits and roots which we found at the other islands; is tolerably cultivated, but thinly inhabited. While I was walking all over it, our people were employed in cutting some grafs for the cattle; and we planted some melon seeds, with which the natives seemed much pleased, and inclosed them with branches. On our return to the boat, we passed by two or three ponds of dirty water, which was more or less brackish in each of them; and saw one of their burying-places, which was much neater than those that were met with at Hapaee.

On the 4th, at seven in the morning, we weighed; and, with a fresh gale at East South East, stood away for Annamooka, where we anchored, next morning, nearly in the same station which we had so lately occupied.

I went

1777.
June.

I went on shore soon after, and found the inhabitants very busy in their plantations, digging up yams to bring to market; and, in the course of the day, about two hundred of them had assembled on the beach, and traded with as much eagerness, as during our late visit. Their stock appeared to have been recruited much, though we had returned so soon; but, instead of bread-fruit, which was the only article we could purchase on our first arrival, nothing was to be seen now but yams, and a few plantains. This shews the quick succession of the seasons, at least of the different vegetables produced here, at the several times of the year. It appeared also that they had been very busy, while we were absent, in cultivating; for we now saw several large plantain fields, in places which we had, so lately, seen lying waste. The yams were now in the greatest perfection; and we procured a good quantity, in exchanges for pieces of iron.

These people, in the absence of Toobou, whom we left behind us at Kotoo, with Poulaho and the other Chiefs, seemed to be under little subordination. For we could not perceive, this day, that one man assumed more authority than another. Before I returned on board, I visited the several places where I had sown melon seeds, and had the mortification to find, that most of them were destroyed by a small ant; but some pine-apple plants, which I had also left, were in a thriving state.

Friday 6.

About noon, next day, Feenou arrived from Vavaoo. He told us, that several canoes, laden with hogs, and other provisions, which had sailed with him from that island, had been lost, owing to the late blowing weather; and that every body

body on board them had perished. This melancholy tale did not seem to affect any of his countrymen who heard it; and, as to ourselves, we were, by this time, too well acquainted with his character, to give much credit to such a story. The truth, probably, was, that he had not been able to procure at Vavaoo the supplies which he expected; or, if he got any there, that he had left them at Hapaee, which lay in his way back, and where he could not but receive intelligence that Poulaho had been with us; who, therefore, he knew, would, as his superior, have all the merit and reward of procuring them, though he had not any share of the trouble. The invention of this loss at sea was, however, well imagined. For there had lately been very blowing weather; in so much, that the King, and other Chiefs, who had followed us from Hapaee to Kotoo, had been left there, not caring to venture to sea when we did; but desired I might wait for them at Annamooka, which was the reason of my anchoring there, this second time, and of my not proceeding directly to Tongataboo.

The following morning, Poulaho, and the other Chiefs who had been wind-bound with him, arrived. I happened, at this time, to be ashore in company with Feenou; who now seemed to be sensible of the impropriety of his conduct, in assuming a character that did not belong to him. For he not only acknowledged Poulaho to be King of Tongataboo, and the other isles; but affected to insist much on it, which, no doubt, was with a view to make amends for his former presumption. I left him, to visit this greater man, whom I found sitting with a few people before him. But, every one hastening to pay court to him, the circle increased pretty fast. I was very desirous of observing Feenou's behaviour on this occasion; and had the most convincing proof of his superiority; for he placed himself amongst the rest that sat before Poulaho, as attendants on his majesty. He seemed, at first, rather abashed; as some of us were present who had been used to see him act a different part; but he soon recovered himself. Some little conversation passed between these two Chiefs, which none of us understood; nor were we satisfied with Omai's interpretation of it. We were, however, by this time, sufficiently undeceived as to Feenou's rank. Both he and Poulaho went on board with me to dinner; but only the latter sat at table. Feenou, having made his obeisance, in the usual way, saluting his sovereign's foot with his head and hands, retired out of the cabin *. The king had before told us, that this would happen; and it now appeared, that Feenou could not even eat nor drink in his royal presence.

Sunday 1. At eight o'clock, next morning, we weighed and steered for Tongataboo, having a gentle breeze at North East. About fourteen or fifteen sailing vessels, belonging to the natives, set out with us; but every one of them outrun the ships considerably. Feenou was to have taken his passage in the Resolution; but preferred his own canoe; and put two men on

---

* Marks of profound respect, very similar to those paid by natives of the Friendly Islands to their sovereign, are also paid to the principal Chiefs, or *Tamoles* of the Caroline Islands, as appears from father Cantova's account here transcribed. "Lorsqu'un *Tamole* donne audience, il paroit assis sur une table elevée: les peuples s'inclinent devant lui jusqu'à terre, & de plus loin qu'ils arrivent, ils marchent le corps tout courbé, & la tête presqu'entre les genoux, jusqu'à ce qu'ils soient auprès de sa personne; alors ils s'asseyent à plate terre, &, les yeux baissés, ils reçoivent ses ordres avec le plus profond respect. Quand le *Tamole* les congedie, ils se retirent, en se courbant de la même manière que quand ils sont venus, & ne se relevent que lorsqu'ils sont hors de sa presence. Ses paroles sont autant d'oracles qu'on revere; on rend à ses ordres une obeissance aveugle; enfin, on baise les mains & les pieds, quand on lui demande quelque grace."

Lettres Edifiantes & Curieuses, Tom. xv. p. 312, 313.

board,

board, to conduct us to the best anchorage. We steered South by West by compass.

At five in the afternoon we saw two small islands, bearing West, about four leagues distant. Our pilots called the one Hoonga Hapaee, and the other Hoonga Tonga. They lie in the latitude of 20° 36'; and ten or eleven leagues from the West point of Annamooka, in the direction of South, 46° West. According to the account of the islanders on board, only five men reside upon Hoonga Hapaee; and Hoonga Tonga is uninhabited; but both of them abound with sea-fowl.

We continued the same course till two o'clock next morning, when, seeing some lights ahead, and not knowing whether they were on shore, or on board the canoes, we hauled the wind, and made a short trip, each way, till day-break. We then resumed our course to the South by West; and, presently after, saw several small islands before us, and Eooa and Tongataboo beyond them. We had, at this time, twenty-five fathoms water, over a bottom of broken coral and sand. The depth gradually decreased as we drew near the isles above mentioned, which lie ranged along the North East side of Tongataboo. By the direction of our pilots we steered for the middle of it, and for the widest space between the small isles which we were to pass; having our boats ahead, employed in sounding. We were, insensibly, drawn upon a large flat, upon which lay innumerable coral rocks, of different depths, below the surface of the water. Notwithstanding all our care and attention to keep the ship clear of them, we could not prevent her from striking on one of these rocks. Nor did the Discovery, though behind us, escape any better. Fortunately, neither of the ships stuck fast,

fast, nor received any damage. We could not get back without increasing the danger, as we had come in almost before the wind. Nor could we cast anchor, but with the certainty of having our cables instantly cut in two by the rocks. We had no other resource but to proceed. To this, indeed, we were encouraged, not only by being told, but by seeing, that there was deeper water between us and the shore. However, that we might be better informed, the moment we found a spot where we could drop the anchor, clear of rocks, we came to; and sent the Masters, with the boats, to found.

Soon after we had anchored, which was about noon, several of the inhabitants of Tongataboo came off in their canoes to the ships. These, as well as our pilots, assured us, that we should find deep water farther in, and a bottom free from rocks. They were not mistaken; for, about four o'clock, the boats made the signal for having found good anchorage. Upon this we weighed, and stood in till dark, and then anchored in nine fathoms, having a fine, clear, sandy bottom.

During the night we had some showers of rain; but toward the morning, the wind shifted to the South, and South East, and brought on fair weather. At day-break we weighed, and, working in to the shore, met with no obstructions, but such as were visible, and easily avoided.

While we were plying up to the harbour, to which the natives directed us, the king kept sailing round us in his canoe. There were, at the same time, a great many small canoes about the ships. Two of these, which could not get out of the way of his royal vessel, he run quite over, with as little concern, as if they had been bits of wood.

wood. Amongst many others who came on board the Resolution, was Otago [*], who had been so useful to me when I visited Tongataboo during my last voyage; and one Toobou, who, at that time, had attached himself to Captain Furneaux. Each of them brought a hog, and some yams, as a testimony of his friendship; and I was not wanting, on my part, in making a suitable return.

At length, about two in the afternoon, we arrived at our intended station. It was a very snug place, formed by the shore of Tongataboo on the South East, and two small islands on the East and North East. Here we anchored in ten fathoms water, over a bottom of oozy sand; distant from the shore one-third of a mile.

[*] See a print of him in Captain Cook's Voyage, Vol. I. p. 197.

CHAP. VII.

Friendly Reception at Tongataboo.—Manner of distributing a baked Hog and Kava to Poulaho's Attendants.—The Observatory, &c. erected.—The Village where the Chiefs reside, and the adjoining Country, described.—Interviews with Mareewagee, and Toobou, and the King's Son.—A grand Haiva, or Entertainment of Songs and Dances, given by Mareewagee.—Exhibition of Fireworks.—Manner of Wrestling and Boxing.—Distribution of the Cattle.—Thefts committed by the Natives.—Poulaho, and the other Chiefs, confined on that Account.—Poulaho's Present, and Haiva.

1777.
June.
Tuesday 10.

SOON after we had anchored, having first dined, I landed, accompanied by Omai, and some of the Officers. We found the king waiting for us upon the beach. He, immediately, conducted us to a small neat house, situated a little within the skirts of the woods, with a fine large area before it. This house, he told me, was at my service, during our stay at the island; and a better situation we could not wish for.

We had not been long in the house, before a pretty large circle of the natives were assembled before us, and seated upon the area. A root of the *kava* plant being brought, and laid down before the king, he ordered it to be split into pieces, and distributed to several people of both sexes, who began

the

the operation of chewing it; and a bowl of their favourite liquor was soon prepared. In the mean time, a baked hog, and two baskets of baked yams, were produced, and afterward divided into ten portions. These portions were then given to certain people present; but how many were to share in each, I could not tell. One of them, I observed, was bestowed upon the king's brother; and one remained undisposed of, which, I judged, was for the king himself, as it was a choice bit. The liquor was next served out; but Poulaho seemed to give no directions about it. The first cup was brought to him, which he ordered to be given to one who sat near him. The second was also brought to him, and this he kept. The third was given to me; but their manner of brewing having quenched my thirst, it became Omai's property. The rest of the liquor was distributed to different people, by direction of the man who had the management of it. One of the cups being carried to the king's brother, he retired with this, and with his mess of victuals. Some others also quitted the circle with their portions; and the reason was, they could neither eat nor drink in the royal presence; but there were others present, of a much inferior rank, of both sexes, who did both. Soon after, most of them withdrew, carrying with them what they had not eat of their share of the feast.

I observed, that not a fourth part of the company had tasted either the victuals or the drink; those who partook of the former, I supposed to be of the king's household. The servants, who distributed the baked meat, and the *kava*, always delivered it out of their hand sitting, not only to the king, but to every other person. It is worthy of remark, though this was the first time of our landing, and a great many people were present who had never seen us before, yet

yet no one was troublesome; but the greatest good order was preserved, throughout the whole assembly.

Before I returned on board, I went in search of a watering place, and was conducted to some ponds, or rather holes, containing fresh water, as they were pleased to call it. The contents of one of these, indeed, were tolerable; but it was at some distance inland, and the supply to be got from it was very inconsiderable. Being informed, that the little island of Pangimodoo, near which the ships lay, could better furnish this necessary article, I went over to it, next morning, and was so fortunate as to find there a small pool, that had rather fresher water, than any we had met with amongst these islands. The pool being very dirty, I ordered it to be cleaned; and here it was that we watered the ships.

As I intended to make some stay at Tongataboo, we pitched a tent, in the forenoon, just by the house which Poulaho had assigned for our use. The horses, cattle, and sheep, were afterward landed, and a party of marines, with their Officer, stationed there as a guard. The observatory was then set up, at a small distance from the other tent; and Mr. King resided on shore, to attend the observations, and to superintend the several operations necessary to be conducted there. For the sails were carried thither, to be repaired; a party was employed in cutting wood for fuel, and plank for the use of the ships; and the gunners of both, were ordered to remain upon the spot, to conduct the traffic with the natives, who thronged from every part of the island, with hogs, yams, cocoa-nuts, and other articles of their produce. In a short time, our land post was like a fair, and the ships were so crowded with visiters, that we had hardly room to stir upon the decks.

Feenou

Feenou had taken up his refidence in our neighbourhood; but he was no longer the leading man. However, we ſtill found him to be a perſon of confequence, and we had daily proofs of his opulence and liberality, by the continuance of his valuable prefents. But the king was equally attentive in this refpect; for fcarcely a day paſſed, without receiving from him fome confiderable donation. We now heard, that there were other great men of the iſland, whom we had not, as yet, feen. Ota'go and Toobou, in particular, mentioned a perſon named Mareewagee, who, they faid, was of the firſt confequence in the place, and held in great veneration; nay, if Omai did not mifunderſtand them, fuperior even to Poulaho, to whom he was related; but, being old, lived in retirement; and, therefore, would not viſit us. Some of the natives even hinted, that he was too great a man to confer that honour upon us. This account exciting my curioſity, I, this day, mentioned to Poulaho, that I was very defirous of waiting upon Mareewagee; and he readily agreed to accompany me, to the place of his refidence, the next morning.

Accordingly, we ſet out, pretty early, in the pinnace; and Captain Clerke joined me in one of his own boats. We proceeded round, that is, to the Eaſtward of the little iſles that form the harbour, and then, turning to the South, according to Poulaho's directions, entered a ſpacious bay or inlet, up which we rowed about a league, and landed amidſt a confiderable number of people, who received us with a fort of acclamation, not unlike our huzzaing. They immediately feparated, to let Poulaho paſs, who took us into a ſmall inclofure, and ſhifted the piece of cloth he wore, for a new piece, neatly folded, that was carried by a young man. An old woman affiſted in dreſſing him, and put a mat over his cloth; as we supposed, to prevent its being dirtied when he sat down. On our now asking him where Mareewagee was, to our great surprize, he said, he had gone from the place, to the ship, just before we arrived. However, he desired us to walk with him to a *malaee*, or house of public resort, which stood about half a mile up the country. But when we came to a large area before it, he sat down in the path, and desired us to walk up to the house. We did so, and seated ourselves in front, while the crowd that followed us filled up the rest of the space. After sitting a little while, we repeated our inquiries, by means of Omai, Whether we were to see Mareewagee? But receiving no satisfactory information, and suspecting that the old Chief was purposely concealed from us, we went back to our boats, much piqued at our disappointment; and when I got on board, I found that no such person had been there. It afterward appeared, that, in this affair, we had laboured under some gross mistakes, and that our interpreter Omai had either been misinformed, or, which is more likely, had misunderstood what was told him about the great man, on whose account we had made this excursion.

The place we went to was a village, most delightfully situated on the bank of the inlet, where all, or most of the principal persons of the island reside; each having his house in the midst of a small plantation, with lesser houses, and offices for servants. These plantations are neatly fenced round; and, for the most part, have only one entrance. This is by a door, fastened, on the inside, by a prop of wood; so that a person has to knock, before he can get admittance. Public roads, and narrow lanes, lie between each plantation; so that no one trespasseth upon another. Great part of some of these inclosures is laid out in grass-plots, and

planted

planted with fuch things as feem more for ornament than ufe. But hardly any were without the *kava* plant, from which they make their favourite liquor. Every article of the vegetable produce of the ifland, abounded in others of thefe plantations; but thefe, I obferved, are not the refidence of people of the firft rank. There are fome large houfes near the public roads, with fpacious fmooth grafs-plots before them, and unenclofed. Thefe, I was told, belonged to the king; and, probably, they are the places where their public affemblies are held. It was to one of thefe houfes, as I have already mentioned, that we were conducted, foon after our landing at this place.

About noon, the next day, this Mareewagee, of whom we had heard fo much, actually came to the neighbourhood of our poft on fhore; and, with him, a very confiderable number of people of all ranks. I was informed, that he had taken this trouble, on purpofe to give me an opportunity of waiting upon him; having, probably, heard of the difpleafure I had fhewn, on my difappointment the day before. In the afternoon, a party of us, accompanied by Feenou, landed, to pay him a vifit. We found a perfon fitting under a large tree, near the fhore, a little to the right of the tent. A piece of cloth, at leaft forty yards long, was fpread before him, round which a great number of people, of both fexes, were feated. It was natural to fuppofe, that this was the great man; but we were undeceived by Feenou; who informed us, that another, who fat on a piece of mat, a little way from this Chief, to the right hand, was Mareewagee, and he introduced us to him, who received us very kindly, and defired us to fit down by him. The perfon, who fat under the tree, fronting us, was called Toobou; and, when I have occafion to fpeak of him afterward, I fhall call him

him old Toobou, to distinguish him from his namesake, Captain Furneaux's friend. Both he and Mareewagee had a venerable appearance. The latter is a slender man, and, from his appearance, seems to be considerably above threescore years of age. The former is rather corpulent, and almost blind with a disorder of his eyes; though not so old.

Not expecting to meet with two Chiefs, on this occasion, I had only brought on shore a present for one. This I now found myself under a necessity of dividing between them; but it happened to be pretty considerable, and both of them seemed satisfied. After this, we entertained them, for about an hour, with the performance of two French horns, and a drum. But they seemed most pleased with the firing off a pistol, which Captain Clerke had in his pocket. Before I took my leave, the large piece of cloth was rolled up, and, with a few cocoa-nuts, presented to me.

Saturday 14. The next morning, old Toobou returned my visit on board the ship. He also visited Captain Clerke; and if the present we made to him, the evening before, was scanty, the deficiency was now made up. During this time, Mareewagee visited our people ashore; and Mr. King shewed to him every thing we had there. He viewed the cattle with great admiration; and the cross-cut saw fixed his attention for some time.

Toward noon, Poulaho returned from the place where we had left him two days before, and brought with him his son, a youth about twelve years of age. I had his company at dinner; but the son, though present, was not allowed to sit down with him. It was very convenient to have him for my guest. For when he was present, which was generally the case while we stayed here, every other native was

excluded

excluded from the table; and but few of them would remain in the cabin. Whereas, if, by chance, it happened, that neither he nor Feenou were on board, the inferior Chiefs would be very importunate to be of our dining party, or to be admitted into the cabin at that time; and then we were so crowded, that we could not sit down to a meal with any satisfaction. The king was very soon reconciled to our manner of cookery. But still, I believe, he dined thus frequently with me, more for the sake of what we gave him to drink, than for what we set before him to eat. For he had taken a liking to our wine, could empty his bottle as well as most men, and was as cheerful over it. He now fixed his residence at the house, or *Malaee*, by our tent; and there he entertained our people, this evening, with a dance. To the surprise of every body, the unwieldy Poulaho endeavoured to vie with others, in that active amusement.

In the morning of the 15th, I received a message from Old Toobou, that he wanted to see me ashore. Accordingly Omai and I went to wait upon him. We found him, like an ancient patriarch, seated under the shade of a tree, with a large piece of the cloth, made in the island, spread out at full length before him; and a number of respectably looking people sitting round it. He desired us to place ourselves by him; and then he told Omai, that the cloth, together with a piece of red feathers, and about a dozen cocoa-nuts, were his present to me. I thanked him for the favour; and desired he would go on board with me, as I had nothing on shore to give him in return.

Omai now left me, being sent for by Poulaho; and, soon after, Feenou came, and acquainted me that young Fattafaihe, Poulaho's son, desired to see me. I obeyed the summons, and found the prince, and Omai, sitting under a large

large canopy of the finer sort of cloth; with a piece of the coarser sort, spread under them and before them, that was seventy-six yards long, and seven and a half broad. On one side was a large old boar; and on the other side a heap of cocoa-nuts. A number of people were seated round the cloth; and, amongst them, I observed Mareewagee, and others of the first rank. I was desired to sit down by the prince; and then Omai informed me, that he had been instructed by the king to tell me, that, as he and I were friends, he hoped that his son might be joined in this friendship; and that, as a token of my consent, I would accept of his present. I very readily agreed to the proposal; and, it being now dinner-time, I invited them all on board.

Accordingly, the young prince, Mareewagee, old Toobou, three or four inferior Chiefs, and two respectable old ladies of the first rank, accompanied me. Mareewagee was dressed in a new piece of cloth, on the skirts of which were fixed six pretty large patches of red feathers. This dress seemed to have been made, on purpose, for this visit; for, as soon as he got on board, he put it off, and presented it to me; having, I guess, heard that it would be acceptable, on account of the feathers. Every one of my visiters received from me such presents, as, I had reason to believe, they were highly satisfied with. When dinner came upon table, not one of them would sit down, or eat a bit of any thing that was served up. On expressing my surprise at this, they were all *taboo*, as they said; which word has a very comprehensive meaning; but, in general, signifies that a thing is forbidden. Why they were laid under such restraints, at present, was not explained. Dinner being over, and, having gratified their curiosity, by shewing to them every part of the ship, I then conducted them ashore.

As soon as the boat reached the beach, Feenou, and some others, instantly stepped out. Young Fattafaihe following them, was called back by Mareewagee, who now paid the heir apparent the same obeisance, and in the same manner, that I had seen it paid to the king. And when old Toobou, and one of the old ladies, had shewn him the same marks of respect, he was suffered to land. This ceremony being over, the old people stepped from my boat, into a canoe, that was waiting to carry them to their place of abode.

I was not sorry to be present on this occasion, as I was thus furnished with the most unequivocal proofs of the supreme dignity of Poulaho and his son, over the other principal Chiefs. Indeed, by this time, I had acquired some certain information about the relative situations of the several great men, whose names have been so often mentioned. I now knew, that Mareewagee and old Toobou were brothers. Both of them were men of great property in the island, and seemed to be in high estimation with the people; the former, in particular, had the very honourable appellation given to him, by every body, of *Motooa Tonga*; that is to say, Father of Tonga, or of his Country. The nature of his relationship to the king was also no longer a secret to us; for we now understood, that he was his father-in-law; Poulaho having married one of his daughters, by whom he had this son; so that Mareewagee was the prince's grandfather. Poulaho's appearance having satisfied us, that we had been under a mistake, in considering Feenou as the sovereign of these islands, we had been, at first, much puzzled about his real rank; but that was, by this time, ascertained. Feenou was one of Mareewagee's sons; and Tooboueitoa was another.

On

1777.
June.

On my landing, I found the king, in the house adjoining to our tent, along with our people who resided on shore. The moment I got to him, he bestowed upon me a present of a large hog, and a quantity of yams. About the dusk of the evening, a number of men came, and, having sat down in a round group, began to sing in concert with the music of bamboo drums, which were placed in the centre*. There were three long ones, and two short. With these they struck the ground endwise, as before described. There were two others, which lay on the ground, side by side, and one of them was split or shivered; on these a man kept beating with two small sticks. They sung three songs while I stayed; and, I was told, that, after I left them, the entertainment lasted till ten o'clock. They burnt the leaves of the *wharra* palm for a light; which is the only thing I ever saw them make use of for this purpose.

While I was passing the day in attendance on these great men, Mr. Anderson, with some others, made an excursion into the country, which furnished him with the following remarks: "To the Westward of the tent, the country is totally uncultivated for near two miles, though quite covered with trees and bushes, in a natural state, growing with the greatest vigour. Beyond this is a pretty large plain, on which are some cocoa-trees, and a few small plantations that appear to have been lately made; and, seemingly, on ground that has never been cultivated before. Near the creek, which runs to the Westward of the tent, the land is quite flat, and partly overflowed by the sea every

* The same sort of evening concert is performed round the house of the Chief, or *Tamole*, at the Caroline Islands. " Le *Tamole* ne s'endort qu'au bruit d'un concert " de musique que forme une troupe de jeunes gens, qui s'assemblent le soir, autour de ". sa maison, & qui chantent, à leur manière, certaines poesies." *Lettres Edifiantes & Curieuses*, Tom. xv. p. 314.

tide.

tide. When that retires, the surface is seen to be composed of coral rock, with holes of yellowish mud scattered up and down; and toward the edges, where it is a little firmer, are innumerable little openings, from which issue as many small crabs, of two or three different sorts, which swarm upon the spot, as flies upon a carcase; but are so nimble, that, on being approached, they disappear in an instant, and baffle even the natives to catch any of them.

At this place is a work of art, which shews, that these people are capable of some design, and perseverance, when they mean to accomplish any thing. This work begins, on one side, as a narrow causeway, which, becoming gradually broader, rises, with a gentle ascent, to the height of ten feet, where it is five paces broad, and the whole length seventy-four paces. Joined to this is a sort of circus, whose diameter is thirty paces, and not above a foot or two higher than the causeway that joins it, with some trees planted in the middle. On the opposite side, another causeway of the same sort descends; but this is not above forty paces long, and is partly in ruin. The whole is built with large coral stones, with earth on the surface, which is quite overgrown with low trees and shrubs; and, from its decaying in several places, seems to be of no modern date. Whatever may have been its use formerly, it seems to be of none now; and all that we could learn of it from the natives was, that it belonged to Poulaho, and is called *Etchee.*"

On the 16th, in the morning, after visiting the several works now carrying on ashore, Mr. Gore, and I, took a walk into the country; in the course of which nothing remarkable appeared, but our having opportunities of seeing the whole process of making cloth, which is the principal manufacture

manufacture of these islands, as well as of many others in this Ocean. In the narrative of my first Voyage *, a minute description is given of this operation, as performed at Otaheite; but the process, here, differing in some particulars, it may be worth while to give the following account of it:

The manufacturers, who are females, take the slender stalks or trunks of the paper-mulberry, which they cultivate for that purpose; and which seldom grows more than six or seven feet in height, and about four fingers in thickness. From these they strip the bark, and scrape off the outer rind with a muscle-shell. The bark is then rolled up to take off the convexity which it had round the stalk, and macerated in water for some time (they say, a night). After this, it is laid across the trunk of a small tree squared, and beaten with a square wooden instrument, about a foot long, full of coarse grooves on all sides; but, sometimes, with one that is plain. According to the size of the bark, a piece is soon produced; but the operation is often repeated by another hand, or it is folded several times, and beat longer, which seems rather intended to close than to divide its texture. When this is sufficiently effected, it is spread out to dry; the pieces being from four to six, or more, feet in length, and half as broad. They are then given to another person, who joins the pieces, by smearing part of them over with the viscous juice of a berry, called *tooo*, which serves as a glue. Having been thus lengthened, they are laid over a large piece of wood, with a kind of stamp, made of a fibrous substance pretty closely interwoven, placed beneath. They then take a bit of cloth, and dip it in a juice,

* Hawkesworth's Collection of Voyages, Vol. ii. p. 210.

expressed from the bark of a tree, called *kulla*, which they rub briskly upon the piece that is making. This, at once, leaves a dull brown colour, and a dry gloss upon its surface; the stamp, at the same time, making a slight impression, that answers no other purpose that I could see, but to make the several pieces, that are glued together, stick a little more firmly. In this manner they proceed, joining and staining by degrees, till they produce a piece of cloth, of such length and breadth as they want; generally leaving a border, of a foot broad, at the sides, and longer at the ends, unstained. Throughout the whole, if any parts of the original pieces are too thin, or have holes, which is often the case, they glue spare bits upon them, till they become of an equal thickness. When they want to produce a black colour, they mix the soot procured from an oily nut, called *doodooe*, with the juice of the *kulla*, in different quantities, according to the proposed depth of the tinge. They say, that the black sort of cloth, which is commonly most glazed, makes a cold dress, but the other a warm one; and, to obtain strength in both, they are always careful to join the small pieces lengthwise, which makes it impossible to tear the cloth in any direction but one.

On our return from the country, we met with Feenou, and took him, and another young Chief, on board to dinner. When our fare was set upon the table, neither of them would eat a bit; saying, that they were *taboo avy*. But, after enquiring how the victuals had been dressed, having found that no *avy* (water) had been used in cooking a pig and some yams, they both sat down, and made a very hearty meal; and, on being assured that there was no water in the wine, they drank of it also. From this we conjectured, that, on some account or another, they were, at

this

1777.
June.

this time, forbidden to use water; or, which was more probable, they did not like the water we made use of, it being taken up out of one of their bathing-places. This was not the only time of our meeting with people that were *taboo avy*; but, for what reason, we never could tell with any degree of certainty.

Tuesday 17.

Next day, the 17th, was fixed upon by Mareewagee, for giving a grand *Haiva*, or entertainment; to which we were all invited. For this purpose a large space had been cleared, before the temporary hut of this Chief, near our post, as an area where the performances were to be exhibited. In the morning, great multitudes of the natives came in from the country, every one carrying a pole, about six feet long, upon his shoulder; and at each end of every pole, a yam was suspended. These yams and poles were deposited on each side of the area, so as to form two large heaps, decorated with different sorts of small fish, and piled up to the greatest advantage. They were Mareewagee's present to Captain Clerke and me; and it was hard to say, whether the wood for fuel, or the yams for food, were of most value to us. As for the fish, they might serve to please the sight, but were very offensive to the smell; part of them having been kept two or three days, to be presented to us on this occasion.

Every thing being thus prepared, about eleven o'clock they began to exhibit various dances, which they call *mai*. The music * consisted, at first, of seventy men as a chorus, who sat down; and amidst them were placed three instruments, which we called drums, though very unlike them. They are large cylindrical pieces of wood, or trunks of

* Mr. Anderson's description of the entertainments of this day being much fuller than Captain Cook's, it has been adopted as on a former occasion.

trees,

trees, from three to four feet long, some twice as thick as an ordinary sized man, and some smaller, hollowed entirely out, but close at both ends, and open only by a chink, about three inches broad, running almost the whole length of the drums; by which opening, the rest of the wood is certainly hollowed, though the operation must be difficult. This instrument is called *nassa*; and, with the chink turned toward them, they sit and beat strongly upon it, with two cylindrical pieces of hard wood, about a foot long, and as thick as the wrist; by which means they produce a rude, though loud and powerful sound. They vary the strength and rate of their beating, at different parts of the dance; and also change the tones, by beating in the middle, or near the end, of their drum.

The first dance consisted of four ranks, of twenty-four men each, holding in their hands a little, thin, light, wooden instrument, above two feet long, and, in shape, not unlike a small oblong paddle. With these, which are called *pagge*, they made a great many different motions; such as pointing them toward the ground on one side, at the same time inclining their bodies that way, from which they were shifted to the opposite side in the same manner; then passing them quickly from one hand to the other, and twirling them about very dexterously; with a variety of other manoeuvres, all which were accompanied by correspondoning attitudes of the body. Their motions were, at first, slow, but quickened as the drums beat faster; and they recited sentences, in a musical tone, the whole time, which were answered by the chorus; but at the end of a short space they all joined, and finished with a shout.

After ceasing about two or three minutes, they began as before, and continued, with short intervals, above a quarter of an hour; when the rear rank dividing, shifted themselves very slowly round each end, and, meeting in the front, formed the first rank; the whole number continuing to recite the sentences as before. The other ranks did the same successively, till that which, at first, was the front, became the rear; and the evolution continued, in the same manner, till the last rank regained its first situation. They then began a much quicker dance (though slow at first), and sung for about ten minutes, when the whole body divided into two parts, retreated a little, and then approached, forming a sort of circular figure, which finished the dance; the drums being removed, and the chorus going off the field at the same time.

The second dance had only two drums, with forty men for a chorus; and the dancers, or rather actors, consisted of two ranks, the foremost having seventeen, and the other fifteen persons. Feenou was at their head, or in the middle of the front rank, which is the principal place in these cases. They danced and recited sentences, with some very short intervals, for about half an hour, sometimes quickly, sometimes more slowly, but with such a degree of exactness, as if all the motions were made by one man, which did them great credit. Near the close, the back rank divided, came round, and took the place of the front, which again resumed its situation, as in the first dance; and when they finished, the drums and chorus, as before, went off.

Three drums (which, at least, took two, and sometimes three men to carry them) were now brought in; and seventy men sat down as a chorus to the third dance. This consisted of two ranks, of sixteen persons each, with young Toobou at their head, who was richly ornamented with a

sort

fort of garment covered with red feathers. Thefe danced, fung, and twirled the *pagge*, as before; but, in general, much quicker, and performed fo well, that they had the conftant applaufes of the fpectators. A motion that met with particular approbation, was one in which they held the face afide, as if afhamed, and the *pagge* before it. The back rank clofed before the front one, and that again refumed its place, as in the two former dances; but then they began again, formed a triple row, divided, retreated to each end of the area, and left the greateft part of the ground clear. At that inftant, two men entered very haftily, and exercifed the clubs which they ufe in battle. They did this, by firft twirling them in their hands, and making circular ftrokes before them with great force and quicknefs; but fo fkilfully managed, that, though ftanding quite clofe, they never interfered. They fhifted their clubs from hand to hand, with great dexterity; and, after continuing a little time, kneeled, and made different motions, tolling the clubs up in the air, which they caught as they fell; and then went off as haftily as they entered. Their heads were covered with pieces of white cloth, tied at the crown (almoft like a night-cap) with a wreath of foliage round the forehead; but they had only very fmall pieces of white cloth tied about their waifts; probably, that they might be cool, and free from every incumbrance or weight. A perfon with a fpear, dreffed like the former, then came in, and in the fame hafty manner; looking about eagerly, as if in fearch of fomebody to throw it at. He then ran haftily to one fide of the crowd in the front, and put himfelf in a threatening attitude, as if he meant to ftrike with his fpear at one of them, bending the knee a little, and trembling, as it were with rage. He continued in this manner only a few feconds, when he moved to the

other

other fide, and having flood in the fame pofture there, for the fame fhort time, retreated from the ground, as faft as when he made his appearance. The dancers, who had divided into two parties, kept repeating fomething flowly all this while; and now advanced, and joined again, ending with univerfal applaufe. It fhould feem, that this dance was confidered as one of their capital performances, if we might judge from fome of the principal people being engaged in it. For one of the drums was beat by Futtafaihe, the brother of Poulaho, another by Feenou, and the third, which did not belong to the chorus, by Mareewagee himfelf, at the entrance of his hut.

The laft dance had forty men, and two drums, as a chorus. It confifted of fixty men, who had not danced before, difpofed in three rows, having twenty-four in front. But, before they began, we were entertained with a pretty long preliminary harangue, in which the whole body made refponfes to a fingle perfon who fpoke. They recited fentences (perhaps verfes) alternately with the chorus, and made many motions with the *pagge*, in a very brifk mode, which were all applauded with *mareeai!* and *fufogge!* words expreffing two different degrees of praife. They divided into two bodies, with their backs to each other; formed again, fhifted their ranks, as in the other dances; divided and retreated, making room for two champions, who exercifed their clubs as before; and after them two others: the dancers, all the time, reciting flowly in turn with the chorus; after which they advanced, and finifhed.

Thefe dances, if they can properly be called fo, lafted from eleven till near three o'clock; and though they were, doubtlefs, intended, particularly, either in honour of us, or to fhew a fpecimen of their dexterity, vaft numbers of

their

their own people attended as spectators. Their numbers could not be computed exactly, on account of the inequality of the ground; but, by reckoning the inner circle, and the number in depth, which was between twenty and thirty in many places, we supposed that there must be near four thousand. At the same time, there were round the trading place at the tent, and straggling about, at least as many more; and some of us computed, that, at this time, there were not less than ten or twelve thousand people, in our neighbourhood; that is, within the compass of a quarter of a mile; drawn together, for the most part, by mere curiosity.

It is with regret I mention, that we could not understand what was spoken, while we were able to see what was acted, in these amusements. This, doubtless, would have afforded us much information, as to the genius and customs of these people. It was observable, that, though the spectators always approved of the various motions, when well made, a great share of the pleasure they received seemed to arise from the sentimental part, or what the performers delivered in their speeches. However, the mere acting part, independently of the sentences repeated, was well worth our notice, both with respect to the extensive plan on which it was executed, and to the various motions, as well as the exact unity, with which they were performed. The drawings which Mr. Webber made of the performances at Hapaee, and which are equally applicable to those exhibited now, will serve much to illustrate the account here given of the order in which the actors range themselves. But neither pencil nor pen can describe the numerous actions and motions, the singularity of which was not greater, than
was

was the ease and gracefulness with which they were performed.

At night, we were entertained with the *heeva*, or night dances, on a space before Feenou's temporary habitation. They lasted about three hours; in which time we had about twelve of them performed, much after the same manner as those at Hapaee. But, in two, that were performed by women, a number of men came and formed a circle within their's. And, in another, consisting of twenty-four men, there were a number of motions with the hands, that we had not seen before, and were highly applauded. The music was, also, once changed, in the course of the night; and in one of the dances, Feenou appeared at the head of fifty men who had performed at Hapaee, and he was well dressed with linen, a large piece of gauze, and some little pictures hung round his neck. But it was evident, after the diversions were closed, that we had put these poor people, or rather that they had put themselves, to much inconvenience. For being drawn together on this uninhabited part of their island, numbers of them were obliged to lie down and sleep under the bushes, by the side of a tree, or of a canoe; nay many either lay down in the open air, which they are not fond of, or walked about all the night.

The whole of this entertainment was conducted with far better order, than could have been expected in so large an assembly. Amongst such a multitude, there must be a number of ill-disposed people; and we, hourly, experienced it. All our care and attention did not prevent their plundering us, in every quarter; and that, in the most daring and insolent manner. There was hardly any thing that they did not attempt to steal; and yet, as the crowd was always so great,

great, I would not allow the fentries to fire, left the innocent fhould fuffer for the guilty. They once, at noon day, ventured to aim at taking an anchor from off the Difcovery's bows; and they would certainly have fucceeded, if the fluke had not hooked one of the chain plates in lowering down the fhip's fide, from which they could not difengage it by hand; and tackles were things they were unacquainted with. The only act of violence they were guilty of, was the breaking the fhoulder bone of one of our goats, fo that fhe died foon after. This lofs fell upon themfelves, as fhe was one of thofe that I intended to leave upon the ifland; but of this, the perfon who did it, was ignorant.

Early in the morning of the 18th, an incident happened, that ftrongly marked one of their cuftoms. A man got out of a canoe into the quarter gallery of the Refolution, and ftole from thence a pewter bafon. He was difcovered, purfued, and brought along-fide the fhip. On this occafion, three old women, who were in the canoe, made loud lamentations over the prifoner, beating their breafts and faces in a moft violent manner, with the infide of their fifts; and all this was done without fhedding a tear. This mode of expreffing grief is what occafions the mark which almoft all this people bear on the face, over the cheek bones. The repeated blows which they inflict upon this part, abrade the fkin, and make even the blood flow out in a confiderable quantity; and when the wounds are recent, they look as if a hollow circle had been burnt in. On many occafions, they actually cut this part of the face with an inftrument; in the fame manner as the people of Otaheite cut their heads.

This day, I beftowed on Mareewagee fome prefents, in return for thofe we had received from him the day before;

and

and as the entertainments which he had then exhibited for our amusement, called upon us to make some exhibition in our way, I ordered the party of marines to go through their exercise, on the spot where his dances had been performed; and, in the evening, played off some fireworks at the same place. Poulaho, with all the principal Chiefs, and a great number of people, of all denominations, were present. The platoon firing, which was executed tolerably well, seemed to give them pleasure; but they were lost in astonishment when they beheld our water rockets. They paid but little attention to the fife and drum, or French horns, that played during the intervals. The king sat behind every body, because no one is allowed to sit behind him; and, that his view might not be obstructed, nobody sat immediately before him; but a lane, as it were, was made by the people from him, quite down to the space allotted for the fireworks.

In expectation of this evening shew, the circle of natives about our tent being pretty large, they engaged, the greatest part of the afternoon, in boxing and wrestling; the first of which exercises they call *fongatoa*, and the second *foobow*. When any of them chooses to wrestle, he gets up from one side of the ring, and crosses the ground in a sort of measured pace, clapping smartly on the elbow joint of one arm, which is bent, and produces a hollow sound; that is reckoned the challenge. If no person comes out from the opposite side to engage him, he returns, in the same manner, and sits down; but sometimes stands clapping, in the midst of the ground, to provoke some one to come out. If an opponent appear, they come together with marks of the greatest good-nature, generally smiling, and taking time to adjust the piece of cloth which is fastened round the waist.

They

They then lay hold of each other by this girdle, with a hand on each side; and he who succeeds in drawing his antagonist to him, immediately tries to lift him upon his breast, and throw him upon his back; and if he be able to turn round with him two or three times, in that position, before he throws him, his dexterity never fails of procuring plaudits from the spectators. If they be more equally matched, they close soon, and endeavour to throw each other by entwining their legs, or lifting each other from the ground; in which struggles they shew a prodigious exertion of strength, every muscle, as it were, being ready to burst with straining. When one is thrown, he immediately quits the field, but the victor sits down for a few seconds, then gets up, and goes to the side he came from, who proclaim the victory aloud, in a sentence delivered slowly, and in a musical cadence. After sitting a short space, he rises again and challenges; when sometimes several antagonists make their appearance; but he has the privilege of choosing which of them he pleases to wrestle with; and has, likewise, the preference of challenging again, if he should throw his adversary, until he himself be vanquished; and then the opposite side sing the song of victory in favour of their champion. It also often happens, that five or six rise from each side, and challenge together; in which case, it is common to see three or four couple engaged on the field at once. But it is astonishing to see what temper they preserve in this exercise; for we observed no instances of their leaving the spot, with the least displeasure in their countenances. When they find, that they are so equally matched as not to be likely to throw each other, they leave off by mutual consent. And if the fall of one is not fair, or if it does not appear very clearly who has had the advantage,

both

both sides sing the victory, and then they engage again. But no person, who has been vanquished, can engage with his conqueror a second time.

The boxers advance side-ways, changing the side at every pace, with one arm stretched fully out before, the other behind; and holding a piece of cord in one hand, which they wrap firmly about it, when they find an antagonist, or else have done so before they enter. This, I imagine, they do, to prevent a dislocation of the hand or fingers. Their blows are directed chiefly to the head; but sometimes to the sides; and are dealt out with great activity. They shift sides, and box equally well with both hands. But one of their favourite and most dextrous blows, is, to turn round on their heel, just as they have struck their antagonist, and to give him another very smart one with the other hand backward.

The boxing matches seldom last long; and the parties either leave off together, or one acknowledges his being beat. But they never sing the song of victory in these cases, unless one strikes his adversary to the ground; which shews, that, of the two, wrestling is their most approved diversion. Not only boys engage, in both the exercises, but frequently little girls box very obstinately for a short time. In all which cases, it doth not appear, that they ever consider it as the smallest disgrace to be vanquished; and the person overcome sits down, with as much indifference, as if he had never entered the lists. Some of our people ventured to contend with them in both exercises, but were always worsted; except in a few instances, where it appeared, that the fear they were in of offending us, contributed more to the victory, than the superiority of the person they engaged.

† The

The cattle, which we had brought, and which were all on shore, however carefully guarded, I was sensible, run no small risk, when I considered the thievish disposition of many of the natives, and their dexterity in appropriating to themselves by stealth, what they saw no prospect of obtaining by fair means. For this reason I thought it prudent to declare my intention of leaving behind me some of our animals; and even to make a distribution of them previously to my departure.

With this view, in the evening of the 19th, I assembled all the Chiefs before our house, and my intended presents to them were marked out. To Poulaho, the king, I gave a young English bull and cow; to Mareewagee, a Cape ram, and two ewes; and to Feenou, a horse and a mare. As my design, to make such a distribution, had been made known the day before, most of the people in the neighbourhood were then present. I instructed Omai to tell them, that there were no such animals within many months sail of their island; that we had brought them, for their use, from that immense distance, at a vast trouble and expence; that, therefore, they must be careful not to kill any of them, till they had multiplied to a numerous race; and, lastly, that they and their children ought to remember, that they had received them from the men of *Britane*. He also explained to them their several uses, and what else was necessary for them to know, or rather as far as he knew; for Omai was not very well versed in such things himself. As I intended that the above presents should remain with the other cattle, till we were ready to sail, I desired each of the Chiefs to send a man or two to look after their respective animals, along with my people, in order that they might be better acquainted with them, and with the manner

of

of treating them. The king and Feenou did so; but neither Mareewagee, nor any other person for him, took the least notice of the sheep afterward; nor did old Toobou attend at this meeting, though he was invited, and was in the neighbourhood. I had meant to give him the goats, viz. a ram and two ewes; which, as he was so indifferent about them, I added to the king's share.

Friday 12. It soon appeared, that some were dissatisfied with this allotment of our animals; for, early next morning, one of our kids, and two turkey-cocks, were missing. I could not be so simple as to suppose, that this was merely an accidental loss; and I was determined to have them again. The first step I took was to seize on three canoes that happened to be along-side the ships. I then went ashore, and, having found the king, his brother, Feenou, and some other Chiefs, in the house that we occupied, I immediately put a guard over them, and gave them to understand, that they must remain under restraint, till not only the kid and the turkeys, but the other things, that had been stolen from us, at different times, were restored. They concealed, as well as they could, their feelings, on finding themselves prisoners; and, having assured me, that every thing should be restored, as I desired, sat down to drink their *kava*, seemingly much at their ease. It was not long before an axe, and an iron wedge, were brought to me. In the mean time, some armed natives began to gather behind the house; but, on a part of our guard marching against them, they dispersed; and I advised the Chiefs to give orders, that no more should appear. Such orders were accordingly given by them, and they were obeyed. On asking them to go aboard with me to dinner, they readily consented. But some having afterward objected to the king's going, he instantly rose up, and declared he would

would be the first man. Accordingly we came on board. I kept them there till near four o'clock, when I conducted them ashore; and, soon after, the kid, and one of the turkey-cocks, were brought back. The other, they said, should be restored the next morning. I believed this would happen, and released both them and the canoes.

After the Chiefs had left us, I walked out with Omai, to observe how the people about us fared; for this was the time of their meals. I found that, in general, they were at short commons. Nor is this to be wondered at, since most of the yams, and other provisions which they brought with them, were sold to us; and they never thought of returning to their own habitations, while they could find any sort of subsistence in our neighbourhood. Our station was upon an uncultivated point of land; so that there were none of the islanders, who, properly, resided within half a mile of us. But, even at this distance, the multitude of strangers being so great, one might have expected, that every house would have been much crowded. It was quite otherwise. The families residing there were as much left to themselves, as if there had not been a supernumerary visiter near them. All the strangers lived in little temporary sheds, or under trees and bushes; and the cocoa-trees were stripped of their branches, to erect habitations for the Chiefs.

In this walk we met with about half a dozen women, in one place, at supper. Two of the company, I observed, being fed by the others, on our asking the reason, they said *taboo mattee*. On farther inquiry we found, that one of them had, two months before, washed the dead corpse of a Chief; and that, on this account, she was not to handle any food for five months. The other had performed the same

1777.
June.

same office to the corpse of another person of inferior rank, and was now under the same restriction; but not for so long a time. At another place, hard by, we saw another woman fed; and we learnt, that she had assisted in washing the corpse of the above-mentioned Chief.

Saturday 21.

Early the next morning, the king came on board, to invite me to an entertainment, which he proposed to give the same day. He had already been under the barber's hands; his head being all besmeared with red pigment, in order to redden his hair, which was naturally of a dark brown colour. After breakfast, I attended him to the shore; and we found his people very busy, in two places, in the front of our area, fixing, in an upright and square position, thus [::], four very long posts, near two feet from each other. The space between the posts was afterward filled up with yams; and as they went on filling it, they fastened pieces of sticks across, from post to post, at the distance of about every four feet; to prevent the posts from separating, by the weight of the inclosed yams, and also to get up by. When the yams had reached the top of the first posts, they fastened others to them, and so continued till each pile was the height of thirty feet, or upward. On the top of one, they placed two baked hogs; and on the top of the other, a living one; and another they tied by the legs, half-way up. It was matter of curiosity to observe, with what facility and dispatch these two piles were raised. Had our seamen been ordered to execute such a work, they would have sworn that it could not be performed without carpenters; and the carpenters would have called to their aid a dozen different sorts of tools, and have expended, at least, a hundred weight of nails; and, after all, it would have employed them as many days, as it did

these

these people hours. But seamen, like most other amphibious animals, are always the most helpless on land. After they had completed these two piles, they made several other heaps of yams and bread-fruit on each side of the area; to which were added a turtle, and a large quantity of excellent fish. All this, with a piece of cloth, a mat, and some red feathers, was the king's present to me; and he seemed to pique himself on exceeding, as he really did, Feenou's liberality, which I experienced at Hapaee.

About one o'clock they began the *mai*, or dances; the first of which was almost a copy of the first that was exhibited at Mareewagee's entertainment. The second was conducted by Captain Furneaux's Toobou, who, as we mentioned, had also danced there; and in this, four or five women were introduced, who went through the several parts with as much exactness as the men. Toward the end, the performers divided to leave room for two champions, who exercised their clubs, as described on a former occasion. And, in the third dance, which was the last now presented, two more men, with their clubs, displayed their dexterity. The dances were succeeded by wrestling and boxing; and one man entered the lists with a sort of club, made from the stem of a cocoa-leaf, which is firm and heavy; but could find no antagonist to engage him at so rough a sport. At night we had the *boxai* repeated; in which Poulaho himself danced, dressed in English manufacture. But neither these, nor the dances in the day-time, were so considerable, nor carried on with so much spirit, as Feenou's, or Mareewagee's; and, therefore, there is less occasion to be more particular in our description of them.

In order to be present the whole time, I dined ashore. The king sat down with us; but he neither eat nor drank.

I found

I found that this was owing to the presence of a female, whom, at his desire, I had admitted to the dining party; and who, as we afterward understood, had superior rank to himself. As soon as this great personage had dined, she stepped up to the king, who put his hands to her feet; and then she retired. He immediately dipped his fingers into a glass of wine, and then received the obeisance of all her followers. This was the single instance we ever observed of his paying this mark of reverence to any person. At the king's desire, I ordered some fireworks to be played off in the evening; but, unfortunately, being damaged, this exhibition did not answer expectation.

CHAP. VIII.

Some of the Officers plundered by the Natives.—A fishing Party.—A Visit to Poulaho.—A Fiatooka described.— Observations on the Country Entertainment at Poulaho's House.—His Mourning Ceremony.—Of the Kava Plant, and the Manner of preparing the Liquor.—Account of Onevy, a little Island.—One of the Natives wounded by a Sentinel.—Messrs. King and Anderson visit the King's Brother.—Their Entertainment.— Another Mourning Ceremony.—Manner of passing the Night.—Remarks on the Country they passed through.—Preparations made for sailing.—An Eclipse of the Sun, imperfectly observed.—Mr. Anderson's Account of the Island, and its Productions.

AS no more entertainments were to be expected, on either side, and the curiosity of the populace was, by this time, pretty well satisfied; on the day after l'oulaho's *kava*, most of them left us. We still, however, had thieves about us; and, encouraged by the negligence of our own people, we had continual instances of their depredations.

Some of the officers, belonging to both ships, who had made an excursion into the interior parts of the island, without my leave, and, indeed, without my knowledge, returned this evening, after an absence of two days. They had

1777.
June.

Monday 23.

had taken with them their muskets, with the necessary ammunition, and several small articles of the favourite commodities; all which the natives had the dexterity to steal from them, in the course of their expedition. This affair was likely to be attended with inconvenient consequences. For, our plundered travellers, upon their return, without consulting me, employed Omai to complain to the king of the treatment they had met with. He, not knowing what step I should take, and, from what had already happened, fearing left I might lay him again under restraint, went off early the next morning. His example was followed by Feenou; so that we had not a Chief, of any authority, remaining in our neighbourhood. I was very much displeased at this, and reprimanded Omai for having presumed to meddle. This reprimand put him upon his metal to bring his friend Feenou back; and he succeeded in the negociation; having this powerful argument to urge, that he might depend upon my using no violent measures to oblige the natives to restore what had been taken from the gentlemen. Feenou, trusting to this declaration, returned toward the evening; and, encouraged by his reception, Poulaho favoured us with his company the day after.

Tuesday 24.

Both these Chiefs, upon this occasion, very justly observed to me, that, if any of my people, at any time, wanted to go into the country, they ought to be acquainted with it; in which case they would send proper people along with them; and then they would be answerable for their safety. And I am convinced, from experience, that, by taking this very reasonable precaution, a man and his property may be as safe among these islanders, as in other parts of the more civilized world. Though I gave myself no trouble about the recovery of the things stolen upon this occasion, most

of

of them, through Feenou's interpofition, were recovered; except one mufket, and a few other articles of inferior value. By this time alfo, we had recovered the turkey-cock, and moft of the tools, and other matters, that had been ftolen from our workmen.

On the 25th, two boats, which I had fent to look for a channel, by which we might, moft commodioufly, get to fea, returned. The Mafters, who commanded them, reported, that the channel to the North, by which we came in, was highly dangerous, being full of coral rocks from one fide to the other; but that, to the Eaftward, there was a very good channel; which, however, was very much contracted, in one place, by the fmall iflands; fo that a leading wind would be requifite to get through it; that is, a Wefterly wind, which, we had found, did not often blow here. We had now recruited the fhips with wood and water; we had finifhed the repairs of our fails; and had little more to expect from the inhabitants, of the produce of their ifland. However, as an eclipfe of the fun was to happen upon the 5th of the next month, I refolved to defer failing till that time had elapfed, in order to have a chance of obferving it.

Having, therefore, fome days of leifure before me, a party of us, accompanied by Poulaho, fet out, early next morning, in a boat, for Mooa, the village where he and the other great men ufually refide. As we rowed up the inlet, we met with fourteen canoes fifhing in company; in one of which was Poulaho's fon. In each canoe was a triangular net, extended between two poles; at the lower end of which was a cod to receive and fecure the fifh. They had already caught fome fine mullets; and they put about a dozen into

our

our boat. I defired to fee their method of fifhing; which they readily complied with. A fhoal of fifh was fuppofed to be upon one of the banks, which they inftantly inclofed in a long net like a feine, or fet-net. This the fifhers, one getting into the water out of each boat, furrounded with the triangular nets in their hands; with which they fcooped the fifh out of the feine, or caught them as they attempted to leap over it. They fhewed us the whole procefs of this operation (which feemed to be a fure one), by throwing in fome of the fifh they had already caught; for, at this time, there happened to be none upon the bank that was inclofed.

Leaving the prince and his fifhing party, we proceeded to the bottom of the bay, and landed where we had done before, on our fruitlefs errand to fee Mareewagee. As foon as we got on fhore, the king defired Omai to tell me, that I need be under no apprehenfions about the boat, or any thing in her, for not a fingle article would be touched by any one; and we afterward found this to be the cafe. We were immediately conducted to one of Poulaho's houfes not far off, and near the public one, or *malaee*, in which we had been, when we firft vifited Mooa. This, though pretty large, feemed to be his private habitation, and was fituated within a plantation. The king took his feat at one end of the houfe, and the people, who came to vifit him, fat down, as they arrived, in a femicircle at the other end. The firft thing done, was to prepare a bowl of *kava*, and to order fome yams to be baked for us. While thefe were getting ready, fome of us, accompanied by a few of the king's attendants, and Omai as our interpreter, walked out to take a view of a *fatooka*, or burying-place, which we had obferved to be almoft clofe by the houfe, and was much more exten-

five,

five, and seemingly of more consequence, than any we had seen at the other islands. We were told, that it belonged to the king. It consisted of three pretty large houses, situated upon a rising ground, or rather just by the brink of it, with a small one, at some distance, all ranged longitudinally. The middle house of the three first, was, by much, the largest, and placed in a square, twenty-four paces by twenty-eight, raised about three feet. The other houses were placed on little mounts, raised artificially to the same height. The floors of these houses, as also the tops of the mounts round them, were covered with loose, fine pebbles, and the whole was inclosed by large flat stones * of hard coral rock, properly hewn, placed on their edges; one of which stones measured twelve feet in length, two in breadth, and above one in thickness. One of the houses, contrary to what we had seen before, was open on one side; and within it were two rude, wooden busts of men; one near the entrance, and the other farther in. On inquiring of the natives, who had followed us to the ground, but durst not enter here, What these images were intended for? they made us as sensible as we could wish, that they were merely memorials of some Chiefs who had been buried there, and not the representations of any deity. Such monuments, it should seem, are seldom raised; for these had, probably, been erected several ages ago. We were told, that the dead had been buried in each of these houses; but no marks of this appeared. In one of them, was the carved head of an Otaheite canoe, which had been driven ashore on their coast, and deposited here. At the foot of the rising ground, was a large area, or grass-plot, with different trees planted about

* The burying-places of the Chiefs at the Caroline Islands, are also inclosed in this manner. See *Lettres Édifiantes & Curieuses*, Tom. xv. p. 309.

it; amongst which were several of those called *etoa*, very large. These, as they resemble the cypress, had a fine effect in such a place. There was, also, a row of low palms near one of the houses, and behind it a ditch, in which lay a great number of old baskets. Mr. Webber's drawing of this *fatooka*, will supply the defects of my description.

After dinner, or rather after we had refreshed ourselves with some provisions which we had brought with us from our ship, we made an excursion into the country, taking a pretty large circuit, attended by one of the king's ministers. Our train was not great, as he would not suffer the rabble to follow us. He also obliged all those whom we met upon our progress, to sit down, till we had passed; which is a mark of respect due only to their Sovereigns. We found by far the greatest part of the country cultivated, and planted with various sorts of productions; and most of these plantations were fenced round. Some spots, where plantations had been formerly, now produced nothing, lying fallow; and there were places that had never been touched; but lay in a state of nature; and, yet, even these were useful, in affording them timber, as they were generally covered with trees. We met with several large uninhabited houses, which, we were told, belonged to the king. There were many public and well-beaten roads, and abundance of foot-paths leading to every part of the island. The roads being good, and the country level, travelling was very easy. It is remarkable, that when we were on the most elevated parts, at least a hundred feet above the level of the sea, we often met with the same coral rock, which is found at the shore, projecting above the surface, and perforated and cut into all those inequalities which are usually seen in rocks that lie within the wash of the tide. And yet these very

very spots, with hardly any soil upon them, were covered with luxuriant vegetation. We were conducted to several little pools, and to some springs of water; but, in general, they were either stinking or brackish, though recommended to us by the natives as excellent. The former were, mostly, inland, and the latter near the shore of the bay, and below high-water mark; so that tolerable water could be taken up from them, only when the tide was out.

When we returned from our walk, which was not till the dusk of the evening, our supper was ready. It consisted of a baked hog, some fish, and yams, all excellently well cooked, after the method of these islands. As there was nothing to amuse us after supper, we followed the custom of the country, and lay down to sleep, our beds being mats spread upon the floor, and cloth to cover us. The king, who had made himself very happy with some wine and brandy which we had brought, slept in the same house, as well as several others of the natives. Long before daybreak, he and they all rose, and sat conversing by moonlight. The conversation, as might well be guessed, turned wholly upon us; the king entertaining his company with an account of what he had seen, or remarked. As soon as it was day, they dispersed, some one way, and some another; but it was not long before they all returned, and, with them, several more of their countrymen.

They now began to prepare a bowl of *kava*; and, leaving them so employed, I went to pay a visit to Toobou, Captain Furneaux's friend, who had a house hard by, which, for size and neatness, was exceeded by few in the place. As I had left the others, so I found here a company, preparing a morning draught. This Chief made a present to me of a
living

living hog, a baked one, a quantity of yams, and a large piece of cloth. When I returned to the king, I found him and his circle of attendants, drinking the second bowl of *kava*. That being emptied, he told. Omai, that he was going presently to perform a mourning ceremony, called *Toogé*, on account of a son who had been dead some time; and he desired us to accompany him. We were glad of the opportunity, expecting to see somewhat new or curious.

The first thing the Chief did, was to step out of the house, attended by two old women, and put on a new suit of clothes, or rather a new piece of cloth, and, over it, an old ragged mat, that might have served his great grandfather, on some such occasion. His servants, or those who attended him, were all dressed in the same manner, excepting that none of their mats could vie, in antiquity, with that of their master. Thus equipped, we marched off, preceded by about eight or ten persons, all in the above habits of ceremony, each of them, besides, having a small green bough about his neck. Poulaho held his bough in his hand, till we drew near the place of rendezvous, when he also put it about his neck. We now entered a small inclosure, in which was a neat house, and we found one man sitting before it. As the company entered, they pulled off the green branches from round their necks, and threw them away. The king having first seated himself, the others sat down before him, in the usual manner. The circle increased, by others dropping in, to the number of a hundred or upward, mostly old men, all dressed as above described. The company being completely assembled, a large root of *kava*, brought by one of the king's servants, was produced, and a bowl which contained four or five gallons. Several persons now began to chew the root, and this bowl was made brimfull of liquor.

liquor. While it was preparing, others were employed in
making drinking cups of plantain leaves. The first cup
that was filled, was presented to the king, and he ordered
it to be given to another person. The second was also
brought to him, which he drank, and the third was offered
to me. Afterward, as each cup was filled, the man who
filled it, asked, who was to have it? Another then named the
person; and to him it was carried. As the bowl grew low,
the man who distributed the liquor seemed rather at a loss
to whom cups of it should be next sent, and frequently consulted those who sat near him. This mode of distribution
continued, while any liquor remained; and though not
half the company had a share, yet no one seemed dissatisfied. About half a dozen cups served for all; and each, as
it was emptied, was thrown down upon the ground, where
the servants picked it up, and carried it to be filled again.
During the whole time, the Chief and his circle sat, as was
usually the case, with a great deal of gravity, hardly speaking a word to each other.

We had long waited in expectation, each moment, of
seeing the mourning ceremony begin; when, soon after
the *kava* was drank out, to our great surprize and disappointment, they all rose up and dispersed; and Poulaho told
us, he was now ready to attend us to the ships. If this was
a mourning ceremony, it was a strange one. Perhaps, it
was the second, third, or fourth mourning; or, which was
not very uncommon, Omai might have misunderstood what
Poulaho said to him. For, excepting the change of dress,
and the putting the green bough round their necks, nothing seemed to have passed at this meeting, but what we
saw them practise, too frequently, every day.

" We

1777.
June.

"* We had seen the drinking of *kava* sometimes, at the other islands; but, by no means, so frequently as here, where it seems to be the only forenoon employment of the principal people. The *kava* is a species of pepper, which they cultivate for this purpose, and esteem it a valuable article, taking great care to defend the young plants from any injury; and it is commonly planted about their houses. It seldom grows to more than a man's height; though I have seen some plants almost double that. It branches considerably, with large heart-shaped leaves, and jointed stalks. The root is the only part that is used at the Friendly Islands, which, being dug up, is given to the servants that attend, who, breaking it in pieces, scrape the dirt off with a shell, or bit of stick; and then each begins and chews his portion, which he spits into a piece of plantain leaf. The person, who is to prepare the liquor, collects all these mouthfuls, and puts them into a large wooden dish or bowl, adding as much water as will make it of a proper strength. It is, then, well mixed up with the hands; and some loose stuff, of which mats are made, is thrown upon the surface, which intercepts the fibrous part, and is wrung hard, to get as much liquid out from it, as is possible. The manner of distributing it need not be repeated. The quantity which is put into each cup, is commonly about a quarter of a pint. The immediate effect of this beverage is not perceptible on these people, who use it so frequently; but on some of ours, who ventured to try it, though so hastily prepared, it had the same power as spirits have, in intoxicating them; or, rather, it produced that kind of stupefaction, which is

* The following account of *kava*, to the end of this paragraph, is inserted from Mr. Anderson's journal.

†

the consequence of using opium, or other substances of that kind. It should be observed, at the same time, that though these islanders have this liquor always fresh prepared, and I have seen them drink it seven times before noon, it is, nevertheless, so disagreeable, or, at least, seems so, that the greatest part of them cannot swallow it without making wry faces, and shuddering afterward."

As soon as this mourning ceremony was over, we left Mooa, and set out to return to the ships. While we rowed down the *lagoon* or inlet, we met with two canoes coming in from fishing. Poulaho ordered them to be called alongside our boat, and took from them every fish and shell they had got. He, afterward, stopped two other canoes, and searched them, but they had nothing. Why this was done, I cannot say; for we had plenty of provisions in the boat. Some of this fish he gave to me; and his servants sold the rest on board the ship. As we proceeded down the inlet, we overtook a large sailing canoe. Every person on board her, that was upon his legs when we came up, sat down till we had passed; even the man who steered, though he could not manage the helm, except in a standing posture.

Poulaho, and others, having informed me, that there was some excellent water on Onevy, a little island, which lies about a league off the mouth of the inlet, and on the North side of the Eastern channel, we landed there, in order to taste it. But I found it to be as brackish as most that we had met with. This island is quite in a natural state, being only frequented as a fishing place, and has nearly the same productions as Palmerston's Island, with some *etoa* trees. After leaving Onevy, where we dined, in our way to the ship, we took a view of a curious coral rock, which seems to have been thrown upon

the

the reef where it stands. It is elevated about ten or twelve feet above the surface of the sea that surrounds it. The base it rests upon, is not above one-third of the circumference of its projecting summit, which I judged to be about one hundred feet, and is covered with *etoa* and *pandanus* trees.

When we got on board the ship, I found that every thing had been quiet during my absence, not a theft having been committed; of which Feenou, and Futtafaihe, the king's brother, who had undertaken the management of his countrymen, boasted not a little. This shews what power the Chiefs have, when they have the will to execute it; which we were seldom to expect, since, whatever was stolen from us, generally, if not always, was conveyed to them.

The good conduct of the natives was of short duration; for, the next day, six or eight of them assaulted some of our people, who were sawing planks. They were fired upon by the sentry; and one was supposed to be wounded, and three others taken. These I kept confined till night; and did not dismiss them without punishment. After this, they behaved with a little more circumspection, and gave us much less trouble. This change of behaviour, was certainly occasioned by the man being wounded; for, before, they had only been told of the effect of fire-arms, but now they had felt it. The repeated insolence of the natives, had induced me to order the muskets of the sentries to be loaded with small shot, and to authorize them to fire on particular occasions. I took it for granted, therefore, that this man had only been wounded with small shot. But Mr. King and Mr. Anderson, in an excursion into the country, met with him, and found indubitable marks of his having

been

been wounded, but not dangerously, with a musket ball. I never could find out how this musket happened to be charged with ball; and there were people enough ready to swear, that its contents were only small shot.

Mr. Anderson's account of the excursion, just mentioned, will fill up an interval of two days, during which nothing of note happened, at the ships: "Mr. King and I went, on the 30th, along with Futtafaihe as visiters to his house, which is at Mooa, very near that of his brother Poulaho. A short time after we arrived, a pretty large hog was killed; which is done by repeated strokes on the head. The hair was then scraped off, very dextrously, with the sharp edge of pieces of split bamboo; taking the entrails out at a large oval hole cut in the belly, by the same simple instrument. Before this, they had prepared an oven; which is a large hole dug in the earth, filled at the bottom with stones, about the size of the fist, over which a fire is made till they are red hot. They took some of these stones, wrapt up in leaves of the bread-fruit tree, and filled the hog's belly, stuffing in a quantity of leaves, to prevent their falling out, and putting a plug of the same kind in the *anus*. The carcase was then placed on some sticks laid across the stones, in a standing posture, and covered with a great quantity of plantain leaves. After which, they dug up the earth, all round; and having thus effectually closed the oven, the operation of baking required no farther interference.

In the mean time, we walked about the country, but met with nothing remarkable, except a *fuiatta* of one house, standing on an artificial mount, at least thirty feet high. A little on one side of it, was a pretty large open area; and, not far off, was a good deal of uncultivated ground; which, on inquiring, why it lay waste; our guides seemed to say, belonged

belonged to the *fatooka* (which was Poulaho's), and was not, by any means, to be touched. There was also, at no great distance, a number of *etooa* trees, on which clung vast numbers of the large *ternate* bats, making a disagreeable noise. We could not kill any, at this time, for want of muskets; but some, that were got at Annamooka, measured near three feet, when the wings were extended. On our returning to Futtafaihe's house, he ordered the hog, that had been dressed, to be produced, with several baskets of baked yams, and some cocoa-nuts. But we found, that, instead of his entertaining us, we were to entertain him; the property of the feast being entirely transferred to us, as his guests, and we were to dispose of it as we pleased. The same person who cleaned the hog in the morning, now cut it up (but not before we desired him), in a very dexterous manner, with a knife of split bamboo; dividing the several parts, and hitting the joints, with a quickness and skill that surprized us very much. The whole was set down before us, though at least fifty pounds weight, until we took a small piece away, and desired, that they would share the rest amongst the people sitting round. But it was not without a great many scruples they did that at last; and then they asked, what particular persons they should give it to. However, they were very well pleased, when they found, that it was not contrary to any custom of ours; some carrying off the portion they had received, and others eating it upon the spot. It was with great difficulty, that we could prevail upon Futtafaihe himself to eat a small bit.

After dinner, we went with him, and five or six people, his attendants, toward the place where Poulaho's mourning ceremony was transacted, the last time we were at Mooa; but we did not enter the inclosure. Every person who went with us, had the mat tied over his cloth, and some leaves about the neck, as had been done on the former occasion; and when we arrived at a large open boat-house, where a few people were, they threw away their leaves, sat down before it, and gave their cheeks a few gentle strokes with the fist; after which they continued sitting, for about ten minutes, with a very grave appearance, and then dispersed, without having spoken a single word. This explained what Poulaho had mentioned about *Tooge*; though, from the operation only lasting a few seconds, he had not been observed to perform it. And this seems to be only a continuation of the mourning ceremony, by way of condolence. For, upon inquiring, on whose account it was now performed; we were told, that it was for a Chief who had died at Vavaoo, some time ago; that they had practised it ever since, and should continue to do so, for a considerable time longer.

In the evening, we had a pig, dressed as the hog, with yams and cocoa-nuts, brought for supper; and Futtafaihe finding, that we did not like the scruples they had made before, to accept of any part of the entertainment, asked us immediately to share it, and give it to whom we pleased. When supper was over, abundance of cloth was brought for us to sleep in; but we were a good deal disturbed, by a singular instance of luxury, in which their principal men indulge themselves; that of being beat while they are asleep. Two women sat by Futtafaihe, and performed this operation, which is called *tooge tooge*, by beating briskly on his body and legs, with both fists, as on a drum, till he fell asleep, and continuing it the whole night, with some short intervals. When once the person is asleep, they abate a little in the strength and quickness of the beating; but resume it, if they observe any appearance of his awaking. In the morning, we found

that

1777.
June.

that Futtafaihe's women relieved each other, and went to sleep by turns. In any other country, it would be supposed, that such a practice would put an end to all rest; but here it certainly acts as an opiate; and is a strong proof of what habit may effect. The noise of this, however, was not the only thing that kept us awake; for the people, who passed the night in the house, not only conversed amongst each other frequently, as in the day; but all got up before it was light, and made a hearty meal on fish and yams, which were brought to them by a person, who seemed to know very well the appointed time for this nocturnal refreshment.

July,
Tuesday 1.

Next morning we set out with Futtafaihe, and walked down the East side of the bay, to the point. The country, all along this side, is well cultivated; but, in general, not so much inclosed as at Mooa; and amongst many other plantain fields that we passed, there was one at least a mile long, which was in excellent order, every tree growing with great vigour. We found, that, in travelling, Futtafaihe exercised a power, though by no means wantonly, which pointed out the great authority of such principal men; or is, perhaps, only annexed to those of the royal family. For he sent to one place for fish; to another for yams; and so on, at other places; and all his orders were obeyed with the greatest readiness, as if he had been absolute master of the people's property. On coming to the point, the natives mentioned something of one, who, they said, had been fired at by some of our people; and, upon our wishing to see him, they conducted us to a house, where we found a man, who had been shot through the shoulder, but not dangerously; as the ball had entered a little above the inner part of the collar bone, and passed out obliquely backward.

We

We were sure, from the state of the wound, that he was the person who had been fired at by one of the sentinels, three days before; though positive orders had been given, that none of them should load their pieces with any thing but small shot. We gave some directions to his friends how to manage the wound, to which no application had been made; and they seemed pleased, when we told them it would get well in a certain time. But, on our going away, they asked us to send the wounded man some yams, and other things for food; and in such a manner, that we could not help thinking they considered it to be our duty to support him, till he should get well.

In the evening we crossed the bay to our station, in a canoe, which Futtafaihe had exercised his prerogative in procuring, by calling to the first that passed by. He had also got a large hog at this place; and brought a servant from his house with a bundle of cloth, which he wanted us to take with us, as a present from him. But the boat being small, we objected; and he ordered it to be brought over to us the next day."

I had prolonged my stay at this island, on account of the approaching eclipse; but, on the 2d of July, on looking at the micrometer belonging to the board of longitude, I found some of the rack work broken, and the instrument useless till repaired; which there was not time to do before it was intended to be used. Preparing now for our departure, I got on board, this day, all the cattle, poultry, and other animals, except such as were destined to remain. I had designed to leave a turkey-cock and hen; but having now only two of each undisposed of, one of the hens, through the ignorance of one of my people, was strangled, and

and died upon the spot. I had brought three turkey-hens to these islands. One was killed, as above mentioned; and the other, by an useless dog belonging to one of the officers. These two accidents put it out of my power to leave a pair here; and, at the same time, to carry the breed to Otaheite, for which island they were originally intended. I was sorry, afterward, that I did not give the preference to Tongataboo, as the present would have been of more value there than at Otaheite; for the natives of the former island, I am persuaded, would have taken more pains to multiply the breed.

Thursday 3. The next day we took up our anchor, and moved the ships behind Pangimodoo, that we might be ready to take the advantage of the first favourable wind, to get through the narrows. The king, who was one of our company, this day, at dinner, I observed, took particular notice of the plates. This occasioned me to make him an offer of one, either of pewter, or of earthen ware. He chose the first; and then began to tell us the several uses to which he intended to apply it. Two of them are so extraordinary, that I cannot omit mentioning them. He said, that, whenever he should have occasion to visit any of the other islands, he would leave this plate behind him at Tongataboo, as a sort of representative, in his absence, that the people might pay it the same obeisance they do to himself in person. He was asked, what had been usually employed for this purpose, before he got this plate; and we had the satisfaction of learning from him, that this singular honour had hitherto been conferred on a wooden bowl in which he washed his hands. The other extraordinary use to which he meant to apply it in the room of his wooden bowl, was to discover a thief. He said, that, when any thing was stolen, and the thief

thief could not be found out, the people were all assembled together before him, when he washed his hands in water in this vessel; after which it was cleaned, and then the whole multitude advanced, one after another, and touched it in the same manner that they touch his foot, when they pay him obeisance. If the guilty person touched it, he died immediately upon the spot, not by violence, but by the hand of Providence; and if any one refused to touch it, his refusal was a clear proof that he was the man.

In the morning of the 5th, the day of the eclipse, the weather was dark and cloudy, with showers of rain; so that we had little hopes of an observation. About nine o'clock the sun broke out at intervals for about half an hour; after which it was totally obscured, till within a minute or two of the beginning of the eclipse. We were all at our telescopes, viz. Mr. Bayly, Mr. King, Captain Clerke, Mr. Bligh, and myself. I lost the observation, by not having a dark glass at hand, suitable to the clouds that were continually passing over the sun; and Mr. Bligh had not got the sun into the field of his telescope; so that the commencement of the eclipse was only observed by the other three gentlemen; and by them, with an uncertainty of several seconds, as follows:

	H.	M.	S.	
By Mr. Bayly, at	11	46	23½	⎫
Mr. King, at	11	46	28	⎬ Apparent time.
Capt. Clerke, at	11	47	5	⎭

Mr. Bayly and Mr. King observed, with the achromatic telescopes, belonging to the board of longitude, of equal magnifying powers; and Captain Clerke observed with one of the reflectors. The sun appeared at intervals, till about the middle of the eclipse; after which it was seen no more during

during the day; so that the end could not be observed. The disappointment was of little consequence, since the longitude was more than sufficiently determined, independently of this eclipse, by lunar observations, which will be mentioned hereafter.

As soon as we knew the eclipse to be over, we packed up the instruments, took down the observatories, and sent every thing on board that had not been already removed. As none of the natives had taken the least notice or care of the three sheep allotted to Mareewagee, I ordered them to be carried back to the ships. I was apprehensive, that, if I had left them here, they run great risk of being destroyed by dogs. That animal did not exist upon this island, when I first visited it in 1773; but I now found they had got a good many, partly from the breed then left by myself, and partly from some, imported since that time, from an island not very remote, called Feejee. The dogs, however, at present, had not found their way into any of the Friendly Islands, except Tongataboo; and none but the Chiefs there had, as yet, got possession of any.

Being now upon the eve of our departure from this island, I shall add some particulars about it, and its productions, for which I am indebted to Mr. Anderson. And, having spent as many weeks there, as I had done days * when I visited it in 1773, the better opportunities that now occurred, of gaining more accurate information, and the skill of that gentleman, in directing his inquiries, will, in some measure, supply the imperfection of my former account of this island.

" Amsterdam, Tongataboo, or (as the natives also very frequently called it) Tonga, is about twenty leagues in circuit,

* From the 4th to the 7th of October.

circuit, somewhat oblong, though, by much, broadest at the East end; and its greatest length from East to West. The South shore, which I saw in 1773, is straight, and consists of coral rocks, eight or ten feet high, terminating perpendicularly, except in some places where it is interrupted by small sandy beaches; on which, at low water, a range of black rocks may be seen. The West end is not above five or six miles broad, but has a shore somewhat like that of the South side; whereas the whole North side is environed with shoals and islands, and the shore within them low and sandy. The East side or end is, most probably, like the South; as the shore begins to assume a rocky appearance, toward the North East point, though not above seven or eight feet high.

The island may, with the greatest propriety, be called a low one, as the trees, on the West part, where we now lay at anchor, only appeared; and the only eminent part, which can be seen from a ship, is the South East point; though many gently rising and declining grounds are observable by one who is ashore. The general appearance of the country does not afford that beautiful kind of landscape that is produced from a variety of hills and valleys, lawns, rivulets, and cascades; but, at the same time, it conveys to the spectator an idea of the most exuberant fertility, whether we respect the places improved by art, or those still in a natural state; both which yield all their vegetable productions with the greatest vigour, and perpetual verdure. At a distance, the surface seems entirely clothed with trees of various sizes; some of which are very large. But, above the rest, the tall cocoa-palms always raise their tufted heads; and are far from being the smallest ornament to any country that produces them. The *bongo*, which is a
species

species of fig, with narrow pointed leaves, is the largest sized tree of the island; and on the uncultivated spots, especially toward the sea, the most common bushes and small trees are the *pandanus*; several sorts of *hibiscus*; the *faitanoo*, mentioned more than once in the course of our voyage; and a few others. It ought also to be observed, that though the materials for forming grand landscapes are wanting, there are many of what might, at least, be called near prospects, about the cultivated grounds and dwelling-places; but, more especially, about the *fiatookas*; where sometimes art, and sometimes nature, has done much to please the eye.

From the situation of Tongataboo, toward the tropic, the climate is more variable, than in countries farther within that line; though, perhaps, that might be owing to the season of the year, which was now the winter solstice. The winds are, for the most part, from some point between South and East; and, when moderate, are commonly attended with fine weather. When they blow fresher, the weather is often cloudy, though open; and, in such cases, there is frequently rain. The wind sometimes veers to the North East, North North East, or even North North West, but never lasts long, nor blows strong from thence; though it is commonly accompanied by heavy rain, and close sultry weather. The quick succession of vegetables has been already mentioned; but I am not certain that the changes of weather, by which it is brought about, are considerable enough to make them perceptible to the natives as to their method of life, or rather that they should be very sensible of the different seasons. This, perhaps, may be inferred from the state of their vegetable productions, which are never so much affected, with respect to the foliage, as to shed

that

that all at once; for every leaf is succeeded by another, as fast as it falls; which causes that appearance of universal and continual spring found here.

The basis of the island, as far as we know, is entirely a coral rock, which is the only sort that presents itself on the shore. Nor did we see the least appearance of any other stone, except a few small blue pebbles strewed about the *fatoskus*; and the smooth, solid black stone, something like the *lapis lydius*, of which the natives make their hatchets. But these may, probably, have been brought from other islands in the neighbourhood; for a piece of flatey, iron-coloured stone was bought at one of them, which was never seen here. Though the coral projects in many places above the surface, the soil is, in general, of a considerable depth. In all cultivated places, it is, commonly, of a loose, black colour; produced, seemingly, in a great measure, from the rotten vegetables that are planted there. Underneath which is, very probably, a clayey *stratum* for a soil of that kind is often seen both in the low, and in the rising grounds; but especially in several places toward the shore, where it is of any height, and, when broken off, appears sometimes of a reddish, though oftener of a brownish yellow colour, and of a pretty stiff consistence. Where the shore is low, the soil is commonly sandy, or rather composed of triturated coral; which, however, yields bushes growing with great luxuriance; and is sometimes planted, not unsuccessfully, by the natives.

Of cultivated fruits, the principal are plantains; of which they have fifteen different sorts or varieties; bread-fruit; two sorts of fruit found at Otaheite, and known there under the names of *jambu* and *eevee*; the latter a kind of plumb;

plumb; and vast numbers of shaddocks, which, however, are found as often in a natural state, as planted.

The roots are yams, of which are two sorts; one black, and so large, that it often weighs twenty or thirty pounds; the other white, and long, seldom weighing a pound; a large root, called *kappe*; one not unlike our white potatoes, called *mawbaba*; the *talo*, or *coccos* of other places; and another, named *jeejee*.

Besides vast numbers of cocoa-nut trees, they have three other sorts of palms, two of which are very scarce. One of them is called *beeoo*; which grows almost as high as the cocoa-tree, has very large leaves plaited like a fan, and clusters or bunches of globular nuts, not larger than a small pistol ball, growing amongst the branches, with a very hard kernel, which is sometimes eat. The other is a kind of cabbage-tree, not distinguishable from the cocoa, but by being rather thicker, and by having its leaves more ragged. It has a cabbage three or four feet long; at the top of which are the leaves, and at the bottom the fruit, which is scarcely two inches long, resembling an oblong cocoa-nut, with an insipid tenacious kernel, called, by the natives, *seeoogoola*, or red cocoa-nut, as it assumes a reddish cast when ripe. The third sort is called *ongo ongo*, and much commoner, being generally found planted about their *fiatookas*. It seldom grows higher than five feet, though sometimes to eight; and has a vast number of oval compressed nuts, as large as a pippin, sticking immediately to the trunk, amongst the leaves, which are not eat. There is plenty of excellent sugar-cane, which is cultivated; gourds; bamboo; turmeric; and a species of fig, about the size of a small cherry, called *matte*, which, though wild, is sometimes eat. But the catalogue

talogue of uncultivated plants is too large to be enumerated here. Besides the *pemphis decaspermum*, *mallococca*, *maba*, and some other new *genera*, described by Dr. Foster [*], there are a few more found here; which, perhaps, the different seasons of the year, and his short stay, did not give him an opportunity to take notice of. Although it did not appear, during our longer stay, that above a fourth part of the trees, and other plants, were in flower; a circumstance absolutely necessary, to enable one to distinguish the various kinds.

The only quadrupeds, besides hogs, are a few rats, and some dogs, which are not natives of the place, but produced from some left by us in 1773, and by others got from Feejee. Fowls, which are of a large breed, are domesticated here.

Amongst the birds, are parrots, somewhat smaller than the common grey ones, of an indifferent green on the back and wings, the tail bluish, and the rest of a sooty or chocolate brown; parroquets, not larger than a sparrow, of a fine yellowish green, with bright azure on the crown of the head, and the throat and belly red; besides another sort as large as a dove, with a blue crown and thighs, the throat and under part of the head crimson, as also part of the belly, and the rest a beautiful green.

There are owls about the size of our common sort, but of a finer plumage; the cuckoos, mentioned at Palmerston's Island; king fishers, about the size of a thrush, of a greenish blue, with a white ring about the neck; and a bird of the thrush kind, almost as big, of a dull green colour, with two yellow wattles at the base of the bill, which is the only singing one we observed here; but it compensates a good deal

[*] See his *Characteres Generum Plantarum*. Lond. 1776.

for the want of others by the strength and melody of its notes, which fill the woods at dawn, in the evening, and at the breaking up of bad weather.

The other land birds are rails, as large as a pigeon, of a variegated grey colour, with a rusty neck; a black sort with red eyes, not larger than a lark; large violet-coloured coots, with red bald crowns; two sorts of fly-catchers; a very small swallow; and three sorts of pigeons, one of which is *le ramier cuivre* of Monf. Sonnerat*; another, half the size of the common sort, of a light green on the back and wings, with a red forehead; and a third, somewhat less, of a purple brown, but whitish underneath.

Of water-fowl, and such as frequent the sea, are the ducks seen at Annamooka, though scarce here; blue and white herons; tropic birds; common noddies; white terns; a new species of a leaden colour, with a black crest; a small bluish curlew; and a large plover, spotted with yellow. Besides the large bats, mentioned before, there is also the common sort.

The only noxious or disgusting animals of the reptile or insect tribe, are sea snakes, three feet long, with black and white circles alternately, often found on shore; some scorpions, and *centipedes*. There are fine green *guanoes*, a foot and a half long; another brown and spotted lizard, about a foot long; and two other small sorts. Amongst the other insects are some beautiful moths; butterflies; very large spiders; and others; making, in the whole, about fifty different sorts.

The sea abounds with fish, though the variety is less than might be expected. The most frequent sorts are mullets;

* *Voyage à la Nouvelle Guinée*, Tab. CII.

several

several sorts of parrot-fish; silver fish; old wives; some beautifully spotted soles; leather-jackets; bonnetos; and albicores; besides the eels mentioned at Palmerston's Island; some sharks; rays; pipe-fish; a sort of pike; and some curious devil-fish.

The many reefs and shoals on the North side of the island, afford shelter for an endless variety of shell-fish; amongst which are many that are esteemed precious in Europe. Such as the true hammer oyster; of which, however, none could be obtained entire; a large indentated oyster, and several others; but none of the common sort; panamas; cones; a sort of gigantic cockle, found also in the East Indies; pearl shell oysters; and many others; several of which, I believe, have been hitherto unknown to the most diligent inquirers after that branch of natural history. There are, likewise, several sorts of sea-eggs; and many very fine star-fish; besides a considerable variety of corals; amongst which are two red sorts; the one most elegantly branched, the other tubulous. And there is no less variety amongst the crabs and cray fish, which are very numerous. To which may be added, several sorts of sponge; the sea hare, *boletburis*, and the like."

C H A P.

CHAP. IX.

A grand Solemnity, called NATCHE, *in Honour of the King's Son, performed.—The Proceſſions and other Ceremonies, during the firſt Day, deſcribed.—The Manner of paſſing the Night at the King's Houſe.—Continuation of the Solemnity, the next Day.—Conjectures about the Nature of it.—Departure from Tongataboo, and Arrival at Eooa.—Accounts of that Iſland, and Tranſactions there.*

1777.
July.
‾‾‾‾
Sunday 6.

WE were now ready to ſail; but the wind being Eaſterly, we had not ſufficient day light to turn through the narrows, either with the morning, or with the evening flood; the one falling out too early, and the other too late. So that, without a leading wind, we were under a neceſſity of waiting two or three days.

Monday 7.
Tueſday 8.

I took the opportunity of this delay, to be preſent at a public ſolemnity, to which the king had invited us, when we went laſt to viſit him, and which, he had informed us, was to be performed on the 8th. With a view to this, he and all the people of note, quitted our neighbourhood on the 7th, and repaired to Mooa, where the ſolemnity was to be exhibited. A party of us followed them, the next morning. We underſtood, from what Poulaho had ſaid to us, that his ſon and heir was now to be initiated into certain

privileges;

privileges; amongst which was, that of eating with his father; an honour he had not, as yet, been admitted to.

We arrived at Mooa about eight o'clock, and found the
king, with a large circle of attendants fitting before him,
within an inclofure fo fmall and dirty, as to excite my wonder that any fuch could be found in that neighbourhood.
They were Intent upon their ufual morning occupation, in
preparing a bowl of *kava*. As this was no liquor for us, we
walked out to vifit fome of our friends, and to obferve what
preparations might be making for the ceremony, which was
foon to begin. About ten o'clock, the people began to affemble,
in a large area, which is before the *malaee*, or great houfe, to
which we had been conducted the firft time we vifited Mooa.
At the end of a road, that opens into this area, ftood fome
men with fpears and clubs, who kept conftantly reciting, or
chanting, fhort fentences, In a mournful tone, which conveyed fome idea of diftrefs, and as if they called for fomething. This was continued about an hour; and, in the
mean time, many people came down the road, each of them
bringing a yam, tied to the middle of a pole, which they
laid down, before the perfons who continued repeating the
fentences. While this was going on, the king and prince
arrived, and feated themfelves upon the area; and we were
defired to fit down by them, but to pull off our hats, and
to untie our hair. The bearers of the yams being all come
in, each pole was taken up between two men, who carried
it over their fhoulders. After forming themfelves into companies, of ten or twelve perfons each, they marched acrofs
the place, with a quick pace; each company, headed by a
man bearing a club or fpear, and guarded, on the right, by
feveral others, armed with different weapons. A man carrying a living pigeon on a perch, clofed the rear of the
proceffion,

procession, in which about two hundred and fifty persons walked.

Omai was desired by me, to ask the Chief, to what place the yams were to be thus carried, with so much solemnity? but, as he seemed unwilling to give us the information we wanted, two or three of us followed the procession, contrary to his inclination. We found, that they stopped before a *morai* or *fiatooka* * of one house standing upon a mount, which was hardly a quarter of a mile from the place where they first assembled. Here we observed them depositing the yams, and making them up into bundles; but for what purpose, we could not learn. And, as our presence seemed to give them uneasiness, we left them, and returned to Poulaho, who told us, we might amuse ourselves by walking about, as nothing would be done for some time. The fear of losing any part of the ceremony, prevented our being long absent. When we returned to the king, he desired me to order the boat's crew not to stir from the boat; for, as every thing would, very soon, be *taboo*, if any of our people, or of their own, should be found walking about, they would be knocked down with clubs; nay *matteed*, that is, killed. He also acquainted us, that we could not be present at the ceremony; but that we should be conducted to a place, where we might see every thing that passed. Objections were made to our dress. We were told, that, to qualify us to be present, it was necessary that we should be naked as low as the breast, with our hats off, and our hair untied. Omai offered to conform to these requisites, and began to strip; other objections were then started; so that the exclusion was given to him equally with ourselves.

* This is the *fiatooka* mentioned above by Mr. Anderson, p. 311.

I did

I did not much like this restriction; and, therefore, stole out, to see what might now be going forward. I found very few people stirring, except those dressed to attend the ceremony; some of whom had in their hands small poles, about four feet long, and to the under-part of these were fastened two or three other sticks, not bigger than one's finger, and about six inches in length. These men were going toward the *morai* just mentioned. I took the same road, and was, several times, stopped by them, all crying out *taboo*. However, I went forward, without much regarding them, till I came in sight of the *morai*, and of the people who were sitting before it. I was now urged, very strongly, to go back; and, not knowing what might be the consequence of a refusal, I complied. I had observed, that the people, who carried the poles, passed this *morai*, or what I may, as well, call temple; and guessing, from this circumstance, that something was transacting beyond it, which might be worth looking at, I had thoughts of advancing, by making a round, for this purpose; but I was so closely watched by three men, that I could not put my design in execution. In order to shake these fellows off, I returned to the *malaee*, where I had left the king, and, from thence, made an elopement a second time; but I instantly met with the same three men; so that it seemed, as if they had been ordered to watch my motions. I paid no regard to what they said or did, till I came within sight of the king's principal *futocka* or *morai*, which I have already described [*], before which a great number of men were sitting, being the same persons whom I had just before seen pass by the other *morai*, from which this was but a little distant. Observing, that I could watch the proceedings of this company from the

[*] See p. 313.

king's plantation, I repaired thither, very much to the satisfaction of those who attended me.

As soon as I got in, I acquainted the gentlemen who had come with me from the ships, with what I had seen; and we took a proper station, to watch the result. The number of people, at the *fatoka*, continued to increase for some time; and, at length, we could see them quit their sitting posture, and march off in procession. They walked in pairs, one after another, every pair carrying, between them, one of the small poles above-mentioned, on their shoulders. We were told, that the small pieces of sticks, fastened to the poles, were yams; so that, probably, they were meant to represent this root emblematically. The hindmost men of each couple, for the most part, placed one of his hands to the middle of the pole, as if, without this additional support, it were not strong enough to carry the weight that hung to it, and under which they all seemed to bend, as they walked. This procession consisted of one hundred and eight pairs, and all, or most of them, men of rank. They came close by the fence behind which we stood; so that we had a full view of them.

Having waited here, till they had all passed, we then repaired to Poulaho's house, and saw him going out. We could not be allowed to follow him; but were, forthwith, conducted to the place allotted to us, which was behind a fence, adjoining to the area of the *fatoka* where the yams had been deposited in the forenoon. – As we were not the only people who were excluded from being publicly present at this ceremony, but allowed to peep from behind the curtain, we had a good deal of company; and I observed, that all the other inclosures, round the place, were filled with people.

people. And, yet, all imaginable care seemed to be taken, that they should see as little as possible; for the fences had not only been repaired that morning, but, in many places, raised higher than common; so that the tallest man could not look over them. To remedy this defect in our station, we took the liberty to cut holes in the fence, with our knives; and, by this means, we could see, pretty distinctly, every thing that was transacting on the other side.

On our arrival at our station, we found two or three hundred people, sitting on the grass, near the end of the road that opened into the area of the *morai*; and the number continually increased, by others joining them. At length, arrived a few men carrying some small poles, and branches or leaves of the cocoa-nut tree; and, upon their first appearance, an old man seated himself in the road, and, with his face toward them, pronounced a long oration in a serious tone. He then retired back, and the others advancing to the middle of the area, began to erect a small shed, employing, for that purpose, the materials above-mentioned. When they had finished their work, they all squatted down, for a moment, before it, then rose up, and retired to the rest of the company. Soon after, came Poulaho's son, preceded by four or five men, and they seated themselves a little aside from the shed, and rather behind it. After them, appeared twelve or fourteen women of the first rank, walking slowly in pairs, each pair carrying between them, a narrow piece of white cloth extended, about two or three yards in length. These marched up to the prince, squatted down before him; and, having wrapped some of the pieces of the cloth they had brought, round his body, they rose up, and retired in the same order, to some distance on his left, and there seated themselves. Poulaho himself soon made his appearance,
preceded

preceded by four men, who walked two and two abreast, and sat down on his son's left hand, about twenty paces from him. The young prince, then, quitting his first position, went and sat down under the shed, with his attendants; and a considerable number more placed themselves on the grass, before this royal canopy. The prince himself sat facing the people, with his back to the *morai*. This being done, three companies, of ten or a dozen men in each, started up from amongst the large crowd, a little after each other, and running hastily to the opposite side of the area, sat down for a few seconds; after which, they returned, in the same manner, to their former stations. To them succeeded two men, each of whom held a small green branch in his hand, who got up and approached the prince, sitting down, for a few seconds, three different times, as they advanced; and then, turning their backs, retired in the same manner, inclining their branches to each other as they sat. In a little time, two more repeated this ceremony.

The grand procession, which I had seen march off from the other *morai*, now began to come in. To judge of the circuit they had made, from the time they had been absent, it must have been pretty large. As they entered the area, they marched up to the right of the shed, and, having prostrated themselves on the grass, deposited their pretended burthens (the poles above-mentioned), and faced round to the prince. They then rose up, and retired in the same order, closing their hands, which they held before them, with the most serious aspect, and seated themselves along the front of the area. During all the time that this numerous band were coming in, and depositing their poles, three men, who sat under the shed, with the prince, continued pronouncing

separate

separate sentences, in a melancholy tone. After this, a profound silence ensued, for a little time, and then a man, who sat in the front of the area, began an oration (or prayer), during which, at several different times, he went and broke one of the poles, which had been brought in by those who had walked in procession. When he had ended, the people, sitting before the shed, separated, to make a lane, through which the prince and his attendants passed, and the assembly broke up.

Some of our party, satisfied with what they had already seen, now returned to the ships; but I, and two or three more of the officers, remained at Mooa, to see the conclusion of the solemnity, which was not to be till the next day; being desirous of omitting no opportunity, which might afford any information about the religious or the political institutions of this people. The small sticks or poles, which had been brought into the area, by those who walked in procession, being left lying on the ground, after the crowd had dispersed, I went and examined them. I found, that to the middle of each, two or three small sticks were tied, as has been related. Yet we had been repeatedly told by the natives, who stood near us, that they were young yams; insomuch that some of our gentlemen believed them, rather than their own eyes. As I had the demonstration of my senses to satisfy me, that they were not real yams, it is clear, that we ought to have understood them, that they were only the artificial representations of these roots.

Our supper was got ready about seven o'clock. It consisted of fish and yams. We might have had pork also; but we did not choose to kill a large hog, which the king had given to us for that purpose. He supped with us, and drank pretty freely of brandy and water; so that he went to bed with

with a sufficient dose. We passed the night in the same house with him, and several of his attendants.

Wedaef. 9. About one or two o'clock in the morning they waked, and conversed for about an hour, and then went to sleep again. All, but Poulaho himself, rose at day-break, and went, I know not whither. Soon after, a woman, one of those who generally attended upon the Chief, came in, and inquired where he was. I pointed him out to her; and she immediately sat down by him, and began the same operation, which Mr. Anderson had seen practised upon Futtafaihe, tapping or beating gently, with her clinched fists, on his thighs. This, instead of prolonging his sleep, as was intended, had the contrary effect; however, though he awaked, he continued to lie down.

Omai, and I, now went to visit the prince, who had parted from us early in the evening. For he did not lodge with the king; but in apartments of his own, or, at least, such as had been allotted to him, at some distance from his father's house. We found him with a circle of boys, or youths, about his own age, sitting before him; and an old woman, and an old man, who seemed to have the care of him, sitting behind. There were others, both men and women, employed about their necessary affairs, in different departments; who, probably, belonged to his household.

From the prince we returned to the king. By this time he had got up, and had a crowded circle before him, composed chiefly of old men. While a large bowl of *kava* was preparing, a baked hog and yams, smoking hot, were brought in; the greatest part of which fell to our share, and was very acceptable to the boat's crew: for these people

eat

eat very little in a morning; especially the *kava* drinkers. I afterward walked out, and visited several other Chiefs; and found, that all of them were taking their morning draught, or had already taken it. Returning to the king, I found him asleep in a small retired hut, with two women tapping on his breech. About eleven o'clock he arose again; and then some fish and yams, which tasted as if they had been stewed in cocoa-nut milk, were brought to him. Of these he eat a large portion, and lay down once more to sleep. I now left him, and carried to the prince a present of cloth, beads, and other articles, which I had brought with me from the ship for the purpose. There was a sufficient quantity of cloth to make him a complete suit; and he was immediately decked out with it. Proud of his dress, he first went to shew himself to his father; and then conducted me to his mother; with whom were about ten or a dozen other women of a respectable appearance. Here the prince changed his apparel, and made me a present of two pieces of the cloth manufactured in the island. By this time, it was past noon, when, by appointment, I repaired to the palace to dinner. Several of our gentlemen had returned, this morning, from the ships; and we were all invited to the feast, which was presently served up, and consisted of two pigs and yams. I roused the drowsy monarch, to partake of what he had provided for our entertainment. In the mean time, two mullets, and some shell-fish, were brought to him, as I supposed, for his separate portion. But he joined it to our fare, sat down with us, and made a hearty meal.

When dinner was over, we were told that the ceremony would soon begin; and were strictly enjoined not to walk out. I had resolved, however, to peep no longer from behind the curtain, but to mix with the actors themselves, if possible. With this view, I stole out from the plantation, and walked toward the *morai*, the scene of the solemnity. I was, several times, desired to go back, by people whom I met; but I paid no regard to them; and they suffered me to pass on. When I arrived at the *morai*, I found a number of men seated on the side of the area, on each side of the road that leads up to it. A few were sitting on the opposite side of the area; and two men in the middle of it, with their faces turned to the *morai*. When I got into the midst of the first company, I was desired to sit down; which I accordingly did. Where I sat, there were lying a number of small bundles or parcels, composed of cocoa-nut leaves, and tied to sticks made into the form of hand-barrows. All the information I could get about them was, that they were *taboo*. Our number kept continually increasing; every one coming from the same quarter. From time to time, one or another of the company turned himself to those who were coming to join us, and made a short speech; in which I could remark that the word *areckee*, that is King, was generally mentioned. One man said something that produced bursts of hearty laughter from all the crowd; others, of the speakers, met with public applause. I was, several times, desired to leave the place; and, at last, when they found that I would not stir, after some seeming consultation, they applied to me to uncover my shoulders as theirs were. With this request I complied; and then they seemed to be no longer uneasy at my presence.

I sat a full hour, without any thing more going forward, beside what I have mentioned. At length the prince, the women, and the king, all came in, as they had done the day before. The prince, being placed under the shed, after his father's arrival, two men, each carrying a piece of mat, came, repeating something seriously, and put them about him. The assembled people now began their operations; and first, three companies ran backward and forward across the area, as described in the account of the proceedings of the former day. Soon after, the two men, who sat in the middle of the area, made a short speech or prayer; and then the whole body, amongst whom I had my place, started up, and ran and seated themselves before the shed under which the prince, and three or four men, were sitting. I was now partly under the management of one of the company, who seemed very assiduous to serve me. By his means, I was placed in such a situation, that, if I had been allowed to make use of my eyes, nothing that passed could have escaped me. But it was necessary to sit with down-cast looks, and demure as maids.

Soon after, the procession came in, as on the day before; each two persons bearing on their shoulders a pole, round the middle of which, a cocoa-nut leaf was plaited. These were deposited with ceremonies similar to those observed on the preceding day. This first procession was followed by a second; the men composing which, brought baskets, such as are usually employed by this people to carry provisions in, and made of palm leaves. These were followed by a third procession, in which were brought different kinds of small fish; each fixed at the end of a forked stick. The baskets were carried up to an old man, whom I took to be the Chief Priest, and who sat on the prince's right-hand, without the shed. He held each in his hand, while he made a short speech or prayer; then laid it down, and called for another, repeating the same words as before; and thus he went through the whole number of baskets. The fish were
presented,

presented, one by one, on the forked sticks, as they came in, to two men, who sat on the left; and who, till now, held green branches in their hands. The first fish they laid down on their right, and the second on their left. When the third was presented, a stout looking man, who sat behind the other two, reached his arm over between them, and made a snatch at it; as also did the other two, at the very same time. Thus they seemed to contend for every fish that was presented; but as there were two hands against one, besides the advantage of situation, the man behind got nothing but pieces; for he never quitted his hold, till the fish was torn out of his hand; and what little remained in it, he shook out behind him. The others laid what they got, on the right and left alternately. At length, either by accident or design, the man behind got possession of a whole fish, without either of the other two so much as touching it. At this, the word *mareeai*, which signifies *very good*, or *well done*, was uttered in a low voice throughout the whole crowd. It seemed, that he had performed now all that was expected from him; for he made no attempt upon the few fish that came after. These fish, as also the baskets, were all delivered, by the persons who brought them in, sitting; and, in the same order and manner, the small poles, which the first procession carried, had been laid upon the ground.

The last procession being closed, there was some speaking or praying, by different persons. Then, on some signal being given, we all started up, ran several paces to the left, and sat down with our backs to the prince, and the few who remained with him. I was desired not to look behind me. However, neither this injunction, nor the remembrance of Lot's wife, discouraged me from facing about.

I now

I now saw that the prince had turned his face to the *morai*. But this last movement had brought so many people between him and me, that I could not perceive what was doing. I was afterward assured, that, at this very time, the prince was admitted to the high honour of eating with his father; which, till now, had never been permitted to him; a piece of roasted yam being presented to each of them for this purpose. This was the more probable, as we had been told, before-hand, that this was to happen during the solemnity; and as all the people turned their backs to them, at this time, which they always do when their monarch eats.

After some little time, we all faced about, and formed a semicircle before the prince, leaving a large open space between us. Presently there appeared some men coming toward us, two and two, bearing large sticks, or poles, upon their shoulders, making a noise that might be called singing, and waving their hands as they advanced. When they had got close up to us, they made a shew of walking very fast, without proceeding a single step. Immediately after, three or four men started up from the crowd, with large sticks in their hands, who ran toward those new-comers. The latter instantly threw down the poles from their shoulders, and scampered off; and the others attacked the poles; and, having beat them most unmercifully, returned to their places. As the pole-bearers ran off, they gave the challenge that is usual here in wrestling; and, not long after, a number of stout fellows came from the same quarter, repeating the challenge as they advanced. These were opposed by a party, who came from the opposite side almost at the same instant. The two parties paraded about the area for a few minutes, and then retired, each to their own side. After this,

this, there were wrestling and boxing-matches for about half an hour. Then two men seated themselves before the prince, and made speeches, addressed, as I thought, entirely to him. With this the solemnity ended, and the whole assembly broke up.

I now went and examined the several baskets which had been presented; a curiosity that I was not allowed before to indulge; because every thing was then *taboo*. But the solemnity being now over, they became, simply, what I found them to be, empty baskets. So that, whatever they were supposed to contain, was emblematically represented. And so, indeed, was every other thing which had been brought in procession, except the fish.

We endeavoured, in vain, to find out the meaning, not only of the ceremony in general, which is called *Natche*, but of its different parts. We seldom got any other answer to our inquiries, but *taboo*; a word, which, I have before observed, is applied to many other things. But, as the prince was, evidently, the principal person concerned in it; and as we had been told by the king, ten days before the celebration of the *Natche*, that the people would bring in yams for him and his son to eat together; and as he even described some part of the ceremony, we concluded, from what he had then said, and from what we now saw, that an oath of allegiance, if I may so express myself, or solemn promise, was, on this occasion, made to the prince, as the immediate successor to the regal dignity, to stand by him, and to furnish him with the several articles that were here emblematically represented. This seems the more probable, as all the principal people of the island, whom we had ever seen, assisted in the processions. But, be this as it may, the whole was conducted with a great deal of mysterious solemnity; and, that there was a mixture of religion in the institution, was evident, not only from the place where it was performed, but from the manner of performing it. Our dress and deportment had never been called in question, upon any former occasion whatever. Now, it was expected that we should be uncovered as low as the waist; that our hair should be loose, and flowing over our shoulders; that we should, like themselves, sit cross-legged; and, at times, in the most humble posture, with down-cast eyes, and hands locked together; all which requisites were most devoutly observed by the whole assembly. And, lastly, every one was excluded from the solemnity, but the principal people, and those who assisted in the celebration. All these circumstances were to me a sufficient testimony, that, upon this occasion, they considered themselves as acting under the immediate inspection of a Supreme Being.

The present *Natche* may be considered, from the above account of it, as merely figurative. For the small quantity of yams, which we saw the first day, could not be intended as a general contribution; and, indeed, we were given to understand, that they were a portion consecrated to the *Otooa*, or Divinity. But we were informed, that, in about three months, there would be performed, on the same account, a far more important and grander solemnity; on which occasion, not only the tribute of Tongataboo, but that of Hapaee, Vavaoo, and of all the other islands, would be brought to the Chief, and confirmed more awfully, by sacrificing ten human victims from amongst the inferior sort of people. A horrid solemnity indeed! and which is a most significant instance of the influence of gloomy and ignorant superstition, over the minds of one of the most benevolent and humane

mane nations upon earth. On inquiring into the reasons of so barbarous a practice, they only said, that it was a necessary part of the *Natche*; and that, if they omitted it, the Deity would certainly destroy their king.

Before the assembly broke up, the day was far spent; and as we were at some distance from the ships, and had an intricate navigation to go through, we were in haste to set out from Mooa. When I took leave of Poulaho, he pressed me much to stay till the next day, to be present at a funeral ceremony. The wife of Mareewagee, who was mother in-law to the king, had lately died; and her corpse had, on account of the *Natche*, been carried on board a canoe that lay in the *lagoon*. Poulaho told me, that, as soon as he had paid the last offices to her, he would attend me to Fooa; but, if I did not wait, that he would follow me thither. I understood, at the same time, that, if it had not been for the death of this woman, most of the Chiefs would have accompanied us to that island; where, it seems, all of them have possessions. I would gladly have waited to see this ceremony also, had not the tide been now favourable for the ships to get through the narrows. The wind, besides, which, for several days past, had been very boisterous, was now moderate and settled; and to have lost this opportunity, might have detained us a fortnight longer. But what was decisive against my waiting, we understood that the funeral ceremonies would last five days, which was too long a time, as the ships lay in such a situation, that I could not get to sea at pleasure. I, however, assured the king, that, if we did not sail, I should certainly visit him again the next day. And so we all took leave of him, and set out for the ships, where we arrived about eight o'clock in the evening.

I had

I had forgot to mention, that Omai was present at this second day's ceremony, as well as myself; but we were not together; nor did I know that he was there, till it was almost over. He afterward told me, that, as soon as the king saw that I had stolen out from the plantation, he sent several people, one after another, to desire me to come back. Probably, these messengers were not admitted to the place where I was; for I saw nothing of them. At last, intelligence was brought to the Chief, that I had actually stripped, in conformity to their custom; and then he told Omai, that he might be present also, if he would comply with all the necessary forms. Omai had no objection, as nothing was required of him, but to conform to the custom of his own country. Accordingly, he was furnished with a proper dress, and appeared at the ceremony as one of the natives. It is likely, that one reason of our being excluded at first, was an apprehension, that we would not submit to the requisites to qualify us to assist.

While I was attending the *Natche* at Mooa, I ordered the horses, bull and cow, and goats, to be brought thither; thinking that they would be safer there, under the eyes of the Chiefs, than at a place that would be, in a manner, deserted, the moment after our departure. Besides the abovementioned animals, we left, with our friends here, a young boar, and three young sows, of the English breed. They were exceedingly desirous of them, judging, no doubt, that they would greatly improve their own breed, which is rather small. Feenou also got from us two rabbits, a buck and a doe; and, before we failed, we were told, that young ones had been already produced. If the cattle succeed, of which I make no doubt, it will be a vast acquisition to these islands;

1777.
July.

islands; and, as Tongataboo is a fine level country, the horses cannot but be useful.

Thursday 10. On the 10th, at eight o'clock in the morning, we weighed anchor, and, with a steady gale at South East, turned through the channel, between the small isles called Makkahaa and Monooafai; it being much wider than the channel between the last mentioned island and Pangimodoo. The flood set strong in our favour, till we were the length of the channel leading up to the *lagoon*, where the flood from the Eastward meets that from the West. This, together with the indraught of the *lagoon*, and of the shoals before it, causeth strong riplings and whirlpools. To add to these dangers, the depth of water in the channel exceeds the length of a cable; so that there is no anchorage, except close to the rocks, where we meet with forty and forty-five fathoms, over a bottom of dark sand. But then, here, a ship would be exposed to the whirlpools. This frustrated the design which I had formed, of coming to an anchor, as soon as we were through the narrows, and of making an excursion to see the funeral. I chose rather to lose that ceremony, than to leave the ships in a situation, in which I did not think them safe. We continued to ply to windward, between the two tides, without either gaining or losing an inch, till near high water, when, by a favourable slant, we got into the Eastern tide's influence. We expected, there, to find the ebb to run strong to the Eastward in our favour; but it proved so inconsiderable, that, at any other time, it would not have been noticed. This informed us, that most of the water, which flows into the *lagoon*, comes from the North West, and returns the same way. About five in the afternoon, finding that we could not get to sea before it was

dark,

dark, I came to an anchor, under the shore of Tongataboo, in forty-five fathoms water; and about two cables length from the reef, that runs along that side of the island. The Discovery dropped anchor under our stern; but before the anchor took hold, she drove off the bank, and did not recover it till after midnight.

We remained at this station, till eleven o'clock, the next day, when we weighed, and plyed to the Eastward. But it was ten at night, before we weathered the East end of the island, and were enabled to stretch away for Middleburg, or Eooa (as it is called by the inhabitants), where we anchored, at eight o'clock, the next morning, in forty fathoms water, over a bottom of sand, interspersed with coral rocks; the extremes of the island extending, from North, 40° East, to South, 22° West; the high land of Eooa, South, 45° East; and Tongataboo, from North, 70° West, to North, 19° West; distant about half a mile from the shore; being nearly the same place where I had my station in 1773, and then named by me, *English Road*.

We had no sooner anchored, than Taoofa the Chief, and several other natives, visited us on board, and seemed to rejoice much at our arrival. This Taoofa * had been my *Taye*, when I was here, during my last voyage; consequently, we were not strangers to each other. In a little time, I went ashore with him, in search of fresh water; the procuring of which, was the chief object that brought me to Eooa. I had been told, at Tongataboo, that there was here a stream, running from the hills into the sea; but this was not the case now. I was first conducted to a brackish spring, between low and high water mark, amongst rocks, in the

---

* In the account of Captain Cook's former voyage, he calls the only Chief he then met with, at this place, *Tioony*. See Vol. I. p. 192.

cove

cove where we landed, and where no one would ever have thought of looking for what we wanted. However, I believe, the water of this spring might be good, were it possible to take it up, before the tide mixes with it. Finding that we did not like this, our friends took us a little way into the island; where, in a deep chasm, we found very good water; which, at the expence of some time and trouble, might be conveyed down to the shore, by means of spouts or troughs, that could be made with plantain leaves, and the stem of the tree. But, rather than to undertake that tedious task, I resolved to rest contented with the supply the ships had got at Tongataboo.

Before I returned on board, I set on foot a trade for hogs and yams. Of the former, we could procure but few; but, of the latter, plenty. I put ashore, at this island, the ram and two ewes, of the Cape of Good Hope breed of sheep; intrusting them to the care of Taoofa, who seemed proud of his charge. It was fortunate, perhaps, that Mareewagee, to whom I had given them, as before-mentioned, slighted the present. Eooa, not having, as yet, got any dogs upon it, seems to be a properer place than Tongataboo for the rearing of sheep.

As we lay at anchor, this island bore a very different aspect from any we had lately seen, and formed a most beautiful landscape. It is higher than any we had passed, since leaving New Zealand (as Kao may justly be reckoned an immense rock), and from its top, which is almost flat, declines very gently toward the sea. As the other isles, of this cluster, are level, the eye can discover nothing but the trees that cover them; but here the land, rising gently upward, presents us with an extensive prospect, where groves of trees are only intersperfed at irregular distances, in

beautiful

beautiful diforder, and the reft covered with grafs. Near
the fhore, again, it is quite fhaded with various trees,
amongft which are the habitations of the natives; and to
the right of our ftation, was one of the moft extenfive groves
of cocoa-palms we had ever feen.

The 13th, in the afternoon, a party of us made an excur-
fion to the higheft part of the ifland, which was a little to
the right of our fhips, in order to have a full view of the
country. About half way up, we croffed a deep valley, the
bottom and fides of which, though compofed of hardly any
thing but coral rock, were clothed with trees. We were
now about two or three hundred feet above the level of the
fea, and yet, even here, the coral was perforated into all the
holes and inequalities, which ufually diverfify the furface
of this fubftance within the reach of the tide. Indeed, we
found the fame coral, till we began to approach the fummits of the higheft hills; and, it was remarkable, that
thefe were chiefly compofed of a yellowifh, foft, fandy
ftone. The foil, there, is, in general, a reddifh clay; which,
in many places, feemed to be very deep. On the moft elevated part of the whole ifland, we found a round platform,
or mount of earth, fupported by a wall of coral ftones; to
bring which, to fuch a height, muft have coft much labour.
Our guides told us, that this mount had been erected by
order of their Chief; and that they, fometimes, met there
to drink *kava*. They called it *Etebee*; by which name, an
erection, which we had feen at Tongataboo, as already
mentioned, was diftinguifhed. Not many paces from it,
was a fpring of excellent water; and, about a mile lower
down, a running ftream, which, we were told, found its
way to the fea, when the rains were copious. We alfo met
with

with water, in many little holes; and, no doubt, great plenty might be found, by digging.

From the elevation, to which we had afcended, we had a full view of the whole ifland, except a part of the South point. The South Eaſt fide, from which the higheſt hills, we were now upon, are not far diſtant, rifes with very great inequalities, immediately from the fea; fo that the plains and meadows, of which there are here fome of great extent, lie all on the North Weſt fide; and, as they are adorned with tufts of trees, intermixed with plantations, they form a very beautiful landfcape, in every point of view. While I was furveying this delightful profpect, I could not help flattering myfelf with the pleafing idea, that fome future navigator may, from the fame ſtation, behold thefe meadows ſtocked with cattle, brought to thefe iflands by the ſhips of England; and that the completion of this fingle benevolent purpofe, independently of all other confiderations, would fufficiently mark to poſterity, that our voyages had not been ufelefs to the general interefts of humanity. Befides the plants common on the other neighbouring iflands, we found, on the height, a fpecies of *acroſticum*, *melaſtoma*, and fern tree; with a few other ferns and plants, not common lower down.

Our guides informed us, that all, or moſt of the land, on this ifland, belonged to the great Chiefs of Tongataboo; and that the inhabitants were only tenants, or vaffals, to them. Indeed, this feemed to be the cafe at all the other neighbouring iſles, except Annamooka, where there were fome Chiefs, who feemed to act with fome kind of independence. Omai, who was a great favourite with Feenou, and thefe people in general, was tempted with the offer of being

being made Chief of this island, if he would have staid amongst them; and it is not clear to me, that he would not have been glad to stay, if the scheme had met with my approbation. I own, I did disapprove of it; but not because I thought that Omai would do better for himself in his own native isle.

On returning from my country expedition, we were informed that a party of the natives had, in the circle where our people traded, struck one of their own countrymen with a club, which laid bare, or, as others said, fractured his skull, and then broke his thigh with the same; when our men interposed. He had no signs of life, when carried to a neighbouring house; but afterward recovered a little. On my asking the reason of so severe a treatment, we were informed, that he had been discovered in a situation rather indelicate, with a woman who was *taboo'd*. We, however, understood, that she was no otherwise *taboo'd*, than by belonging to another person, and rather superior in rank to her gallant. From this circumstance, we had an opportunity of observing, how these people treat such infidelities. But the female sinner has, by far, the smaller share of punishment for her misdemeanor; as they told us, that she would only receive a slight beating.

The next morning, I planted a pine-apple, and sowed the seeds of melons, and other vegetables in the Chief's plantation. I had some encouragement, indeed, to flatter myself, that my endeavours of this kind would not be fruitless; for, this day, there was served up at my dinner, a dish of turnips, being the produce of the seeds I had left here during my last voyage.

1777.
July.

Monday 14.

I had

1777.
July.
Tuesday 15.

I had fixed upon the 15th for sailing, till Taoofa pressed me to stay a day or two longer, to receive a present he had prepared for me. This reason, and the daily expectation of seeing some of our friends from Tongataboo, induced me to defer my departure.

Wednes. 16.

Accordingly, the next day, I received the Chief's present; consisting of two small heaps of yams, and some fruit, which seemed to be collected by a kind of contribution, as at the other isles. On this occasion, most of the people of the island had assembled at the place; and, as we had experienced on such numerous meetings amongst their neighbours, gave us not a little trouble to prevent them from pilfering whatever they could lay their hands upon. We were entertained with cudgelling, wrestling, and boxing-matches; and in the latter, both male and female combatants exhibited. It was intended to have finished the shew with the *bomai*, or night-dance; but an accident either put a total stop to it, or, at least, prevented any of us from staying ashore to see it. One of my people, walking a very little way, was surrounded by twenty or thirty of the natives, who knocked him down, and stripped him of every thing he had on his back. On hearing of this, I immediately seized two canoes, and a large hog; and insisted on Taoofa's causing the clothes to be restored, and on the offenders being delivered up to me. The Chief seemed much concerned at what had happened; and forthwith took the necessary steps to satisfy me. This affair so alarmed the assembled people, that most of them fled. However, when they found that I took no other measures to revenge the insult, they returned. It was not long before one of the offenders was delivered up to me, and a shirt and a pair of trowsers
restored

reftored. The remainder of the ftolen goods not coming in before night, I was under a neceffity of leaving them to go aboard; for the fea run fo high, that it was with the greateft difficulty the boats could get out of the creek with daylight, much lefs in the dark.

The next morning, I landed again, having provided myfelf with a prefent for Taoofa, in return for what he had given me. As it was early, there were but few people at the landing-place, and thofe few not without their fears. But on my defiring Omai to affure them, that we meant no harm; and, in confirmation of this affurance, having reftored the canoes, and releafed the offender, whom they had delivered up to me, they refumed their ufual gaiety; and, prefently, a large circle was formed, in which the Chief, and all the principal men of the ifland, took their places. The remainder of the clothes were now brought in; but, as they had been torn off the man's back, by pieces, they were not worth carrying on board. Taoofa, on receiving my prefent, fhared it with three or four other Chiefs, keeping only a fmall part for himfelf. This prefent exceeded their expectation fo greatly, that one of the Chiefs, a venerable old man, told me, that they did not deferve it, confidering how little they had given to me, and the ill treatment one of my people had met with. I remained with them, till they had finifhed their bowl of *kava*; and having then paid for the hog, which I had taken the day before, returned on board, with Taoofa, and one of Poulaho's fervants, by whom I fent, as a parting mark of my efteem and regard for that Chief, a piece of bar iron; being as valuable a prefent as any I could make to him.

VOL. I. 3 A Soon

1777.
July.

Soon after, we weighed, and with a light breeze at South East, stood out to sea; and then Taoofa, and a few other natives, that were in the ship, left us. On heaving up the anchor, we found, that the cable had suffered considerably by the rocks; so that the bottom, in this road, is not to be depended upon. Besides this, we experienced, that a prodigious swell rolls in there from the South West.

We had not been long under sail, before we observed a sailing canoe coming from Tongataboo, and entering the creek before which we had anchored. Some hours after, a small canoe, conducted by four men, came off to us. For, as we had but little wind, we were, still, at no great distance from the land. These men told us, that the sailing canoe, which we had seen arrive from Tongataboo, had brought orders to the people of Eooa, to furnish us with a certain number of hogs; and that, in two days, the king, and other Chiefs, would be with us. They, therefore, desired we would return to our former station. There was no reason to doubt the truth of what these men told us. Two of them had actually come from Tongataboo, in the sailing canoe; and they had no view in coming off to us, but to give this intelligence. However, as we were now clear of the land, it was not a sufficient inducement to bring me back; especially as we had, already, on board, a stock of fresh provisions, sufficient, in all probability, to last during our passage to Otaheite. Besides Taoofa's present, we had got a good quantity of yams at Eooa, in exchange chiefly for small nails. Our supply of hogs was also considerably increased there; though, doubtless, we should have got many more, if the Chiefs of Tongataboo had been with us, whose property they mostly were. At the approach of night, these men,

men, finding that we would not return, left us; as also some others, who had come off in two canoes, with a few cocoa-nuts, and shaddocks, to exchange them for what they could get; the eagerness of these people to get into their possession more of our commodities, inducing them to follow the ships out to sea, and to continue their intercourse with us to the last moment.

CHAP. X.

*Advantages derived from visiting the Friendly Islands.—
Best Articles for Traffic.—Refreshments that may be
procured.—The Number of the Islands, and their Names.
—Keppel's and Boscawen's Islands belong to them.—Account of Vavaoo—of Hamoa—of Feejee.—Voyages of
the Natives in their Canoes.—Difficulty of procuring
exact Information.—Persons of the Inhabitants of both
Sexes.—Their Colour.—Diseases.—Their general Character.—Manner of wearing their Hair—of puncturing their Bodies.—Their Clothing and Ornaments.—
Personal Cleanliness.*

1777. July.

THUS we took leave of the Friendly Islands, and their inhabitants, after a stay of between two and three months; during which time, we lived together in the most cordial friendship. Some accidental differences, it is true, now and then happened, owing to their great propensity to thieving; but, too often, encouraged by the negligence of our own people. But these differences were never attended with any fatal consequences; to prevent which, all my measures were directed; and, I believe, few, on board our ships, left our friends here without some regret. The time, employed amongst them, was not thrown away. We expended very little of our sea provisions; subsisting, in general, upon the produce of the islands, while we staid; and carrying away with us a quantity of refreshments sufficient

to

to laſt till our arrival at another ſtation, where we could depend upon a freſh ſupply. I was not ſorry, beſides, to have had an opportunity of bettering the condition of theſe good people, by leaving the uſeful animals, before-mentioned, among them; and, at the ſame time, thoſe deſigned for Otaheite, received freſh ſtrength in the paſtures of Tongataboo. Upon the whole, therefore, the advantages we received, by touching here, were very great; and I had the additional ſatisfaction to reflect, that they were received, without retarding, one moment, the proſecution of the great object of our voyage; the ſeaſon, for proceeding to the North, being, as has been already obſerved, loſt, before I took the reſolution of bearing away for theſe iſlands.

But, beſides the immediate advantages, which both the natives of the Friendly Iſlands, and ourſelves, received by this viſit, future navigators from Europe, if any ſuch ſhould ever tread our ſteps, will profit by the knowledge I acquired of the geography of this part of the Pacific Ocean; and the more philoſophical reader, who loves to view human nature in new ſituations, and to ſpeculate on ſingular, but faithful repreſentations of the perſons, the cuſtoms, the arts, the religion, the government, and the language of uncultivated man, in remote and freſh diſcovered quarters of the globe, will, perhaps, find matter of amuſement, if not of inſtruction, in the information which I have been enabled to convey to him, concerning the inhabitants of this Archipelago. I ſhall ſuſpend my narrative, of the progreſs of the voyage, while I faithfully relate what I had opportunities of collecting on theſe ſeveral topics.

We found, by our experience, that the beſt articles for traffic, at theſe iſlands, are iron tools in general. Axes and hatchets; nails, from the largeſt ſpike down to tenpenny ones;

ones; rasps, files; and knives, are much sought after. Red cloth; and linen, both white and coloured; looking-glasses, and beads, are also in estimation; but, of the latter, those that are blue, are preferred to all others; and white ones are thought the least valuable. A string of large blue beads would, at any time, purchase a hog. But it must be observed, that such articles as are merely ornaments, may be highly esteemed at one time, and not so at another. When we first arrived at Annamooka, the people there would hardly take them in exchange even' for fruit; but when Feenou came, this great man set the fashion, and brought them into vogue, till they rose in their value to what I have just mentioned.

In return for the favourite commodities which I have enumerated, all the refreshments may be procured that the islands produce. These are, hogs, fowls, fish, yams, bread-fruit, plantains, cocoa-nuts, sugar-cane, and, in general, every such supply as can be met with at Otaheite, or any of the Society Islands. The yams of the Friendly islands are excellent, and, when grown to perfection, keep very well at sea. But their pork, bread fruit, and plantains, though far from despicable, are, nevertheless, much inferior in quality to the same articles at Otaheite, and in its neighbourhood.

Good water, which ships, on long voyages, stand so much in need of, is scarce at these islands. It may be found, it is true, on them all; but, still, either in too inconsiderable quantities, or in situations too inconvenient, to serve the purposes of navigators. However, as the islands afford plenty of provisions, and particularly of cocoa-nuts, ships may make a tolerable shift with such water as is to be got; and if one is not over-nice, there will be no want. While we lay at anchor, under Kotoo, on our return from Hapaee,
some

some people, from Kao, informed us, that there was a stream of water there, which, pouring down from the mountain, runs into the sea, on the South West side of the island; that is, on the side that faces Toofoa, another island remarkable for its height, as also for having a considerable volcano in it, which, as has been already mentioned, burnt violently all the time that we were in its neighbourhood. It may be worth while for future navigators, to attend to this intelligence about the stream of water at Kao; especially as we learned that there was anchorage on that part of the coast. The black stone, of which the natives of the Friendly Islands make their hatchets, and other tools, we were informed, is the production of Toofoa.

Under the denomination of Friendly Islands, we must include, not only the group at Hapaee, which I visited, but also all those islands, that have been discovered nearly under the same meridian, to the North, as well as some others that have never been seen, hitherto, by any European navigators; but are under the dominion of Tongataboo, which, though not the largest, is the capital, and seat of government.

According to the information that we received there, this Archipelago is very extensive. Above one hundred and fifty islands were reckoned up to us by the natives, who made use of bits of leaves to ascertain their number; and Mr. Anderson, with his usual diligence, even procured all their names. Fifteen of them are said to be high, or hilly, such as Toofoa, and Eooa; and thirty-five of them large. Of these, only three were seen this voyage; Hapaee (which is considered by the natives as one island), Tongataboo, and Eooa: of the size of the unexplored thirty-two, nothing more can be mentioned, but that they must
be

be all larger than Annamooka; which thofe, from whom we had our information, ranked amongft the fmaller iſles. Some, or indeed feveral, of this latter denomination, are mere fpots, without inhabitants. Sixty-one of thefe iſlands have their proper places and names marked upon our chart of the Friendly Iſlands, and upon the ſketch of the harbour of Tongataboo, to both which I refer the reader. But it muſt be left to future navigators, to introduce into the geography of this part of the South Pacific Ocean, the exact fituation and fize of near a hundred more iſlands in this neighbourhood, which we had not an opportunity to explore; and whofe exiſtence we only learnt from the teſtimony of our friends, as above-mentioned. On their authority, the following liſt of them was made; and it may ſerve as a ground-work for farther inveſtigation.

Names of the Friendly Iſlands, and others, in that Neighbourhood, mentioned by the Inhabitants of Annamooka, Hapaee, and Tongataboo.

Komooefeeva,	Noogoofaceou,	Novababoo,
Kullalona,	Koreemou,	Golabbe,
Felongaboonga,	Failemaia,	Vagaeetoo,
Koverectoa,	Koweeka,	Gowakka,
Fonogoocatta,	Konookoonama,	*Goofoo*,
Modooanoogoo noo-	Kooonoogoo,	Mafanna,
goo,	Geenageena,	Kolloooa,
Tongooa,	Kowourogoheefo,	Tabanna,
Koona,	. Kottejeea,	Morooha,
Fonooa eeka,	Kokabba,	Looakabba,

* Thofe Iſlands, which the natives repreſented as large ones, are diſtinguiſhed in Italics.

Vavaoo,

Vavaoo,	Boloa,	Toofanaetollo,	1777. July.
Koloa,	Toofagga,	Toofanaelaa,	
Fafeene,	Loogoobabanga,	Kogoopoloo,	
Taoonga,	Taoola,	Havaereeke,	
Kobakeemotoo,	Maneenceta,	Tootooeela,	
Kongahoonoho,	Fonooaooma,	Mawoka,	
Komalla,	Fonooonneonne,	Laftainga,	
Konoababoo,	Wegaffa,	Poppataia,	
Konnetalle,	Fooamotoo,	Lonbatta,	
Komongoraffa,	Fonooalaiee,	Oloo,	
Kotoolooa,	Tattahoi,	Takomsove,	
Kologobeele,	Lane,	Kopaoo,	
Kollokolahee,	Newafo,	Kovoosea,	
Marageefaia,	Feejee,	Kongaireekee,	
Mallajee,	Oowaia,	Tafeedoowaia,	
Mallalahee,	Kongaiaraloi,	Humea,	
Gonoogoolaiee,	Kateoboeo,	Neeoaiaboutaboo,	
Toonabai,	Komotte,	Fotoona,	
Konnevy,	Kvmoarra,	Vytoobeo,	
Konnevao,	Kolaiva,	Latooma,	
Moggodoo,	Kofoona,	Toggelao,	
Looamoggo,	Konnagillelaivoo,	Talava.	

I have not the least doubt, that Prince William's Islands, discovered, and so named by Tasman, are included in the foregoing list. For while we lay at Hapaee, one of the natives told me, that, three or four days sail from thence, to the North West, there was a cluster of small islands, consisting of upward of forty. This situation corresponds very well with that assigned, in the accounts we have of Tasman's voyage, to his Prince William's Islands[*].

[*] Tasman saw eighteen or twenty of these small islands, every one of which was surrounded with sands, shoals, and rocks. They are also called, in some charts,

Vol. I. 3 B Heemskirk's

We have also very good authority to believe, that Keppel's and Bofcawen's Iflands, two of Captain Wallis's difcoveries in 1765, are comprehended in our lift; and that they are not only well known to thefe people, but are under the fame fovereign. The following information feemed to me decifive as to this. Upon my inquiring, one day, of Poulaho the king, in what manner the inhabitants of Tongataboo had acquired the knowledge of iron, and from what quarter they had procured a fmall iron tool, which I had feen amongft them, when I firft vifited their ifland, during my former voyage, he informed me, that they had received this iron from an ifland, which he called Neeootabootaboo. Carrying my inquiries further, I then defired to know, whether he had ever been informed, from whom the people of Neeootabootaboo had got it. I found him perfectly acquainted with its hiftory. He faid, that one of thofe iflanders fold a club, for five nails, to a fhip which had touched there; and that thefe five nails afterward were fent to Tongataboo. He added, that this was the firft iron known amongft them; fo that, what Tafman left of that metal, muft have been worn out, and forgot long ago. I was very particular in my inquiries about the fituation, fize, and form of the ifland; expreffing my defire to know when this fhip had touched there; how long fhe ftaid; and whether any more were in company. The leading facts appeared to be frefh in his memory. He faid, that there was but one fhip; that fhe did not come to an anchor, but left the ifland after her boat had been on fhore. And from many circumftances, which he mentioned, it could not be many years fince this

Horsburgh's Bonds. See Dalrymple's Collection of Voyages to the South Pacific Ocean, Vol. ii. p. 83.; and Campbell's edition of Harris's, Vol. i. p. 325.

had

had happened. According to his information, there are two iflands near each other, which he himfelf had been at. The one he defcribed as high, and peaked like Kao, and he called it Kootahee; the other, where the people of the fhip landed, called Neeooiabootaboo, he reprefented as much lower. He added, that the natives of both are the fame fort of people with thofe of Tongataboo; built their canoes in the fame manner; that their iflands had hogs and fowls; and, in general, the fame vegetable productions. The fhip, fo pointedly referred to, in this converfation, could be no other than the Dolphin; the only fingle fhip from Europe, as far as we have ever learned, that had touched, of late years, at any ifland in this part of the Pacific Ocean, prior to my former vifit of the Friendly Iflands *.

But the moft confiderable iflands in this neighbourhood, that we now heard of (and we heard a great deal about them), are Hamoa, Vavaoo, and Feejee. Each of thefe was reprefented to us as larger than Tongataboo. No European, that we know of, has, as yet, feen any one of them. Tafman, indeed, lays down in his chart, an ifland nearly in the fituation where I fuppofe Vavaoo to be; that is, about the latitude of 19° †. But, then, that ifland is there marked

as

---

* See Captain Wallis's Voyage, in Hawkefworth's Collection, Vol. i. p. 492—494. Captain Wallis there calls both thefe iflands *high* even. But the fuperior height of one of them may be inferred, from his faying, that it appears *like a fugarloaf*. This ftrongly marks its refemblance to Kao. From comparing Poulaho's intelligence to Captain Cook, with Captain Wallis's account, it feems to be paft all doubt, that Bofcawen's Ifland is our Kootahee, and Keppel's Ifland our Neeooiabootaboo. The laft is one of the large iflands marked in the foregoing lift. The reader, who has been already appriz'd of the variations of our people in writing down what the natives pronounced, will hardly doubt that Kotteyeta and Kootahee are the fame.

† Neither Dalrymple nor Campbell, in their accounts of Tafman's voyage, take any particular notice of his having feen fuch an ifland. The chart here referred to,

as a very small one; whereas Vavaoo, according to the united testimony of all our friends at Tongataboo, exceeds the size of their own island, and has high mountains. I should certainly have visited it; and have accompanied Feenou from Hapaee, if he had not then discouraged me, by representing it to be very inconsiderable, and without any harbour. But Poulaho, the king, afterward assured me, that it was a large island; and that it not only produced every thing in common with Tongataboo, but had the peculiar advantage of possessing several streams of fresh water, with as good a harbour as that which we found at his capital island. He offered to attend me, if I would visit it; adding, that, if I did not find every thing agreeing with his representation, I might kill him. I had not the least doubt of the truth of his intelligence; and was satisfied that Feenou, from some interested view, attempted to deceive me.

Hamoa, which is also under the dominion of Tongataboo, lies two days sail North West from Vavaoo. It was described to me, as the largest of all their islands; as affording harbours and good water; and as producing, in abundance, every article of refreshment found at the places we visited. Poulaho, himself, frequently resides there. It should seem, that the people of this island are in high estimation at Tongataboo; for we were told, that some of the songs and dances, with which we were entertained, had been copied from theirs; and we saw some houses, said to be built after their fashion. Mr. Anderson, always inquisitive about such

by Captain Cook, is, probably, Mr. Dalrymple's, in his Collection of Voyages, where Tasman's track is marked accurately; and several very small spots of land are laid down in the situation here mentioned.

matters, learnt the three following words of the dialect of Hamoa.

  Tamolao*, a chief man.
  Tamatty, a chief woman.
  Solle, a common man.

             Feejee,

---

* In two or three preceding notes, extracts have been made from the *Lettres Edifiantes & Curieuses*, as marking a strong resemblance between some of the customs of the inhabitants of the Caroline Islands, and those which Captain Cook describes as prevailing at an immense distance, in the islands which he visited in the South Pacific Ocean. Possibly, however, the presumption, arising from this resemblance, that all these islands were peopled by the same nation, or tribe, may be refuted, under the plausible pretence, that customs very similar prevail amongst very distant people, without inferring any other common source, besides the general principles of human nature; the same in all ages, and every part of the globe. The reader, perhaps, will not think this pretence applicable to the matter before us, if he attends to the following very obvious distinction: Those customs which have their foundation in wants that are common to the whole human species, and which are confined to the contrivance of means to relieve those wants, may well be supposed to bear a strong resemblance, without warranting the conclusion, that they who use them have copied each other, or have derived them from one common source; human sagacity being the same every where, and the means adapted to the relief of any particular natural want, especially in countries similarly uncultivated, being but few. Thus the most distant tribes, as widely separated as Terra del Fuego is from the islands East of Kamtschatka, may, both of them, produce their fire, by rubbing two sticks upon each other, without giving us the least foundation for supposing, that either of them imitated the other, or derived the invention from a source of instruction common to both. But this seems not to be the case, with regard to those customs to which no general principle of human nature has given birth, and which have their establishment solely from the endless varieties of local whim, and national fashion. Of this latter kind, those customs obviously are, that belong both to the North, and to the South Pacific Bands, from which, we would infer, that they were originally one nation; and the men of Mangeea and the men of the New Philippines, who pay their respects to a person whom they mean to honour, by rubbing his hand over their faces, but fair to have learnt their mode of salutation in the same school. But if this observation should not have removed the doubts of the sceptical reader, probably he will hardly venture to persist in denying the identity of race, contended for in the present instance, when he shall observe, that, to the proof drawn from affinity of customs, we have it in our power to add that most unexceptionable one, drawn from affinity of language. *Tamolao*, we now know, is the word used at Hamoa, one of the Friendly Islands, to signify a Chief; and whoever looks into the *Lettres Edifiantes & Curieuses*, will see, that this is the very name by which the inhabitants of the Caroline Islands

1777.
July.

Feejee, as we were told, lies three days fail from Tongataboo, in the direction of North West by West. It was described to us as a high, but very fruitful island; abounding with hogs, dogs, fowls, and all the kinds of fruit and roots that are found in any of the others; and as much larger than Tongataboo; to the dominion of which, as was represented to us, it is not subject, as the other islands of this archipelago are. On the contrary, Feejee and Tongataboo frequently make war upon each other. And it appeared, from several circumstances, that the inhabitants of the latter are much afraid of this enemy. They used to express their sense of their own inferiority to the Feejee men, by bending the body forward, and covering the face with their hands. And it is no wonder, that they should be under this dread; for those of Feejee are formidable on account of the dexterity with which they use their bows and slings; but much more so, on account of the savage practice to which they are addicted, like those of New Zealand, of eating their enemies, whom they kill in battle. We were satisfied, that this was not a misrepresentation. For we met with several Feejee people at Tongataboo, and, on inquiring of them, they did not deny the charge.

Now, that I am again led to speak of cannibals, let me ask those who maintain, that the want of food first brings men to feed on human flesh, What is it that induceth the

---

distinguish their principal men. We have, in two preceding notes, inserted passages from Father Cantova's account of them, where their *Tamoles* are spoken of; and he repeats the word at least a dozen times, in the course of a few pages. But I cannot avoid transcribing, from him, the following very decisive testimony, which renders any other quotation superfluous. " L'autorité du Gouvernement se partage entre " plusieurs familles nobles, dont les Chefs s'appellent *Tamoles*. Il y a outre cela, " dans chaque province, un principale *Tamole*, auquel tous les autres sont soumis."
Lettres Edifiantes & Curieuses, Tom. xv. p. 312.

Feejee people to keep it up, in the midst of plenty? This practice is detested, very much, by those of Tongataboo, who cultivate the friendship of their savage neighbours of Feejee, apparently out of fear; though they sometimes venture to skirmish with them, on their own ground; and carry off red feathers, as their booty, which are in great plenty there, and, as has been frequently mentioned, are in great estimation amongst our Friendly Islanders. When the two islands are at peace, the intercourse between them seems to be pretty frequent; though they have, doubtless, been but lately known to each other; or we may suppose, that Tongataboo, and its adjoining islands, would have been supplied, before this, with a breed of dogs, which abound at Feejee, and had not been introduced at Tongataboo, so late as 1773, when I first visited it. The natives of Feejee, whom we met with here, were of a colour that was a full shade darker, than that of the inhabitants of the Friendly Islands in general. One of them had his left ear slit, and the lobe was so distended, that it almost reached his shoulder; which singularity I had met with at other islands of the South Sea, during my second voyage. It appeared to me, that the Feejee men, whom we now saw, were much respected here; not only, perhaps, from the power, and cruel manner of their nation's going to war, but, also, from their ingenuity. For they seem to excel the inhabitants of Tongataboo in that respect, if we might judge from several specimens of their skill in workmanship, which we saw; such as clubs and spears, which were carved in a very masterly manner; cloth beautifully chequered; variegated mats; earthen pots; and some other articles; all which had a cast of superiority in the execution.

I have

I have mentioned, that Feejee lies three days sail from Tongataboo, because these people have no other method of measuring the distance from island to island, but by expressing the time required to make the voyage, in one of their canoes. In order to ascertain this, with some precision, or, at least, to form some judgment, how far these canoes can sail, in a moderate gale, in any given time, I went on board one of them, when under sail, and, by several trials with the log, found that she went seven knots, or miles, in an hour, close hauled, in a gentle gale. From this I judge, that they will sail, on a medium, with such breezes as generally blow in their sea, about seven or eight miles in an hour. But the length of each day is not to be reckoned at twenty-four hours. For when they speak of one day's sail, they mean no more than from the morning to the evening of the same day; that is, ten or twelve hours at most. And two days sail, with them, signifies from the morning of the first day, to the evening of the second; and so for any other number of days. In these navigations, the sun is their guide by day, and the stars by night. When these are obscured, they have recourse to the points from whence the winds and the waves came upon the vessel. If, during the obscuration, both the wind and the waves should shift (which, within the limits of the trade-wind, seldom happens at any other time), they are then bewildered, frequently miss their intended port, and are never heard of more. The history of Omai's countrymen, who were driven to Wateeoo, leads us to infer, that those not heard of, are not always lost.

Of all the harbours and anchoring places I have met with, amongst these islands, that of Tongataboo is, by far, the best;

best, not only on account of its great security, but of its capacity, and of the goodness of its bottom. The risk that we ran, in entering it from the North, ought to be a sufficient caution, to every future Commander, not to attempt that passage again with a ship of burden; since the other, by which we left it, is so much more easy and safe. To sail into it, by this Eastern channel, steer in for the North East point of the island, and keep along the North shore, with the small isles on your starboard, till you are the length of the East point of the entrance into the *lagoon*; then edge over for the reef of the small isles; and, on following its direction, it will conduct you through between Makkahaaa and Monooafai, or the fourth and fifth isles, which you will perceive to lie off the West point of the *lagoon*. Or you may go between the third and fourth islands, that is, between Pangimodoo and Monooafai; but this channel is much narrower than the other. There runs a very strong tide in both. The flood, as I have observed before, comes in from the North West, and the ebb returns the same way; but I shall speak of the tides in another place. As soon as you are through either of these channels, haul in for the shore of Tongataboo, and anchor between it and Pangimodoo, before a creek leading into the *lagoon*; into which boats can go at half flood.

Although Tongataboo has the best harbour, Annamooka furnishes the best water; and yet, it cannot be called good. However, by digging holes near the side of the pond, we can get what may be called tolerable. This island, too, is the best situated for drawing refreshments from all the others, as being nearly in the centre of the whole group. Besides the road in which we anchored, and the harbour within the South West point, there is a creek in the reef,

1777.
July.

before the Eastern sandy cove, on the North side of the island, in which two or three ships may lie very securely, by mooring head and stern, with their anchors or moorings fast to the rocks.

I have already described the Hapaee islands; and shall only add to that description, by mentioning, that they extend South West by South, and North East by North, about nineteen miles. The North end lies in the latitude of 19° 39' South, and 33' of longitude to the East of Annamooka. Between them, are a great many small islands, sand-banks, and breakers; so that the safest way to arrive at Hapaee, is either by the course I held, or round by the North; according to the situation of the ship bound thither. Lefooga, off which we anchored, is the most fertile isle of those that are called Hapaee; and, consequently, is the best inhabited. There is anchorage along the North West side of this island; but it will be necessary to examine the ground well before you moor. For, although the lead may bring up fine sand, there are, nevertheless, some sharp coral rocks, that would soon destroy the cables.

They who want a more particular description of the Friendly Islands, must have recourse to the chart that we constructed. There, every thing is delineated with as much accuracy as circumstances would permit. Recourse must, also, be had, to the same chart, for the better tracing the several stations of the ships, and their route from the one island to the other. To have swelled my journal with a minute account of bearings, tackings, and the like, would neither have been entertaining nor instructive.

What has been here omitted, concerning the geography of these islands, will be found in the narrative of my
last

last voyage*. To that narrative I must also refer†, for such particulars concerning the inhabitants, their manners, and arts, as I had observed then, and about which I saw no reason to change my judgment. At present, I shall confine myself to such interesting particulars, as either were not mentioned in that narrative, or were imperfectly and incorrectly represented there; and to such as may serve to explain some passages in the foregoing account of our transactions with the natives.

It may, indeed, be expected, that, after spending between two and three months amongst them, I should be enabled to clear up every difficulty, and to give a tolerably satisfactory account of their customs, opinions, and institutions, both civil and religious; especially as we had a person on board, who might be supposed qualified to act the part of an interpreter, by understanding their language and ours. But poor Omai was very deficient. For unless the object or thing we wanted to inquire about, was actually before us, we found it difficult to gain a tolerable knowledge of it, from information only, without falling into a hundred mistakes; and to such mistakes Omai was more liable than we were. For, having no curiosity, he never gave himself the trouble to make remarks for himself; and, when he was disposed to explain matters to us, his ideas appeared to be so limited, and, perhaps, so different from ours, that his accounts were often so confused, as to perplex, instead of instructing us. Add to this, that it was very rare that we found, amongst the natives, a person, who united the ability and the inclination to give us the information we wanted; and, we found, that most of them hated to be

---

* Cook's Voyage, Vol. i. p. 211. 213.   † Ibid. p. 213. 225.

troubled

troubled with what they, probably, thought idle questions. Our situation at Tongataboo, where we remained the longest, was, likewise, unfavourable. It was in a part of the country, where there were few inhabitants, except fishers. It was always holiday with our visiters, as well as with those we visited; so that we had but few opportunities of observing, what was really the domestic way of living of the natives. Under these disadvantages, it is not surprizing, that we should not be able to bring away with us satisfactory accounts of many things; but some of us endeavoured to remedy those disadvantages, by diligent observation; and I am indebted to Mr. Anderson, for a considerable share of what follows, in this and in the following chapter. In other matters, I have only expressed, nearly in his words, remarks that coincided with mine; but what relates to the religion and language of these people, is entirely his own.

The natives of the Friendly Islands seldom exceed the common stature (though we have measured some, who were above six feet); but are very strong, and well made; especially as to their limbs. They are generally broad about the shoulders; and though the muscular disposition of the men, which seems a consequence of much action, rather conveys the appearance of strength than of beauty, there are several to be seen, who are really handsome. Their features are very various; insomuch, that it is scarcely possible to fix on any general likeness, by which to characterize them, unless it be a fullness at the point of the nose, which is very common. But, on the other hand, we met with hundreds of truly European faces, and many genuine Roman noses, amongst them. Their eyes and teeth are good; but the last neither so remarkably white, nor so well

well set as is often found amongst Indian nations; though, to balance that, few of them have any uncommon thickness about the lips, a defect as frequent as the other perfection.

The women are not so much distinguished from the men by their features as by their general form, which is, for the most part, destitute of that strong fleshy firmness that appears in the latter. Though the features of some are so delicate, as not only to be a true index of their sex, but to lay claim to a considerable share of beauty and expression, the rule is, by no means, so general as in many other countries. But, at the same time, this is frequently the most exceptionable part; for the bodies and limbs of most of the females are well proportioned; and some, absolutely, perfect models of a beautiful figure. But the most remarkable distinction in the women, is the uncommon smallness and delicacy of their fingers, which may be put in competition with the finest in Europe.

The general colour is a cast deeper than the copper brown; but several of the men and women have a true olive complexion; and some of the last are even a great deal fairer; which is probably the effect of being less exposed to the sun; as a tendency to corpulence, in a few of the principal people, seems to be the consequence of a more indolent life. It is also amongst the last, that a soft clear skin is most frequently observed. Amongst the bulk of the people, the skin is, more commonly, of a dull hue, with some degree of roughness, especially the parts that are not covered; which, perhaps, may be occasioned by some cutaneous disease. We saw a man and boy at Hapaee, and a child at Annamooka, perfectly white. Such have been found amongst all
black

black nations; but, I apprehend, that their colour is rather a diseafe, than a natural phænomenon.

There are, nevertheless, upon the whole, few natural defects or deformities to be found amongst them; though we saw two or three with their feet bent inward; and some afflicted with a sort of blindness, occasioned by a diseafe of the *cornea*. Neither are they exempt from some other diseases. The most common of which is the tetter, or ringworm, that seems to affect almost one half of them, and leaves whitish serpentine marks, every where, behind it. But this is of less consequence than another diseafe, which is very frequent, and appears on every part of the body, in large broad ulcers with thick white edges, discharging a thin, clear matter; some of which had a very virulent appearance, particularly those on the face, which were shocking to look at. And yet we met with some who seemed to be cured of it, and others in a fair way of being cured; but this was not effected without the lofs of the nose, or of the best part of it. As we know for a certainty * (and the fact is acknowledged by themselves), that the people of these islands were subject to this loathsome diseafe before the English first visited them, notwithstanding the similarity of symptoms, it cannot be the effect of the venereal contagion; unless we adopt a supposition, which I could wish had sufficient foundation in truth, that the venereal disorder was not introduced here from Europe, by our ships in 1773. It, assuredly, was now found to exist amongst them; for we had not been long there, before some of our people received

* See Vol. ii. p. 20. of Captain Cook's Voyage, where he gives a particular account of meeting with a person afflicted with this diseafe, at Annamooka, on his landing there in 1773.

the

the infection; and I had the mortification to learn from thence, that all the care I took, when I first visited these islands, to prevent this dreadful disease from being communicated to their inhabitants, had proved ineffectual. What is extraordinary, they do not seem to regard it much; and as we saw few signs of its destroying effects, probably the climate, and the way of living of these people, greatly abate its virulence. There are two other diseases frequent amongst them; one of which is an indolent firm swelling, which affects the legs and arms, and increases them to an extraordinary size in their whole length. The other is a tumour of the same sort, in the testicles, which sometimes exceed the size of the two fists. But, in other respects, they may be considered as uncommonly healthy; not a single person having been seen, during our stay, confined to the house, by sickness of any kind. On the contrary, their strength and activity are, every way, answerable to their muscular appearance; and they exert both, in their usual employment, and in their diversions, in such a manner, that there can be no doubt of their being, as yet, little debilitated by the numerous diseases that are the consequence of indolence, and an unnatural method of life.

The graceful air and firm step with which these people walk, are not the least obvious proof of their personal accomplishments. They consider this as a thing so natural, or so necessary to be acquired, that nothing used to excite their laughter sooner, than to see us frequently stumbling upon the roots of trees, or other inequalities of the ground.

Their countenances very remarkably express the abundant mildness, or good nature, which they possess; and are entirely free from that savage keenness which marks nations in a barbarous state. One would, indeed, be apt to fancy, that they had been bred up under the severest restrictions, to acquire an aspect so settled, and such a command of their passions, as well as steadiness in conduct. But they are, at the same time, frank, cheerful, and good-humoured; though, sometimes, in the presence of their Chiefs, they put on a degree of gravity, and such a serious air as becomes stiff and awkward, and has an appearance of reserve.

Their peaceable disposition is sufficiently evinced, from the friendly reception all strangers have met with, who have visited them. Instead of offering to attack them openly, or clandestinely, as has been the case with most of the inhabitants of these seas, they have never appeared, in the smallest degree, hostile; but, on the contrary, like the most civilized people, have courted an intercourse with their visiters, by bartering, which is the only medium that unites all nations in a sort of friendship. They understand barter (which they call *fakkatoo*) so perfectly, that, at first, we imagined they might have acquired this knowledge of it by commercial intercourse with the neighbouring islands; but we were afterward assured, that they had little or no traffic, except with Feejee, from which they get the red feathers, and the few other articles, mentioned before. Perhaps, no nation in the world traffic with more honesty and less distrust. We could always safely permit them to examine our goods, and to hand them about, one to another; and they put the same confidence in us. If either party repented of the bargain, the goods were re-exchanged with mutual consent and good-humour. Upon the whole, they seem possessed of many of the most excellent qualities that adorn the human mind; such as industry, ingenuity, perseverance, affability,

and,

and, perhaps, other virtues which our short stay with them might prevent our observing.

The only defect sullying their character, that we know of, is a propensity to thieving; to which, we found, those of all ages, and both sexes, addicted; and to an uncommon degree. It should, however, be considered, that this exceptionable part of their conduct seemed to exist merely with respect to us; for, in their general intercourse with one another, I had reason to be of opinion, that thefts do not happen more frequently (perhaps less so) than in other countries, the dishonest practices of whose worthless individuals are not supposed to authorize any indiscriminate censure on the whole body of the people. Great allowances should be made for the foibles of these poor natives of the Pacific Ocean, whose minds we overpowered with the glare of objects, equally new to them, as they were captivating. Stealing, amongst the civilized and enlightened nations of the world, may well be considered as denoting a character deeply stained with moral turpitude, with avarice unrestrained by the known rules of right, and with profligacy producing extreme indigence, and neglecting the means of relieving it. But at the Friendly and other islands which we visited, the thefts, so frequently committed by the natives, of what we had brought along with us, may be fairly traced to less culpable motives. They seemed to arise, solely, from an intense curiosity or desire to possess something which they had not been accustomed to before, and belonging to a sort of people so different from themselves. And, perhaps, if it were possible, that a set of beings, seemingly as superior in our judgment, as we are in theirs, should appear amongst us, it might be doubted, whether our natural regard to justice would be able to restrain

1777.
July.

strain many from falling into the same error. That I have assigned the true motive for their propensity to this practice, appears from their stealing every thing indiscriminately at first sight, before they could have the least conception of converting their prize to any one useful purpose. But, I believe, with us, no person would forfeit his reputation, or expose himself to punishment, without knowing, before hand, how to employ the stolen goods. Upon the whole, the pilfering disposition of these islanders, though certainly disagreeable and troublesome to strangers, was the means of affording us some information as to the quickness of their intellects. For their small thefts were committed with much dexterity; and those of greater consequence with a plan or scheme suited to the importance of the objects. An extraordinary instance of the last sort, their attempts to carry away one of the Discovery's anchors, at mid-day, has been already related.

Their hair is, in general, straight, thick, and strong; though a few have it bushy or frizzled. The natural colour, I believe, almost without exception, is black; but the greatest part of the men, and some of the women, have it stained of a brown, or purple colour; and a few of an orange cast. The first colour is produced by applying a sort of plaster of burnt coral, mixed with water; the second, by the raspings of a reddish wood, which is made up with water into a poultice, and laid over the hair; and the third is, I believe, the effect of *turmeric* root.

When I first visited these islands, I thought it had been an universal custom for both men and women to wear the hair short; but, during our present longer stay, we saw a great many exceptions. Indeed, they are so whimsical in their fa-

shions

fhions of wearing it, that it is hard to tell which is most in vogue. Some have it cut off one fide of the head, while that on the other fide remains long; fome have only a portion of it cut fhort, or, perhaps, fhaved; others have it entirely cut off, except a fingle lock, which is left commonly on one fide; or, it is fuffered to grow to its full length, without any of thefe mutilations. The women, in general, wear it fhort. The men have their beards cut fhort; and both men and women ftrip the hair from their armpits. The operation by which this is performed has been already defcribed. The men are ftained from about the middle of the belly, to about half way down the thighs, with a deep blue colour. This is done with a flat bone inftrument, cut full of fine teeth, which, being dipped in the ftaining mixture, prepared from the juice of the *dooe dooe*, is ftruck into the fkin with a bit of ftick; and, by that means, indelible marks are made. In this manner they trace lines and figures, which, in fome, are very elegant, both from the variety, and from the arrangement. The women have only a few fmall lines or fpots, thus imprinted, on the infide of their hands. Their kings, as a mark of diftinction, are exempted from this cuftom, as alfo from inflicting on themfelves any of thofe bloody marks of mourning, which fhall be mentioned in another place.

The men are all circumcifed, or rather fupercifed; as the operation confifts in cutting off only a fmall piece of the forefkin, at the upper part; which, by that means, is rendered incapable, ever after, of covering the *glans*. This is all they aim at; as they fay, the operation is practifed from a notion of cleanlinefs.

The drefs of both men and women is the fame; and confifts of a piece of cloth or matting (but moftly the former),

former), about two yards wide, and two and a half long; at least, so long as to go once and a half round the waist, to which it is confined by a girdle or cord. It is double before, and hangs down, like a petticoat, as low as the middle of the leg. The upper part of the garment, above the girdle, is plaited into several folds; so that, when unfolded, there is cloth sufficient to draw up and wrap round the shoulders; which is very seldom done. This, as to form, is the general dress; but large pieces of cloth, and fine matting, are worn only by the superior people. The inferior sort are satisfied with small pieces; and, very often, wear nothing but a covering made of leaves of plants, or the *maro*, which is a narrow piece of cloth, or matting, like a sash. This they pass between the thighs, and wrap round the waist; but the use of it is chiefly confined to the men. In their great *haivas*, or entertainments, they have various dresses made for the purpose; but the form is always the same; and the richest dresses are covered, more or less, with red feathers. On what particular occasion their Chiefs wear their large red feather-caps, I could not learn. Both men and women sometimes shade their faces from the sun with little bonnets, made of various materials.

As the clothing, so are the ornaments, worn by those of both sexes, the same. The most common of these are necklaces, made of the fruit of the *pandanus*, and various sweet-smelling flowers, which go under the general name of *tabulla*. Others are composed of small shells, the wing and leg-bones of birds, shark's teeth, and other things; all which hang loose upon the breast. In the same manner, they often wear a mother-of-pearl shell, neatly polished, or a ring of the same substance carved, on the upper part of of the arm; rings of tortoise-shell on the fingers; and a number of these, joined together, as bracelets on the wrists.

1777.
July.

The lobes of the ears (though, most frequently, only one) are perforated with two holes, in which they wear cylindrical bits of ivory, about three inches long, introduced at one hole, and brought out of the other; or bits of reed of the same size, filled with a yellow pigment. This seems to be a fine powder of *turmeric*, with which the women rub themselves all over, in the same manner as our ladies use their dry rouge upon the cheeks.

Nothing appears to give them greater pleasure than personal cleanliness; to produce which, they frequently bathe in the ponds, which seem to serve no other purpose*. Though the water in most of them stinks intolerably, they prefer them to the sea; and they are so sensible that salt water hurts their skin, that, when necessity obliges them to bathe in the sea, they commonly have some cocoa-nut shells, filled with fresh water, poured over them, to wash it off. They are immoderately fond of cocoa-nut oil for the same reason; a great quantity of which they not only pour upon their head and shoulders, but rub the body all over, briskly, with a smaller quantity. And none but those who have seen this practice, can easily conceive how the appearance of the skin is improved by it. This oil, however, is not to be procured by every one; and the inferior sort of people, doubtless, appear less smooth for want of it.

---

* So at the Caroline Islands. "Ils sont accoutumés a se baigner trois fois, le jour, le matin, à midi, & sur le soir."
Lettres Edifiantes & Curieuses, Tom. xv. p. 314.

CHAP.

CHAP. XI.

*Employments of the Women, at the Friendly Islands.—
Of the Men.—Agriculture.—Construction of their
Houses.—Their working Tools.—Cordage, and fishing
Implements.—Musical Instruments.—Weapons.—Food,
and Cookery.—Amusements.—Marriage.—Mourning
Ceremonies for the Dead.—Their Divinities.—Notions
about the Soul, and a future State.—Their Places of
Worship.—Government.—Manner of paying Obeisance
to the King.—Account of the Royal Family.—Remarks
on their Language, and a Specimen of it.—Nautical,
and other Observations.*

1777.
July.

THEIR domestic life is of that middle kind, neither so laborious as to be disagreeable, nor so vacant as to suffer them to degenerate into indolence. Nature has done so much for their country, that the first can hardly occur, and their disposition seems to be a pretty good bar to the last. By this happy combination of circumstances, their necessary labour seems to yield, in its turn, to their recreations, in such a manner, that the latter are never interrupted by the thoughts of being obliged to recur to the former, till satiety makes them wish for such a transition.

The employment of the women is of the easy kind, and, for the most part, such as may be executed in the house. The manufacturing their cloth, is wholly consigned to their care.

care. Having already defcribed the procefs, I fhall only add, that they have this cloth of different degrees of finenefs. The coarfer fort, of which they make very large pieces, does not receive the impreffion of any pattern. Of the finer fort, they have fome that is ftriped, and chequered, and of other patterns differently coloured. But how thefe colours are laid on, I cannot fay, as I never faw any of this fort made. The cloth, in general, will refift water, for fome time; but that which has the ftrongeft glaze will refift longeft.

The manufacture next in confequence, and alfo within the department of the women, is that of their mats, which excel every thing I have feen at any other place, both as to their texture and their beauty. In particular, many of them are fo fuperior to thofe made at Otaheite, that they are not a bad article to carry thither, by way of trade. Of thefe mats, they have feven or eight different forts, for the purpofes of wearing or fleeping upon; and many are merely ornamental. The laft are chiefly made from the tough, membraneous part of the ftock of the plantain tree; thofe that they wear, from the *pandanus*, cultivated for that purpofe, and never fuffered to fhoot into a trunk; and the coarfer fort, which they fleep upon, from a plant called *evarra*. There are many other articles of lefs note, that employ the fpare time of their females; as combs, of which they make vaft numbers; and little bafkets made of the fame fubftance as the mats, and others of the fibrous cocoanut hufk, either plain, or interwoven with fmall beads; but all, finifhed with fuch neatnefs and tafte in the difpofition of the various parts, that a ftranger cannot help admiring their affiduity and dexterity.

The province allotted to the men is, as might be expected, far more laborious and extensive than that of the women. Agriculture, architecture, boat-building, fishing, and other things that relate to navigation, are the objects of their care*. Cultivated roots and fruits being their principal support, this requires their constant attention to agriculture, which they pursue very diligently, and seem to have brought almost to as great perfection as circumstances will permit. The large extent of the plantain fields has been taken notice of already; and the same may be said of the yams; these two together, being, at least, as ten to one, with respect to all the other articles. In planting both these, they dig small holes for their reception, and, afterward, root up the surrounding grass, which, in this hot country, is quickly deprived of its vegetating power, and, soon rotting, becomes a good manure. The instruments they use for this purpose, which they call *huo*, are nothing more than pickets or stakes of different lengths, according to the depth they have to dig. These are flattened and sharpened to an edge at one end; and the largest have a short piece fixed transversely, for pressing it into the ground with the foot. With these, though they are not more than from two to four inches broad, they dig and plant ground of many acres in extent. In planting the plantains and yams, they observe so much exactness, that, whichever way you look, the rows present themselves regular and complete.

* How remarkably does Captain Cook's account of the employments of the women and men here, agree with Father Cantova's, of the Caroline Islanders?—" La " principale occupation des hommes, est de construire des barques, de pecher, & de " cultiver la terre. L'affaire des femmes est de faire la cuisine, & de mettre en " œuvre un espece de plante sauvage, &un arbre,—pour en faire de la toile."
Lettres Edifiantes & Curieuses, Tom. xv. p. 313.

The

The cocoa-nut and bread-fruit trees are scattered about, without any order, and seem to give them no trouble, after they have attained a certain height. The same may be said of another large tree, which produces great numbers of a large, roundish, compressed nut, called *eefee*; and of a smaller tree, that bears a rounded oval nut, two inches long, with two or three triangular kernels, tough and insipid, called *mabba*, most frequently planted near their houses.

The *tappe* is, commonly, regularly planted, and in pretty large spots; but the *mawbaba* is interspersed amongst other things, as the *jeejee* and *yams* are; the last of which, I have frequently seen, in the interspaces of the plantain trees, at their common distance. Sugar-cane is commonly in small spots, crowded closely together; and the mulberry, of which the cloth is made, though without order, has sufficient room allowed for it, and is kept very clean. The only other plant, that they cultivate for their manufactures, is the *pandanus*; which is generally planted in a row, close together, at the sides of the other fields; and they consider it as a thing so distinct in this state, that they have a different name for it; which shews, that they are very sensible of the great changes brought about by cultivation.

It is remarkable, that these people, who, in many things, shew much taste and ingenuity, should shew little of either in building their houses; though the defect is rather in the design, than in the execution. Those of the lower people are poor huts, scarcely sufficient to defend them from the weather, and very small. Those of the better sort, are larger and more comfortable; but not what one might expect. The dimensions of one of a middling size, are about thirty feet long, twenty broad, and twelve high. Their house is, properly speaking, a thatched roof or shed, supported

ported by posts and rafters, disposed in a very judicious manner. The floor is raised with earth smoothed, and covered with strong, thick matting, and kept very clean. The most of them are closed on the weather side (and some more than two-thirds round), with strong mats, or with branches of the cocoa-nut tree, plaited or woven into each other. These they fix up edgewise, reaching from the eaves to the ground; and thus they answer the purpose of a wall. A thick, strong mat, about two and one half or three feet broad, bent into the form of a semicircle, and set upon its edge, with the ends touching the side of the house, in shape resembling the fender of a fire hearth, incloses a space for the master and mistress of the family to sleep in. The lady, indeed, spends most of her time, during the day, within it. The rest of the family sleep upon the floor, wherever they please to lie down; the unmarried men and women apart from each other. Or, if the family be large, there are small huts adjoining, to which the servants retire in the night; so that privacy is as much observed here, as one could expect. They have mats made on purpose for sleeping on; and the clothes that they wear in the day, serve for their covering in the night. Their whole furniture consists of a bowl or two, in which they make *kava*; a few gourds; cocoa-nut shells; some small wooden stools, which serve them for pillows; and, perhaps, a large stool for the Chief, or Master, of the family to sit upon.

The only probable reason I can assign for their neglect of ornamental architecture, in the construction of their houses, is their being fond of living much in the open air. Indeed, they seem to consider their houses, within which they seldom eat, as of little use but to sleep in, and to retire to in bad weather. And the lower sort of people, who spend a great part

part of their time in close attendance upon the Chiefs, can have little use for their own houses, but in the last case.

They make amends for the defects of their houses, by their great attention to, and dexterity in, naval architecture, if I may be allowed to give it that name. But I refer to the narrative of my last voyage, for an account of their canoes, and their manner of building and navigating them.*

The only tools which they use, to construct these boats, are hatchets, or rather thick adzes, of a smooth black stone that abounds at Toofoa; augres, made of shark's teeth, fixed on small handles; and rasps, of a rough skin of a fish, fastened on flat pieces of wood, thinner on one side, which also have handles. The labour and time employed in finishing their canoes, which are the most perfect of their mechanical productions, will account for their being very careful of them. For they are built and preserved under sheds; or they cover the decked part of them with cocoa-leaves, when they are hauled on shore, to prevent their being hurt by the sun.

The same tools are all they have for other works; if we except different shells, which they use as knives. But there are few of their productions that require these, unless it be some of their weapons; the other articles being chiefly their fishing materials, and cordage.

The cordage is made from the fibres of the cocoa-nut husk, which, though not more than nine or ten inches long, they plait, about the size of a quill, or less, to any length

---

* Cook's Voyage, Vol. i. p. 215, 216. The reader, by comparing that account, with what Cantova says of the islanders of the Caroline Islands, will find, in this instance, also, the greatest similarity. See *Lettres Edifiantes & Curieuses*, p. 286.

that

1777.
July.

that they pleafe, and roll it up in balls; from which the larger ropes are made, by twifting feveral of thefe together. The lines, that they fifh with, are as ftrong and even as the beft cord we make, refembling it almoft in every refpect. Their other fifhing implements, are large and fmall hooks. The laft are compofed entirely of pearl-fhell; but the firft are only covered with it on the back; and the points of both, commonly, of tortoife-fhell; thofe of the fmall being plain, and the others barbed. With the large ones, they catch bonnetos and albicores, by putting them to a bamboo rod, twelve or fourteen feet long, with a line of the fame length, which refts in a notch of a piece of wood, fixed in the ftern of the canoe for that purpofe, and is dragged on the furface of the fea, as fhe rowes along, without any other bait than a tuft of flaxy ftuff near the point. They have alfo great numbers of pretty fmall feines, fome of which are of a very delicate texture. Thefe they ufe to catch fifh with, in the holes on the reefs, when the tide ebbs.

The other manual employments, confift chiefly in making mufical reeds, flutes, warlike weapons, and ftools, or rather pillows, to fleep on. The reeds have eight, nine, or ten pieces placed parallel to each other, but not in any regular progreffion; having the longeft, fometimes, in the middle, and feveral of the fame length; fo that I have feen none with more than fix notes; and they feem incapable of playing any mufic on them, that is diftinguifhable by our ears*. The flutes are a joint of bamboo, clofe at both ends, with a hole near each, and four others; two of which, and one of the firft only, are ufed in playing. They apply the thumb

* See a drawing of one of thefe mufical reeds, in Captain Cook's Voyage, Vol. I. p. 221. Plate XXI.

of the left hand, to close the left nostril, and blow into the hole at one end, with the other. The middle finger of the left hand is applied to the first hole on the left, and the forefinger of the right, to the lowest hole on that side. In this manner, though the notes are only three, they produce a pleasing, yet simple, music, which they vary much more than one would think possible, with so imperfect an instrument. Their being accustomed to a music which consists of so few notes, is, perhaps, the reason why they do not seem to relish any of ours, which is so complex. But they can taste what is more deficient than their own; for, we observed, that they used to be well pleased with hearing the chant of our two young New Zealanders, which consisted rather in mere strength, than in melody of expression.

The weapons, which they make, are clubs of different sorts (in the ornamenting of which they spend much time), spears, and darts. They have also bows and arrows; but these seemed to be designed only for amusement, such as shooting at birds, and not for military purposes. The stools are about two feet long, but only four or five inches high, and near four broad, bending downward in the middle, with four strong legs, and circular feet; the whole made of one piece of black or brown wood, neatly polished, and sometimes inlaid with bits of ivory. They also inlay the handles of fly-flaps with ivory, after being neatly carved; and they shape bones into small figures of men, birds, and other things, which must be very difficult, as their carving instrument is only a shark's tooth.

Yams, plantains, and cocoa nuts, compose the greatest part of their vegetable diet. Of their animal food, the chief articles are hogs, fowls, fish, and all sorts of shell-fish; but the lower people eat rats. The two first vegetable articles, with

with bread-fruit, are, what may be called, the basis of their food, at different times of the year, with fish and shell-fish; for hogs, fowls, and turtle, seem only to be occasional dainties, reserved for their Chiefs. The intervals between the seasons of these vegetable productions must be, sometimes, considerable, as they prepare a sort of artificial bread from plantains, which they put under ground before ripe, and suffer them to remain, till they ferment, when they are taken out, and made up into small balls; but so sour and indifferent, that they often said our bread was preferable, though somewhat musty.

Their food is, generally, dressed by baking, in the same manner as at Otaheite; and they have the art of making, from different kinds of fruit, several dishes, which most of us esteemed very good. I never saw them make use of any kind of sauce; nor drink any thing at their meals but water, or the juice of the cocoa-nut; for the *ava* is only their morning draught. I cannot say, that they are cleanly either in their cookery, or manner of eating. The generality of them will lay their victuals upon the first leaf they meet with, however dirty it may be; but when food is served up to the Chiefs, it is, commonly, laid upon green plantain leaves. When the king made a meal, he was, for the most part, attended upon by three or four persons. One cut large pieces of the joint, or of the fish; another divided it into mouthfuls; and others stood by with cocoa-nuts, and whatever else he might want. I never saw a large company sit down to what we should call a sociable meal, by eating from the same dish. The food, be what it will, is always divided into portions, each to serve a certain number; these portions are again subdivided; so that one seldom sees above two or three persons eating together. The women are

are not excluded from eating with the men; but there are
certain ranks or orders amongst them, that can neither eat
nor drink together. This distinction begins with the king;
but where it ends, I cannot say.

They seem to have no set time for meals; though it
should be observed, that, during our stay amongst them,
their domestic œconomy was much disturbed by their constant attention to us. As far as we could remark, those of
the superior rank, only drink *kava* in the forenoon, and the
others eat, perhaps, a bit of yam; but we commonly saw all
of them eat something in the afternoon. It is probable that
the practice of making a meal in the night is pretty common,
and their rest being thus interrupted, they frequently sleep
in the day. They go to bed as soon as it is dark, and rise
with the dawn in the morning *.

They are very fond of associating together; so that it is
common to find several houses empty, and the owners of
them convened in some other one, or, rather, upon a convenient spot in the neighbourhood, where they recreate
themselves by conversing, and other amusements. Their
private diversions are chiefly singing, dancing, and music
performed by the women. When two or three women sing
in concert, and snap their fingers, it is called *oobai*; but
when there is a greater number, they divide into several
parties, each of which sings on a different key, which makes
a very agreeable music, and is called *brevo*, or *baiva*. In the
same manner, they vary the music of their flutes, by playing on those of a different size; but their dancing is much
the same as when they perform publickly. The dancing

* Cantova says of his Islanders, "Ils prennent leur repas dès que le soleil est couché,
" & ils se levent avec l'aurore." *Lettres Édifiantes & Curieuses*, Tom. xv. p. 314.

A VOYAGE TO

1777.
July.

of the men (if it is to be called dancing), although it does not consist much in moving the feet, as we do, has a thousand different motions with the hands, to which we are entire strangers; and they are performed with an ease and grace which are not to be described, nor even conceived, but by those who have seen them. But I need add nothing to what has been already said on this subject, in the account of the incidents that happened during our stay at the islands*.

Whether their marriages be made lasting by any kind of solemn contract, we could not determine with precision; but

---

* If, to the copious descriptions that occur in the preceding pages, of the particular entertainments exhibited in Hapaee and Tongataboo, we add the general view of the usual amusements of the inhabitants of these islands, contained in this paragraph, and compare it with the quotation from the Jesuit's Letters, in a former note (p. 255.), we shall be still more forcibly struck with the reasonableness of tracing such singularly resembling customs to one common source. The argument, in confirmation of this, drawn from identity of language, has been already illustrated, by observing the remarkable coincidence of the name, by which the Chiefs at the Caroline Islands, and those at Hamoa, one of the Friendly ones, are distinguished. But the argument does not rest on a single instance, though that happens to be a very striking one. Another of the very few specimens of the dialect of the North Pacific Islanders, preferred by father Cantova, furnishes an additional proof. Immediately after the passage above referred to, he proceeds thus: " Ce divertissement s'appelle, en leur " langue, *tanger ifaifil*; qui veut dire, la plainte des femmes." *Lettres Édifiantes & Curieuses*, Tom. xv. p. 315. Now it is very remarkable, that we learn from Mr. Anderson's collection of words, which will appear in this chapter, that *la plainte des femmes*, or, in English, *the mournful fong of the women*, which the inhabitants of the Caroline Islands express in their language *tanger ifaifil*, would, by those of Tongataboo, be expressed *tanger vefoine*.

If any one should still doubt, in spite of this evidence, it may be recommended to his consideration, that long separation, and other causes, have introduced greater variations in the mode of pronouncing these two words, at places confessedly inhabited by the same race, than subsists in the specimen just given. It appears, from Mr. Anderson's vocabulary, printed in Captain Cook's second voyage, that what is pronounced *tangee* at the Friendly Islands, is *taa* at Otaheite; and the *vefoine* of the former, is the *wahine* of the latter.

it

it is certain, that the bulk of the people satisfied themselves with one wife. The Chiefs, however, have, commonly, several women *; though some of us were of opinion, that there was only one that was looked upon as the mistress of the family.

As female chastity, at first sight, seemed to be held in no great estimation, we expected to have found frequent breaches of their conjugal fidelity; but we did them great injustice. I do not know that a single instance happened during our whole stay †. Neither are those of the better sort, that are unmarried, more free of their favours. It is true, there was no want of those of a different character; and, perhaps, such are more frequently met with here, in proportion to the number of people, than in many other countries. But it appeared to me, that the most, if not all of them, were of the lowest class; and such of them as permitted familiarities to our people, were prostitutes by profession.

Nothing can be a greater proof of the humanity of these people, than the concern they shew for the dead ‡. To use a common expression, their mourning is not in words but deeds. For, besides the *touge* mentioned before, and burnt circles and scars, they beat the teeth with stones, strike a shark's tooth into the head until the blood flows in streams, and thrust spears into the inner part of the thigh, into their

---

* Cantova says of his Caroline islanders, " La pluralité des femmes est non " seulement permise à tous ces insulaires, elle est encore une marque d'honneur & " de distinction. Le Tamole de l'isle d'Huogoleu en a neuf."
       Lettres Edifiantes & Curieuses, Tom. xv. p. 310.
† At the Caroline Islands, " Ils ont horreur de l'adultere, comme d'une grand " peché." *Ibid.* Tom. xv. p. 310.
‡ How the inhabitants of the Caroline Islands express their grief on such occasions, may be seen, *Ibid.* Tom. xv. p. 308.

sides below the arm-pits, and through the cheeks into the mouth. All these operations convey an idea of such rigorous discipline, as must require either an uncommon degree of affection, or the grossest superstition, to exact. I will not say, that the last has no share in it; for, sometimes, it is so universal, that many could not have any knowledge of the person for whom the concern is expressed. Thus we saw the people of Tongataboo mourning the death of a Chief at Vavaoo; and other similar instances occurred during our stay. It should be observed, however, that the more painful operations are only practised on account of the death of those most nearly connected with the mourners. When a person dies, he is buried, after being wrapped up in mats and cloth, much after our manner. The Chiefs seem to have the *fiatookas* appropriated to them as their burial-places; but the common people are interred in no particular spot*. What part of the mourning ceremony follows, immediately after, is uncertain; but, that there is something besides the general one, which is continued for a considerable length of time, we could infer, from being informed, that the funeral of Mareewagee's wife, as mentioned before, was to be attended with ceremonies that were to last five days; and in which all the principal people were to commemorate her.

Their long and general mourning, proves that they consider death as a very great evil. And this is confirmed by a

---

* Cantova's account of the practice of the Caroline Islands is as follows: "Lors-qu'il meurt quelque personne d'un rang distingué, ou qui leur est chere par d'autres endroits, ses obseques se font avec pompe. Il y en a qui renferment le corps du défunct dans un petit edifice de pierre, qu'ils gardent au-dedans de leur maisons. D'autres les enterrent loin de leurs habitations."

Lettres Edifiantes & Curieuses, Tom. xv. p. 308, 309.

very

very odd cuſtom which they practiſe to avert it. When I firſt viſited theſe Iſlands, during my laſt voyage, I obſerved that many of the inhabitants had one or both of their little fingers cut off; and we could not then receive any ſatisfactory account of the reaſon of this mutilation *. But we now learned, that this operation is performed when they labour under ſome grievous diſeaſe, and think themſelves in danger of dying. They ſuppoſe, that the Deity will accept of the little finger, as a ſort of ſacrifice efficacious enough to procure the recovery of their health. They cut it off with one of their ſtone hatchets. There was ſcarcely one in ten of them whom we did not find thus mutilated, in one or both hands; which has a diſagreeable effect, eſpecially as they ſometimes cut ſo cloſe, that they encroach upon the bone of the hand which joins to the amputated finger †.

From the rigid ſeverity with which ſome of theſe mourning and religious ceremonies are executed, one would expect to find, that they meant thereby to ſecure to themſelves felicity beyond the grave; but their principal object relates to things merely temporal. For they ſeem to have little conception of future puniſhment for faults committed in this life. They believe, however, that they are juſtly puniſhed upon earth; and, conſequently, uſe every method to render their divinities propitious. The Supreme Author of moſt things they call *Kallafootonga*; who, they ſay, is a female, reſiding in the ſky, and directing the thunder, wind, rain; and, in general, all the changes of weather. They

* See Cook's Voyage, Vol. i. p. 222.
† It may be proper to mention here, on the authority of Captain King, that it is common for the inferior people to cut off a joint of their little finger, on account of the ſickneſs of the Chiefs to whom they belong.

believe,

believe, that when she is angry with them, the productions of the earth are blasted; that many things are destroyed by lightning; and that they themselves are afflicted with sickness and death, as well as their hogs and other animals. When this anger abates, they suppose that every thing is restored to its natural order; and it should seem, that they have a great reliance on the efficacy of their endeavours to appease their offended divinity. They also admit a plurality of deities, though all inferior to *Kollefeotonga*. Amongst them, they mention *Toofooa-bolotoo*, God of the clouds and fog; *Talletcboo*, and some others, residing in the heavens. The first in rank and power, who has the government of the sea, and its productions, is called *Futtafaihe*, or, as it was sometimes pronounced, *Foot-fooa*; who, they say, is a male, and has for his wife *Fykava kajeea*: and here, as in heaven, there are several inferior potentates, such as *Vahea fonooa*, *Tarreava*, *Mattaba*, *Evaroo*, and others. The same religious system, however, does not extend all over the cluster of the Friendly Isles; for the supreme God of *Hapaee*, for instance, is called *Alo Alo*; and other isles have two or three, of different names. But their notions of the power, and other attributes of these beings, are so very absurd, that they suppose they have no farther concern with them after death.

They have, however, very proper sentiments about the immateriality and the immortality of the soul. They call it life, the living principle, or, what is more agreeable to their notions of it, an *Otooa*; that is, a divinity, or invisible being. They say, that, immediately upon death, the souls of their Chiefs separate from their bodies, and go to a place called *Boolootoo*; the Chief, or god, of which, is *Goolebo*. This *Goolebo* seems to be a personification of death; for they used to say to us, " You, and the men of Feejee (by this junc-

" tion, meaning to pay a compliment, expressive of their
" confession of our superiority over themselves), are also
" subject to the power and dominion of G*shba*." His
country, the general receptacle of the dead, according to
their mythology, was never seen by any person; and yet,
it seems, they know that it lies to the Westward of Feejee;
and that they who are once transported thither, live for
ever; or, to use their own expression, are not subject to
death again; but feast upon all the favourite products of
their own country, with which this everlasting abode is
supposed to abound. As to the souls of the lower sort of
people, they undergo a sort of transmigration; or, as they
say, are eat up by a bird called *loata*, which walks upon
their graves for that purpose.

I think I may venture to assert, that they do not worship
any thing that is the work of their own hands, or any visible part of the creation. They do not make offerings of
hogs, dogs, and fruit, as at Otaheite, unless it be emblematically; for their *morais* were perfectly free from every
thing of the kind. But that they offer real human sacrifices,
is, with me, beyond a doubt. Their *morais*, or *fiatookas* (for
they are called by both names, but mostly by the latter),
are, as at Otaheite, and many other parts of the world, bu-
rying-grounds, and places of worship; though some of
them seemed to be only appropriated to the first purpose;
but these were small, and, in every other respect, inferior
to the others.

Of the nature of their government, we know no more than
the general outline. A subordination is established among
them, that resembles the feudal system of our progenitors
in Europe. But of its subdivisions, of the constituent parts,
and

and in what manner they are connected, so as to form a body politic, I confess myself totally ignorant. Some of them told us, that the power of the king is unlimited, and that the life and property of the subject is at his disposal. But the few circumstances that fell under our observation, rather contradicted than confirmed the idea of a despotic government. Mareewagee, old Tooboo, and Feenou, acted each like petty sovereigns, and frequently thwarted the measures of the king; of which he often complained. Neither was his court more splendid than those of the two first, who are the most powerful Chiefs in the islands; and, next to them, Feenou, Mareewagee's son, seemed to stand highest in authority. But, however independent on the despotic power of the king the great men may be, we saw instances enough to prove, that the lower order of people have no property, nor safety for their persons, but at the will of the Chiefs to whom they respectively belong.

Tongataboo is divided into many districts; of above thirty of which we learned the names. Each of these has its particular Chief, who decides differences, and distributes justice within his own district. But we could not form any satisfactory judgment about the extent of their power in general, or their mode of proportioning punishments to crimes. Most of these Chiefs have possessions in other islands, from whence they draw supplies. At least, we know this is so with respect to the king, who, at certain established times, receives the product of his distant domains at Tongataboo; which is not only the principal place of his residence, but, seemingly, of all the people of consequence amongst these isles. Its inhabitants, in common conversation, call it the Land of Chiefs; while the subordinate isles are distinguished by the appellation of Lands of Servants.

These

These Chiefs are, by the people, styled not only Lords of the Earth, but of the Sun and Sky; and the king's family assume the name of Futtafaihe, from the God so called, who is probably their tutelary patron, and perhaps their common ancestor. The sovereign's peculiar earthly title is, however, simply *Tooee Tonga*.

There is a decorum observed in the presence of their principal men, and particularly of their king, that is truly admirable. Whenever he sits down, whether it be in an house, or without, all the attendants seat themselves, at the same time, in a semicircle before him; leaving always a convenient space between him and them, into which no one attempts to come, unless he has some particular business. Neither is any one allowed to pass, or sit, behind him, nor even near him, without his order or permission; so that our having been indulged with this privilege, was a significant proof of the great respect that was paid us. When any one wants to speak with the king, he advances and sits down before him; delivers what he has to say in a few words; and, having received his answer, retires again to the circle. But if the king speaks to any one, that person answers from his seat, unless he is to receive some order; in which case he gets up from his place, and sits down before the Chief with his legs across; which is a posture to which they are so much accustomed, that any other mode of sitting is disagreeable to them [*]. To speak to the king standing, would be accounted here as a striking mark of rudeness, as it would be, with us, for one to sit down and put on his hat, when he addresses himself to his superior, and that superior on his feet, and uncovered.

[*] This is peculiar to the men; the women always sitting with both legs thrown a little on one side. We owe this remark to Captain King.

1777.
July.

It does not, indeed, appear, that any of the most civilized nations, have ever exceeded this people, in the great order observed, on all occasions; in ready compliance with the commands of their Chiefs; and in the harmony that subsists throughout all ranks, and unites them, as if they were all one man, informed with, and directed by, the same principle. Such a behaviour is remarkably obvious, whenever it is requisite that their Chiefs should harangue any body of them collected together, which is frequently done. The most profound silence and attention is observed during the harangue, even to a much greater degree than is practised amongst us, on the most interesting and serious deliberations of our most respectable assemblies. And, whatever might have been the subject of the speech delivered, we never saw an instance, when any individual present, shewed signs of his being displeased, or that indicated the least inclination to dispute the declared will of a person who had a right to command. Nay, such is the force of these verbal laws, as I may call them, that I have seen one of their Chiefs express his being astonished, at a person's having acted contrary to such orders; though it appeared, that the poor man could not possibly have been informed, in time, to have observed them *.

Though some of the more potent Chiefs may vie with the king in point of actual possessions, they fall very short in rank, and in certain marks of respect, which the collective body have agreed to pay the monarch. It is a particular privilege annexed to his sovereignty, not to be punctured,

* Cantova gives us the same account of the profound submission of the Caroline Islanders, to the orders of the Tamole. "Ils reçoivent ses ordres avec le plus profond respect. Ses paroles sont autant d'oracles, qu'on revere."
Lettres Edifiantes & Curieuses, Tom. xv. p. 312.

nor circumcifed, as all his fubjects are. Whenever he walks out, every one whom he meets muft fit down till he has paffed. No one is allowed to be over his head; on the contrary, all muft come under his feet; for there cannot be a greater outward mark of fubmiffion, than that which is paid to the fovereign, and other great people of thefe iflands, by their inferiors. The method is this; the perfon who is to pay obeifance, fquats down before the Chief, and bows the head to the fole of his foot; which, when he fits, is fo placed, that it can be eafily come at; and, having tapped, or touched it with the under and upper fide of the fingers of both hands, he rifes up, and retires. It fhould feem, that the king cannot refufe any one who choofes to pay him this homage, which is called *moe mora*; for the common people would frequently take it into their heads to do it when he was walking; and he was always obliged to ftop, and hold up one of his feet behind him, till they had performed the ceremony. This, to a heavy unwieldy man, like Poulaho, muft be attended with fome trouble and pain; and I have, fometimes, feen him make a run, though very unable, to get out of the way, or to reach a place where he might conveniently fit down. The hands, after this application of them to the Chief's feet, are, in fome cafes, rendered ufelefs for a time; for, until they be wafhed, they muft not touch any kind of food. This interdiction, in a country where water is fo fcarce, would feem to be attended with fome inconvenience; but they are never at a lofs for a fuccedaneum; and a piece of any juicy plant, which they can eafily procure immediately, being rubbed upon them, this ferves for the purpofe of purification, as well as wafhing them with water. When the hands are in this ftate,

Vol. I.   3 G   they

they call it *taboo rema*. *Taboo*, in general, signifies forbidden; and *rema* is their word for hand.

When the *taboo* is incurred, by paying obeisance to a great personage, it is thus easily washed off. But, in some other cases, it must necessarily continue for a certain time. We have frequently seen women, who have been *taboo rema*, fed by others. At the expiration of the time, the interdicted person washes herself in one of their baths, which are dirty holes, for the most part, of brackish water. She then waits upon the king, and, after making her obeisance in the usual way, lays hold of his foot, and applies it to her breast, shoulders, and other parts of her body. He then embraces her on each shoulder; after which she retires, purified from her uncleanness. I do not know, that it is always necessary to come to the king for this purpose; though Omai assured me it was. If this be so, it may be one reason why he is, for the most part, travelling from island to island. I saw this ceremony performed, by him, two or three times; and once by Feenou, to one of his own women; but as Omai was not then with me, I could not ask the occasion.

Taboo, as I have before observed, is a word of an extensive signification. Human sacrifices are called *tangata taboo*; and when any thing is forbidden to be eat, or made use of, they say, that it is *taboo*. They tell us, that, if the king should happen to go into a house belonging to a subject, that house would be *taboo*, and could never more be inhabited by the owner; so that, wherever he travels, there are particular houses for his reception. Old Toobou, at this time, presided over the *taboo*; that is, if Omai comprehended the matter rightly, he and his deputies inspected all the produce of the island; taking care that every man should cultivate

tivate and plant his quota; and ordering what should be eat, and what not. By this wife regulation, they effectually guard against a famine; a sufficient quantity of ground is employed in raising provisions; and every article, thus raised, is secured from unnecessary waste.

By another prudent regulation, in their Government, they have an officer over the police; or something like it. This department, when we were amongst them, was administered by Feenou; whose business, we were told, it was, to punish all offenders, whether against the state, or against individuals. He was also Generalissimo, and commanded the warriors, when called out upon service; but, by all accounts, this is very seldom. The king, frequently, took some pains to inform us of Feenou's office; and, among other things, told us, that if he himself should become a bad man, Feenou would kill him. What I understood, by this expression of being a bad man, was, that, if he did not govern according to law, or custom, Feenou would be ordered, by the other great men, or by the people at large, to put him to death. There should seem to be no doubt, that a Sovereign, thus liable to be controuled, and punished for an abuse of power, cannot be called a despotic monarch.

When we consider the number of islands that compose this little state, and the distance at which some of them lie from the seat of Government, attempts to throw off the yoke, and to acquire independency, it should seem, might be apprehended. But they tell us, that this never happens. One reason why they are not thus disturbed, by domestic quarrels, may be this: That all the powerful Chiefs, as we have already mentioned, reside at Tongataboo. They also secure the dependence of the other islands, by the celerity of their operations; for if, at any time, a troublesome and

popular

popular man should start up, in any of them, Feenou, or whoever holds his office, is immediately difpatched thither to kill him. By this means, they crush a rebellion in its very infancy.

The orders, or claffes, amongft their Chiefs, or thofe who call themfelves fuch, feemed to be almoft as numerous as amongft us; but there are few, in comparifon, that are lords of large diftricts of territory; the reft holding their lands under thofe principal barons, as they may be called. I was, indeed, told, that when a man of property dies, every thing he leaves behind him falls to the king; but that it is ufual to give it to the eldeft fon of the deceafed, with an obligation to make a provifion, out of it, for the reft of the children. It is not the cuftom here, as at Otaheite, for the fon, the moment he is born, to take from the father the homage and title; but he fucceeds to them, at his deceafe; fo that their form of government is not only monarchical, but hereditary.

The order of fucceffion to the crown, has not been of late interrupted; for we know, from a particular circumftance, that the Futtafaihes (Poulaho being only an addition, to dif- tinguifh the king from the reft of his family) have reigned, in a direct line, for, at leaft, one hundred and thirty-five years. Upon inquiring, whether any account had been preferved amongft them, of the arrival of Tafman's fhips, we found, that this hiftory had been handed down to them, from their anceftors, with an accuracy which marks, that oral tradition may fometimes be depended upon. For they defcribed the two fhips, as refembling ours; mentioning the place where they had anchored; their having ftaid but a few days; and their moving from that ftation to Annamooka. And, by way of informing us how long ago this had

had happened, they told us the name of the Futtafaihe who was then king, and of those who had succeeded, down to Poulaho, who is the fifth since that period; the first being an old man, at the time of the arrival of the ships.

From what has been said of the present king, it would be natural to suppose, that he had the highest rank of any person in the islands. But, to our great surprize, we found it is not so; for Latoolibooloo, the person who was pointed out to me as king, when I first visited Tongataboo, and three women, are, in some respects, superior to Poulaho himself. On our inquiring, who these extraordinary personages were, whom they distinguish by the name and title of *Tammaha**? we were told, that the late king, Poulaho's father, had a sister of equal rank, and elder than himself; that she, by a man who came from the island of Feejee, had a son and two daughters; and that these three persons, as well as their mother, rank above Futtafaihe the king. We endeavoured, in vain, to trace the reason of this singular pre-eminence of the *Tammahas*; for we could learn nothing besides this account of their pedigree. The mother, and one of the daughters, called Tooeela-kaipa, live at Vavaoo. Latoolibooloo, the son, and the other daughter, whose name is Moungoula-kaipa, reside at Tongataboo. The latter, is the woman who is mentioned to have dined with me on the 21st of June. This gave occasion to our discovering her superiority over the king, who would not eat in her presence; though she made no scruple to do so before him, and received from him the customary obeisance, by touching her foot. We never had an opportunity of seeing him pay this

---

* The reader need not be reminded that *Tameaha*, which signifies a Chief, in the dialect of Hamoa, and *Tammaha*, become the same word, by the change of a single letter, the articulation of which is not very strongly marked.

mark of respect to Latooliboolo; but we have observed him leave off eating, and have his victuals put aside, when the latter came into the same house. Latooliboolo assumed the privilege of taking any thing from the people, even if it belonged to the king; and yet, in the ceremony called *Natche*, he assisted only in the same manner as the other principal men. He was looked upon, by his countrymen, as a madman; and many of his actions seemed to confirm this judgment. At Eooa, they shewed me a good deal of land, said to belong to him; and I saw there a son of his, a child, whom they distinguished by the same title as his father. The son of the greatest Prince in Europe could not be more humoured and caressed than this little *Toomaba* was.

The language of the Friendly Islands, has the greatest affinity imaginable to that of New Zealand, of Wateeoo, and Mangeea; and, consequently, to that of Otaheite, and the Society Islands. There are also many of their words the same with those used by the natives of Cocos Island, as appears from the vocabulary collected there by Le Maire and Schouten*. The mode of pronunciation differs, indeed, considerably, in many instances, from that both of New Zealand, and Otaheite; but, still, a great number of words

---

* See this vocabulary, at the end of Vol. II. of Dalrymple's Collection of Voyages. And yet, though Tasman's people used the words of this vocabulary, in speaking to the natives of Tongataboo (his Amsterdam), we are told, in the accounts of his voyage, that they did not understand one another. A circumstance worth observing, as it shews how cautious we should be, upon the scanty evidence afforded by such transient visits as Tasman's, and, indeed, as those of most of the subsequent navigators of the Pacific Ocean, to found any argument about the affinity, or want of affinity, of the languages of the different islands. No one, now, will venture to say, that a Cocos man, and one of Tongataboo, could not understand each other. Some of the words of Horn Island, another of Schouten's discoveries, also belong to the dialect of Tongataboo. See *Dalrymple*, as above.

are

are either exactly the same, or so little changed, that their common original may be satisfactorily traced. The language, as spoken at the Friendly Islands, is sufficiently copious, for all the ideas of the people; and we had many proofs of its being easily adapted to all musical purposes, both in song and in recitative; besides being harmonious enough in common conversation. Its component parts, as far as our scanty acquaintance with it enabled us to judge, are not numerous; and, in some of its rules, it agrees with other known languages. As, for instance, we could easily discern the several degrees of comparison, as used in the Latin; but none of the inflections of nouns and verbs.

We were able to collect several hundreds of the words; and, amongst these, are terms that express numbers as far as a hundred thousand; beyond which they never would reckon. It is probable, indeed, that they are not able to go farther; for, after having got thus far, we observed, that they commonly used a word which expresses an indefinite number. A short specimen, selected from the larger vocabulary, is here inserted, with the corresponding words, of the same signification, as used at Otaheite, on the opposite column; which, while it will give, as we may say, ocular demonstration of their being dialects of the same language, will, at the same time, point out the particular letters, by the insertion, omission, or alteration of which, the variations of the two dialects, from each other, have been effected.

It must be observed, however, that our vocabularies, of this sort, must necessarily be liable to great mistakes. The ideas of those, from whom we were to learn the words, were

were so different from ours, that it was difficult to fix them to the object of inquiry. Or, if this could be obtained, to learn an unknown tongue, from an instructor who did not know a single word of any language that his scholar was conversant with, could not promise to produce much. But even, when these difficulties were surmounted, there still remained a fruitful source of mistake. I mean, inaccuracy in catching, exactly, the true sound of a word, to which our ears had never been accustomed, from persons whose mode of pronunciation was, in general, so indistinct, that it seldom happened that any two of us, in writing down the same word, from the same mouth, made use of the same vowels, in representing it. Nay, we even, very commonly, differed about consonants, the sounds of which are least liable to ambiguity. Besides all this, we found, by experience, that we had been led into strange corruptions of some of the most common words, either from the natives endeavouring to imitate us, or from our having misunderstood them. Thus, *cheeto* was universally used by us, to express a thief, though totally different from the real word, in the language of Tongataboo. The mistake arose from a prior one, into which we had run, when at New Zealand. For though the word that signifies thief there, be absolutely the same that belongs to the dialect of the Friendly Islands (being *kaeehaa* at both places), yet, by some blunder, we had used the word *teete*, first at New Zealand, and, afterward, at Tongataboo, on our arrival there. The natives, endeavouring to imitate us, as nearly as they could, and so fabricating the word *cheeto*, this, by a complication of mistakes, was adopted by us as their own. All possible care has been taken to make the following table as correct as possible:

English.

English.	Friendly Islands.	Otaheite.
The sun,	Elaa,	Eraa.
Fire,	Eafoi,	Eahoi.
Thunder,	Fatoore,	Pateere.
Rain,	Ooha,	Eooa.
The wind,	Matangee,	Mataee.
Warm,	Mafanna,	Mahanna.
The clouds,	Ao,	Eao.
Land,	Fonooa,	Fenooa.
Water,	Avy,	Evy.
Sleep,	Mohe,	Moe.
A man,	Tangata,	Taata.
A woman,	Vefaine,	Waheine.
A young girl,	Taheine,	Toonea.
A servant, or person of mean rank,	Tooa,	Toutou, or teou.
The dawn, or day-break,	Aho,	Aou.
The hair,	Fooroo,	Eroroo.
The tongue,	Elelo,	Erero.
The ear,	Tareenga,	Tareea.
The beard,	Koomoo,	Ooma.
The sea,	Tahee,	Tace.
A boat, or canoe,	Wakka,	Evaa.
Black,	Oole,	Ere.
Red,	Goola,	Oora, oora.
A lance, or spear,	Tao,	Tao.
A parent,	Motooa,	Madooa.
What is that?	Kohaeea?	Yahaeea?
To hold fast,	Amou,	Mou.
To wipe, or clean any thing,	Horo,	Horoee.

English.

English.	Friendly Islands.	Otaheite.
To rife up,	Etoo,	Atoo.
To cry, or fhed tears,	Tangee,	Taee.
To eat, or chew,	Eky,	Ey.
Yes,	Ai,	Ai.
No,	Kaee,	Aee.
Yes,	Koe,	Oe.
I,	Ou,	Wou.
Ten,	Ongofooroo,	Ahooroo.

Having now concluded my remarks on thefe iflands and people, I fhall take my final leave of them, after giving fome account of the aftronomical and nautical obfervations that were made during our ftay.

And, firft, I muft take notice, that the difference of longitude, between Annamooka and Tongataboo, is fomewhat lefs than was marked in the chart and narrative of my laft voyage. This error might eafily arife, as the longitude of each was then found without any conneftion with the other. But, now, the diftance between them is determined to a degree of precifion, that excludes all poffibility of miftake; which the following table will illuftrate:

The latitude of the obfervatory at Tongataboo, by the mean of feveral obfervations, - - - 21° 0' 19" South.

The longitude, by the mean of one hundred and thirty-one fets of lunar obfervations, amounting to above a thoufand obferved diftances, between the moon, fun, and ftars, - - - - 184 55 18 Eaft.

The difference of longitude, made
by the time-keeper, between the
above observatory, and that at
Annamooka, - - - 0° 16′ 0″
Hence, the longitude of Annamo-
ka is - - - - 185 11 18 East.
By the time- ⎰ Greenwich rate, - 186 12 27
keeper it is, ⎱ New Zealand rate, 184 37 0
Its latitude - - - 20 15 0

N. B. The observatory at Tongataboo was near the middle of the North side of the island; and that at Annamooka, on its West side; but the chart will elucidate this.

The time-keeper was too slow for mean time at Greenwich, on the first of July at noon, by $12^h\ 34'\ 55'',2$; and her daily rate, at that time, was losing, on mean time, $1'',783$ per day. This rate will now be used for finding the longitude by the time-keeper; and $1^{c}4'\ 55'\ 18''$, or $12^h\ 19^m\ 41'',2$, will be taken as the true longitude of Tongataboo, East from Greenwich.

By the mean of several observations, the South end of the needle was found to dip

At ⎰ Lefooga, one of the Hapaee islands, 30° 55′
⎱ Tongataboo, - - - 39 1¼.

The variation of the compass was found to be

⎰ Annamooka, on board, - - 8° 30′ 3½″ East.
⎪ Anchor off Kotoo, between ⎱ - 8 12 29¼
At ⎨   Annamooka and Hapaee, ⎰
⎪ Anchor off Lefooga, - - 10 11 40
⎪ Tongataboo, on board, - 9 44 5½
⎱ Ditto, on shore, - - - 10 12 58

A VOYAGE TO

1777.
July.

I can assign no reason why the variation is so much less at, and near, Annamooka, than at either of the other two places. I can only say, that there is no fault in the observations; and that the variation ought to be more at Annamooka than the above, as it has been found to be so to the Northward, Southward, Eastward, and Westward of it. But disagreements in the variation, greater than this, even in the same needle, have been often observed. And I should not have taken notice of this instance, but from a belief that the cause, whatever it is, exists in the place, and not in the needles; for Mr. Bayly found the same, or rather more difference.

The tides are more considerable at these islands, than at any other of my discoveries in this ocean, that lie within the tropics. At Annamooka it is high water, on the full and change days, nearly at six o'clock; and the tide rises and falls there, upon a perpendicular, about six feet. In the harbour of Tongataboo, it is high water, on the full and change days, at fifty minutes past six. The tide rises and falls, on those days, four feet nine inches; and three feet six inches at the Quadratures. In the channels between the islands, which lie in this harbour, it flows near tide and half tide; that is, the flood continues to run up near three hours, after it is high water by the shore; and the ebb continues to run down, after it is flood by the shore. It is only in these channels, and in a few other places near the shores, that the motion of the water or tide is perceivable; so that I can only guess at the quarter from which the flood comes. In the road of Annamooka, it sets West South West, and the ebb the contrary; but it falls into the harbour of Tongataboo from the North West,

passes

passes through the two narrow channels, on each side of
Hoolalva, where it runs with considerable rapidity, and
then spends itself in the *lagoon*. The ebb returns the
same way, and runs with rather greater force. The North
West tide is met, at the entrance of the *lagoon*, by one
from the East; but this, as I have before observed, was
found to be very inconsiderable.

END OF THE FIRST VOLUME.

www.ingramcontent.com/pod-product-compliance
Lightning Source LLC
Chambersburg PA
CBHW031945290426
44108CB00011B/677